'It is a very good book indeed and the chapter on the economy, a swift butchering of the economic record, sundering ribs and hacking vertebrae, is of especial value . . . Few men so combine grace with implacability.' Edward Pearce, *Guardian*

'His quiet voice tells an icy truth, a truth to send a shiver down a blue-rinsed spine.' Jad Adams, *The Times Educational Supplement*

'An impassioned retrospective crusade against the policies to which he had so unwillingly lent his name . . . written with feeling.' John Biffen, *The Spectator*

'[Gilmour] uses the full power of his scalpel-like intellect, his sense of history and his discriminating scholarship to unflesh the bones of Thatcherism – and a fairly repellent skeleton is revealed.' Lord St John of Fawsley, *Sunday Express*

'*Dancing with Dogma* proves that Thatcherite petulance offered no more of an escape from economic entropy than Wilsonite paranoia.' Roy Porter, *The Sunday Times*

'The author has mercilessly exposed the madness and intellectual impoverishment of Thatcherite policy and its destructive consequences . . . this important book may help us retrace the ground we have lost by walking for so many years in the wrong direction.' Godfrey Hodgson, *Independent*

'This is a devastating and highly entertaining critique of the Thatcher years . . . Written with rare verve and vigour by a former member of Mrs Thatcher's Cabinet, this should be compulsory reading for the Labour front bench.' Tariq Ali, *The Oldie*

'Lord Gilmour has written a powerful, searing polemic about the 1980s whic̶h̶ ̶ will ̶ ̶ ̶ ̶dard work in the arguments a̶ ̶ ̶ ̶ism.' Gordon Greig, *Daily M̶a̶*

'He has written ̶ ̶ ̶ ̶ ̶ ̶ ̶ ̶ngs with a wit

and elegance so often lacking in his peers.' Julian Critchley, *Evening Standard*

'A sprightly and delightfully barbed account of the Thatcher years from an insider who must have ground his teeth to a fine dust while serving in her government.' Jeremy Paxman, *Independent*

'[Gilmour] has expounded his critique of the Tory reversion to Victorian economic values many times before – but never so well as in his new book, the most elegant polemic against Mrs Thatcher and everything she stood for yet published . . . John Smith will want to learn the best passages in this book by heart.' Ben Pimlott, *Independent on Sunday*

'Unlike almost all other ministerial litterateurs from the 1980s, too many of whom have inflicted bad books on a gullible public, Gilmour is a professional writer. On that account alone his book stands out, being well put together, scrupulously sourced and elegantly composed . . . He is numerate as well as literate. He makes the case his eponymous anti-heroine will have to answer if her own memoirs are to be taken seriously . . . As an indictment of what happened, if not as an account of what might have been, it could scarcely be bettered.' Hugo Young, *The Tablet*

'A tale of woe, a sober, analytical chronicle of the political era, a detailed critique of Thatcherism of which any left-wing historian might be proud.' Rupert Morris, *The Sunday Times*

'There is much that is entertaining here, nothing that is rude, little that is bitter.' Douglas Hurd, *Daily Telegraph*

'Any reader who has an old-fashioned desire to find out what "actually happened" can do so. It breaks one scholarly convention however – it is gracefully and wittily written. One of the strengths of *Dancing with Dogma* is Lord Gilmour's readiness to see Thatcherism as a system of persuasion as well as an ideology and his willingness to say plain things at a time when others have not been so willing – that such a thoughtful and rebellious book can be written from within the Conservative Party is a cause for hope.' Ross McKibbin, *London Review of Books*

'Anyone tempted to buy Lawson . . . should buy Gilmour, for the same reason that wise folk buy Alka-Seltzer at the same time as the Christmas pud.' Ian Aitken, *Observer*

'This book is, without doubt, the best argued criticism of Margaret Thatcher's period in office that has yet been published.' Vernon Bogdanor, *The Times Higher Educational Supplement*

About the Author

IAN GILMOUR was the Editor of *Spectator* from 1954–59. He was a Conservative MP from 1962–92, firstly for Norfolk Central and then Chesham and Amersham. At the Ministry of Defence throughout the Heath Government, he ended up as Defence Secretary. He was Chairman of the Conservative Research Department 1974–75. Under Mrs Thatcher he was Shadow Home Secretary, Shadow Defence Secretary and Lord Privy Seal from 1979–81.

His previous books are *The Body Politic*; *Inside Right, A Study of Conservatism*; *Britain Can Work*; and *Riot, Risings and Revolution, Governance and Violence in Eighteenth Century England*.

Dancing with Dogma

Britain under Thatcherism

IAN GILMOUR

POCKET BOOKS

New York   London   Toronto   Sydney   Tokyo   Singapore

First published in Great Britain by
Simon & Schuster Ltd in 1992
First published in Pocket Books, an imprint
of Simon & Schuster Ltd, in 1993
A Paramount Communications Company

Simon & Schuster Ltd
West Garden Place
Kendal Street
London W2 2AQ

Simon & Schuster of Australia Pty Ltd
Sydney

A CIP catalogue record for this book is
available from the British Library
ISBN 0-671-85094-6

Typeset in Sabon 10.5/12.5 by
Hewer Text Composition Services, Edinburgh
Printed and bound in Great Britain by
HarperCollins Manufacturing

Illustration credits:
pictures 2, 4, 5, 6, 7, 9: Press Association;
picture 1: Solo Syndication; picture 3: Associated Press;
picture 8: Associated Press/Topham;
picture 11: Popperfoto/Reuter.

To the officers, agents and members
of the Chesham and Amersham
Conservative Association 1972–1992.

Contents

Preface & Acknowledgements

NOT LONG AFTER she had ceased to be Prime Minister, Margaret Thatcher reported that she still had 'invitations to go the world over to try to teach them to do some of the things which we did during the Thatcher years'.[1]

This book examines some of the lessons of those 'Thatcher years'. It is only very partly a product of hindsight. From the start I held strong opinions about Thatcherism in action and continued to hold them throughout the Thatcher era. Of course, only those who are impervious to events can retain exactly the same political opinions, yet my views have not greatly changed in the years since 1979. Hence I have drawn on speeches I made at the time and articles that I contributed to various papers. The frequent references in the notes at the end of the book to my speeches and articles and to *Britain Can Work*, a book I wrote in 1983, are included only to substantiate the point about hindsight. They do not claim to be authority for anything else.

Many people have helped me, above all Dr Mark Garnett and Jane Pleydell Bouverie. Mark Garnett, who suggested I write the book, has given very freely of his own ideas and has been a tireless critic of mine; he has also traced many references as well as compiling the index. Jane Pleydell Bouverie did a vast amount of work on the social chapters, and in addition to helping to form those, she has done much to better the others.

John Grigg has yet again been a fruitful source of help and encouragement. He, William Keegan, Professor Keith Middlemas, David Gilmour and Andrew Gilmour, who thought of the title, read all or most of the typescript; Christopher Barclay, Professor Wynne Godley, David Knox, Professor Anthony King, Hermione Parker and Rob Shepherd read parts of it. I am deeply indebted to all of them for their valuable suggestions and amendments and for their zeal in spotting errors. I am also greatly obliged to Richard Brisbourne, Dr Barrington Cooper, Dr Emma Gilmour, Ron Kibble, Dr J J McMullan, Sara Morrison, Chris Pond, Stephen Sharp, Geoffrey Williams and Dr James Willis — as well as a few other people who had better remain unnamed — for kindly reading various chapters and giving me the benefit of their expertise. The errors which remain after all that generous and variegated scrutiny are of course mine alone, as are the opinions.

I must also thank Dr David Butler, and Professors Tony Atkinson, Jonathan Bradshaw, Robert Eccleshall and R A W Rhodes for their prompt and helpful responses to my pleas for assistance. As always the House of Commons Library did everything that was asked of it with its customary efficiency.

Last and most, I am profoundly grateful to Diane Craig for once more spoiling her eyesight, but not her temper, by solving the puzzles set by my handwriting and for speedily typing and retyping many drafts.

Ian Gilmour
1 July 1992

I

Introduction: Harmony and Discord

THE CONSERVATIVE GOVERNMENT that came into office in 1979 claimed to be, and indeed was, very different from its Conservative predecessors. Unlike them it would not stoop to shabby compromise, pander to consensus, or delay decisive action by trying to remedy any lack of knowledge. Instead the 1979 government had an ideology (or something very like one), and it already knew all that it wanted to know.[1] Hence Royal Commissions would be an expensive waste of time, and attempts to reach consensus or compromise would merely adulterate truth with error and reproduce the deficiencies of previous governments. Statistics were no longer necessary. The problems after all were simple, the solutions even more so. In the past, conviction had been lacking. Now it was abundantly present. In consequence Britain's post-war crisis was about to be ended.

Before long, it seemed to some, the long-running crisis had indeed been resolved, and Mrs Thatcher had succeeded in changing the national mood. Prior to her arrival in No 10, the national disposition had been predominantly one of dejection and acceptance of British decline. In 1979 Britannia seemed to be sinking beneath the waves; after a few years of Mrs Thatcher Britannia seemed once more to be ruling them. The Prime Minister, many people believed, had engendered a new spirit of self-confidence. That in itself, true or not, was an impressive accomplishment.

For the Prime Minister's first words in Downing Street a speech-writer had thoughtfully primed her with a nineteenth-century pastiche of St Francis of Assisi:

> Where there is discord, may we bring harmony,
> Where there is error, may we bring truth,
> Where there is doubt, may we bring faith,
> Where there is despair, may we bring hope.[2]

Margaret Thatcher unquestionably possessed faith and hope, and she had no doubts about the truth. Harmony might prove more difficult. But that was (at best) a secondary consideration. So, spurred on by a right-wing popular press which could scarcely have been more fawning if it had been state-controlled – and indeed a liberal use of the honours system to knight editors and ennoble proprietors produced much the same effect – the new Thatcher government confidently set out to solve the problems that had defied all its predecessors since 1945.[3]

Those predecessors had long been derided by the new Conservative leadership, even by those parts of it that had served in them without demur. For obvious reasons Conservatives normally seek to build on their past, not to decry it. Yet the new right-wing Conservatism poured scorn on previous Tory governments as well as on the socialist enemy. Not only had the Heath government (in Mrs Thatcher's words) 'failed the people', the governments of the thirteen Conservative years had also been sadly deluded; unwittingly they had helped to foster the growth of a socialist state. A heavy helping of myth, of course, was needed for this repudiation of the Conservative past. But in ideological as in other wars truth is the first casualty, and a rewriting of the history of the very recent past, if not of the present, was also a conspicuous feature of the Thatcher years in government.[4]

The most distinguished of the new Conservative missionaries, Sir Keith Joseph, who had sat in the Conservative cabinets of Harold Macmillan and Alec Douglas-Home as well as of Edward Heath, announced in between the two

1974 elections that it was only in 1974 that he had been converted to true Conservatism — as a result, apparently, of the good offices of Sir Alfred Sherman, himself also a convert, though from rather more distant ideological shores. (Sir Keith had indeed undergone a 'conversion' — though not to Conservatism but to mid-Victorian Liberalism.) Anyhow belief in monetarism, it emerged, was now a prerequisite not only for controlling inflation but for being a real Conservative. Following Mrs Thatcher's election to the party leadership in 1975, many other Conservative politicians were also born again, some of them overnight. Those who resisted conversion and clung instead to traditional Tory principles were soon regarded as, at best, suspect infidels or, at worst, the enemy within.[5]

These primitive or now heretical Conservatives, especially those like myself who were members of Mrs Thatcher's first cabinet, together with the policies they favoured, came to be designated 'wet', as opposed to the right-wing Thatcherites who were 'dry' and who were, in the Prime Minister's phraseology, 'on my side' or 'one of us'. According to Michael Foot, writing in 1984, the term 'wet' was — and was intended to be — 'deeply offensive', though he believed that some of the wets nevertheless gloried in it.[6] I certainly thought it odd to dub the main Tory tradition 'wet': Baldwin, Churchill, Eden, Macmillan, Butler and Macleod were, in the sense meant by the neologism, wets to a man; and since for at least the earlier part of his ministerial career Neville Chamberlain, whom Mrs Thatcher in the words of one of her most reverential biographers 'much resembled in terms of social and political style', was also undoubtedly wet, the last unequivocally 'dry' Prime Minister had been Bonar Law.[7]

Furthermore the coinage of the word introduced an element of confusion. After all, the word 'wet' when used of people (as of the weather) had previously had a meaning that was perfectly clear: of people, it denoted futility and weakness. Now in its new application it could carry almost the exact opposite meaning. Thus for Conservatives to remain silent about those parts of the government's policy which they considered misguided and old-fashioned would have been wet in the proper sense of the word, while for them to voice criticism or disagreement was now wet in its new spurious sense.[8]

The first Thatcher cabinet, with its complement of wets, dries, and those who were too intelligent, cautious, fearful or uncommitted to be either, was palpably not a happy and united body; probably, indeed, as Jim Prior has said, it was 'the most divided Conservative cabinet ever'. Emphatically, too, it was not the sort of cabinet that Mrs Thatcher had undertaken to form. In a celebrated interview shortly before coming into office, she had laid down that she was 'not a *consensus* politician or a *pragmatic* politician' but 'a *conviction* politician', and had affirmed her intention of having in her cabinet 'only the people who want to go in the direction in which every instinct tells me we have to go . . . It must be a Cabinet that works on something much more than pragmatism or consensus. It must be a "conviction Cabinet".' The cabinet had to go in an agreed and clear direction. 'As Prime Minister,' Mrs Thatcher added, 'I could not waste time having any internal arguments.'[9] But in 1979 she was not yet in total control of the Conservative party and did not have full freedom of choice, so the cabinet that she formed was far from being a conviction cabinet, and did not agree with the direction the Prime Minister wished to go. This might have been inconvenient, but it turned out not to matter very much, as only rarely were the most important issues permitted to reach the cabinet.[10]

Mrs Thatcher regarded her first cabinet (and, I suspect, also her other cabinets) not as an aid to good government but as an obstacle to be surmounted. Her belief that dialogue was a waste of time rather than a means of arriving at an agreed course of action was part of her rejection of consensus politics. Consensus, the Prime Minister later proclaimed, was achieved only by 'abandoning all beliefs, principles and values. Whoever won a battle,' she asked, 'under the banner

"I stand for consensus"?' In her mind, of course, 'conviction' was diametrically opposed to 'consensus'. Certainly her own convictions were hostile to consensus. But in fact nearly every politician has convictions, and some of them have the strong conviction that consensus as such should not be despised.[11]

Naturally 'consensus' does not mean that the opposing parties are in agreement. There were continuing differences between the parties throughout the thirty years after the war, though those differences, Winston Churchill wrote without regret in 1954, were 'now mainly those of emphasis'. But, as Churchill's words suggest, consensus implies a desire to keep party controversy within limits and a willingness to consider the convictions of opponents. And in Britain, at least, consensus politicians have recognized that, under our unusual system which normally gives the whole of the executive and the control of the legislature to one party even if it has won only a minority of the votes, the winning party does not have *carte blanche* to do whatever its extremists may happen to want.[12]

However much it was despised by some in the seventies and eighties, consensus has usually been considered one of the marks that distinguish liberal democracies from less civilized states. 'The ethics of democracy regarded mutual concession and compromise,' Professor G H Sabine wrote some years ago, 'not as defections from principle but as ways of reaching agreements which on the whole were more satisfactory than any that could be reached by the dominance of one interest . . . one party' or, he might have added, one dogma.[13]*

For supporters of consensus, convictions are of course fine, provided that they are based on facts; but if they are based

---

* Michael Oakeshott, whom Mrs Thatcher admired but may not have closely read, wrote that the kind of society favoured by a libertarian found 'its guide in a principle of *continuity* (which is a diffusion of power between past, present and future) and in a principle of *consensus* (which is a diffusion of power between the different legitimate interests of the present)'.[14]

on dogma or whim, consensus politicians regard them as little more than self-indulgence or as delusions which may well cause havoc. Perhaps the chief difference, therefore, between consensus and conviction politicians is that the former weigh the consequences of carrying their convictions into practice or law, while the latter are determined to implement their convictions whatever the cost to other people.

In any case, instead of trying to achieve a consensus in her cabinet, thus bringing harmony to where there was discord, as she had recently promised, the Prime Minister governed by clique and committee, where 'conviction' could have its head. According to one of her biographers, who took it to be a virtue, Mrs Thatcher was uniquely unsuited to a cabinet system. She therefore 'removed the most vital aspects of policy-making from Cabinet discussion'.[15] Collective decision-making was severely truncated and with it, inevitably, collective responsibility.[16]

Nevertheless the cabinet's role in economic policy-making could not quite be reduced to the purely formal one of registering decisions taken elsewhere, like that of a cathedral chapter in 'electing' its bishop. Decisions on public expenditure, for instance, had to come before it, and in July 1981 the Prime Minister found herself in a minority of four. Apart from her, only Keith Joseph backed the Treasury team's risible proposals to make yet more cuts in public spending. That humiliation, though the Downing Street propaganda machine managed to pass it off to the press in the same style as it had dismissed an earlier cabinet discussion as a 'Quick win for Maggie', speeded up Mrs Thatcher's strategy, in operation since the previous January, of progressively neutering and virtually eliminating the 'wets'.[17]

Mr Gladstone doubted whether a prime minister had the right to require a cabinet minister to resign. Indeed the constitutional convention in the nineteenth century was that no cabinet minister could be dismissed for differing with the prime minister, only for delinquency or incompetence. But practice had long made such scruples and restraints redundant. A prime minister, as Lord Randolph Churchill once put it, could if he was so minded form a cabinet with waiters from the Carlton Club. So Mrs Thatcher was well within her rights in dispatching the wets, and in my case at least she can certainly be excused. 'He takes every chance to do me down,' she complained of me to a journalist she had knighted. 'He is against me on every issue that comes before the Cabinet.' That was characteristically over-personalized but otherwise only a little exaggerated.[18]

Mrs Thatcher later achieved cabinets better attuned to her wishes, but they had a different and possibly even greater handicap than the presence of some opponents of her most cherished ideas. Though she was against consensus, she was, she professed, 'in favour of agreement'.[19] The difference of course is that 'consensus' demands adjustment of views by everybody involved in order to achieve an acceptable compromise, whereas 'agreement' here meant everybody save one surrendering their views – a process more suited, perhaps, to absolute monarchy than parliamentary democracy; and indeed some Thatcherite writing suggested that her followers saw her more as a monarch than a parliamentary democrat, which presumably helped to foster monarchical tendencies.[20]

'Agreement' effectively meant a one-woman consensus, a state of affairs which rendered debate superfluous. The so-called Community Charge met none of the requirements of a tolerable tax and was likely to be politically disastrous as well as socially indefensible.[21] Yet when the Chancellor of the Exchequer, Nigel Lawson, put a paper to a cabinet committee pointing out that a poll tax would be 'completely unworkable' only his number two, the Chief Secretary, supported him. And when the poll tax came before the full cabinet, even Nigel Lawson fell silent. Only one minister – Peter Walker – spoke up against it. The doubts of many others were stifled by their awareness of the Prime Minister's enthusiasm for what she conceived to be 'the flagship' of her policies.[22] Thus, as the cabinet became 'drier' in the word's new sense, that is to say more right wing, it became 'wetter' in the proper sense of that word, rather a weekly festival of sycophancy than an organ of government. Mrs Thatcher never quite got round to filling her cabinet with waiters from the Carlton Club, but she did appoint a number of courtiers or placemen whose function was not so different.[23]

'We must have an ideology', Mrs Thatcher had earlier told another gathering, the Conservative Philosophy Group. 'The other side has got an ideology they can test their policies against. We must have one as well.' Whether this deeply felt need to keep up with the ideological Joneses, the Labour party, actually produced an ideology called 'Thatcherism' is debatable. But Mrs Thatcher undoubtedly inserted into Conservative policy an ideological, if not religious, fervour and a dogmatic tone that had previously been lacking. 'Thatcherism' and 'Thatcherite' entered the language, becoming terms both of praise and abuse; and unlike John Wilkes who told George III he had never been a Wilkite, Karl Marx who denied being a Marxist, and President de Gaulle who repudiated Gaullism, Mrs Thatcher gloried in the existence of an 'ism' that bore her name.[24]

And not only Mrs Thatcher. Plenty of people in Britain and overseas also gloried in Thatcherism. They saw Britain's first woman prime minister and her opinions and activities as the promise of a revitalized Britain and of a renewal of freedom both at home and abroad. Part of the British adulation might be ascribed to what Richard Shepherd, MP, called the 'hallelujah chorus' of a press that saluted everything the government did.[25] In the past, Britain's Conservative newspapers had often criticized Tory prime ministers for not being sufficiently right wing. That was not a complaint that could be laid against Mrs Thatcher; and the right-wing press – many of its publications could not be described either as Tory or even as newspapers – were in a state of perpetual thanksgiving to and for the Prime Minister.

Yet Mrs Thatcher's appeal was not confined to the United Kingdom or even to the United States where her prestige was soon immense. In Eastern Europe, too, she became easily the most-admired foreign politician, her visit to the Soviet Union being among the most successful ever paid by a leading statesman to another country. Abroad many people regretted that their own political leaders were not as determined and dominant as Mrs Thatcher. Had statesmen been as internationally tradeable as footballers or film stars, the British Prime Minister would have commanded a record transfer fee.

Equally, many at home would have willingly given her a free transfer to another country. Mrs Thatcher's popularity in Britain varied enormously during her years at the top, but it was mainly low. In the seventies the voters much preferred a man as prime minister, and her stridency was distrusted. Although she fought a good campaign in 1979, the Conservative party won that election more despite than because of her, polls indicating that the party would have fared far better under Ted Heath than Margaret Thatcher. By the end of the campaign, indeed, she was nineteen points behind the Labour leader, James Callaghan; and in 1981 she became the most unpopular prime minister since records began. Yet not long afterwards she enjoyed huge popularity in the wake of the Falklands victory. And the Conservatives under her leadership won two more elections triumphantly, though her personal standing remained depressed. Taking the whole of her three terms into account, she was, apart from Ted Heath, the least well-regarded of all post-war prime ministers.[26]

Yet, whatever the state of her fluctuating poll ratings, Margaret Thatcher dominated British politics for more than a decade in a way that few, if any, politicians have done this century. The history of 'the Thatcher years' must wait a while, and the depiction of Mrs Thatcher's sterling qualities can be safely entrusted to her biographers, whose number is already legion. But now that the leading 'conviction politician' has left Downing Street, it is not inappropriate, I think, to examine the effects of those convictions, especially as Mrs Thatcher announced that she hoped to exert matriarchal influence over her successor and from time to time she issues edicts telling him not to 'undo what I've done'.[27]

Thatcherism can be viewed as ideology, style, mood, 'I must have my own way', monarchism, nineteenth-century Liberalism, millenarian revivalism, right-wingery, a method of controversy, a set of moral values, statecraft, or as a combination of all of them. This book attempts to assess its impact on the country and on Conservative policy during Mrs Thatcher's eleven-year reign, the longest continuous occupation of Downing Street of any prime minister since Lord Liverpool's in the early nineteenth century. We can then judge which parts of Thatcherism have benefited Britain and can be safely taught 'the world over' and which parts should in future be zealously avoided both at home and abroad.[28]

II

Economic Policy to 1981

Experience shows that the only sure way of tackling
inflation is to keep the money supply closely related to
the output of goods and services.

Margaret Thatcher, 28 February 1980[1]

Our present troubles ... are not of a monetary character, and are not to be cured by monetary means.

Sir John Hicks[2]

THATCHERISM LARGELY CONSISTED of nineteenth-
century individualism dressed up in twentieth-century
clothes. As with the Manchester Liberalism of the last century,
economic dogma was at its core. For a British government
(and nearly every other government) such dogmatism was
unusual. In formulating their policies, previous British governments had traditionally avoided the extremes of a command
economy on the left and of uncontrolled market forces on
the right.

Whatever their ideological banner, Labour governments
have never attempted a fully socialist economy, and indeed
have often shown at least as much respect for traditional
orthodoxy and market forces as their opponents. Philip

Snowden, the Chancellor of the Exchequer in the two pre-war Labour governments, was a rigid old-fashioned liberal, whose primary allegiance was to free trade and retrenchment. 'The Treasury mind and the Snowden mind,' wrote Winston Churchill, 'embraced each other with the fervour of two long-separated kindred lizards.' Not surprisingly, therefore, the 1929–31 Labour government took no socialist (or any other) steps to reduce spiralling unemployment. The Attlee government's much-vaunted belief in planning did not translate itself into a planned economy, and it was that government not its Conservative successor which first lit 'a bonfire of controls'.[3]

Harold Wilson ensured the failure of his first government by refusing to devalue in 1964, and once again a Labour government proved 'unable, even unwilling, to plan'. Despite its heavily interventionist election manifesto, the economic policy of the 1974 Wilson government was similarly confused rather than socialist, and Tony Benn's 'alternative economic strategy', known to colleagues as 'Benn's follies', gained minimal support. Finally, in 1976, Wilson's successor James Callaghan was happy to please the International Monetary Fund by proclaiming, in words written by his monetarist son-in-law, Peter Jay, that we could no longer spend ourselves out of a recession.[4]

Much the same is true of right-wing governments, though in the past Britain was sometimes much nearer pure *laissez-faire* than total regulation. Yet, even in the nineteenth century, *laissez-faire* was never the doctrine of the Conservative party. Protectionism was a recurring strand in Tory thinking, and many Tories (and a number of Liberals) saw that government interference was needed to make capitalism more or less tolerable to the mass of the people; otherwise women and small children would have continued to work down coal mines and for long hours in factories. Unrestrained market forces, they realized, benefited only the rich and powerful. Hence the Factory Acts, improvements in public health, and other causes championed by that archetypal Tory 'wet', the seventh Earl of Shaftesbury.[5]

In 1872 Disraeli reminded his audience at the Crystal Palace that 'many years ago the Tory Party believed ... that you might elevate the condition of the people by the reduction of their toil and the mitigation of their labour and at the same time inflict no injury on the wealth of the nation.' The Liberal leaders had replied with all the economists' dogma that the result would be to 'diminish capital' and hence employment, which would lead 'ultimately to the impoverishment of the kingdom'. But economic dogma had been proved wrong, Disraeli continued; and the Tories had been right.[6]

Over the years the Conservative party oscillated, and Tories differed among themselves over where the balance should be struck between individualism and state regulation, but nearly all of them agreed that a balance was required. As Anthony Eden later said, 'we opposed [the *laissez-faire* school] decade after decade.'[7]

Between the wars Britain's economic growth was higher than it had been between 1899 and 1913, and predominantly Conservative governments continued the development of the social services. Free trade was abandoned, and economic policy in the 1930s became heavily interventionist, yet ministers paid little attention to the writings of Keynes, and their economic views (though not their actions) were still broadly in line with those of the classical economists.[8]

After 1945 Keynesian managed capitalism – or from the other point of view 'Keynesian social democracy'[9] – was adopted by all the main parties, though they differed on the proportions of management and capitalism that they favoured. Exactly what comprises the right mix of market forces and government regulation is obviously a matter of argument and, presumably, it differs from time to time. But humanity and common sense and indeed economic theory, too, require a mixture. There is no warrant in experience or, as our leading economic theorist, Professor Frank Hahn, recently pointed out, even in theory (except on impossibly unrealistic assumptions) for believing that unrestricted market forces will necessarily produce the best outcome. Government intervention is required not only to make social conditions acceptable but also to make market economies work. *Laissez-faire* is not, in practice, a serious option.[10]

By the mid 1970s the post-war compromise had broken down. But it was anyway alien to the Thatcherites. In their view Britain's troubles stemmed from the attempts of successive governments to tamper with the sacred market system. To them, Keynesianism was anathema. Nineteenth-century liberalism was their ideal and, intent on letting market forces have full rein, Thatcherites adopted the particularly dogmatic form of classical economics, Friedmanite monetarism, which was currently fashionable. A number of other countries also adopted a monetarist approach, but none of them became such fundamentalist devotees of the Friedmanite scriptures. In consequence, of all the leading right-wing European democratic parties, most of which in the 1970s also moved to the right, the British Conservative party became far and away the most dogmatic.[11]

Ironically, however, it was the last Labour government which in 1976 had introduced some aspects of monetarist policy into England. Labour's flirtation was reluctant and unsatisfactory, but it constituted a break with the past. Full employment was abandoned in practice and, partly, even in theory.[12] Over-mighty trade unions looked after themselves with as little regard for the common good as any nineteenth-century rogue capitalist. Not surprisingly, over half the country thought Jack Jones, the leader of the Transport and General Workers' Union, the most powerful man in the country; only 25 per cent thought that accolade should be awarded to the Prime Minister, James Callaghan. On many counts Labour's performance was lamentable. By 1979, both economically and politically, the Labour government was worn out.[13]

The next Conservative government, it was widely agreed, would have to move towards a more market economy and curb trade-union power. Even so, the ascendancy that monetarism quickly gained in the Conservative party, traditionally the home of caution and pragmatism and of hostility to abstract ideas, was remarkable. To the new breed of Conservative, pragmatism and caution became dirty words. The new Conservative leaders gloried in being subject to fashionable intellectual influences. They were not even, in Keynes's famous words, 'madmen in authority . . . distilling their frenzy from some academic scribbler of a few years back'.[14] Their favourite academic scribbler, Professor Milton Friedman of Chicago University, was a far from defunct contemporary.

Monetarism

The details of the distilled monetarist 'frenzy' that swept through much of the Conservative party with the force of revelation need not now detain us. Its essence can be conveyed in five assumptions or propositions: (1) that the quantity of money in the economy can be defined; (2) that the demand for money is stable and therefore its velocity of circulation is nearly constant;[15] (3) that its supply can be controlled and (4) that there is a causal link between the money supply and inflation – so, in the Friedmanite view, a reduction in the money supply will be followed (about two years later) by a fall in inflation (and vice versa). Fifthly, following the classical economists, monetarists believe that a market economy is fundamentally self-regulating. Hence it should be left alone as much as possible, thereby enabling its inbuilt equilibrating mechanisms to do their work. Accordingly, the government should concern itself with its own finances – the balance between income and expenditure in the public sector and the Public Sector Borrowing Requirement – with removing rigidities and distortions in the market, with enlarging incentives and with improving and promoting the system of private enterprise and, of course, with controlling the money supply. It should not concern itself with attempting to manage aggregate demand for goods and services in the economy as a whole. Indeed, the concept of demand management is dangerously inappropriate, monetarists believe or believed, and should be discarded. Similarly the government should withdraw from just about every sphere of activity except law and order and defence.[16]

In sum, stripped of all technicalities the message of monetarism in the late 1970s was simple and optimistic. Provided that a number of straightforward rules were followed, inflation would be eliminated within two years or so; after a temporary rise, unemployment would be reduced as inflationary expectations adjusted; and sustained economic growth would be achieved as attitudes changed under the strong incentive of economic gain. That was the monetarist prospectus.

The fervent Thatcherite espousal of that prospectus was all the more remarkable in that there was virtually no empirical evidence to support Friedmanite monetarism, and both Professor Friedman's theory and his facts had been battered, even before 1979, both by other economists such as Sir John Hicks, Professor James Tobin and Lord Kaldor, and by events. Switzerland had to suspend its monetary targets in 1978 to prevent its exchange rate going too high; and West Germany had over a twenty-year period seen a persistent rate of growth in the money supply in excess of the rise in money income, at the same time contriving (in direct contravention of Friedman's precepts) to preserve a consistently low inflation rate.[17] In addition the Thatcherites had been frequently warned by moderate Conservatives of the dangers of slavishly following fashion and of wholeheartedly embracing an economic doctrine.[18] But just as Christian fundamentalists remain impervious to modern biblical criticism, the monetarist zealots in the new Conservative government did not allow irksome facts or the existence of differing monetarist sects to disturb their faith in the Chicago prophet.[19]*

Their faith in Milton Friedman – or perhaps Margaret Thatcher – was just that. It was not based on profound knowledge, diligent research or, even, consultation with the Bank of England.[20] The late Lord Rothschild, when head of the Heath government's think-tank, always used to refer to one of the more intellectual cabinet members, who had a penchant for economic theory, as 'A-level economics' (sic). In Mrs Thatcher's shadow cabinet that former minister had a number of fellow students; unhappily they made scant progress in their studies. Even by 1988, according to Professor Hahn, Thatcherism's 'simple-minded text-book economics' for all its 'strident certainty' had produced 'no coherent economic arguments' at all.[21]

To Milton Friedman, of course, things looked very different. For him monetary theory was 'like a Japanese garden. It has aesthetic unity born of variety; an apparent simplicity that conceals a sophisticated reality; a surface view that dissolves in ever deeper perspectives. Both can be fully appreciated only if examined from many different angles . . .'[22] But monetarism was not only beautiful, it was also true. Friedman's writings are replete with wide-ranging certainty: 'Inflation is always and everywhere a monetary phenomenon', an *ex cathedra* pronouncement that ignored the English inflations of the sixteenth and seventeenth centuries as well as more recent experience.[23] Of course admissions of doubt or ignorance would have been inappropriate intruders into Friedman's theorizing. He was not, after all, putting forward a hypothesis or just another theory. His theory was infallibly true; it was both faith and science. He suspected, for example, that the 'invariable link' between 'substantial changes in the

---

* According to Friedman himself, 'Margaret Thatcher [was] not in terms of beliefs a Tory. She is a nineteenth-century liberal.'[24] Sir John Nott, Francis Pym's successor as Defence Secretary, said much the same thing of her and of himself.

stock of money over short periods and in prices . . . in the same direction [was a] uniformity of the same order as many of the uniformities that form the basis of the physical sciences.' For Friedman a theory which evidently combined every known virtue provided a complete economic system and a political ideology as well.[25]

As for Friedman, so for his Thatcherite followers. All five of Friedmanite monetarism's basic propositions were at best dubious. Yet the Thatcherites accepted them as indubitable laws. In 1980 Sir Henry Phelps Brown was disturbed to find that the Chancellor of the Exchequer had 'treated monetarism not as one theory among others but as an incontrovertible principle like the law of gravitation'. Another Treasury minister was even more confident. In the House of Lords he likened monetarism to the simple truth that 'if twice one is two, then twice two is four'.[26] Admittedly Keith Joseph had earlier conceded that monetarism was not enough. Yet this was only because he thought that by itself it would not take the country sufficiently far towards *laissez-faire*. Sir Keith was signalling not a retreat but an 'advance from monetarism'. Hence, though monetary control was still deemed a pre-essential for everything desirable and necessary, cuts in public spending and taxation were also needed to release entrepreneurial energies, revitalize the economy and make the system perfect.[27]

Monetarism, then, was the Thatcherite equivalent of the Marxist materialist conception of history. Much as, according to Marxist tenets, the destruction of capitalism and the advent of socialism would revolutionize social, political and economic relations, so would the introduction of monetarism quickly transform the British economy, permanently banish inflation and profoundly alter the beliefs and attitudes of the British people. Unfortunately monetarism, like Marxism, suffered the only fate that for a theory is worse than death: it was put into practice.

That it was Britain which was pioneering a strict monetarist experiment with no concessions to the squeamish was given an ironic welcome by Professor J K Galbraith. He thought Britain's political experience and social cohesion would enable her to stand the strain.[28] The British were like the pigs that were driven across minefields in the First World War to clear the way for those marginally more fortunate beings, the poor bloody infantry. This time, however, not only the pigs were blown up; monetarism, as the Professor expected, was also a casualty.

Indeed the doctrine of monetarism was so comprehensively disproved by its practice that both a considerable effort of memory and a suspension of disbelief are needed to recall that, in the opening years of the Thatcher government, monetarism was its guiding doctrine and principle. And not only the government succumbed to the new orthodoxy. With very few exceptions nearly everyone of influence became a monetarist or at least a fellow-traveller. Yet so discredited is Friedmanite monetarism today in Britain that only a few professors of economics, well accustomed, perhaps, to banishing experience of real life from their speculations,* and some clever amiable eccentrics like Lord Rees-Mogg and Mr Nicholas Budgen, MP, still cling to it. Rarely if ever has a doctrine risen so quickly and fallen so heavily.

Friedmanite monetarism rose because it was thought to provide a simple solution to the problems of inflation, over-mighty trade unions and excessive government intervention in the economy. It fell because it failed. The attempt to control the growth of money proved to be incompatible with the progressive deregulation of the financial system and the consequent growth of credit. The relationship between the growth of money and inflation, which supposedly had been scientifically proved, completely broke down – if indeed it ever existed. And thirdly the (unsuccessful) attempt to control

---

* In 1986 Sir Alan Walters, like Professor Tim Congdon before him, managed to discuss the monetary expansion of the early, and the inflation of the middle, 1970s without mentioning the Arab–Israeli war of 1973 and the quadrupling of the price of oil.[29]

the money supply helped to produce an exceptionally large, rapid and enduring rise in unemployment. But that lay in the future.[30]

The 1979 Budget

In the summer of 1979, in full monetarist innocence, the Thatcherite ministers began their assault on the intractable problems of the British economy. Unsurprisingly, apart from Jim Prior at Employment, monetarist enthusiasts occupied all the key economic posts in the 1979 government. And Margaret Thatcher was, in fact as well as in title, very much the 'First Lord of the Treasury' – so much so indeed that the crucial economic decisions emanated more from No 10 than from No 11 Downing Street.[31]

In 1979, as in most subsequent years, inflation was identified as the chief Conservative enemy. Yet it was far from being the only prominent adversary. Britain's economic performance in comparison with that of our neighbours had long been grim. As well as an inflation rate which was over 10 per cent and rising, the incoming Conservative government inherited a gravely weakened industry, unemployment that had doubled to over a million since 1974, a demoralized public sector and poisoned industrial relations. Furthermore in the election campaign the Conservatives had promised to accept the recommendations of the Clegg Commission on public-service pay – a pledge which despite the dangers of a pay explosion the new government honourably kept.[32]

From one point of view all this made the British economy a suitable subject for experiment: a cure was urgently needed. From another point of view any experimentation was dangerous: although the balance of payments was beginning to be strengthened by the fast-growing extraction of North Sea oil – a bonus which no other government had enjoyed and one which Thatcherite commentators tend to pass over very lightly[33] – the economy had otherwise been weakened, and the patient might well be killed, not cured, by drastic surgery.

In any event the Friedmanite zealots had no doubts. The money supply had quickly to be brought under control, come what might. There was nothing Augustinian about the Thatcherites' craving for what they quaintly called 'monetary continence'. Future chastity was not enough; they wanted it now. Accordingly no time was lost in driving the economy into the monetarist minefield.

Unfortunately, as if wary of finding their task too easy, the Thatcherites almost immediately devised an additional sort of mine, or rather a booby-trap, for themselves. Shortly before Geoffrey Howe's first budget a leading commentator asked me if it was true that VAT was going to be virtually doubled. I said that I had no idea of the contents of the budget – there had been no question of any kind of cabinet consultation in even the broadest terms[34] – but that it was surely inconceivable that anything so silly could even be contemplated. That showed how out of touch I was. The columnist, the late Peter Jenkins, ill-advisedly abandoned his story, and on budget day the Chancellor of the Exchequer revealed to the cabinet that income tax was being substantially cut and VAT was to be increased from 8 per cent (or 12.5 per cent in some cases) to 15 per cent. And that was not the end of it. In the first display of the government's free-market zeal John Nott and Norman Tebbit at the Department of Trade had abolished price controls, and now the budget put up nationalized industries' prices and the tax on petrol. All in all the first budget of the anti-inflation crusaders propelled the retail price index upwards by almost six percentage points. The right-wing American economist, Arthur Laffer, predicted it would cause a disastrous recession.[35]

Admittedly Labour had raised taxation on big incomes to vindictively self-defeating heights, and it was difficult to reduce those rates without giving a substantial morsel to other income tax-payers as well. Moreover the Thatcherites held a strong belief in the therapeutic properties of lower direct taxation which would, they thought, galvanize hitherto complacent businessmen into dramatic entrepreneurial activity.* Yet the government's overriding economic aim was to lower inflation, and most people are fairly well aware that the best way to bring inflation down is not to put prices up – especially when inflationary pressures are already intense. The Treasury had warned its ministers of the likely effect of the VAT increase on wage claims, and Jim Prior had similarly warned Mrs Thatcher. Those warnings were ignored, and the reassurances of monetarist economists were accepted.[36]

What was plain to almost everybody else could not be seen by the monetarist elect, blinkered as they were by dogma. As Milton Friedman had laid down that inflation was always caused by excessive monetary growth, they were blind to the important distinction between a 'demand pull and a cost push' inflation, 'which on the most casual survey of inflationary experience,' wrote Sir John Hicks, 'simply leaps to the eye.' Yet, even after presumably rather more careful study, it was invisible to the Thatcherites. According to their theology, incredibly enough, neither tax nor wage increases would raise the inflation rate;[37] inflation could only be caused by an increase in the money supply, and that was going to be rigidly controlled by the government. Hence the hike in VAT would have, if anything, a benign impact on inflation. Writing in 1986, between stints as Mrs Thatcher's economic advisor, Sir Alan Walters defended the VAT increase on the grounds first that it should have led to rational 'expectations' of lower price increases in the future, and second that 'price increases *remove* inflationary pressure; they do not add to it.'[38]

Regrettably, trade unionists were not well versed in monetarist doctrine and had no such expectations, rational or otherwise. They therefore responded to the price rises in the way everybody but the monetarists knew they would: by putting in larger wage claims. The result was that inflation reached a peak of 21.9 per cent in May 1980. So a government

---

* John Biffen, however, feared that the chief upswing might be seen in their golf. He was probably right.[39]

whose chief objective was to defeat inflation had in its first year succeeded in doubling it.[40]

The Medium-Term Financial Strategy

The Thatcherites' first extremist budget[41] – their first foray into monetarism – caused heavy losses. But it was a mere skirmish compared with the struggle to control the money supply and lower public expenditure.

Early in 1917 the relatively inexperienced General Nivelle, who had recently succeeded General Joffre as the French Commander-in-Chief, decided to launch a major offensive against the German salient in Champagne. Believing he had discovered the secret of victory, Nivelle discarded the old plodding strategy in favour of greater audacity and simplicity. He was going to fight a decisive battle and he was confident of success. Unfortunately, the weather turned nasty, the attack was delayed, and surprise was lost. Knowing what was going to happen, the Germans withdrew their forces from the salient to the Hindenburg line. Yet though almost all the relevant circumstances had changed, General Nivelle still launched his offensive almost exactly as he had originally planned it. Inevitably his attack soon ended in costly defeat. Much of the French army mutinied, and Nivelle was replaced by General Pétain.[42]

The Thatcherites' attack on the money supply and public spending bore a strong resemblance to General Nivelle's offensive. Like him they thought they had discovered a magic formula, and like him they were certain of success. Like him, they had planned their attack long in advance, ignored warnings of likely disaster and failed to change their plans despite radically altered conditions. And like him they, too, suffered calamitous failure. Almost the only differences were that just a few of their troops mutinied, the Thatcherites continued the battle despite the mounting casualties, and while General Nivelle did at least attack the right enemy, the Thatcherites attacked the wrong one; finally

Mrs Thatcher was the supreme authority, so there was no one to dismiss her.

In 1979–80 Britain's economic circumstances were transformed by a sharp rise in the price of oil, by Britain becoming a large-scale oil producer, by the Clegg Commission and by the government's own budget. During 1979 and the first half of 1980 oil prices nearly tripled as a result of the Ayatollah Khomeini's revolution in Iran. For Britain, fast becoming a major exporter instead of an importer of oil, the oil price increase was far from all bad. It would improve our relative position and was of immediate benefit to the government's own finances.[43] Yet the jump in the oil price obviously added to industry's costs and to inflationary pressures, already stoked up by the government's acceptance of the Clegg Commission and by its own budget. Worst of all, it also created the virtual certainty of a world recession.

Such a fundamental change in economic conditions might have been expected to produce a marked effect on economic policy. After all, to conduct a monetarist experiment concurrently with a three-fold rise in oil prices and an eruption of wage claims would seem to be less than rational. The Thatcherites proved no more capable, however, of acting in accordance with 'rational expectations' than did the trade unions. Undeterred by the prospect of a world recession abroad, they proceeded to create their own far worse recession at home.[44]

In his budget Geoffrey Howe had put up interest rates by two points, and tightened the monetary target for M3 from the previous government's range. In November 1979 interest rates were raised by a further three percentage points. This massive rise proved even more damaging to industry than the increase in VAT. The pound rose sharply – all the more so because it was now a petro-currency. Yet the main cause of its upward surge, to the dismay of exporters and the delight of importers, was the high interest rates, which attracted a flood of foreign money.[45]

According to monetarist dogma the exchange rate should

be left to the market to determine; the government should concern itself with the money supply and let the pound look after itself. Exchange controls were abolished in October 1979.* At the time I thought the decision was sensible since it seemed likely to slow sterling's climb. But, in the event, it scarcely did. In any case the decision owed less to concern at the pound's rise than to the Thatcherites' ideological belief in the invariable beneficence of market forces. Yet this ideological triumph was won at the expense of a far more important ideological objective, for the dismantling of exchange controls made the government's primary objective – control of the money supply – virtually unattainable.[46]

Industry found itself in a multiple squeeze: an artificially high pound, high interest rates, greatly increased costs, caused by high oil prices and the wage explosion, and a sharp fall in demand at home and abroad. Company profits fell by 20 per cent during 1980, output fell by nearly 6 per cent, manufacturing output fell by 15 per cent and unemployment rose from 1.3 million to over two million. Laffer's prediction was all too accurate.[47]

As early as February 1980 the outlook was so bleak that I made the first of my public criticisms of Thatcherite economic policy. The speech was a lecture on Conservatism that I had agreed to give before the election. As I had not changed my views and had a heavy workload at the Foreign Office it was inevitably, as Mrs Thatcher fairly said, largely a rehash of my previous books. Nobody in the 1979 cabinet thought the economy could have continued as it had in the 1970s. We were all aware of Britain's relative decline. Everybody agreed that changes to a freer economy were needed, and at Cambridge I reaffirmed that view. But amidst a good deal of Burke and a smattering of Salisbury and the Younger Pitt, I also derided dogmatic reliance on market forces alone and disregard of

* Like many other cabinet ministers I learned of it from the newspapers. Secrecy had to be preserved of course, but that should not have ruled out a general discussion of the issue in cabinet.[48]

their social and political consequences; I said there should be no Conservative hostility to the state in general, and I defended the welfare state in particular.[49]

According to constitutional doctrine, cabinet members who disagree with government policy should not criticize it but resign. I did not follow that course, firstly because the government's economic policy was not that of the cabinet as a whole but of a secretive monetarist clique – since collective decision-making had been abandoned, it followed in my view that collective responsibility had also been relaxed.[50] My second reason was political. In a piece which I had originally written for an introduction to our 1979 election manifesto by the leader of the party, and which was instead published separately as a message from Margaret Thatcher, *Now is the Time to Choose*, I had said: 'We shall unite the country by the politics of common sense. And we shall restore the economy by the economics of common sense.'[51] Ridiculous as it seems now, like many colleagues I still had lingering if fading hopes that common sense (or Conservatism in Arthur Balfour's well-known view of it) would soon be introduced into the conduct of economic policy and that the economic ministers would in the end digest the lessons of events.

That was a vain hope. Events certainly did all that was expected of them, but the Thatcherites failed to respond to such mundane considerations. They were too absorbed in their doctrine to be educated by mere events. So common sense remained absent, and instead of moderating a policy which had already caused devastation, the economic ministers institutionalized and perpetuated it. In March 1980 the Treasury unveiled the so-called Medium-Term Financial Strategy, to a fanfare of self-congratulation. Its reception by the cabinet was less than ecstatic, a number of us thinking that what was needed was a medium- *and* short-term strategy to deal with unemployment. Full employment, however, was not a government objective; monetarist dogma taught that government could not, and should not try to, control that sort of thing.[52]

Regardless of the recession, the essence of the MTFS was 'progressively [to] reduce the growth of the money stock'. Gradually declining targets for the money supply and for the Public Sector Borrowing Requirement were set for the next four years without spelling out how they would be attained. The MTFS was thus a series of signposts without a road. Despite this omission, the government rashly concluded its exposition of its strategy with the pledge that 'there would be no question of departing from the money supply policy, which is essential to the success of any anti-inflationary strategy'.[53] Fortunately, that resounding promise was soon safely buried in Treasury verbiage. Even as it was, the MTFS caused mayhem, but nothing like as much as it would have created if the government had succeeded in adhering to it.[54]

Shortly afterwards Nigel Lawson, the Financial Secretary and by far the ablest exponent of Thatcherite economics, set out the government's thinking, confidently laying down 'two basic propositions: The first is that changes in the quantity of money determine at the end of the day changes in the general price level; the second is that government is able to determine the quantity of money.'[55] Unfortunately both the Financial Secretary's basic propositions turned out to be wrong.

Indeed everything about the MTFS turned out to be mistaken. The Thatcherites were attacking the wrong enemies. The money supply and the PSBR, the intermediate targets which the government was certain it could control, turned out to be every bit as elusive as the real targets – employment, growth etc. – and the Treasury was quite unable to control them either. In the first four years none of the targets originally set in 1980 for M3 and the PSBR was ever hit. The growth of M3 in the first three years of the MTFS was respectively 74 per cent, 37 per cent, and 23 per cent above the top of the ranges set in 1980.[56] In consequence the government kept on setting new targets. But – to move from archery to football – even this widening of the goal posts produced no goals for some time. Eventually in 1982 the Thatcherites implicitly admitted defeat. M3 was dethroned, and the government announced that it would 'take account of' two other monetary aggregates as well. This was not so much a matter of moving the goalposts as of erecting them all round the pitch. Under such conditions even Neasden United under the management of the ashen-faced Ron Knee[57] might on some occasions have found the net. And indeed the government at long last managed to score an occasional goal.*

The second main feature of the MTFS – the determination to cut the PSBR, 'that most myopic of indicators',[58] in order to bring down inflation – was if anything even more peculiar than the idolatry of sterling M3. It was based on two elementary mistakes. The first delusion was that, as was laid down in the first sentence of the government's first White Paper on the subject, 'Public expenditure is at the heart of Britain's present economic difficulties.' In fact, apart from Greece, Britain's ratio of public expenditure to GDP was then the lowest in the European Community. The second delusion was the government's deeply held conviction that a high PSBR produced an enlarged money supply. That, too, was simply wrong, Lord Kaldor having shown conclusively that there had recently been no correlation whatever between the two.[59] He of course was a Keynesian left winger. But even Friedman himself told a House of Commons committee that there was 'no necessary relation between the size of PSBR and monetary growth', adding that emphasis on the PSBR diverted attention from 'the really important aspects of government fiscal policy'.[60]

Thus, much more fundamentalist than their own prophet, the Thatcherites sought to secure a reduction in the PSBR – which was supposed to bring inflation down – by increasing indirect taxation which put inflation up. The same thing happened elsewhere. In order to lower the PSBR the nationalized industries were made to increase their prices and charges. In

* With unintentional irony Sir Alan Walters described the feat of bringing all the monetary aggregates within the new target range set for 1982–83 as one of Geoffrey Howe's 'remarkable coups'.[61]

other words the government's pursuit of its intermediate targets did not merely cause a slump, it initially raised inflation as well, while placing additional burdens on those least able to bear them.[62] Monetarist doctrine was wrong-headed enough without the Thatcherite ministers adding to the damage by misunderstanding it.

The reason for their extraordinary misconception lay in the belief, particularly associated with the Prime Minister,[63] that the nation's borrowing should be treated as it would be in an ordinary household. Yet, as John Stuart Mill pointed out long ago, analogies between the individual and the nation are inapplicable;[64] certainly the analogy with the prudent (or imprudent) housewife was inappropriate. For one thing, a housewife knows what her income and expenses are. The 1979 government did not; its estimates of the PSBR were massively wide of the mark. More important, if a housewife cuts her household expenses, she does not thereby cut her income. Not so a national government. Unlike a housewife, a government has responsibilities not only for its own finances but also for the national economy. And when a government spends less, it indirectly causes its own income to fall. A government which cuts its spending on goods or services reduces national income and increases unemployment. As a consequence, it has to spend more on unemployment benefit and receives lower income from taxes. The loss of government revenue and the higher recession-induced expenditure largely cancel out the effects of the previous cuts in spending, so that the gap between expenditure and income, the PSBR, remains wide.

Hence the eight or nine attempts of various sorts to cut government expenditure between 1979 and 1981 resulted in the Treasury always seeking to balance the books at an ever-lower level of economic activity. The PSBR was not allowed to play its proper role of helping to stabilize the economy.[65]

In contrast with its attitude to the PSBR the government's treatment of cost–push inflation[66] as though it was an inflation caused by excessive demand was in full accordance with Friedmanite dogma. Yet 'deflation', as Keynes warned in 1925, does not reduce wages 'automatically'. 'It reduces them', he continued, 'by causing unemployment. The proper object of dear money is to check an incipient boom. Woe to those whose faith leads them to use it to aggravate a depression.'[67] That was exactly what the Thatcherites were doing, bringing in consequence a large amount of woe to the ever-growing army of the unemployed. That woe would have been yet more widespread if the Bank of England had not pumped billions of pounds into the financial system. By doing so, it saved the whole financial system from ruin – while at the same time frustrating the government's scheme of controlling the money supply.[68]

Although the economy declined sharply throughout 1980, the Treasury asked the cabinet in November to agree yet again to substantial cuts in public expenditure. Remarkably, the 'wets' to much Thatcherite irritation largely succeeded in foiling the Treasury's attempt. We had gained a temporary victory.[69]

By November 1980 I was so alarmed by what was being done by a government of which I was a member that I decided to make another speech critical of its economic policy. Dining with Roy Jenkins, the President of the Commission, during a Foreign Affairs Council in Luxemburg, I outlined what I was going to say. He asked why I had to say anything at all about the economy.* Clearly a second mutinous speech was tantamount to ministerial suicide, but I thought it preferable to acquiescent silence.

The occasion was a celebration of Lord Butler's thirty years as President of Cambridge University Conservative Association, and I spoke on Rab Butler and the continuity of

---

* One of Mrs Thatcher's objections to me was my being a friend of Roy Jenkins. 'Why,' she later asked Sir John Junor, 'does he have Roy Jenkins to dinner?' She might have been less resentful had she known that over dinner he had recommended more restrained opposition.[70]

post-war Conservatism. This time doing without the Burkean covering fire, I maintained that the claim that there were no alternatives to the government's economic policy was not true, suggested that monetarism was a passing fad, and warned that if we allowed our society to become divided between a fortunate skilled majority (who could get work) and an unfortunate unskilled minority (for whom employment prospects remained bleak), we risked the creation of a 'Clockwork Orange' society with its attendant alienation and misery.[71] Shortly afterwards at a party at No 10 the Prime Minister, very understandably, made several complaints about my speech and asked why I never made any speeches supporting the government.*

Towards the end of 1980 the Thatcherites, increasingly puzzled by the conjunction of a slump and a soaring M3, commissioned a monetarist expert to investigate the prevailing monetary conditions and report whether they were indeed as tight as the severe recession suggested or as loose as the spiralling-upwards M3 indicated. The fact that any inquiry at all was felt to be necessary was in itself revealing. Most people, after all, if confronted with a contradiction between a heavy thunder-storm plainly visible through their window and a barometer inside their house certifying 'fair weather' would have little difficulty in concluding that their barometer was faulty; and at the end of 1980 nobody could doubt the existence of astronomically high unemployment and a cascade of bankruptcies. Yet so strong was the hold of dogma that only after a Swiss monetarist, Professor Jürg Niehans, had reported that what was happening in real life to the real economy was the correct indicator and M3 the wrong one did the Treasury ministers and many monetarists

---

* At the same party Jim Prior at full volume congratulated me on coining the description of the government's policies 'the economics of the madhouse'. Although it was not my phrase, it was a good and accurate one, so my disavowal was muted and amounted to asking whether he was not its true father. In fact it was almost certainly Peter Walker's child.

tacitly concede that monetary conditions were far tighter than they had intended. They had, in other words, made a terrible mistake, and in consequence had caused, quite unnecessarily, far and away the worst recession since the war.[72]

That monetary blunder set the scene for the 1981 budget. Another scene-setter was the 'wets'' victory in November on public spending; a third was the economic naivety of much of the City of London, made greater by years of monetarist indoctrination. Mrs Thatcher and Professor Walters, the Prime Minister's economic advisor, who had himself been convinced long before the Niehans report that monetary conditions were far too tight, evidently decided that the way to deal with all these factors was to squeeze the economy still further by reducing the PBSR from an expected £14 billion to £10.5 billion. The bold stratagem of introducing a heavily deflationary budget during a slump would help to conceal the disastrous mishandling of monetary policy and allow a further drop in interest rates. (They had been reduced by 2 per cent in November.) A savage fiscal squeeze would in addition satisfy the City that the Thatcherites were still being tough, and would also wreak suitable vengeance on 'the wets' for foiling them over public spending cuts.[73]

The use of the PSBR as the main engine of deflation instead of the disgraced M3 was thus both a demonstration of Thatcherite virility and an elaborate camouflage for monetarist failure. The squeeze was largely accomplished by cuts in public expenditure on capital programmes and by increases in taxes, the brunt of which, as in previous budgets, was borne by the less well off.

I thought at the time that the 1981 budget would accentuate the recession, causing even more unemployment and spelling even greater destruction for industry, and I was confirmed in that view by the famous letter from 364 economists, which maintained that deflation of demand alone would never generate a recovery. Yet the 1981 budget has long been hailed by the Thatcherites as a counter-Keynesian master stroke, a magic potion which produced a miraculous recovery.

And for a long time, too, the conventional wisdom has been that we were all wrong; that 'ironically' it was just when the economists' letter appeared that the economy was 'bottoming out' and allegedly entering the longest period of uninterrupted growth of the post-war period. The episode has even been taken as marking the final demise of Keynesianism and, equally absurdly, as David Howell has said, as 'some sort of Stalingrad, the moment when the dark forces of public expenditure were finally and heroically turned'.[74]

So what really happened in 1981–82? Economic activity never goes on falling indefinitely, and not even our government could have made permanent the catastrophic depression of 1979–81. Part of the Treasury expected the fall in output to come to an end in the first half of 1981,[75] and the National Institute thought the same. In its February Review it said 'while the decline in economic activity is not expected to continue, GDP is forecast to remain virtually unchanged during 1981 and 1982 with only limited signs of future recovery towards the end of the period. At the same time . . . unemployment [is expected to reach] 3 million by the end of 1982.' That was pretty close to the mark.

Output did rise a little during the course of 1981, but taking the year as a whole GDP was about 1.5 per cent lower than in 1980. There can be no true recovery unless output is rising fast enough to reduce unemployment, that is by at least 3 per cent a year. Instead of recovery after 1981, there was 'a growth recession', with an average growth rate of 2.8 per cent a year between 1981 and 1985, while unemployment (which lags behind output) continued to grow – by one-third, or three-quarters of a million – for five more years after the 1981 budget, only peaking in mid 1986. The militantly monetarist Patrick Minsford was surely right to concede, therefore, that the 1981 budget 'badly worsened the supply-side'. Recoveries from previous recessions were far quicker. Despite all the Thatcherite self-applause, the inverted Keynesianism of the 1981 budget postponed recovery.[76]

Furthermore, such rise in output as did occur in 1981 was

entirely accounted for by the ending of the run-down in stocks. In the last quarter of 1980 stockbuilding had been negative to the tune of nearly £6 billion (at an annual rate), but by the last quarter of 1981 this had reverted to nearly zero, thereby contributing about 2 per cent to the growth of GDP. The further small rise in GDP (1.5 per cent) which took place in 1982 equally does not substantiate claims of spontaneous growth or of the success of the 1981 budget, because so much of it was caused by the fall in personal savings which followed the removal of all controls on consumer credit in the middle of the year. As a result of this decontrol, in the year ending in the second quarter of 1983 consumption of consumer durables rose discontinuously by over 20 per cent. 1982, in other words, saw the beginning of the government's reflation, brought about by a credit boom. Belatedly, the lady was for turning after all. And two weeks after the 1983 election she had to turn again: mortgage rates were increased by 1.5 per cent.[77]

Almost certainly, therefore, the claim of the 364 economists that the government's policies as set out in 1981 would never produce a recovery was right. As, however, the government did not continue with the policy the economists had condemned, but partially adopted their advice while pouring derision upon it, we shall never know for sure.

We do know, though, that the costs of what the government attempted were enormous. Like their opponents, monetarists are fond of military metaphors. Defending the high and rising unemployment in January 1982, Nigel Lawson explained that it was 'a war against inflation that we are fighting. In war, casualties are inescapable. They are neither intended, nor are they unexpected. They are a sign neither of wickedness nor incompetence.'[78] That was misleading since, although there would have anyway been some rise in unemployment because of the increase in the price of oil, the sort of war the government was fighting was neither intended nor expected. Had the Thatcherites actually intended the havoc they caused, they would, in Nigel Lawson's language, have been 'wicked' rather than merely incompetent, and the indictment against them would be far heavier than it is. Nevertheless the French army in 1917 was luckier than the British economy in 1980–81. Having got themselves into a far bloodier and less successful conflict than they had expected, the monetarist commanders unlike the French persisted in their misconceived Thatcherite strategy, thereby maximizing the country's casualties.[79]

In consequence, by the second quarter of 1981 they had doubled the unemployment they inherited.[80] Poverty and misery had similarly increased. Between the election in 1979 and the first half of 1981 output fell by 5 per cent, and manufacturing production fell by 17 per cent. The decline in industrial output was 'the fastest in recorded history'. Most serious of all, between a quarter and a fifth of manufacturing industry was wiped out.[81]

Although this débâcle was both unintended and unexpected, various attempts have been made to maintain that it benefited the economy,[82] rather as the Allies' wartime obliteration of much of German industry led to Germany's economic renaissance in the 1950s. Unfortunately, the application to industry of what might be called the Dr Bodkin Adams school of medicine did not have the curative properties that were claimed for it, as Britain's economic difficulties a decade later conclusively demonstrated. But it undoubtedly did have some beneficial side effects. Many businesses which by good management or good luck survived the treatment did become, as the phrase went, leaner and fitter. The trouble was that the government's continued prescription of starvation as a remedy for anorexia killed off many others, some of them already moribund, some of them previously in good health. And investment by the survivors was heavily reduced. Ironically, therefore, by their policies of cutting demand the proponents of 'supply-side economics' ended up crippling supply.[83]

Thus, despite the apologias that were later dreamed up, Thatcherite monetarism, though tempered (luckily) by incompetence, proved in 1979–81 to be every bit as destructive as had ever been feared by even the gloomiest pessimists.

III

Why the Moderates Lost

I regard [Conservatives who believed in consensus politics] as quislings, as traitors.

Margaret Thatcher in 1978[1]

On I went through this world of wetness.

Logan Pearsall Smith[2]

MANY OF THE better-off did well even out of the earliest Thatcher period. Yet monetarist dogma was so cruelly discredited by its results, and Thatcherite economic policy in its opening years so patently disastrous that the survival of either of them, let alone their continuing relentless implementation, provides cause for surprise. The Tory moderates always held two convictions about an extreme monetarist economic policy: it would be socially divisive and it would not work. With riots in Brixton, Liverpool, Birmingham, Leeds, Bradford and some twenty-five other towns, and more than a thousand policemen injured, and with rocketing bankruptcies and unemployment, we were on both counts proved right.[3]*

* According to Kenneth Harris, whose biography almost canonizes Mrs Thatcher, 'there is general agreement now that the monetary policy envisaged in the MTFS was too simplistic — that the wets were right.'[4]

Why then, it may be asked, did the moderates n
acceptably sensible behaviour by their Thatcherite co.
Why, instead, did we acquiesce in the most damaging s
economic decisions since before the war? Those are, as
say, good questions, to which two answers have been offered
by commentators: the moderates' failure to propose an alternative economic policy and their personal inadequacies – for
instance *inter alia* their weakness, indecision and disunity.[5]

The first answer is palpably mistaken. For one thing, when
policy will in all probability have disastrous results (which
soon become apparent) its opponents are not required to
produce a completely articulated alternative programme. They
are entitled just to oppose what is being done, to point to its
calamitous consequences and to urge its abandonment. The
remedy, after all, for banging your head against the wall is
to stop doing so.

For another, the moderates did have an alternative. We
favoured a policy to bring down inflation, but deplored
the injection into the economy of neo-Liberal dogma which
increased it. We were opposed to the obsessive pursuit of
monetary targets and the frenetic cutting of public expenditure, and we did not think reduced inflation should be the
sole policy objective. We thought that both unemployment
and the pound were far too high. We favoured growth not
slump. In opposition to rampant ideology, our policy was one
of economic common sense.[6]

Our alternative was never a single simple unalterable
blueprint, because the situation was changing and economic
blueprints are never right. Had we produced a blueprint, it
would have been much less damaging than the Friedmanite
fantasy of our opponents, yet to do so would have been to
make much the same mistake that they had made: 'a plan
to resist all planning,' Michael Oakeshott said of Hayek's
The Road to Serfdom, 'may be better than its opposite, but
it belongs to the same style of politics.'[7]

Thirdly, to have produced a blueprint would have been
wholly unrealistic, for it would have been never been discussed.

In the early nineteenth century any member of the cabinet could summon a cabinet meeting, but not today. Prime ministers have long had control of the cabinet's agenda and the circulation of its papers; and Mrs Thatcher would not have permitted the flaunting of heresy in a cabinet paper, let alone discussion of it around the cabinet table.*
In any case, even if the inconceivable had occurred and the moderates had produced an economic blueprint which the Prime Minister had allowed to be circulated and discussed, the debate would not have been productive. People in the grip of dogma are neither susceptible to reason nor prone to the admission of error. The moderates' proposals would have been shouted down, contradicted with inaccurate 'facts', pelted with erroneous arguments and then ignored. All in all, therefore, the suggestion that the right wing prevailed because the moderates did not produce an alternative can be dismissed.[9]

The second answer – the personal inadequacies of the wets – is more plausible. Indeed it is probably correct. Within the ranks of the moderates were men of great weight, ability and experience. Yet they allowed themselves to be defeated by people, who, the Prime Minister apart, matched them in none of these, and who furthermore were possessed by ideology and delusion. The verdict therefore must be: 'guilty of grave dereliction of duty'; but, before returning it, one or two pleas in mitigation should be entered and a few words of explanation allowed.

The circumstances were unprecedented. Never before had a prime minister and a few close associates embarked upon so disastrous an economic experiment while keeping the cabinet at a distance. The nearest equivalent, which had similarly unhappy results, is probably Neville Chamberlain

---

* Three weeks after the 1979 election Jim Prior sent Mrs Thatcher a paper on incomes policy. The paper was not circulated or discussed. It was merely returned to Jim Prior with some rude comments by the Prime Minister.[8]

and the so-called Big Four's running of foreign policy in the
few weeks before the Munich agreement in 1938.[10]

'The Prime Minister,' according to a leading Thatcherite,
'carries the responsibility of the executive, just as the President
of the USA does.' Nicholas Ridley may well have been accurately describing (or rationalizing) Mrs Thatcher's attitude
and behaviour, but he was not giving a recognizable picture
of the British constitution, at least prior to 1979. Except in
very exceptional circumstances the prime minister is of course
much the most powerful member of the cabinet. That has been
so for a long time; writing in 1889 John Morley thought the
premier occupied 'a position which so long as it lasts is one
of exceptional and peculiar authority'. Other ministers are
effectively tenants of the prime minister with no security of
tenure. Nevertheless the prime minister is not a president, and
the executive is a collective one. That is the difference between
the parliamentary and the presidential systems. Indeed Enoch
Powell went so far as to say that 'it is the collective view which
is at the back of the mind of the individual minister all the
time'.[11]

Mrs Thatcher, however, seldom had anywhere in her mind
any sort of 'collective view', or even any apparent desire for
one. No doubt the idea smacked too much of the dreaded
'consensus politics'. Since she regarded those Conservatives
who 'believed in consensus politics . . . as quislings, as
traitors', a search for agreement or compromise with them
was unthinkable. To the Prime Minister, ideological affinity
was imperative.[12]

The normal conventions of cabinet government were therefore disregarded – if indeed they ever entered her consciousness
– to facilitate the translation of her monetarist convictions
and neo-Liberal ideology into government policy. Margaret
Thatcher's dominant characteristic was, and remained, a
compulsive need always to have her own way. This can
be regarded either as heroic resolve on a Churchillian
scale or as childish obstinacy stemming from deep-seated
insecurity. Whichever it was, it had important constitutional

implications, which will be considered lower down. Here we are only concerned with the considerable difficulty it presented to her most senior colleagues, who were accustomed to dealing with people at least partially amenable to facts and arguments, and with prime ministers who respected, more or less, the constitutional conventions of cabinet government. Those venerable gentlemen were also at an additional and unprecedented disadvantage. Mrs Thatcher, in the words of Anthony King, had 'long ago observed that well brought-up Englishmen . . . have no idea what to do with a strong, assertive woman.'[13]

Faced with a Prime Minister who disliked cabinet government and sought to evade it in order always to prevail, her most senior colleagues had either to acquiesce in what was going on – in so far as they knew what it was – or present her with an ultimatum that unless she changed tack they would resign their offices. Since to act in such a way might well have split the Conservative party, they would have been in a serious dilemma, had they ever confronted it. In fact they did not. All able and honourable men, none of them counted economics as his strongest suit. So apart from the occasional intervention at the rare cabinet discussions of economic policy – even the Permanent Secretary to the Treasury was shocked by his Chancellor of the Exchequer's secretiveness – all they ever did was to hope that the results of Mrs Thatcher's policy would turn out better than ever seemed probable.[14]

The second plea in mitigation is that the sheer weight of departmental business told against the moderates. Most cabinet members had so much to do in their own departments that they had only limited time for sorting out the mistakes made by their colleagues. There is nothing new of course about ministers' preoccupation with their own departments. Lord Salisbury, when both Prime Minister and Foreign Secretary, devoted most of his time to the Foreign Office; 'the Prime Ministership' got whatever was left over. In the early fifties Harold Macmillan, to his subsequent regret, was too engrossed with the Ministry of Housing to press the

European issue. Since then, the volume of ministerial work has grown.[15]

Thirdly a group that does not include the prime minister has difficulty in combining, more especially when the cause of the trouble is not a sudden event or crisis but a long-running policy. Nowadays only the prime minister can summon meetings without taint of disloyalty, and Mrs Thatcher had her group of zealots who met weekly for breakfast. Other ministers could not meet regularly without the fact soon being widely known. They would then have been open to the (justified) charge of forming a cabal which, being contrary to the Tory ethos, would have damaged their cause. So, although our failure to combine was fatal, it was also virtually unavoidable.[16]

Finally it was not a question of tough conviction politicians seeing off a bunch of weak-kneed consensus ones. Our long-held convictions were a good deal more in evidence than those of many of the ministers who had fairly recently changed theirs and who now kept in full consensual step with those of Margaret Thatcher. Peter Carrington was certainly not a weak Foreign Secretary. Jim Prior insisted on going his own way on trade-union reform. If Norman St John Stevas had been influenced by Mrs Thatcher's wishes, he would not have carried through his important reforms of House of Commons procedure. Peter Walker paid very little attention to the Prime Minister on agriculture. And Francis Pym protected the defence budget so tenaciously that she had to move him to another office.[17]

So much for the mitigation. The rest is explanation, not excuse. In one sense the moderates had a majority in Mrs Thatcher's first cabinet. Yet that was only formally true; the majority was mostly silent. In 1915 Sir Edward Carson told his cabinet colleagues that they were 'twenty-three blind mice'. Not all Mrs Thatcher's first cabinet were mice or blind, but many of them were both. As in every cabinet there were ministers who had no wish to become entangled with the Prime Minister; she had appointed them and she had the power to remove them. Some, Hugo Young pointed out at the time, would anyway have had difficulty in engaging in intelligent economic debate, even if they had had the inclination. Hence, the cabinet, which met much more rarely than any of its twentieth-century predecessors, was little more than a semi-detached observer of economic events.[18]

For a different reason Peter Carrington did not wish to become more than marginally embroiled. He was as far from being an ideologue as it is possible to be, but he had his hands full with foreign affairs, and a foreign secretary who dabbles too openly in economic policy is practically inviting the economic ministers to interfere in his domain – something no sensible foreign secretary would willingly contemplate. In addition, in 1979–80, Peter Carrington felt that since every other remedy for the British economy had been tried and failed, monetarism should be given its chance – it could, he felt, scarcely be worse than what had gone before. That of course was an error – things always can be worse, and they soon were – but it was an understandable one. Christopher Soames made much the same judgement. The adroit and deservedly popular Willie Whitelaw also held moderate views. But he seemed to disagree with Harold Macmillan's view that the Conservative party is not a military formation obediently executing orders. The deputy leader of the party, the number two man in the cabinet and the number one fixer, Willie Whitelaw seemingly regarded himself as being like a second-in-command of a battalion with Mrs Thatcher as the commanding officer; he therefore conceived it his duty to support the Prime Minister, right or wrong.[19]

Quintin Hailsham, whose pupil at the bar and, later, PPS I have had the great good luck to be, was likewise a wet. 'I sit there,' he once told me outside the cabinet room, 'quietly oozing.' Much the best Conservative thinker in politics since the war, he had in opposition written a prescient book pointing to the dangers of an 'elective dictatorship'; he decided in 1979, however, that the time was not ripe for his constitutional reforms,[20] and although he made some electric dissenting interventions he, too, thought he should not oppose the Prime Minister. Francis Pym was for much of the first eighteen months kept busy defending with some success the defence budget, which the Treasury was seeking to reduce, notwithstanding that as Shadow Defence Secretary I had spent three years pledging, with Mrs Thatcher's full support, that a Conservative government would increase it.[21] Finally, Michael Heseltine was no monetarist, but he was sensibly selective in his opposition.

Hence, for one reason or another, 'the big beasts of the jungle'[22] had all become domesticated, or rather had built their own cages. In consequence the only marauding beasts still at large were smaller and less dangerous than those who should have been stalking the monetarist ministers and guarding the economy from their depredations. Effectively, indeed, until the spring of 1981, the only four open and consistent dissenters from the right wing's economic policy were Jim Prior, Peter Walker, Norman St John Stevas and myself; and Norman was sacked in January 1981.

No doubt we could have done more, though except in one respect it is not easy even with hindsight to see how. Jim Prior as Employment Minister was the only one clearly involved in economic policy, and even he was excluded from the inner ring of Thatcherite ministers. Peter Walker at Agriculture was only peripherally involved, and I at the Foreign Office was wholly excluded. Even if the three of us had made, as some backbenchers were urging, a sort of 'Relugas Compact' – not an encouraging precedent* – agreeing that if one of us was sacked the other two would resign, we were not, I think, in sufficiently important positions for that to have deterred the Prime Minister. In any case, even if I had especially wished to survive, which I did not, it was plainly not for me, who

---

* By the so-called compact made at Relugas, Grey's fishing lodge in Scotland, Asquith, Haldane and Grey agreed in 1905 not to serve in a Campbell-Bannerman government, unless the Prime Minister consented to go to the House of Lords. Campbell-Bannerman insisted on staying in the Commons, and Asquith, Haldane and Grey all joined his government.[23]

was easily the most vulnerable of the three, to suggest an agreement of that sort.

The night before the 1981 budget, which according to her biographer was 'uniquely shaped by Mrs Thatcher',[24] Jim Prior and I were at the same official dinner. I sat next to Jack Jones who talked a deal of good sense about the economy and unemployment. Jim told me the budget would be appalling, and after dinner we went off to discuss it over a drink. Before we could do so I ran into Rupert Murdoch. He was a press proprietor whom Mrs Thatcher had not felt able to ennoble, but not because he was not 'one of us'. At least as far to the right as the Prime Minister, Murdoch hated the wets, regarding us as 'hypocrites' and 'pissing liberals', and nagged his editors, or rather the one or two of them who required nagging, into being as sycophantic as possible to Mrs Thatcher.[25] Murdoch informed me that nowadays nobody cared about unemployment, including apparently the unemployed, and that inflation was all that mattered. Armed with that wisdom, I listened to Jim's account of the next day's budget, which was indeed astonishingly perverse and bound to lead to prolonged and astronomic unemployment. No wonder the First Lord of the Treasury and the Chancellor of the Exchequer had withheld any hint of their strategy from the Cabinet![26]

The next day the two of us and Peter Walker – he and I were old and close friends and long-time political allies – had breakfast together. Since the first and only cabinet discussion on the budget was later that morning (i.e. just hours before Geoffrey Howe would be on his feet in the House of Commons) the cabinet meeting would be a formality; the budget was a *fait accompli*. Largely for those reasons Jim Prior thought resignation would be futile, and we decided to stay, a decision that was confirmed at a brief meeting with Peter Carrington shortly afterwards. At cabinet we expressed our dissent, and after it the Downing Street propaganda machine (not invented but energetically developed by the Thatcher regime) duly leaked to the press that we were the only ministers who had opposed the budget.[27]

Jim Prior and I later regretted that we had not resigned. Peter Walker thought we were right to stay because our resignations might have damaged sterling and the economy.[28]

Leaving aside the question whether or not we should have resigned, would our joint resignations have made any significant difference? Almost certainly they would have had no direct effect on government policy. Despite its dire results, the Thatcherites remained convinced it was right. The only immediate consequence of our resignations would have been to provide the Prime Minister with the opportunity to pick a cabinet even more amenable to her wishes than the one she achieved six months later. Our resignations might, nonetheless, have had an indirect effect by mobilizing the backbenchers in favour of change. The precedents, though, suggested otherwise.

While there has often been some prominent opposition in the Conservative party to the policies of the leadership, the party has an unrivalled discipline and solidarity – which are of immense benefit to the country when the leadership is going in the right direction, and correspondingly disastrous when it is not. Whether the direction is right or wrong, the Conservative party usually follows its leaders, until it gets rid of them. Even after Munich the Edenite group amounted to only twenty-five out of over 400 Conservative MPs, while Winston Churchill's 'party' consisted of three, one of whom was his son-in-law. Harold Macmillan thought the Conservative MPs of the thirties were servile and accused the government of treating the House of Commons 'as a kind of Reichstag'; Bob Boothby thought the whips had conspired to make the House of Commons 'a paradise of yes-men'. After he had resigned with Eden in 1938, Lord Cranborne was prevented by his local association from speaking in his constituency.[29]

1979–81 resembled those pre-war years, and since 1939 the government's powers of patronage have been greatly extended. The number of parliamentary private secretaries, for example, has multiplied, and they are no longer permitted to dissent in the voting lobbies, as they were even thirty years ago. In addition the Conservative party's solidarity after 1979 was usefully reinforced by broadcasting services that were less sturdily independent than in the past and by a mainly docile press. Finally the rank and file of the parliamentary party had also become more doctrinaire and were at least as conformist as the cabinet. Probably, therefore, even under the leadership of Jim Prior and Peter Walker, the Conservative moderates on the back benches would not have been able to make much impression on the government's policy.

Dismissal

Later on that summer there were persistent reports that a major cabinet reshuffle was pending. They were undoubtedly well-founded. And when on 23 July the Treasury team put forward proposals – almost incredible even from them – to cut public spending by another £5 billion, the cabinet revolted. Apparently I quoted Churchill, 'however beautiful the strategy, you should occasionally look at the results', and pointed out that the cuts would only increase unemployment. Others were still more hostile. The Prime Minister found herself virtually isolated, alone in a laager with Keith Joseph and the two Treasury ministers, Geoffrey Howe and Leon Brittan.[30]

After that débâcle she clearly had to change either her policy or her cabinet. Equally clearly she would find it much easier to throw moderates overboard than to jettison dogma. So obvious was it that I wrote my letter of resignation whilst on holiday, and on my return I gave an interview to Chris Moncrieff, the well-trusted correspondent of the Press Association, to be used when the shuffle was officially announced. At lunch with Peter and Iona Carrington, Peter asked me if I wanted him to intercede for me. I said 'no, thanks', but hoped there would be no attempt by the Downing Street propaganda machine to pretend that my dismissal was due to incompetence rather than policy differences with the Prime Minister – and to be fair no such attempt was made.

The reports of the coming purge were so pervasive – even the day was known – that a friend who later became a very senior member of Mrs Thatcher's cabinet suggested that I should make a pre-emptive resignation. But having failed to resign over the budget in March, I thought to do so in September would be too contrived. Wrongly. Such a resignation might have ensured that future purifications of the cabinet were carried out in a more seemly manner.[31]

A few days before the day appointed for the reshuffle the new French socialist government visited London – when I had told Mrs Thatcher that I thought Mitterrand would beat Giscard she bet me £5 that he would not; she paid up, and I gave her a book on French politics. I had meetings with my French opposite number in the Foreign Office at which we made elaborate plans for future cooperation and further meetings. At the end I asked the officials to leave the room and then told him to disregard everything I had said; we would not be meeting again as I was being sacked on the following Monday. He looked a little mystified.

When the great day came and I had been ushered upstairs at No 10, Mrs Thatcher asked me if I minded the presence of her private secretary. I said I did not, though I thought it oddish. What was odder was that the Prime Minister remained standing throughout the interview. As the room was small and we were only a few feet apart this gave me the feeling of being addressed at a public meeting with the speaker far too near the audience. I contemplated standing up, too, but as I am a bit taller than she is that would merely have reversed the situation. The only solutions would have been for her to sit down or for us both to move to a bigger room, but as I was some way from being the host of the event I did not feel I could suggest either of them.

Margaret Thatcher was perfectly polite. (She had never been rude to me; indeed our personal relations had usually, I think, been rather good. Certainly after something had gone wrong in the Foreign Office on a matter for which I was ultimately responsible, she was cheerfully and briskly understanding when I told her about it.) After she had very reasonably explained her need to make changes with becoming if unconvincing regret, I asked her when she was going to announce them, pointing out that I had been reading about my dismissal for weeks and was anxious to make some comments. She replied with a straight face that the stories had had nothing to do with her, a claim that was too blatantly untrue to be worth disputing.[32]* Otherwise the conversation was friendly.

When I went downstairs I was met successively by the late Ian Gow and by Michael Jopling, both of whom had managed to don a more solemn demeanour than the average undertaker achieves at a funeral. Ian Gow told me it had been decided that there should be an exchange of letters between the departing ministers and Mrs Thatcher. That presented no difficulty, I said, as I had written mine some weeks ago after a good lunch in Italy.†

Since I had cleared my desk the previous week, there was nothing to do at the Foreign Office but give Chris Moncrieff the go-ahead, write a welcoming letter to my successor, read

---

* Both before and after this, Mrs Thatcher did the same thing. When she sacked David Knox as vice-chairman of the party in 1975 and he complained that he had already read about his dismissal in the *Daily Telegraph*, she made the same denial; later two lobby correspondents told him that she had told the lobby. In the eighties Peter Rees, Patrick Jenkin and others were similarly treated.

† In my interview with Chris Moncrieff, I had said that it did no harm to throw a man overboard from time to time but that it did not do much good if the ship was steering straight for the rocks. (David Howell later pointed out to me that I had written the same words about resignations in general in a book I had written a dozen years before; it was an unconscious piece of self-plagiarism.) As Mrs Thatcher went on to win two elections by huge parliamentary, if not popular, majorities, I was in the most obvious and important sense spectacularly wrong. But in another sense what I said was, I think, defensible. Economically and socially, the government was steering for the rocks – and hit them.

the papers, take some telephone calls from journalists, agree to do some interviews and wait for the farewell party I was giving. I was sorry to be leaving the Foreign Office, but relieved to be leaving the government. Indeed, as Michael White said the next day, I had courted dismissal.[33] Had I wanted to stay in the cabinet, after all, it would have been quite easy to do so. I would only have had to keep my mouth shut – apart from voicing regular agreement with Mrs Thatcher.*

Why then had I not resigned instead of patiently waiting to be sacked? That winter (1980–81) Mrs Thatcher's exceptionally competent and assiduous PPS, the late Ian Gow, had on several evenings come round to have a drink with me at the Foreign Office and discuss politics. I liked Ian Gow, but he was not a close friend and we were politically far apart. Neither of us pretended that he was paying a social call. He was on his mistress's business and wanted to know what I thought. On each occasion I told him that I believed our economic policy was a disaster and should be drastically redirected. Much later he mentioned to me that he had told Mrs Thatcher that he thought I would resign on the 1981 budget.

Clearly I should have done so – it was the right thing to do and would have made me feel much better, though

* In 1980 the *Daily Telegraph* alleged that I was 'quite capable of reading a newspaper at the Cabinet table if the subject under discussion does not particularly interest him', a thought which deeply shocked the *Daily Mirror*. Had I done so I would have been in good historical company: Peel used to read them when he did not get his way. In fact I never did while away the time by reading newspapers, though often tempted to do so in order to avoid listening to a tedious discussion of an unimportant subject. My next-door neighbour, Peter Walker, and I attempted to stave off boredom by passing notes to each other, but occasionally even those exchanges failed to keep me awake and I took a nap. In that, I was in less good company: Sidmouth was an habitual sleeper, and, according to Kinglake, at the crucial meeting to decide upon the invasion of Crimea, all of 'the cabinet except a small minority were overcome with sleep'. Even so, had I slept a bit more, I might have been considered a sound and dutiful Thatcherite.[34]

it would probably have had no other effect. Up to that point, however, I still think I was right to stay. Whereas, in a normal cabinet, disagreements with government policy provide a reason for leaving, in the first Thatcher cabinet they provided good cause for staying. The active moderates became well accustomed both to not being consulted on the government's basic strategy and to finding objectionable many of the manifestations of that strategy when we finally learned of them. We knew we were losing the war, but we had the occasional tactical success, and we had reason to think that things would be even worse without us. Just to give up the fight and depart would have been craven.

In addition, of course, there are always strong general arguments against resignation. 'Never resign,' said Winston Churchill, and many lesser men have said the same. Resignations seldom achieve anything except political suicide, particularly when they are that especially rare sort which arise from policies that have nothing to do with the departmental responsibility of the resigning minister.[35]*

Occasionally, nevertheless, hara-kiri is the only proper course. I was well aware that I could not stay much longer in the cabinet – either Margaret Thatcher's intense desire to get rid of me or my own growing exasperation would see to that. By her removal of Norman St John Stevas in January – it was only because of Peter Carrington's intervention that I had not been removed at the same time† – the Prime Minister had given fair warning that she intended to build a conviction cabinet based on her convictions. I was still clearly at the top

---

* 'Resignations will still occur,' I had written twelve years earlier. 'But almost always they will be acts of desperation, a last stand when all is lost, not the beginning of an offensive. They will be actions bringing honour to the men who perform them; seldom will they bring fear to the Prime Minister to whom they are submitted.'[36]

† Peter Carrington strongly advised me not to resign over the 1981 budget. In view of his earlier intervention, his well-meant advice obviously weighed heavily with me – wrongly, as we both later agreed.

of her hit list, though Christopher Soames joined me there in the summer by proving himself right and Mrs Thatcher wrong over how to end the civil-service strike. He knew the terms on which the unions would settle and wanted to offer them. Most of the cabinet supported him, but Mrs Thatcher refused to agree and Willie Whitelaw persuaded the cabinet to let her have her way. After an expensive few weeks she had to climb down and allow Christopher to settle on his original terms – his being right cost him his job; her being wrong cost the country some £500 million.[37]

I had made at least two speeches critical of the government's economic policy. In addition my book *Inside Right*, a defence of traditional Conservatism which pointed to the dangers of getting hooked on monetarism, was reissued in June.[38] Finally, as Willie Whitelaw wrote to me after I was sacked, I was totally disenchanted with the whole direction of government policy.

So, unquestionably, I should have resigned on the 1981 budget or, failing that, manufactured a resignation issue shortly afterwards. Instead, like many ministers before me I had, in the scathing words of Sydney Smith, 'a great deal of patience but no resignation'.[39]

Conclusion

Were then the 'wets', in the proper sense of the word, wet? According to Sir John Nott, Mrs Thatcher thinks all men are 'wimps'.[40] If he is right about that, the behaviour of Conservative politicians during her decade in power provided a great deal of support for her view – she was unwise, though, not to have exempted Michael Heseltine. So the answer to that question then is: yes, the wets were wimps, but less so than most of the other members of Mrs Thatcher's cabinets. Indeed, compared with many of the 'dries' and the silent, admiring majority (the safe, prudent men adept at staying on the winning side) they appear paragons of steadfastness.[41] The wets were evidently less wimpish, too, than were Margaret Thatcher and Keith Joseph in the Heath cabinet where they kept remarkably quiet. Except to cronies, they made no complaint against the government's policies until they were safely in opposition.[42]

The only cabinet that gave Mrs Thatcher any trouble was her first (partly wet) one. Certainly that cabinet would never have submitted to the imposition, say, of the poll tax or the broadcasting bill. The wets may have failed to prevent the follies of 1979–81, but they did at least oppose them.

The answer to the wider question posed at the beginning of this chapter – why did the moderates lose? – is because their 'captains' were non-playing members of the team. For a variety of reasons, none of them discreditable, the most powerful moderates declined to challenge the Prime Minister or her economic policy. In part they were prepared to wait and see what the policy produced; in part they saw that faced with a Prime Minister intent on forcing through her policy, however damaging its results, they could only stop her at the risk of splitting the party and bringing down the government.

The moderates who did actively oppose the Prime Minister could obviously have played their cards better. Yet without the participation of the most senior members of the cabinet those cards were low ones. Though not a president, a British prime minister possesses unrivalled authority, and Mrs Thatcher was particularly powerful for so long as there was, in one sense, truly 'no alternative'– so long, that is to say, that there was no alternative to the Conservative government.

The pathetically debilitated condition of the Labour opposition made the low cards of the active moderates lower still. While every party wants to win the next general election, the Conservative party's will to win is especially strong. Nothing makes it more open-minded than the prospect of being beaten at the polls. Had the government been confronted by a united, aggressive Labour opposition, advocating credible alternatives, the hand of the Conservative moderates would have been immeasurably strengthened. But although the government became increasingly unpopular between 1979 and 1981, the Labour party never looked a convincing alternative. In the throes of Tony Benn's abortive revolution, it had evidently learned nothing from the winter of discontent. With the left wing or, as Chris Patten called them, the socialist 'drys' in the ascendancy, Labour seemed in fast terminal decline and could only win if the government committed suicide (to which it often seemed prone). Furthermore, after Labour's leftward lurch had precipitated the foundation of the SDP, the opposition was divided as well as impotent. In consequence, the extreme left provided powerful assistance to the extreme right.[43]

In the early 1980s the old cliché that competent government requires a strong opposition was never more apposite. The absence of a credible opposing party with a serious chance of turning out the government allowed the Thatcherite ideologues the chance to use the economy as a laboratory for experimenting with their nostrums.[44] All the same, whoever else also deserves a place in the dock, it was we who lost. And history (or rather historians) does not like losers. Unfortunately, the country and the economy were losers too.

IV

Economic Policy from 1981 to 1990

Absolute poppycock. Is he [a former Labour minister] not having any regard for the total industrial and commercial transformation that has taken place in this country, the colossal increase of production, the colossal increase in efficiency in our manufacturing industries, the freeing up of the whole financial services and London being the freest sector? ... Poppycock. Codswallop, bunkum and balderdash. It took someone with real spine to do it.

Margaret Thatcher, October 1990[1]

State-Policy, a Cyclops with one eye, and that in the back of the head! ... Despotism of finance in government and legislation ... of presumption, temerity and hardness of heart in political economy ... The wealth of the nation i.e. of the wealthy individuals thereof [substituted] for the well-being of the people.

Samuel Taylor Coleridge, 1839[2]

THE CONSERVATIVE MODERATES undoubtedly lost the war. Did we also lose the argument? Unlike the other one, that question could be decided only by events, not by patronage. Few now deny that the years 1979–81 were disastrous – we were certainly right about them – but many claim that the later Thatcher years saw an economic miracle. In that case, was that opening period an essential prelude to future economic success? Or, even if it was not, was it redeemed by a subsequent economic triumph?

Before reaching a conclusion we have to decide what was claimed for government policies, what those policies were, what happened, and what was the eventual outcome. My economic convictions did not alter much during the 1980s, nor has my point of view been markedly enriched by hindsight. Yet the perspective of this chapter is necessarily different from earlier ones, since my sacking in September 1981 changed my position from one of dissident insider to that of external critic.

The government and its critics were more or less agreed on the aims of economic policy: sustained economic growth at a level which would keep inflation and unemployment at tolerable levels, together with improvement in the underlying rate at which economic growth could be sustained.[3] The disagreement lay in the methods. The view of the dissidents throughout the 1980s was that, although it would be difficult to achieve, a balance should be sought between government intervention and market forces. I never thought simple reflation was the answer, because it would merely have reproduced the same old problems. For growth to be sustainable, exports need to grow fast enough to pay for imports; hence the importance of manufacturing industry. That remained my consistent theme throughout the eighties – while the Thatcherite position was highly changeable, that of its critics was not.

Trade-union reform, privatization and rising productivity in the mid 1980s improved much of what was left of British industry.* Had those advances been complemented by a sensible, undogmatic economic policy, that combination – together with the enormous boon of North Sea oil – might

* These developments are discussed in chapter V.

well have brought to an end a century of relative economic decline. North Sea oil could have been used to finance a massive increase of investment in industry and in the infra-structure; the social repercussions of economic change could have been cushioned, and industry restructured and made more competitive;[4] at the same time the tax and benefit systems and the system of pay bargaining (all inter-connected) could have been reformed. All that, in the view of the dissidents, might well have produced a decisive change in the British economy.

The Thatcher notion of the right use of economic policy was very different. Thatcherites believed – and on this they were fairly consistent – that the only way to achieve steady and sustainable growth, low inflation and low unemployment was for the government to control the money supply, balance its books, cut income tax and allow market forces to work.[5] That attitude always seemed to me to have an element of witch-doctory about it. On a more elevated level, it was reminiscent of Elijah's challenge to the prophets of Baal to see whether his or their god would produce fire.

> And Elijah said unto the prophets of Baal, 'choose you one bullock for yourselves and dress it first . . . and call the name of your gods, but put no fire under.' And they took the bullock which was given them, and they dressed it, and called on the name of Baal from morning even until noon, saying, 'O Baal hear us'. But there was no voice, nor any that answered. And they leaped upon the altar which was made. And it came to pass at noon, that Elijah mocked them . . . And they cried aloud, and cut themselves after their manner with knives and lancets, till the blood gushed out upon them.[6]

But no fire came to the prophets of Baal.

Did it come to the prophets of Thatcherism? The Thatcherites certainly spoke as though it had; indeed they behaved as though their Baal, the god of the free market, had delivered them a miracle. Were they right? Or, instead of boasting of their miracle, should they have 'cut themselves . . . with knives and scalpels' like their predecessors? Let us first look at what they claimed for their free-market policies.

Thatcherite Claims

From 1981 onwards two themes predominated in Thatcherite rhetoric: the virtues of a free-market economy undistorted by government interference, and the triumph of Thatcherite policies — to the extent even of claiming an economic transformation. Of course, after the devastation of the first two years, the government's claims for the success of its economic stewardship had initially to be modest. It took credit for bringing down inflation from 10 to 3 per cent by controlling the money supply — while omitting to mention that it had initially doubled it — but, with economic growth either negative or very low, Geoffrey Howe could do little more than claim that the government was laying the foundations 'for sustainable growth in output and employment'.[7]

Not until some time after the 1983 election did Thatcherite triumphalism get into its stride. Even then the government could hardly be ecstatic about Friedmanite monetarism. It continued to announce multiple monetary targets until 1986, when its inability to hit them persuaded it to decree their abolition. But while the Thatcherites' allegiance to monetarism became muted by its failure, their dedication to *laissez-faire* economics remained as wholehearted as ever.[8]

Nigel Lawson, Geoffrey Howe's successor, gave a brilliant exposition of the prevailing orthodoxy in his 1984 Mais Lecture. Setting out to reverse what he called 'post-war conventional wisdom', he maintained that it was 'the conquest of inflation, and not the pursuit of growth and employment, which is or should be the objective of macro-economic policy', and that it was 'the creation of conditions conducive to growth and employment, and not the suppression of price rises, which is or should be the objective of micro-economic policy.' In his opinion it was only possible to generate real growth (and thereby reduce unemployment) by adopting what he called a 'micro-policy' which is 'wholeheartedly designed to make the economy work better'. By that he emphatically did not mean the expansion of demand by the government. The role of government, he believed, should be limited to 'removing controls and allowing markets to work better'. Since the economy is self-adjusting, government interference should be avoided.[9]

The Chancellor denied that the government's monetary policy had led to 'overkill'. At the time of his lecture unemployment stood at 2.9 million and went on rising till July 1986, when it peaked at 3.15 million. So if to triple unemployment since 1979 was not 'overkill', it was not exactly 'underkill'. Nevertheless Nigel Lawson contended that the government's policy approach had been 'unequivocally vindicated by events', a claim which he repeated in 1987. And, after paying what had already become a ritual obeisance to the 1981 budget, he made much of 'a sustained economic recovery', which was already in its fourth year.[10]

In the same year, the Prime Minister, the Chancellor and many other ministers began to boast that output, investment, non-oil exports etc. had achieved 'all-time records', and such claims were wearisomely reiterated until the end of the Thatcherite period. If the government was to be believed, its free-market policies (having providentially revived the British economy from its clapped-out state in 1979) had made its term in office the most successful economic period Britain had seen since the war. 'Tory reforms,' said Mrs Thatcher during the 1987 election, 'have transformed a lame duck economy into a bulldog economy.'[11]

The following year her Chancellor made a similar claim, though without the poetic imagery: 'The British economy,' Nigel Lawson told the House of Commons in his budget speech, 'is stronger than at any time since the war', adding that the plain fact was that the economy had been 'transformed'. Indeed Britain was 'now experiencing an economic miracle' comparable to those of West Germany and Japan. More unexpectedly, perhaps, the Chancellor repeated in 1989 his claim of a transformed economy in his last budget speech:

> The government's first 10 years in office have seen a transformation both in the way in which economic policy is conducted and in the results that have been achieved . . . We have been guided by the basic philosophy that the government should set a sound medium-term financial framework and leave the private sector free to operate with confidence within it . . . Inflation is a disease of money; and monetary policy is the cure. The role for fiscal policy is to bring the public accounts into balance and to keep them there, and thus underpin the process of re-establishing sound money.
>
> Strong sustainable growth is achieved, not through any artificial stimulus but by allowing nature to work again and restoring the enterprise culture; by removing unnecessary restrictions and controls and rolling back the frontiers of the state; by reforming trade union law and promoting all forms of capital ownership; and by reforming and reducing taxation . . .
>
> We have the longest period of strong and steady growth since the war. Output in the United Kingdom has grown faster than in all the other main European nations during the 1980s – a marked contrast to the previous two decades, when we were bottom of the league – and this growth had been based on a dramatic and sustained improvement in productivity.[12]

Those high claims were made all the more remarkable by the Chancellor's admission, in the same speech, that inflation would rise to 8 per cent later in the year and that the balance-of-payments deficit would be as high as it had been in the previous year – about £15 billion or some 3 per cent of GDP. Clearly Nigel Lawson had no doubts that the fire had come from heaven and that despite the occasional 'blip' the prophets of Baal had not been disappointed. And he was not alone. His belief that the government's free-market policies had produced an economic miracle was the conventional wisdom.

How true were the Thatcherite claims? In considering that question, not only the degree of success that attended the government's policies needs to be examined; we should also assess how far any success was due to the Thatcherite espousal of *laissez-faire* economics and how widely the government's policies and actions differed from those of its predecessors. Here the answers to those questions will be sought, not by attempting a comprehensive history of the British economy from 1981 to 1990, but by looking at the initial period of slow growth and the decline of inflation after 1981, the government's attitude to manufacturing industry, the boom of 1986–89, and the onset of the second slump.

The Decline of Inflation and Rise of Production

In the autumn of 1981 unemployment was still rising by 40,000 a month. The issue, therefore, was whether the government should do anything to mitigate this social and economic disaster. Though largely cushioned both by a surprising insensitivity to the human costs of their policy[13] and by strong, if diminishing, feelings of dogmatic certainty, the Thatcherite ministers were impaled on a Morton's fork: if the Medium-Term Financial Strategy was expected to produce three million unemployed, then it should not have been adopted; and if it had not envisaged three million unemployed, it had been proved fundamentally wrong and should be abandoned.[14]

In fact it was the second prong that constituted the real one, for no one had envisaged three million unemployed. In the seventies Mrs Thatcher had called Labour 'the natural party of unemployment'; during the 1979 election after saying that there was 'nothing inevitable about rising unemployment' she had promised to reduce it; and in February 1980 she would hardly have criticized the Callaghan government for having doubled unemployment if she had thought that her government on top of that doubling would go on to triple it.[15] Thus only the government's most cynical critics could seriously claim that the Thatcherites had anticipated the disastrous effects of their policies. Misled by their clutch of monetarist economists, they had intended something much more gradual and benign: a change of behaviour brought about by a reduction in trade unionists' 'rational expectations' induced by the government's policies, and a gradual deflation resulting in what Milton Friedman reassuringly called 'only a modest reduction in output and employment'.[16]

That being so, to seek to return to the path from which they had unintentionally strayed was the Thatcherites' natural and proper course. Indeed that was the very least they owed, if not to themselves, to the hundreds of thousands whom they had unnecessarily deprived of their jobs by ill-digested dogma.

In 1981, even more than in 1979, there was 'nothing inevitable about rising unemployment'. Owing to the recession and North Sea oil the balance of payments was in comfortable surplus, and with unemployment at nearly three million there was both plenty of slack in the economy and little danger of increased wage inflation. A change of direction was obviously needed and clearly possible, provided of course that the necessary expansion was not engineered by the time-honoured expedient of setting off a consumer boom.

Accordingly, I put forward in October a package which would have provided at least £500 million of capital investment, some half a million jobs, a reduction in interest rates, and some much needed currency stability by joining the EMS at a rate slightly lower than that currently prevailing. (Although the pound had fallen since the budget, an even lower rate was in fact needed.)* The gross cost of the

---

* One of the architects of the MTFS, Sir Terence Burns, has claimed that 'the exchange rate has been an important feature in interest rate decisions over the whole life of the MTFS.' Yet between 1978 and 1981 the real exchange rate rose by nearly 40 per cent, an overvaluation described by the president of the Bundesbank as 'by far the most excessive . . . in recent monetary history'. The contrary verdict of Mrs Thatcher's economic advisor, Sir Alan Walters, that from 1980 to 1982 'the exchange rate was left very largely to market forces' seems more in accordance with the evidence of the pound's switchback course in those years. In his budget speech in 1985, some two years after a change of policy, Nigel Lawson publicly recanted, conceding that 'benign neglect' of the exchange rate was 'not an option'.[17]

package would have been £5 billion or about 2 per cent of GDP, and it was plainly non-inflationary. There was no shortage of spare resources in the economy, especially in the construction industry.[18]

The country would have been saved a great deal of pain had we entered the EMS at the right rate in 1981 (or 1985). And my package was, if anything, too modest; indeed some monetarists (a little illogically) criticized it on those grounds. It was run through the Treasury model of the economy, which showed that compared with what otherwise would have happened it would add 1 per cent to output in 1982 and 1.5 per cent in 1985, while reducing retail prices in both years. A bigger package was then put through the computer, and it produced greater output and a larger reduction in prices.[19]

Although Treasury ministers could not refute the result of their own model, they were not prepared to accept it, because to do so would have entailed confessions of error and amendments of policy. Instead, bemused by *laissez-faire* dogma, they claimed that any job created by government policy was not a 'real' job, and they refused to mitigate the injurious and unintended consequences of their policies by creating 'false' jobs. The result was the postponement of recovery and rising 'real' unemployment for another five years.[20]

In the course of 1982, as an offset to the unemployment fiasco the government achieved a dramatic success in its main objective, the fight against inflation; in 1983 the inflation rate was down to 4.6 per cent. Yet, despite monetarist claims to the contrary, whatever else brought that success, it was not a decline in the money supply. Monetarists postulated a time lag of about two years between a change in the money supply and a change in the inflation rate. In 1981 the money supply increased by 13.7 per cent. Indeed between 1979 and 1981–82 the growth in M3 quickened, and even in 1982–83 it was higher than it had been in 1978–79. Had Friedmanite monetarism – Nigel Lawson's first basic proposition – been right, inflation would have been about 16 per cent in 1982–83, 11 per cent in 1983–84, and 8 per cent in 1984–85.* In fact (though inflation rose again in the second half of the eighties) in the relevant years it never approached the levels infallibly predicted by monetarist doctrine.[21][†]

Paradoxically, therefore, the achievement of the Thatcherites' principal ambition provided a conclusive rebuttal of their basic dogma. All five of Friedmanite monetarism's main propositions, mentioned at the beginning of chapter II, had turned out to be false, and monetarists were shown to be slaves of what Joseph Schumpeter called 'the Ricardian vice'. That is, in Schumpeter's words, 'the habit of establishing simple relations between aggregates that then acquire a spurious role of causal importance, whereas all the really important (and, unfortunately, complicated) things are being bundled away in or behind these aggregates'. Not only Friedman's belief that the immensely complicated process of inflation is always a purely monetary phenomenon but also Nigel Lawson's first 'basic proposition' that 'changes in the quantity of money determine at the end of the day changes in the general price level' were classic examples of the Ricardian vice. In fact, as Gordon Richardson, then Governor of the Bank of England, had hinted before the monetarist experiment began, the causality usually runs not from money to prices but from prices to money. Hence, wrote Christopher Dow, 'control of money is not a way to control inflation'.[22]

---

* Much the same happened in the United States. Basing himself on the money supply figures, Professor Friedman predicted that inflation would be 'decidedly higher from 1983 to 1985 than it was from 1981 to 1983'. In the event it was decidedly lower.[23]

† There have been forlorn attempts, notably by Professor Tim Congdon, to demonstrate that the figures for M3, published in *Economic Trends* 1989, were wrong or misleading. According to Professor Congdon, the money supply, properly adjusted, barely, if ever, exceeded the government's targets. However, the *Treasury Bulletin* published in December 1991, as if in answer to Professor Congdon, leaves no doubt at all that the targets were indeed missed in the way I have described.[24]

The sharp fall in inflation had two main causes. One was the deep recession produced by the policies followed from 1979 to 1981. Just as any fool can knock another man out if he hits him hard enough on the head with a big enough stick, so any government can reduce inflation if it bankrupts enough businesses and throws sufficient millions out of work. Yet the probably more important cause of inflation's fall was the sharp drop in world commodity prices to a level lower in real terms than at any time since the Korean War. This enabled many countries to reduce inflation; and they did so at much less cost than Britain. The collapse of commodity prices – a highly fortunate development for Britain though disastrous for the Third World – is customarily ignored by Thatcherite commentators; not until 1987 was a Treasury economist allowed to publish a paper emphasizing its importance.[25]

The very welcome fall in inflation provided the government with a victory; it was not, however, a vindication of *laissez-faire* principles. The government did not hit its intermediate targets – the money supply and the PSBR, those totems of their monetarism which were supposed to lead to the conquest of inflation; the lowering of world commodity prices was a windfall for the government; and in so far as lower inflation was achieved by the Thatcherites' deflation it was achieved only by inflicting lasting damage on the British economy.[26]

Did the slow rise in output from 1982 to 1986 have more to do with the free-market nostrums of Thatcherism? Two of the three ingredients of that torpid resumption of growth were directly opposed to them. From the end of 1982 the United States began a marked expansion, founded on the 'supply-side' belief that cuts in taxes would soon be compensated by greatly increased yields. This was what George Bush in 1980 had correctly called 'voodoo economics', yet if supply-side economics was almost as much of a delusion as Thatcherite monetarism, it was, for a time at least, a valuable one. New supply side was but old demand side writ large, and the huge American budget deficit, which was caused by Reagan's policies, produced by mistake an American boom which helped to pull the European economies out of recession.[27]

In 1981–82 a monetary squeeze increased American unemployment from 7.5 to 12 per cent. But when policy was subsequently relaxed and the budget deficit was doubled, unemployment fell sharply back to 7.5 per cent without any significant upturn in inflation. Thus the central doctrine of Nigel Lawson's Mais Lecture – that growth could not be created by a macroeconomic policy which expanded demand and that macroeconomic policy should only deal with inflation – had already been refuted by American experience even before he had enunciated it. Here the policy promulgated by the Chancellor had led to a remorseless rise in unemployment; in the United States the policy damned by him had led to its sharp decline.[28]

Mr Callaghan's remark when prime minister in 1976 that you could no longer spend your way out of a recession was thus disproved. Remarkably, however, Callaghan's dictum, uttered to please our creditors at the IMF at a time of crisis, remained holy writ to the Thatcherites. Even after the alleged miracles wrought on the economy by monetarist magic, the British government continued to believe that the constraints that Mr Callaghan had thought to be present in 1976 were still there; and it gave greater credence to the theory of a former Labour prime minister than to the practice of the current American president, Mrs Thatcher's ideological brother-in-arms, Ronald Reagan.[29]

The second ingredient was also a denial of the Lawson doctrine. This time, however, it was rebutted by British, not American, experience. Any mention of reflation was considered gross impiety in Thatcherite quarters, and Treasury ministers denied that they had injected additional demand into the economy. Yet the government did markedly relax its fiscal policy between 1981–82 and 1983–84, thus reversing the wrong-headed contraction of 1981. The back-door reflation was concealed by that misleading statistic, the PSBR – as Joel Barnett, Labour's Chief Secretary from 1974–79, admitted, 'the Public Sector Borrowing Requirement is about the figure you first thought of!' – but the government had both expanded public spending and reduced the burden of taxes.[30]

The third and most important element of the resumption of growth was fully in accordance with free-market principles. Yet it was a repudiation of monetarism, of housewife's economics and of the Thatcherite claim to be quite different from all previous governments. By far the greatest engine of expansion was the mini boom that the government set off in July 1982 by abolishing hire-purchase restrictions, which was followed by the dismantling of other controls and a massive expansion of consumer and business credit. In addition, the rise in earnings was higher than the now reduced inflation rate. Instead, then, of a balanced expansion or reflation based upon net export demand and investment, which would have required sensible government intervention and would have strengthened the economy, the period after mid 1982 saw an old-fashioned pre-election mini consumer boom of the classic post-war kind. The Thatcherites had repudiated every form of Keynesianism except the worst: 'electoral Keynesianism'.[31] This time the 'go' after the 'stop' mainly consisted of reflation by credit, with the individual not the government doing most of the borrowing. 'Electoral Keynesianism' helped the government to win the 1983 election, though the successful Falklands war and the pitiful state of the Labour party made such assistance scarcely necessary. But whatever had happened to the prudent housewife – in Downing Street or elsewhere? Like Shakespeare's formerly 'careful housewife', Mrs Thatcher had left 'her neglected child' to pursue that previously despised ambition of others, reflation.[32]

The Government's Treatment of Manufacturing Industry

Come to that, whatever had happened to Milton Friedman's monetarism? In embarking upon a consumer-led expansion based on credit the monetarists had, to mix metaphors, almost in one movement discarded their hair shirt and rushed into Sodom and Gomorrah – the prophets of Baal had produced fire by smuggling in petrol and a match. Not, of course, that there is anything wrong with consumption in itself. Personal consumption is the main objective of economic activity, as Adam Smith and many others have pointed out. But Britain's post-war economic history, about which the Thatcherites had long been so contemptuous, is littered with governments indulging in an expansion which had to be brought to a halt because it was based on consumption: inadequate precautions had been taken to ensure sufficient investment to sustain it and sufficient exports to finance it. Hence the much derided stop–go cycles of the past.[33]

Now the Thatcherites were doing precisely the same thing except that their 'go' was even more consumer-led than its predecessors and their previous 'stop' had been easily the most jarring halt since the war. Moreover, because of the disaster of 1979–81, manufacturing investment to boost manufacturing output was more essential than ever before. During the first Thatcher term almost one third of manufacturing plant was destroyed.[34] Thus, in conjuring up a mini consumer boom almost immediately after inflicting heavy losses on industry, the Thatcherites were like a general ordering a cavalry charge just after he had shot his horses. And not only did the Thatcherites shoot their horses, they also refused to do anything to breed new ones. As an inevitable result, much of the consumer boom was spent on imports rather than on domestically produced manufactures; for some time the latter scarcely recovered at all.

At that stage, of course, we were still in 'growth recession' – growth still being far too slow to reduce unemployment. Yet even that modest expansion quickly led to an enormous deterioration in our balance of payments despite the help of North Sea oil. This was readily apparent at least from the end of 1983. Since most other countries help their own manufacturing industries, a government that does not do the same is effectively helping the industries of its competitors.

Yet in Britain *laissez-faire* was left in sole charge. Government support for research and development was reduced together with regional and industrial subsidies, while our competitors in OECD Europe were increasing theirs. As the chairman of United Biscuits, normally a strong supporter of Thatcherism, put it in 1985, 'the present government has in effect made a virtue of not having a vision of the future of British industry and [of having] a positive policy of distancing the state from the industrial sector.'[35]

One possible justification for such 'distancing' was a remarkable improvement in the productivity of British manufacturing industry. Contrary to all previous experience, UK productivity growth since 1980 had been faster than that of any other major industrial country.[36]

This probably bolstered Thatcherite confidence that Baal, or the free market, would provide everything that was required. Certainly the government was not alarmed by the heavily adverse trend of our manufacturing trade, about which of course there was nothing new. Britain's trading performance had been deteriorating since the early 1950s. The incompatibility of full employment with the avoidance of high inflation would have been even more apparent in the late 1970s had it not been for North Sea oil. As already suggested, the rise in oil revenues in the early 1980s could have helped to lessen that incompatibility, if the oil bonanza had been used to put Britain's industry on a proper footing and to provide for its secure future. Unfortunately that opportunity was missed, so the underlying economic decline continued. Indeed after 1979 the decline accelerated. Britain had her first-ever deficit on manufactured goods in 1983. The chairman of ICI told the House of Lords Committee on Overseas Trade that not only had his company, in common with the rest of UK manufacturing industry, suffered a major loss of international competitiveness between 1979 and 1981, it had also lost 20 per cent of its customer base in its petrochemicals and general chemicals business.[37]

Despite Thatcherite doubts, British manufacturing industry

was and remains of critical importance to the UK economy because it is in manufacturing that by far the greatest opportunities exist for the expansion of production and trade. Over 70 per cent of world trade is in manufacturing; at the end of the Thatcher era British manufacturing industry accounted for over 20 per cent of GDP and provided over 60 per cent of our overseas earnings. So any prudent government would do everything in its power to strengthen its manufacturing base, and only one which had caught a severe dose of ideology would think it unimportant. Yet all the Thatcherites did – which was much better than nothing – was to promote the expansion of Japanese investment in this country, especially in the motor-car industry. Similar efforts were not made on behalf of home-owned manufacturing industries, and British investment abroad was far larger than foreign investment in Britain.[38]

The need for action was all the greater in that, whatever had happened to British manufacturing over the years, British consumers had palpably not lost their appetite for manufactured goods. If British industry cannot deliver those goods or if its products are inferior to those of the Germans or the Japanese, the consumer buys imports. Between 1981 and 1984 imports of manufactures increased by more than a third in real terms, while our own manufacturing output rose by a mere 4 per cent. As a result, in the same period, our non-oil balance of trade deteriorated by nearly £11 billion. In other words North Sea oil was being used to finance not industry's convalescence and recovery but something near to the country's euthanasia, making life for a time much more comfortable for the rich, relatively pleasant for those in employment, and just bearable for many of those out of work.[39]

In 1985 the House of Lords Committee on Overseas Trade saw the danger, even if the government did not. Its message was stark: 'it is neither exaggerating, nor irresponsible, to say that the present situation undoubtedly contains the seeds of a major political and economic crisis in the foreseeable future.' In the Committee's view, unless the manufacturing base was enlarged, import penetration controlled and manufacturing exports stimulated, Britain would suffer increasingly damaging effects as oil revenues diminished. Among those effects would be a balance of payments crisis, higher unemployment, a stagnating economy and rising inflation.[40]

The Chancellor of the Exchequer, whose own appearance before the Committee had been marked by an irritable complacency and a resolute refusal to grasp the problem, greeted the report with the comment that it was 'a mixture of special pleading dressed up as analysis and assertions masquerading as evidence'. The suggestion of the need for governmental action if a crisis was to be avoided was anathema to Nigel Lawson. The Lords Committee's forebodings were nevertheless mild compared with those of Wynne Godley's Cambridge Economic group, which predicted, in the words of Peter Jenkins, 'apocalypse in the form of a balance of payments deficit of £20 billion by 1995'. In the event, Godley was over optimistic. The apocalyptic £20 billion deficit arrived in 1989.[41]

The government's failure to heed the warnings of either events or outside observers was on this occasion not simply due to its faith in market forces and in its own infallibility. It was also due to the Thatcherite belief that Britain's future lay with the service industries not with manufacturing. (The boundary between them is often hazy.)[42]

Although services supply a much higher percentage of GDP than manufacturing industry – 63 per cent – and employ far more people, there is a limit to the contribution that many service industries can make to the growth of international trade. The number of foreign tourists, say, that can be comfortably accommodated is not vastly greater than the annual number who already come here. Yet Britain, the chairman of ICI pointed out, would have 'to entertain another six million or 40 per cent more tourists' to make up for the loss of his company. Many services are not tradeable – a haircut can not be exported – and the overseas earnings of service industries, which amount to some 24 per cent of the total, are nowhere near large enough to solve our balance-of-payments difficulties if our manufacturing position does not improve. Finally, the services sector is highly dependent on manufacturing. 'What,' the managing director of GEC wondered, 'will the service industries be servicing when there is no hardware, when no wealth is actually being produced . . . we will supply the changing of the guard, we will supply the Beefeaters round the Tower of London. We will become,' Lord Weinstock added, 'a curiosity.'[43]

The belief that Britain can rely on services to see her through her difficulties is certainly a curiosity.* Despite the Conservative party's susceptibility over a long period to the views and values of the City, only slightly less curious was the Thatcherites' almost systematic belittling of manufacturing industry's importance. Not for them Winston Churchill's wish in 1925 to make 'Finance less proud and Industry more content'. They always put the interests of finance and commerce well above those of industry. The reason is hard to find. Maybe their prejudice against manufacturing was due to their obsession with market forces and free trade: to help industry would constitute interference in the affairs of Baal. Maybe it was just due to very few Thatcherites knowing anything about industry. Maybe they felt guilty about their decimation of it in 1979–81 – years which were worse for manufacturing industry than any in the whole of the nineteenth or twentieth centuries. (Yet some monetarists were downgrading its importance even before

---

* The idea that the British are particularly good at services is no less curious. British banks were as reckless in lending to Latin America as American banks. 'Bankers tend to be a bit like sheep,' said the chief executive of Midland Bank, 'we follow each other.'[45] British banks were similarly sheeplike in their lending to Robert Maxwell. Japanese banks have gained an increasing share of the UK market. Nor do the recent tribulations of Lloyds suggest an overwhelming British talent for insurance. Very possibly, performance in services follows performance in exporting after a time lag. The hypothesis seems in accordance with the facts and with what Lord Weinstock told the Lords Committee.

the 1979 election.) Maybe, analogous to their hatred of
local government, they disliked it because much of it took
place in Labour heartlands, in the belief that the need for a
large manufacturing sector was a specifically socialist idea.
Or maybe the cause was even simpler: Milton Friedman said
in 1980 that our manufacturing industry should be allowed
to fall to bits, and once again the Thatcherites had swallowed
his doctrine whole.[44]

The Lawson Boom

Whatever the reason the government did little to ward off the
crisis foreseen by the House of Lords Committee and many
others. No provision was made for the decline in oil revenues.
Making light of the problem in his 1986 budget speech, the
Chancellor claimed that if we could 'survive unscathed the loss
of half our oil revenues in less than 25 weeks, the prospective
loss of the other half over the remainder of the next 25 years
should not cause us undue concern'. That was doubly to miss
the point. First, a fall in the world price of oil which helped
almost everyone was a very different thing from a fall just
in British oil revenues which harmed only us. And second,
Britain's lack of competitiveness in manufacturing trade had
been manifest long before we had North Sea oil; consequently,
the idea that it would suddenly disappear when North Sea oil
declined was self-evidently implausible.[46]

By its financial and monetary policies the government
brought trouble ever closer. The financial system had been
progressively deregulated. In 1986 and in subsequent years
most of the monetary aggregates rose by between 12 and
20 per cent. This huge growth in the money supply was the
consequence of the mammoth increase in lending. In the year
to June 1986 net lending to the personal sector was 26 per
cent up on the previous year. Yet at the same time interest rates
remained high. Thus by the monetarist criterion monetary
policy was slack, while by the interest rate criterion it was
very tight. So, taken together, the effect of the government's

monetary policy was thoroughly perverse: consumption was stimulated and investment was curtailed.[47]

In one respect however the government did help British industry. In Thatcherite rhetoric, devaluation was an inflationary and ultimately self-defeating expedient. 'I do not believe,' Nigel Lawson told the Treasury Select Committee at the end of November 1985, 'that there is any salvation for this country through progressive depreciation of the currency, progressive devaluation.' Fortunately Thatcherite practice was occasionally different. In 1985 manufacturing output was 6 per cent less than in the first half of 1979, and the average annual growth rate for the whole economy during the previous six years had been a meagre 1 per cent. More was urgently needed. So, almost immediately after Lawson's pronouncement of anti-devaluation doctrine, the dogma was disregarded; and the maintenance of an over-valued exchange rate was abandoned for the time being. The government engineered (perhaps lay back and enjoyed) a substantial devaluation or, as the Chancellor preferred to call it, 'an exchange-rate adjustment'. With the dollar also declining in value, industry's competitiveness was boosted without inflation also jumping upwards.[48]

The exchange rate had gradually become a matter of crucial importance to the Chancellor. As the government had failed to control the money supply, his earlier monetarism had perforce been abated, if not wholly abandoned. 'It can not be said,' the governor of the Bank of England admitted in a tactful understatement, 'that our experience with our chosen framework for monetary policy has been satisfactory.' He doubted if it was worthwhile setting targets for M3 or other broad monetary aggregates. Nigel Lawson, himself, preferred M0 which measured notes and coins in circulation and which Paul Volcker, the chairman of the US Federal Reserve, was not alone in thinking 'meaningless'. So, for the Chancellor (and for Geoffrey Howe), the exchange rate largely took the place of monetarism and monetary targets – a welcome shift towards economic realism. To gain stability Nigel Lawson tried in 1985 to persuade the Prime Minister that Britain should join the ERM. But though heavily outnumbered at the meeting, Mrs Thatcher vetoed entry — thereby, perhaps, providing some justification for Nicholas Ridley's primitive view of the British constitution: 'the responsibility for governing the country is the Prime Minister's and she alone must be allowed to take the ultimate decisions which are important.' In any event the Chancellor did not appeal to the cabinet, and Britain stayed out of the ERM until 1990, when in the last important move of the Thatcher administration she joined at the wrong time and the wrong rate.[49]

Whether all this is best termed pragmatic monetarism or the death of monetarism matters little. The government had not undergone a conversion to Keynesianism, except the electoral variety, yet almost the only features that Nigel Lawson's activities had in common with early Thatcherism were incessant self-congratulations, dogmatic reliance on market forces and faith in *laissez-faire*. Arguably, indeed, the Chancellor's policies combined the worst features of monetarism and Keynesianism. They were monetarist in that unemployment was considered not a matter for the government (though unemployment did at last begin to fall in August 1986) and no attempt was made to devise an industrial strategy, and Keynesian in that the government indulged in an excessive demand reflation — the biggest since the war — without having ensured that there had been sufficient investment beforehand to prevent it causing a balance-of-payments crisis and inflation.[50]

In 1986, with an election in the offing, Thatcherite 'electoral Keynesianism' became more conspicuous than in 1982–83. The economic policies of most governments tend to deteriorate when elections draw near and the urge to bribe the voters becomes more compulsive. In the 1980s the reverse was true. In a time of ideological politics and ideological economics, the voters stayed more level-headed and, economically, more sensible than the politicians. Hence the Thatcher governments' economic policies improved as ideology succumbed to electoral necessity. In 1986–87 not only were monetary targets abandoned, increased public expenditure, for long a cardinal sin in Thatcherite demonology, suddenly became a virtue. Even Nigel Lawson became converted to its benefits, and for once Britain's crumbling infrastructure, both social and material, was less ignored. Unfortunately these election-bed repentances were short lived, and after the voters had been appeased the government reverted to its previous sins; indeed after 1987 it intensified them. Some reformers in the late eighteenth and early nineteenth centuries favoured annual elections as the only way of keeping politicians free from corruption; probably in the 1980s only annual elections could have kept them free from dogma.[51]

In his 1987 budget the Chancellor completed his preparations for the election by reducing income tax by two pence. Every electoral indicator was thus set fair; taxes were down, unemployment though still over three million was declining, inflation was low, interest rates were falling, growth was high, the balance of payments could be claimed to be in broad balance, the economy was booming and most voters' incomes were rising fast. The Chancellor had done a superb job on the electoral economy, making the economy look like a Derby winner throughout the election campaign. The question was whether he had, as it were, doped the economy to produce palpably unsustainable growth, or whether it was genuinely a good horse which would consistently win its races during the next four years.

In the autumn of 1987 Nigel Lawson claimed that as a result of the 'sound policies' he had pursued, we were 'enjoying the benefits of a virtuous circle. Low inflation, public expenditure under control and sound public finances have led to sustained growth and thus the ability to lower tax-rates, which in turn has brought about improved confidence and better business performance.'[52] The economy did continue to win races. The Chancellor handled the Stock Exchange crash of October 1987 with confident skill, and his boom lasted until 1989. With GDP growing by 4.4 per cent in 1987 and 4.7

per cent in 1988, living standards (except at the bottom) improved faster than at any other time since the war. Yet the policies were anything but sound; Lawson had not achieved a virtuous circle; he had merely tried to square one. In other words the horse had been heavily dosed with steroids. Indeed, even well before the election the economy would not have survived a stewards' inquiry; and what a friendly historian had presciently seen in 1986–87 as 'a potentially reckless monetary binge' soon turned into a wild financial orgy.[53]

The boom was fuelled from every direction. The liberalization of financial markets led the banks and the building societies into even more intense competition to lend. Mortgage rationing had disappeared, and mortgages did not have to be spent on buying a house. Mortgage tax relief was retained, a privilege which did not increase the supply of houses, only their price. With real incomes having grown by some 20 per cent between 1983 and 1987 and with wage inflation which had been endemic throughout the decade becoming more rapid, borrowers were not hard to find. Net lending to households by banks and other financial institutions trebled between 1984 and 1987, and from the latter year until 1989 it was equal to about 10 per cent of GDP. That was the scale on which household disposable income was supplemented by the flow of borrowing. In the eighteen months between mid 1986 and 1988 house prices shot up by 40 per cent, at which point they were nearly 4.5 times average earnings.[54]

No attempt was made by the government to curb the explosion in credit. There were no controls of any kind – not even monetary aggregates – and Britain was not a member of the ERM. Speculation of every sort and City scandals proliferated. While all this was still some way from a re-run of the South Sea Bubble, it was a reversion to nineteenth-century Liberalism before the authorities had learned to moderate the trade cycle. Not surprisingly the Lawson boom bore a close resemblance to those recurrent Victorian commercial and financial crises which were caused by excessive credit and which were graphically described by John Stuart Mill. Nigel Lawson was testing free markets and *laissez-faire* principles to destruction.[55]

Instead of at least trying to postpone the destruction, the Chancellor seemed intent on hastening it. In 1988, at the height of his credit boom and with no possible electoral motive, he doped the horse again, by reducing income tax by another two pence and bringing the top rate of tax down from 60 to 40 per cent. Apart from the economic folly, this largesse to the rich – 40 per cent of the tax reductions went to the richest 5 per cent of taxpayers – was not exactly sensitive, coinciding as it did with cuts for many of the poor not in taxes but in their social-security benefits. In addition the government had just enacted the poll tax which entailed a further hefty redistribution of income from the poor to the rich.[56]

The tax cuts were all the more remarkable, because in 1987 there had been a long overdue revival of industrial investment – too late to fill the gap between manufacturing supply and demand (plants were working at the limit of capacity: there just was nothing like enough capacity), but soon enough to drive an already overheated economy towards boiling point.[57]

The Second Slump

The inevitable crisis duly materialized. The country's deficit on current account was over £15 billion in 1988 and £20 billion in 1989. At the same time inflation took off, eventually reaching 10 per cent in 1990.[58]

With the deficit on the balance of payments as high as 4 per cent of GDP, demand clearly had to be cut. The best way of doing so would have been to raise income tax, which would have cut consumption rather than investment. Interest rates could then have been reduced without causing a loss of confidence in sterling. But in Nigel Lawson's eyes the role of fiscal policy was to keep the public accounts in balance and to provide incentives; income tax could only be lowered. According to Thatcherite theory and practice, therefore, you can raise taxes in a recession (1981) but not in a boom. The correct approach, surely, is to lower taxes when you can, and to raise them when you must.[59]

Credit controls which most other countries use should also have been introduced. Unfortunately, like tax increases, they were proscribed by free-market dogma. Thus the Chancellor was reduced to the 'one club', in Ted Heath's well-known phrase, of interest rates; and the crushing of the boom had to be attained purely by monetary means. After being reduced three times in the weeks following the 1988 budget, interest rates were raised some dozen times between June 1988 and October 1989 when they reached 15 per cent. Thus dogma still reigned in the attempt to cure the trouble that dogma had caused. The only permissible way of moderating a boom that had got wildly out of hand was by creating a slump. The first one was the deepest; the second Thatcher recession was the longest since the thirties.

High interest rates carry almost every disadvantage. For a long time they hit investment rather than consumption. They keep the exchange rate high which makes investment in exporting industries, as well as exports themselves, unprofitable. In addition, high interest rates coming at a time when household indebtedness has been encouraged to grow to unprecedented heights cause severe random and unmerited distress. Finally high interest rates are slow to work and then in the end work all too well, causing a deep recession. Nigel Lawson often talked about 'a soft landing'; in fact, quite predictably, he made a crash-landing. Once again the situation he created was reminiscent of a mid-Victorian financial crisis, described by Sir John Hicks: 'the cycle was a financial one. There was a boom, with rising prices and then rising interest rates; it led to a crisis, with a wave of bankruptcies. The unemployment which followed was a consequence of the bankruptcies, or of attempts to avoid them.'[60]

'Only a few months after the glory of the 1988 Budget,'

wrote Nicholas Ridley without irony, 'the Chancellor himself was forced to slam on the brakes. Inflation was starting again on its upward march ... Margaret Thatcher was appalled. She must have felt bitterly disappointed that the top priority of all her ambitions – an end to inflation – should suddenly have gone seriously wrong.'[61] Admittedly the government in its 1987 election manifesto had made the remarkable promise – remarkable because it was both incredible and unnecessary – that 'we will not be content until we have stable prices, with inflation eradicated altogether.' But, as has been seen, minimum attention was paid to that pledge, and so far from being eradicated inflation mounted fast. If ending inflation really was at the top of the Prime Minister's priorities, she surely should have noticed that it was at the bottom of her Chancellor's.*

So the Thatcher government ended, as it began, with a self-induced recession. The first one was unnecessary; the second was necessary only because of the need to take corrective action against a boom that should not have happened. Although Nigel Lawson's monetarist critics concede that the second recession was 'a disaster', they are not yet ready to make a similar admission about the first one. In

---

* Nicholas Ridley's belief that Mrs Thatcher was not to blame for the 'disaster' (except for not having sacked Lawson) does not sit easily with his view, quoted earlier, that like an American president 'the Prime Minister carries the responsibility of the executive.' On a few issues, during Mrs Thatcher's third term, disagreement grew between the Prime Minister and some of her leading ministers, chiefly Geoffrey Howe and Nigel Lawson. Obviously those differences create something of a problem for this book. When Thatcherites fall out, what are the rest of us to think? How do we decide which Thatcherite was articulating and practising true Thatcherism? Here we do not, I think, have to enter into the intra-factional squabbling, to criticize heresy or award marks for ideological orthodoxy. Instead, the true path of Thatcherism is equated with government policy and the course of events. Since Mrs Thatcher was at this period a very 'strong' Prime Minister, usually getting her own way, this seems the fairest as well as the simplest solution.

their eyes it was only in 1987 that 'things did start to go wrong'. Thatcherites are of course more or less driven to that view. Nigel Lawson can then be the sole scapegoat. To find the cause of the disaster in earlier years would involve blaming themselves, too, as well as casting doubt on the entire Thatcher experiment.[62]

As we have seen, Lawson's later policies were very different from those of early Thatcherism. During Mrs Thatcher's first term Geoffrey Howe constantly claimed that the government was laying the foundations 'for sustainable growth in output and employment'. After about four years of foundation-laying I remember telling him that it was high time the government got on with the building. Yet, when the Thatcherites did at last get round to doing some construction, they put their building nowhere near the foundations that for so long had been their pride and joy. Instead they erected it on the same boggy marsh that they had been denouncing previous administrations for floundering in ever since 1945 – in fact on even more treacherous quicksand: easy credit.[63]

The Heath's government's boom of 1971–73 was always a particular object of Thatcherite obloquy. The indictment was that, although it had reduced unemployment, the jobs were not real ones and that the profligate use of monetary and fiscal policy had first created an inflationary crisis and then led to a large increase in unemployment. In July 1981, in the middle of the Liverpool riots when virtually every member of the cabinet, save the Prime Minister and the Treasury team, refused to countenance another round of public spending cuts, Mrs Thatcher angrily asked the cabinet if it wanted another Barber boom. Were we, she inquired in exasperated incomprehension, really prepared to give a higher priority to jobs than to inflation? To ask such questions at the bottom of the worst slump since the war verged on the hysterical. Yet a few years later what Mrs Thatcher and her Treasury team, not the wets, eventually produced was in many ways a close replica of Tony Barber's boom. The chief differences between them, indeed, were all in Lord Barber's favour; his was the more moderate of the two, his was not largely based on credit, in his boom the share of consumption was lower than in Nigel Lawson's, and he hit the buffers at almost full employment, while Lawson crashed into them with unemployment close to two million.[64]

The Lawson credit-consumption boom brought great if ultimately costly benefit to much of the population. In the eighties personal wealth rose by 80 per cent in real terms. In real terms, too, the value of housing rose by 90 per cent and shares by 160 per cent. Real earnings rose by 25 per cent. Borrowing rose much more sharply. The savings ratio fell from twelve in 1979 to 5.5 per cent in 1988, and in 1989 the net indebtedness of householders was 2.5 times higher than it had been in 1982. In those seven years, the average growth of personal consumption was 4.6 per cent, nearly double the average rate of growth of consumption in the twenty years before the Thatcher administration. Between 1979 and 1989 consumption as a percentage of GDP rose by nearly seven points. No wonder the government's economic policies were popular.[65]

There was no doubt, then, about the strength of demand. The trouble was supply. The share in GDP of total investment rose by two points. Manufacturing investment, however, fell by half a point and, as has been seen, manufacturing output did not exceed its 1974 and 1979 levels until 1988 and 1987 respectively. Unsurprisingly the credit explosion did not lead to an explosion in production. In consequence a considerable gap opened up between demand and supply, averaging 6 per cent of GDP over the decade. Domestic demand rose during that period by a third, GDP by a quarter.[66]

Mrs Thatcher and others claimed that it was the Chancellor's policy of shadowing the Deutschmark between March 1987 and March 1988 which had reintroduced inflation. Yet she knew all about it and acquiesced in the shadowing. In any case Lawson's mistake, if mistake it was, was a marginal one, and to think it was the main cause of Britain's difficulties is superficial, even if convenient. In fact the trouble started long before, beginning, as we have seen, with the irreparable, or at least unrepaired, damage done to manufacturing industry in 1979–81.[67]

Nevertheless, would things have been better if the building had been erected on the foundations that were allegedly laid in the first half of the Thatcher era? Like many Thatcherites the governor of the Bank of England believes they would. In the mid 1980s, Robin Leigh Pemberton claimed a year after Mrs Thatcher's resignation, 'we came tantalisingly close to a virtuous circle, but we did not make it . . . the depreciation of Sterling's exchange rate after 1986 led to an undue loosening of monetary conditions and monetary policy was too relaxed in 1987 and 1988 . . .'[68] The claim in other words is that in 1986–87 Nigel Lawson mistakenly abandoned a successful monetarist experiment, and if he had continued with the previous policy all would have been well.

Whatever mistakes Nigel Lawson made in 1987 and subsequent years, he cannot be fairly accused of aborting a successful monetarist policy. Although inflation was 3.5 per cent in 1986, that cannot have been the result of controlling the money supply, for the simple reason that the money supply was not controlled. During 'the monetarist years' (Mrs Thatcher's first term) the money supply grew at an average of 13 per cent a year. By much more important criteria early Thatcherite policy was similarly a failure. The two most notable features of those years were no significant growth at all and a rise in unemployment of 1.6 million.[69]

Few people other than bankers would claim that such comprehensive blundering constituted 'a virtuous circle'. The foundations of sound growth which the first Thatcher government so frequently claimed to be establishing were always flimsy if not wholly imaginary. Fiddling around (unsuccessfully) with monetary aggregates and the PSBR and inadvertently destroying in the process a swathe of British industry had little to do with laying a secure base for building a revived economy. It was more the digging of a crater, out of which only part of British industry was able to climb;

and it was then left at a competitive disadvantage. Had the government continued with its early policies, an over-valued exchange rate and high-wage inflation, British industry would have gone on getting increasingly uncompetitive, growth would not have increased and unemployment would not have started to fall – albeit temporarily. All the same the balance of payments would still have been in trouble. At the end of 1986 British manufacturing output was still lower than it had been in 1979, while manufactured imports had risen by 40 per cent. The sharp slide into deficit began during the monetarist period – a current-account surplus of nearly £7 billion in 1981 had disappeared five years later – and it was in 1985 that the House of Lords Committee on Overseas Trade (and others) realized that unless something was done disaster would follow. The Lawson boom merely brought forward that disaster; it did not cause it.[70]

The blame for the débâcle of the second Thatcherite recession does not therefore lie only on Nigel Lawson but also on those who were responsible for policy during the early monetarist phase. Arguably, of course, a continuation of the monetarist policies would have been better than the Lawson boom and slump. Yet the so-called virtuous circle would have been one of continued slow growth, a permanent three million unemployed and a balance of payments crisis.

Claims and Reality

We are not, I think, called upon to judge which of two sets of policies would have been the worse. We know, after all, that the first set began with disaster and taken as a whole was ill-conceived and unsuccessful, and we know that the second began with superficial success but also was ill-conceived and ended in disaster. In assessing the Thatcher record we have to look at the combination of them both.

During the Thatcher years growth was lower than in any

period of similar length since the war.* Dismal though that performance was, compared with most of Britain's (pretty poor) post-war economic record, when compared with our European competitors in OECD it was, however, relatively better than it had been in the past. Yet those countries, like previous British governments, did not enjoy the enormous advantages that North Sea oil conferred on the Thatcher administration.[71] So Britain's growth rate from the second quarter of 1979 to the fourth quarter of 1990 of 1.8 per cent must be pronounced a miserable performance.

Even allowing for the general rise of unemployment in Europe, the record on unemployment was abysmal – the low growth and the low priority accorded to employment saw to that. From 1,089,100 in May 1979 unemployment continued to fall until the Thatcher government's measures began to take effect; it then rose from December 1979 to a peak of 3,133,200 in July 1986; it fell from August 1986 to 1,596,000 in April 1990 before rising to 1,763,000 in November 1990 (and continued to rise to 2,717,000 in May 1992). Even at its lowest, in 1990, it was 50 per cent higher than the government had inherited; while Mrs Thatcher was in Downing Street, unemployment was below two million for only forty-five months, and was above two million for sixty-six months and above three million for twenty-six months – a record which would look even more appalling

---

* Since growth is usually measured between similar stages in the economic cycle, it is, arguably, unfair to measure the Thatcher record from the beginning to the end of her term of office, which began with Labour's electoral boom and ended at the onset of the second Thatcher recession. Yet both Thatcher recessions were brought on by her governments; they were not caused by the world economy. Secondly, if instead of ending the period with Mrs Thatcher's resignation it was extended for a year or two the results would be even worse. And thirdly, Thatcherites were themselves decidedly arbitrary in their choice of economic periods when seeking to illustrate their claims of success. So, on balance, the period May 1979 to November 1990 is the right one to take and to judge.

but for the government having fiddled the measurement some twenty-two times.[72]

The government's highest priority (for most of the time) was the conquest of inflation, and here its performance was far better than that of the previous Labour government. Inflation was substantially reduced. Yet, considering the help given by North Sea oil (by keeping taxes lower than they would otherwise have been, it helped to moderate wage claims), the astronomically high unemployment, and the high priority given to it because of the Thatcherite belief that in Keith Joseph's words 'inflation is caused by governments', the verdict must be that the government's performance was good rather than brilliant and was achieved at heavy cost.[73]

By ordinary standards the performance of manufacturing productivity was also only good, though by the standards of the late 1970s it was brilliant. During most of the eighties British productivity grew faster than that of all our main competitors, until it slowed at the end of the decade and was surpassed by the Japanese. Our productivity still lagged behind other countries': the lack of skills of the British labour force, often inadequate management, multi-union factories, shortage of cheap long-term finance for industry and low manufacturing investment still prevented us from being as productive as our neighbours; and the narrowing of the gap was due more to the others slowing down than to the British speeding up – the British increase being only slightly higher than the trend set from 1960–74. Furthermore the continuance of the process was far from assured. Yet the relative improvement was a welcome and major achievement.[74]

Unfortunately, greater productivity is only of limited use unless it leads to higher production; producing relatively less while doing it more efficiently merely increases unemployment and redistributes income from those out of work to those still in it. Manufacturing output was less than 6 per cent higher in November 1990 when Mrs Thatcher left Downing Street than it had been when she arrived in May 1979. Even if the terminal dates are taken as the first quarter of 1979 and 1990 as a whole, the increase was 1 per cent a year – a sorry contrast with the years 1961–74 when it grew by 46 per cent. During the Thatcher period manufacturing output grew by 35 per cent in the USA and by 58 per cent in Japan.[75]

The record of investment in manufacturing industry was even worse. It fell sharply in the early 1980s, and as a percentage of GDP manufacturing investment was lower in 1989 than in 1979–80. During the 1980s there was virtually no net investment at all; indeed the net capital stock in manufacturing industry may well have been lower at the end of the Thatcher period than at the beginning. Similarly 'the UK was the only OECD country in which gross domestic expenditure on R & D declined as a percentage of GDP.' No wonder industry could not cope with the Lawson boom, and no wonder the balance of payments deteriorated sharply despite the aid of North Sea oil.[76]

The Lawson consumption boom brought great temporary benefit to most of the population. Yet since the expansion was fuelled by credit and by cuts in income tax, it was the very rich who benefited most of all, cuts in the rate of income tax being the worst way of reducing poverty (especially when offset by increases in VAT and rates or poll tax) and the least effective way of creating jobs. The Thatcher years saw a great leap in inequality. Taxes became less progressive, wages became more unequal, unemployment went up and benefits increasingly lagged behind earnings. Not only did the poorest 10 per cent of the country get relatively poorer, many of them got absolutely poorer as well.[77]

As well as neglecting the poor, both Lawson's and Howe's chancellorships neglected the future. Mrs Thatcher's was not the first government to be guilty of that, but almost certainly hers was the most complacent in sacrificing future prospects to current consumption.[78] Because of the government's obsession with cutting income tax, its dislike of public expenditure and its devotion to *laissez-faire*, the gaping need to improve industrial training and education was not met.

Instead it was largely left to the market. Similarly public expenditure was needed to stop the country's infrastructure collapsing; yet that expenditure, too, was denied. A decayed dogma produced a decaying infrastructure. Mrs Thatcher's veneration for Victorian values is well known, but Victorian sewers and prisons did not have to be treated with similar reverence.[79]

Such then was the record of the years 1979–90. It speaks for itself. But how do we explain the vast discrepancy between what the Thatcherites claimed for their policies and what actually happened? How, moreover, do we explain the acceptance of the Thatcherite version of events by nearly everybody who had an opinion on these matters? Nigel Lawson and Margaret Thatcher were far from alone in their satisfaction with what they had achieved. Their belief that the government's free-market policies had produced an economic miracle was the view of the great majority.

A tidal wave of fashionable opinion drowned most dissent and swept away many dissenters. Even as late as October 1988 when, as Ian Aitken pointed out, it should have been clear to those who had previously been misled that no miracle had occurred, many intelligent Labour supporters were still conceding that the government's economic policies were a success.[80]

Thatcherite propaganda and a servile, ill-informed press supply much of the answers to both questions. Truth was the first victim of this indoctrination, the Thatcherites were the second – and the country was the third. Although the propagandist methods that they used were often dubious, the Thatcherites did not, for most of the time, mean to deceive the country. Very early on, they came to believe their own propaganda, almost always a recipe for disaster. For them indeed it was not propaganda, it was Holy Writ. So (as in the epigraph of this chapter) in the month before her fall, Mrs Thatcher really thought there had been a 'colossal increase of production' – perhaps she still does. If she had been told that growth during the 1970s under her despised predecessors had been greater than under herself in the 1980s, she would have been astonished, if not incredulous; yet that was the fact.*

Thatcherites fooled themselves as well as other people, making the economy's performance look far better than it was, by a constantly misleading use of statistics. Fiddling with the base year was the usual tactic. Thus while growth was measured from 1981, excluding the two years of decline, employment was measured from 1983 and so on.[81]† The Government praised itself for the 'recovery' after 1981, but took no responsibility for the preceding recession. Similarly the reduction in inflation was attributed to government policy, but not the increase in unemployment, which was perhaps an act of God (or the Devil), that is to say the unions.

Most of the government's constant boasts of the 'all-time records' it had set were also highly misleading. If a company had made a practice of producing similarly spurious reports, it would soon have been in trouble with the press and the City. Thus for a time the Chancellor exulted in non-oil exports being at an all-time high; he was more reticent about imports, which had risen much faster than exports, also being at a record level.

Many of the government's other claims of records they had broken were true, and so of course they should have

* As stated earlier, the growth rate during the eleven and a half years (1979_{q2}–1990_{q4}) of Mrs Thatcher's premiership was 1.8 per cent; in the nine years (1970_{q2}–1979_{q2}) of the Heath, Wilson and Callaghan governments it was 2.4 per cent. In the eleven and a half years prior to 1979_{q2} it was 2.6 per cent.

† Because of the 1980–81 depression, the dates chosen make a crucial difference. For example the increase in UK manufacturing output from 1980 to 1989 was 22 per cent, larger than Germany, Italy and France; but the increase from 1979 to the third quarter of 1990 was only 11.9 per cent, the lowest of the four countries.[82] As argued above, 1979–90 seems the right span, though cases can be made for other dates. What was indefensible was the government's choice of a whole range of different dates depending on which one happened to suit it best.

been. After all, unless they have been very ill, the height and weight of our children or grandchildren reach all-time record levels every year, but we don't boast to our friends about this growth as though it were a remarkable occurrence. We take it very much for granted. And the same should be true of the economy. It grows (or should grow) every year, and we should take that for granted. What deserves attention is not the fact of growth but its rate.[83]

About the middle of the decade the constant deluge of Thatcherite bombast reminded me of an American newspaper report of one of the many unsuccessful attempts to deprive the great Joe Louis of his crown of heavyweight champion of the world. 'Leading briskly with his chin,' the report ran, 'the challenger inflicted a sharp blow on the champion's right hand before passing out.' 'A minute or so later,' the account might have continued, 'the challenger got to his feet and acknowledged the frenzied applause of his fans for regaining consciousness and staggering from the ring nursing a broken jaw.' The government's claims for its economic stewardship were less deadpan, but otherwise similar to that report of the Joe Louis fight. Thus the knock-out to industry in the first two years was either ignored or welcomed as a necessary stimulant to effort. And the country was regaled with glowing accounts of the last few years' 'recovery' and of the many records that were being broken.[84]

Seldom was even the mildest scepticism voiced about the government's entitlement to be the economic champions of the post-war world. The City of London was an enthusiastic acolyte of Thatcherite economics – a Thatcherite government at that time being for the square mile almost as good as a licence to print money, which indeed, after the burial of monetarism, was what many of the banks were doing. The press was similarly supportive, having been largely squared, the opposition was split between Labour and the Alliance, while the Labour element of it was incompetent and incredible. Yet even allowing for the well-off profiting so substantially from the Thatcher years and for political opposition being so weak, astonishingly few people were consistently critical of Thatcherite economic policies.

Ted Heath made a number of excellent speeches, but his attacks tended to be discounted because Downing Street's press lackeys unfairly, but successfully, spread the impression that sour grapes were their cause and that ex-prime ministers should never oppose their successors – a view that was less confidently expressed in the months after November 1990. William Keegan was a persistent and witty opponent in the *Observer*; apart from Christopher Huhne he was, though, almost alone in Fleet Street. Professor Wynne Godley and his Cambridge Economic Policy Group were expert and damaging critics until the team was dispersed by the Economic and Social Research Council's unfathomable decision, highly convenient to the government, to decimate its grant. Godley himself, fortunately, was far from silenced, remaining the most authoritative and trenchant academic opponent of the government. And a small number of parliamentary critics including myself voiced their opposition. In general, however, there was what Alan Watkins has called 'a tendency to bow down before Mrs Thatcher' or a 'collective self-abasement'. In consequence Thatcherite ideology reigned, and minds were closed while pockets were filled.[85]

In addition to swallowing Thatcherite propaganda and pocketing the proceeds, fellow travellers – most opinion-formers and the overwhelming majority of the richer elements of the country – had some more respectable reasons for joining in the worship of Baal and believing that he had brought triumphant success to the government's economic policy. However false they were in fact, the government's claims to have produced the most durable recovery since the war were superficially plausible. The economy did grow from 1981 onwards, and the success of some of the government's other policies, chiefly privatization and trade-union reform which brought a larger measure of industrial peace than the country had known for a long time, suggested that Britain's economy had been changed very much for the better by the government's courageous injection of free-market philosophy and policies into a previously arthritic economy. Furthermore many companies – and not only those in the financial sector – were undoubtedly prospering, and their managers testified to the greatly improved climate in industry, to enhanced productivity and to their spectacular successes.

Happily, all that those companies said was true. But, inevitably, we only heard from the survivors. No doubt some children survived their education at Dotheboys Hall unscathed or even strengthened, but not even the New Right has yet adopted Mr Wackford Squeers as their ideal educationist. Similarly, many of those companies which survived 1979–81 and subsequent Thatcherite vagaries became more efficient, as of course did their competitors abroad. But to argue that because some companies had become stronger, industry as a whole and indeed the entire economy had been strengthened was unwarranted, though understandable, and embodied the fallacy of composition. Anybody who argued in such a fashion ignored the attrition of Britain's industrial base.

Similarly none of the three factors which provided great scope for the expansion in the 1980s that deceived many observers had anything to do with the alleged success of Thatcherite policies. Firstly, the unexampled severity of the 1979–81 slump created an enormous amount of slack in the economy. Secondly, a divided opposition and an unelectable Labour party made it electorally feasible to run the economy with a far higher level of unemployment than any previous government could have dared risk.[86] And thirdly, the great growth in the production of North Sea oil provided a substantial boost to our exports and to the government's revenue: between 1979 and 1984 oil production rose by 50 per cent, the balance of trade in oil improved by £7.5 billion, and between 1979–80 and 1984–85 the government's oil revenues rose sixfold to some £12 billion, or nearly one tenth of the chancellor's budget. Thus the three restraints – the inflationary, the political and the balance of payments –

which had hamstrung all previous post-war governments had in the 1980s all been removed – for a time. Unfortunately all that was forgotten or ignored. While what Harold Perkin calls 'the double helix of economic decline and rising prosperity' continued, the prosperity was more conspicuous than the decline, and the legend of the triumph of free-market policies hid, from Thatcherites and fellow travellers alike, the reality of a shaky economy enjoying an unsustainable credit-consumer boom.[87]

The answer then to the original question is, 'No, the wets were not wrong.' They were right about the Thatcherites' blunders from 1979 to 1981, and they were right about the fundamental flaws in the subsequent policies. Thatcherite claims were untrue. So far from their having wrought an economic miracle, their economic record was wretched. Dogmatic *laissez-faire* policies did not work, and when they were perforce changed to ones similar to those of previous governments which Thatcherites had always despised, these did not work either. Baal in all his forms proved a false god, and like his early prophets the Thatcherites should have had the grace to 'cut themselves after their manner with knives and lancets, till the blood gushed out upon them'. Instead, 'they leaped upon the altar which was made' and worshipped not only Baal but themselves.[88]

V

Trade Union Reform, the Miners' Strike and Privatization

> They used, when I first came in, to talk about us in terms of the British disease. Now they talk about us and say, 'Look, Britain has got the cure. Come to Britain to see how Britain has done it.' That is an enormous turn-round.
>
> Mrs Thatcher in 1988, when becoming the longest-serving twentieth-century prime minister[1]

> We had to fight an enemy without in the Falklands. We always have to be aware of the enemy within, which is more difficult to fight and more dangerous to liberty.
>
> Margaret Thatcher on the striking miners, 19 July 1984[2]

AWAY FROM MAINSTREAM economic policy the story was often very different. One of the two major successes of the early Thatcher years was the sale of council homes.* The other main Thatcherite success in the early years was still more striking. In the seventies many people wondered, both in private and aloud, if Britain had not become ungovernable. Many felt, too, that the country was in inexorable decline.

---

* See chapter VII below.

The widely leaked farewell dispatch of our Ambassador in Paris, Sir Nicholas Henderson, well described how far we had fallen behind our neighbours economically and how little we counted internationally.[3] Many travellers found themselves pitied and patronized abroad; others became almost ashamed to confess themselves British.

Fully justified or not, such thoughts and feelings had by 1979 become common. After only a few years as Prime Minister, Mrs Thatcher had banished them – a major achievement. She re-asserted the authority of government – so much so indeed that, instead of worrying whether a British government possessed enough power to govern, some soon began to fear that it had acquired too much. No longer were holiday-makers and others ashamed of their country. Britain's decline, it was widely felt, had at last been arrested.

Most of the anxiety felt in the seventies that Britain was ungovernable and its economy in decay stemmed from the visible damage, both political and economic, wrought by trade-union power. Both the 1966 Labour and the 1970 Conservative administrations had been brought down or critically wounded by the trade unions. The succeeding Labour government sought to avoid a similar fate, not by curbing the power of its powerful trade-union allies, but by heaping additional immunities upon them. Indeed ministers often seemed mere flunkeys of the unions whose already high membership continued to climb; by 1979 it was over thirteen million. Increasingly the TUC seemed to have power without responsibility, and the Labour government responsibility without power.[4]

This process culminated in 'the winter of discontent' of 1978–79. James Callaghan announced in July 1978 a pay norm of just 5 per cent for the coming year. What he later called a 'fateful figure' had 'popped out' in a television interview. Five per cent was far too low to be acceptable to the unions, whose advice had not been sought; its only useful role was to impress the voters who, with the ending of the Lib–Lab pact and the government's consequent loss of a parliamentary majority, were surely about to be consulted and asked for their verdict. Yet, unaccountably, the Prime Minister failed to call an election either in the summer or the autumn (when he might well have won). Even more than the 5 per cent, that was a fateful decision; it inflicted almost terminal damage on the Labour party.[5]

Following Callaghan's announcement that there would be no general election until the following year, the unions with no thought of tomorrow (or Mrs Thatcher) set about busting his norm. Many demanded increases of 25 or 30 per cent; the local authority manual workers and some others raised the bidding to 40 per cent. One after another the unions won settlements three or four times higher than Mr Callaghan's 5 per cent. Yet, after all the blood and aggression, their members ended up, because of inflation, with a smaller rise in real income than they had achieved in the previous wage round.[6]

In winning this famous victory, union militants went out of their way to offend almost everybody, including most of their union brethren. The TUC was almost as powerless and supine as the government. The cold brutality of the pickets, widely seen on television, did lasting damage to trade unionism and to the Labour party. Schools were closed; old men were left in the snow; cancer patients were expelled from Birmingham Hospital. Labour's Health Secretary, who was a patient in Westminster Hospital, was 'a legitimate target for industrial action', one shop steward exulted. 'Ennals is now beginning to take his own medicine,' this self-appointed physician continued, 'he won't get tea or soup.' 'If people die', said another, 'so be it.' Rubbish was left in the streets, the welfare of schoolchildren was ignored, and the dead were left unburied.* Characteristically, the union leader

---

* Some observers believe that, however momentous was their political effect, the real impact of the public sector strikes was overstated. Certainly in 1979 the media had a field day. In 1988, in another gravediggers' strike, more bodies were left unburied in Liverpool than in the winter of discontent, yet the dispute was barely reported.[7]

involved, Alan Fisher, refused the government's appeal to use his influence to get the gravediggers to return to work.[8]

Mr Callaghan himself, a popular and hitherto competent prime minister, had no ideas and offered no leadership. He seemed paralysed not just by the damage the unions were doing to the country but by the fact that they were doing it to him; after he had spent a lifetime stroking the unions (he had in 1969 wrecked the Wilson government's attempt to deal with the union problem), they had turned and bitten him. Moses (as his son-in-law called Callaghan), instead of stumbling towards the Promised Land, had been engulfed in the Red Sea. He dithered and did nothing, not even declaring a state of emergency. Eventually he reached a 'concordat' with the union leaders. The word 'concordat', previously confined to agreements between the Papacy and national governments, might normally have been thought a trifle over-fulsome when applied to one made with the TUC. Here, however, it flattered the government. The agreement was more like 'the Capitulations', under which the Ottoman Empire was forced to grant privileges to foreigners, who were thereby exempted from the law of the land and granted their own jurisdictions. The Labour government had heaped privileges upon the trade unions, and was now powerless to bring them back within the law of the land.[9]

The Ottoman Empire found its 'Capitulations' increasingly onerous; the British people found the same with theirs. The excesses of the winter of discontent did much to bring the Conservative government to office. If the unions could not work even with an indulgent Labour government, with whom they were supposed to have a 'special relationship' the electorate might as well try a Conservative one. Well before that, the Conservative party had come to the conclusion that trade-union power and pay determination were the central issues of British politics. (Mrs Thatcher herself conceded that 'pay policies are of course extremely important'.) The party was agreed that the trade unions were much too strong for their own good — and for everybody else's.* Accordingly, the Tory policy was to cripple the unions' power of disruption by removing their legal right to do things which virtually nobody thought they should be allowed to do anyway. In addition it was a Tory aim to create a forum 'where the major participants in the economy can sit down calmly together to consider the implications of the government's fiscal and monetary policy'.[10]

The idea of a forum was soon abandoned. Monetarism, the Thatcherites decided, would make it unnecessary. As a result, instead of calmly sitting together round a table, the chief participants shouted at each other from afar; neither side listened, and unemployment rocketed.[11] Nevertheless the main objective was secured. Trade-union law was reformed, and Mrs Thatcher succeeded where her predecessors had failed. Her task was admittedly easier than theirs. By their arrogance in affronting the nation and destroying the Callaghan government, the union leaders and their deluded followers had made an unanswerable case for curbing strikes and reforming industrial relations. They had diligently built their own scaffold and presented themselves for punishment upon it. Yet they were not quite their own executioners; some competent persons were still needed to adjust the noose and pull the lever. Those essential functions were lovingly and efficiently performed by the Conservative government, and overweening trade-union power belatedly met its doom.[12]

Successful trade-union reform was Margaret Thatcher's most important achievement. Yet it was initially carried out in a way that was not at all to the liking of the Prime Minister. Jim Prior, the Employment Secretary, was

---

* Trade unionists thought the same. In 1976 two out of three trade unionists thought that trade unions had too much power, and well over half thought that the unions were 'controlled by a few extremists and militants'.[13]

determined to avoid an all-out war with the unions and to gain the reforms permanent acceptance; he therefore adopted a cautious strategy, much to Mrs Thatcher's annoyance and impatience. His Employment Bill provided government money when union business such as elections and strike calls were conducted by secret ballot; restricted picketing to a striker's place of work and also restricted the unions' legal immunity for secondary action; chipped away at the closed shop; and banned the coercive recruitment tactics used by some unions.[14]

Even some of his firmest supporters like myself thought Jim Prior could have been a bit bolder, while the Thatcherites in the cabinet, on the backbenches and in the press became ever more frustrated. The Chancellor of the Exchequer, Sir Geoffrey Howe, was a leading opponent both in committee and in public speeches of Prior's step-by-step approach. He had been one of the architects of the wholesale union reforms brought in by Ted Heath's government. The fact that they had in the end been unsuccessful did not deter Geoffrey Howe from wanting to repeat them. The employers in what was then called Fleet Street had long since proved themselves craven and incompetent in dealing with their own unions. They had for years had just about the worst industrial relations in the entire country, while almost invariably surrendering to the unions at the first whiff of trouble. Yet that black record similarly did not deter the right-wing press from pontificating on trade-union reform, urging fiercer measures, describing Jim Prior's proposals as weak and inadequate, and dubbing their author 'Pussyfoot Prior'.[15]

Much more damaging of course, was Mrs Thatcher's known opposition to the policy of her Employment Secretary. After Jim Prior had made an ill-judged remark about the chairman of British Steel, an indiscretion for which he had already apologized to the cabinet, Mrs Thatcher quite unnecessarily waded into him in a television interview. Under the headline 'Slapped Down – Maggie's TV rap for three top men',* the *Sun* reported that 'Mrs Thatcher stormed: "I think it was a mistake. Jim Prior was very, very sorry indeed. But you don't sack a chap for one mistake." '[16]

The Prime Minister's hostility to what Jim Prior was trying to do was normally less open but still a matter of public knowledge. His civil servants knew she did not support him. The Thatcherite press was primed, and right-wing MPs were stirred up by the Prime Minister's minions to urge him to go much further. Mrs Thatcher's PPS was heard asking backbenchers whether they supported Jim Prior or the Prime Minister. Prior faced continual trouble from his own side in both Houses of Parliament and from the CBI. Almost the only people who supported him were a majority of the cabinet, but that together with his own determination was enough for him to defeat all his opponents.[17]

Jim Prior, it is now clear, was right, and the doubters and opponents wrong. Aided, admittedly, by the very high unemployment which he and his allies deplored, trade-union reform did win acceptance from trade unionists, and after Prior had been shipped off to Northern Ireland Norman Tebbit, building on his achievement, was able to go much further.

Tebbit was rancorous where Prior was emollient, but beneath his acrimonious style his approach was similar to Jim's. In consequence he, too, ran into criticism from the right-wing press, being called, of all things, 'timid tiptoe Tebbit' by the *Daily Express*. Norman Tebbit's strategy, as he later wrote, was 'first to form public opinion and to be always just a little behind rather than ahead of it as I legislated'. In his 1982 act he rejected, like his predecessor, pleas to 'ban' the closed shop, on the grounds of impracticability, but he

---

* The other two who were 'rapped' were John Biffen, who had recently predicted that Britain faced three years of 'unparalleled austerity', and myself who had just made a speech critical of the government's economic policy. Mrs Thatcher's remarks about me were in fact surprisingly mild and wholly unexceptionable.

further undermined it; he removed the legal immunities of trade unions except in 'pursuit or furtherance' of a 'trades dispute', and he considerably narrowed the definition of a 'trades dispute' so that 'political' strikes lost their immunity. As he said, that was a tougher package than Jim would have brought in, but it still represented a step-by-step approach and was not ahead of public opinion or that of most trade unionists. Sensibly, Norman Tebbit was determined that no trade unionist would ever be able to get himself imprisoned and martyred as a result of the government's legislation.[18]

Before succeeding Cecil Parkinson as Trade and Industry Secretary shortly after the 1983 election, Tebbit had laid down the main provisions of the next piece of trade-union legislation. The 1984 Trade Union Act required the governing bodies of unions to be elected by secret ballot every five years; removed a union's legal immunity from any strike which had not been approved by its members in a secret ballot; and required all unions with political funds to gain its members' regular approval of them in a secret ballot. Apart from a much less important act in 1988 which strengthened the position of individual trade unionists against their leaders, that concluded the union legislation of the Thatcher governments.[19]

The government's legislation was not of course the sole cause of the precipitate decline in trade-union power – to such a degree that the unions were weaker than they had been at any time since 1927. Trade unionism lost influence in many other countries which did not change their union laws. In a sense the succession of British acts of parliament registered rather than caused the decline of the unions. The behaviour of the trade unions in 1978–79 lost them both their legitimacy and their little remaining popularity. Again the astronomically high unemployment of the early 1980s was both cause and effect of lost trade-union power. It led to both a much lower union membership, which fell even further than unemployment rose – both the T and G and the AEU lost some 40 per cent of their members between 1979 and 1989 – and to reduced trade-union influence over the rank and file. Finally the eclipse of the Labour party as a possible alternative government until well after 1987 was a body blow to the unions. The Conservative government treated the TUC with neglectful disdain, and there was no chance of it being replaced by a Labour one.[20]

All the same, one thing that neither three million unemployed nor trade-union reform was able to achieve was the bringing down of annual wage claims to the levels achieved by our rivals. Dogma prevented any arrangements for wage bargaining other than ministerial exhortation, ill-treatment of the public sector and unemployment. Unfortunately, even when unemployment was over three million, the annual wage round did not fall below 8 per cent. Clearly, therefore, leaving everything to the market and shouting at the unions, instead of talking to them, did not work. The intended 'forum', which was dropped in 1979, could hardly have failed to be an improvement on what happened without it.[21]

Nevertheless the Thatcher–Prior–Tebbit union reforms were a vital element in the changed constitutional, political and economic environment. For better or worse, the unions were no longer an estate of the realm and undoubtedly for better, at least after the defeat of the miners' strike, they were no longer a threat to constitutional government. Britain's industrial relations were improved, the trade unions democratized, and the number of pointless strikes diminished.[22]

The sharp reduction in strikes also probably owed as much to high unemployment as to changes in the law. In any case, in the last year of Mrs Thatcher's premiership, the number of days lost through industrial disputes was only a little over two million compared with thirty million in the winter of discontent. Because of the change in the balance of power on the shop floor, over-manning was curtailed, restrictive practices were cut down, and more flexible patterns of working were introduced. The changed climate of industrial relations helped to bring a sharp increase in productivity. In the later seventies UK productivity growth had stagnated; in the eighties it returned to its pre 1974 rate. By the end of the

1980s in manufacturing it was still around 20 per cent less on average than in continental Europe, but the chasm had narrowed.[23]

The Miners' Strike

One unintended result of the union reforms was to rehabilitate trade unions both with their members and with the general public. In the votes now required for the establishment of political funds, trade unionists in every case voted, contrary to the government's hopes, in favour of retaining them. The unions had become much more popular than they had been for many years. Nevertheless, the winter of discontent and its disastrous repercussions did not diminish the death wish of all trade unionists. Both the miners (or rather their leaders) and the print workers were still intent on suicide.[24]

The general acceptance of the Thatcher government's trade-union reforms was sealed by the outcome of the miners' strike. Paradoxically, however, the ultimate success of those reforms hinged on the government not using them during that strike.

Early in its life the government had clearly signalled that Mrs Thatcher had no stomach for beer and sandwiches with union leaders at No 10. In the new year of 1980 the steel workers struck. They had been offered a wage increase of 2 per cent at a time when the miners were being offered nearly 20 per cent and the engineers had settled for just under 15 per cent. The government proclaimed that management must manage and that it would not itself intervene; as it had made perfectly clear to the British Steel Corporation how much money was available, not much further intervention was required. To teach the unions a lesson, the right wingers in the government welcomed a lengthy strike; so the damaging dispute continued for thirteen weeks, after which the steel workers emerged with 16 per cent. Had they been offered anything over 10 per cent to begin with, there would have been no strike. Much the same happened over the civil-service strike in 1981. But in both cases the government demonstrated that it was not prepared to pay up in order to avoid a strike, no matter how much damage was done to the industry concerned or to the whole economy, though in the end, of course, it had to pay up anyway.[25]

Admittedly, one apparently contrary signal was given early in 1981. In February when the chairman of the Coal Board, Sir Derek Ezra, told the National Union of Miners that twenty to fifty pits would have to be closed – a remarkably foolish admission to make, unless he was seeking to coerce the government into slowing down the pit-closure programme – the NUM, still led by Joe Gormley, threatened a national strike. The Energy Secretary originally backed the Coal Board and declined to intervene, but stocks of coal were low, the miners clearly backed the moderate Gormley and were ready to strike, and the government was both acutely unpopular and ill-prepared to take on the union which had brought down the previous Conservative government. Accordingly, Mrs Thatcher and the cabinet very sensibly executed a smart U-turn and surrendered to the miners. The projected closure of uneconomic pits was cancelled, and taxpayers' money was shovelled into the industry.[26]

Arthur Scargill, who had organized the flying pickets in the 1972 strike and who succeeded Gormley in 1982, seems sometimes to have thought that he could force a reprise of 1981. He had no excuse, however, for misunderstanding the government's behaviour on that occasion. Steeped in the history of the general strike of 1926, he consciously modelled himself on A J Cook, the ultra-left-wing and disastrous miners' leader throughout that dispute. The year before the general strike, Stanley Baldwin had similarly climbed down. Asked why the government had done so, he replied, 'we were not ready'. Mrs Thatcher was far from being a Baldwinesque figure, lacking both Baldwin's defects and his virtues. But Scargill should have realized that even less with her than with Baldwin did a retreat from one confrontation imply that a second challenge would be similarly shirked.[27]

The government well used the time it had gained. Coal stocks were built up by David Howell and his two successors, Nigel Lawson (who initially criticized the high stocks) and Peter Walker; and much of the coal was held in the vital power stations without the NUM challenging, or apparently even noticing, what was happening. The Central Electricity Generating Board was asked to produce a plan to counter a strike, and recommended increased oil burning at power stations and other measures to make electricity supplies less vulnerable to a coal dispute. Meanwhile the government was making its own plans to preserve public order: machinery for coordinating the country's many police forces was made permanent. The widespread riots in 1981 in Liverpool, London and many other towns and cities had provided a valuable trial run, demonstrating that even those government policies that produce the most deplorable results can have some useful unforeseen consequences. 'If we hadn't had the Toxteth riots,' Willie Whitelaw said later, 'I doubt if we could have dealt with Arthur Scargill.'[28]

The government's preparations were what any prudent government would have set in hand. They do not mean that Mrs Thatcher and the government sought a pitched battle with the miners. I was a member of the committee, set up by Mrs Thatcher in 1975 and chaired by Peter Carrington, to inquire into the causes of the fall of the Heath government and recommend ways of avoiding a repeat performance. Nobody on the committee wanted another confrontation with the miners, and the same, I am sure, was true of the government when it came into office. When Mrs Thatcher asked Peter Walker to be Energy Secretary in 1983 – one of her cleverest appointments – she told him she was expecting a major challenge from Arthur Scargill. But there is all the difference between spoiling for a fight and making sure that if a fight comes you win it.[29]

Not that the government or the Coal Board went out of their way to avoid either indirect or direct provocation. The unnecessarily silly banning of trade unions at GCHQ,

Cheltenham, was an indirect provocation that destroyed the moderating influence (and virtually ended the career) of the general secretary of the TUC, Len Murray. The appointment of Ian MacGregor (for whom the government had paid a large transfer fee to Lazard Fréres in New York when he was made chairman of British Steel, a job which he did remarkably well) as chairman of the Coal Board was also far from conciliatory. In addition the government's seeming indifference to the rise of unemployment to alpine heights, largely caused by its own policies, was indirectly provocative; but only indirectly, since the government pledged there would be no compulsory redundancies of miners and offered them generous terms for voluntary redundancy.[30]

The only direct provocation was the botched proposal on 1 March 1984 to close Cortonwood, the first announcement of the closure of a Yorkshire pit without the NUM's consent since the government's retreat in 1981. Less than a year before, the Coal Board had said Cortonwood would remain open until 1989; in the last few months it had spent more than £1 million there on improved washing and other facilities; it had recently brought in another eighty miners from another colliery; and Cortonwood was not a militant pit. No wonder Peter Walker was surprised by the announcement, and thought the affair had been mishandled; and no wonder that it brought the Yorkshire miners, who were already in dispute over mealtimes, out on strike.[31]

Nevertheless, the chief aggressor was unquestionably Arthur Scargill. The president of the NUM had described the Conservative general election victory in 1983 as 'the worst national disaster for a hundred years'. So much for Gallipoli, Passchendaele, the fall of Singapore, Suez and the general strike. But not merely Scargill's rhetoric was half-baked. He saw himself as the British Lenin, blissfully ignorant of the reality that he no more resembled Lenin than Thatcher's Britain resembled Tsarist Russia. Scargill had no time for parliamentary or democratic politics. 'Extra-parliamentary action,' he told his union's conference in 1983, 'will be the only course open to the working class and the labour movement.' He was an old-fashioned class warrior and, if the working class and the Labour movement did not know what was good for them, he did. Socialism was what was good for them, and trade-union action was the way to provide it, with the NUM, of course, in the vanguard of the struggle and Arthur Scargill as the Commander-in-Chief.[32]

Scargill's aim was to bring down the government by a national strike called on the issue of uneconomic pits. In Scargill's official view there was no such thing as an uneconomic pit: however much money a pit lost it should not be closed, because he was 'more interested in the investment which our men have put into this industry'.* Before March he had made three attempts to call out the miners on this issue but had failed each time. The rules of the NUM unambiguously laid down that a national strike of miners could not be official unless preceded by a national ballot in which at least 55 per cent voted for strike action. In none of his three attempts had Scargill come near to achieving that 55 per cent; in two of them he lost by 39 to 61 per cent.[34]

In March 1983 on the same issue Arthur Scargill had tried to call a national strike without balloting his members, making the implausible claim that under rule 41 each area could call out its own men without a vote. On that occasion Sir Norman Siddall was still chairman of the Coal Board, and Scargill's proposal was narrowly defeated by his own executive. The appointment of Ian MacGregor as Siddall's successor destroyed the position of the NUM's moderates, and by 1984 Scargill was as much in control of his executive as Mrs Thatcher was of her cabinet. This time the executive made no difficulties. The union's constitution was broken and

---

* In fact an uneconomic pit had been closed in Yorkshire in December 1979, when the president of the Yorkshire miners was Arthur Scargill. Similarly Scargill's official view was that no trade unionist should cross a picket line, but when his staff at the NUM headquarters struck in January 1983, Scargill crossed the picket lines of his employees.[33]

a strike called without members of the union being given a chance to vote on the matter.[35]

The refusal to hold a ballot is often regarded as Scargill's crucial mistake. But that is to miss the point. It was no mistake. Scargill did not hold a ballot, because he would have lost it. His previous failures had shown how reluctant the majority of his union was to strike. That reluctance was no less marked in 1984. Nine areas did obey their union's rules and held ballots of their own in March. In only one of them, Northumberland, was a majority in favour of a strike, and the 52 per cent achieved there was under the union's rules insufficient. In the other eight areas which balloted, only in Derbyshire was the majority against a strike a narrow one. Elsewhere the majority against ranged from 59 to 89 per cent. Altogether 18,000 men voted for a strike and 40,550 voted against. A full union vote would have meant peace. Arthur Scargill insisted upon a strike; therefore he could not hold a national ballot. His vice-president, Mick McGahey, well expressed the Communist contempt for democratic processes when he said that the NUM leadership was not to be constitutionalized out of a strike.[36]

If holding a ballot would have ensured there was no strike, not holding one ensured the strike was lost – though at times, most notably when the Coal Board hamfistedly came very close to bringing the colliery supervisors out on strike in support of the NUM, it was a close-run thing. Without a legitimizing ballot, the NUM leadership had to rely on flying pickets and violence to intimidate its reluctant members into joining the strike. Coercion took the place of consent, and the coercion was massive and ferocious.[37]

With the miners reluctant to join their own leadership's strike, the members of other unions were still more averse to supporting somebody else's. Disinclined to endanger their own jobs, they were shocked by Scargill's refusal of a ballot and the violence he promoted. Had the electricity workers in the coal-fired power stations supported the miners with industrial action, Scargill would have won in an afternoon.

Eric Hammond, the leader of the electricians' union, told the NUM leadership that if it staged and won a secret national ballot, abjured violence and renounced its political objective of bringing down the government by the strike, he would hold a ballot of his members in the coal-fired power stations and urge them to strike in support of the miners. Mr Hammond was presumably pretty certain when he made his offer that the NUM leaders would refuse his conditions, and they duly did so.[38]

Most other unions made little real effort to help the NUM leadership. The miners' traditional allies were to some extent an exception. The rail unions cut the 300 coal trains normally run each day by British Rail to some forty a day; the equivalent of another hundred trains a day went by road. The Transport and General Workers' Union was another that assisted the miners, but many of the lorry drivers who helped break the strike were members of that union. The T and G also called two dock strikes, but soon had to abandon both of them because of its members' refusal of support. In general the unions and the TUC contented themselves with merely vocal support of the miners; Eric Hammond was too honest to offer even that.[39]

Apart from the use of troops, the only thing that would probably have changed the attitude of the trade-union movement from mere ostensible sympathy to genuine support would have been the government's use of its new powers under the 1980 and 1982 Trade Union Acts. The NUM was open to legal action in the courts. Secondary picketing no longer enjoyed legal immunity, nor did unlawful acts which had been authorized by senior union officials; and though the 1984 Act, requiring a ballot before beginning a strike, was not yet operative, the NUM's own constitution prevented a strike that was undertaken without a ballot from being made official and lawful.[40]

Nevertheless Peter Walker was determined not to use the new legislation, and he secured the Prime Minister's firm support; that was more than enough to thwart hard-liners like

Norman Tebbit who wished to fire off the government's new legal armaments. Walker believed that the NUM leadership would be able to avoid being sued and penalized for the secondary picketing by pretending that some other body such as the Sheffield Trades Council, which had no funds, was responsible for it. A more important reason for not taking advantage of the new laws was that to do so might well have driven or encouraged other unions to take sympathetic action.[41]

Both British Railways and British Steel had good legal cases against the NUM under the 1980 and 1982 legislation; but both were strongly discouraged from resorting to the courts. Peter Walker was anxious to avoid 'a second front' being opened. So the boards of these nationalized industries eschewed the legal remedies that were available to them. In addition British Rail, again with government encouragement, took an accommodating attitude to railwaymen who refused to work coal trains.[42]

The Coal Board had an equally strong legal case, and in the early days of the strike it was granted an injunction restricting the Yorkshire miners' picketing of the Nottinghamshire pits. Not having been consulted, Walker could not stop the Board seeking the injunction, but he prevented it from going further. The injunction was never activated.[43]

Private firms, individuals and, above all, miners themselves were in a different position. Peter Walker could not have stopped them taking action even if he had wanted to, which he did not. He strongly favoured it. Legal action by people not under government control or influence carried few dangers of opening up a second front, partly because it was directed at the NUM rather than against other unions and partly because the government was not involved. Action in the courts by miners and others did much to cripple the NUM and defeat the strike.[44]

The government's refusal to risk bringing the full weight of its new legal weaponry to bear on Arthur Scargill and the NUM cast a heavy burden on the police. Many complaints

were made of the use of police power, and many others were
lodged against the conduct of some police officers. No doubt
some police behaviour was reprehensible; anything else would
be a matter for astonishment. To expect thousands of police
officers, often hundreds of miles away from their ordinary
place of work, often subjected to dangerous violence and
severe provocation – 1,392 policemen were injured during
the strike – to turn the other cheek, to avoid violent retaliation
and return good for evil would be impossibly utopian. That
said, some police officers lost all restraint and left deep scars
in the mining communities.[45]

As many as 10,000 pickets confronted the police at
Orgreave on 18 June, the anniversary of the Battle of
Waterloo. Apart from some doubt over which side was
the aggressor, the Battle of Orgreave anyway had less in
common with Waterloo than with Agincourt; the charge of
mounted policemen against the miners was reminiscent of the
French nobility's more colourful but less successful charge in
Laurence Olivier's film. In one week in May, 18,000 pickets
came into Nottinghamshire; on 2 May there were 8,000 at
one pit. The large amount of violence used against working
miners and their families and against Coal Board staff not
on strike as well as against the police is well documented and
undoubted.[46]

A weightier complaint was that the government was using
the police as 'a public order body rather than a law enforce-
ment body'. The police, one inspector later told the Police
Federation Conference, 'were used by the Coal Board to do
all their dirty work. Instead of seeking the civil remedies
under the existing civil law, they relied completely on the
police to solve their problems by implementing the criminal
law.' The police, he went on, were being incessantly abused
and violently assaulted in order to allow the government 'to
maintain a low profile for political purposes'.[47]

All that was largely true, but it ignored the point that had
the government used its legal weapons and thus caused an
extension of the dispute, the position of the police would

have been still less enviable. Those outside the police force who attacked the government's use of the police and who were also opposed to the presence in the statute book of the government's trade-union legislation were on much weaker ground. What was the government expected to do? The only alternative to using the police in mass defence of the law was to call in the army, which other than the government's full employment of its new legal powers was the most likely way of persuading other unions to come out in support of the NUM. To use neither the army nor the police, to allow the miners' violence to prevail and to permit intimidation of the non-striking miners (who were exercising their democratic right to continue working unless called out on strike after the holding of a secret ballot) would have been a capitulation to mob rule and to a political strike.[48]

But for Scargill's Leninism and the violence, the NUM would have had a fully arguable case. The NCB clearly did have plans for massive closures, and not surprisingly many miners felt that they were struggling to defend a way of life. The strictly economic arguments were also mixed. Scargill was hostile to the ideas of economic efficiency as normally expressed, yet the miners' strike was enormously costly to the country. And the long-term benefits of running down the coal industry are doubtful. There is plenty of coal available now; yet in the not-so-distant future the policy of closing most of the country's mines may well seem shortsighted. But all that was obliterated by Arthur Scargill's decision to use genuine anxieties and an arguable case as a springboard for attempted revolution.

The resulting strike failed because of, to use an appropriately Marxist phrase, its own internal contradictions. The NUM launched what one union leader later called 'essentially a revolutionary strike', intended to mobilize the trade unions to take power by industrial means, against a government which had less than a year earlier been re-elected with an enormous majority. Furthermore Scargill's methods and objective precluded support from the rest of the union movement, and did not even secure majority support from his own union, whose rules he broke. Hence Scargill's strike did not break the government. Instead it split the NUM and led to the setting up of the Union of Democratic Miners.[49]

The contradictions of the strike were not only internal. 'Any general worth his salt,' said George Liddell, the Notts vice-president, 'knows that the timing of the commencement of a battle is crucially important.' The NUM began its battle against a recently re-elected government at the end, not the beginning, of winter and at a time when coal stocks were higher than they had ever been. Hence, while the miners were 'the finest body of men' Harold Macmillan had ever known, they were also, in Eric Hammond's words, borrowed from General Hoffman's description of the British army in the 1914–18 war, 'lions led by donkeys'. At least, however, the earlier donkeys had not started the First World War. The NUM's donkey started the coal strike and chose the worst possible time to do it.[50]

Like the earlier donkeys, however, the NUM's leadership was faced by competent generals. Mrs Thatcher and Peter Walker conducted the war brilliantly. Their cleverest tactic was to make out that the government was scarcely involved in it. In July at a meeting of the Conservative party's 1922 Committee – whose meetings used to be private but now carry press releases – the Prime Minister let the mask slip. She talked of 'the enemy within', comparing the miners to the Argentinians in the Falkland War. How unwise, I thought, when I heard her say it; had the remark been specifically applied to the NUM leadership rather than to the miners as a whole, it would have been unobjectionable. (Unlike Harold Macmillan in his maiden speech in the House of Lords, Mrs Thatcher never brought herself to say anything magnanimous about the strikers or their families.) But I need not have worried. The remark turned out not to matter.[51]

Three months later, Mrs Thatcher's prestige and popularity were greatly boosted by the magnificent courage and imperturbability she displayed after her narrow escape from being killed by an IRA bomb at Brighton. She similarly, together with the Energy Secretary, kept her nerve and her head throughout the miners' strike. She and Peter Walker maintained a firm grip on public opinion and prevented the strike from spreading to other industries. In so doing they not only won a notable political and constitutional victory, they set a firm seal on the trade-union reforms enacted by the government. Henceforward trade unionists expected to be given the chance to vote before they were called out on strike.[52]

In the end only two men, Arthur Scargill and Tony Benn, were under any illusion about the outcome. 'The miners' strike,' said Benn, 'was the greatest piece of political radicalisation I've seen; there have never been so many socialists in the country in my lifetime' – or, he could have added a little later, so few miners. 'We're only half-way between Dunkirk and D-Day,' was Benn's conclusion. Scargill was similarly deluded, claiming that the strike had 'changed the course of British history [and had] ... resounded round the world.'[53] Much courage was shown during the strike by the working miners and the families of strikers who bore great hardship for months, but if the strike changed the course of British history it changed it to the opposite direction desired by Arthur Scargill. Uneconomic pits were closed at growing speed, and the NUM was enfeebled and split. So far from being radicalized, the miners showed themselves wholly averse to taking part in any more of Scargill's strikes. Trade-union reform was generally accepted and, the biggest irony of all, the strike opened the way to the eventual privatization of the coal industry.

Nationalization

Of Thatcherism's three successive 'flagships' – Friedmanite monetarism, privatization and the poll tax – the first was never seaworthy and, after a disastrous maiden voyage, its crew had to take to the boats. The third, the poll tax, imperilled not merely its crew but the entire fleet; hence, after the admiral had been forced to walk the plank, it was quickly scuttled. Only the second flagship is still afloat. Possessing almost none of the weakness of its sister ships, privatization has attracted much admiration both here and abroad.

After the Second World War public corporations quickly became identified with socialism and the Labour party. They were, nevertheless, a capitalist invention; the two anti-socialist parties had led the way. The Port of London Authority was created by a Liberal government in 1908; the Central Electricity Board, the BBC and the Racecourse Betting Control Board by a Conservative government in the 1920s and, in 1928, the Liberal Yellow Book expressed support for the idea of the public corporation. The Labour party was therefore the last of the three to be converted to that peculiar institution, though in those days it worked quite well. Not until Herbert Morrison decided to use the Central Electricity Board as a model for his London Passenger Transport Board did Labour finally come to the surprising conclusion that a capitalist device pointed the way to socialism or was even, perhaps, its embodiment.[54]

Morrison's nationalization of London Transport was carried into law, appropriately enough, by a Conservative-dominated coalition in 1933. Coal deposits were nationalized in 1938, and pre-war nationalization ended with the Chamberlain government's creation of the British Overseas Airways Board in 1939.

Despite this pre-war consensus the Labour leaders were not anxious to extend nationalization at the end of the war. Maybe they realized that a public corporation and the creation of state monopolies had little or nothing to do with socialism, being much more akin to state capitalism. In any case, the main economic resolution put forward by the Labour leadership at the party's conference in 1944 did not so much as mention public ownership. In moving it Emmanuel Shinwell said that the National Executive did not think nationalization essential for post-war reconstruction.

Only a revolt from the floor, led by the left winger, Ian Mikardo, and supported by the young James Callaghan, foisted nationalization upon the Labour leadership and the country.[55]

Despite this unpromising start, Labour became indissolubly wedded to nationalization in a state of unholy deadlock. The continuing blatant failure of the nationalized industries to come anywhere near the expectations of even their least enthusiastic champions was insufficient to secure a divorce. 'Particularly to the miners I would say,' Herbert Morrison had told the House of Commons on the third reading of the Coal Nationalization Bill, 'emancipate yourselves from the understandable inhibitions created by the past, emancipate yourselves from the mentality thrust upon you by a crude capitalism. This is vital, this is essential, if this socialized industry is to take with it miners and managements, to become co-operators and partners in a great and worthy adventure for the common good.'[56]

But, in real life, neither the miners nor workers in the other nationalized concerns felt emancipated by the change of ownership in their industries. Nor did they become partners or cooperators, while concern for the common good was seldom visible, let alone conspicuous. Yet, although it became increasingly difficult to see how such ungainly edifices as nationalized corporations could possibly be regarded as the true fulfilment of the socialist utopia, even those Labour members who were opposed to further nationalization never produced an alternative to the Morrison model. As late as 1968 when the nationalized monopoly corporation had been shown to be at least as obsolete as Mr Henry Ford's Model T, the Wilson government set up yet another one: it turned the Post Office and telecommunications into a single giant state monopoly concern.[57] The act of the 1970s Labour governments setting up nationalized corporations to run the shipbuilding and aerospace industries showed a similar poverty of imagination and a similarly dogmatic defiance of all previous experience.

In theory, nationalization of 'the commanding heights of the economy' was not part of the post-war consensus; the Conservative party was always opposed to it. But in practice it accepted nationalization. The Conservative government of 1951 denationalized only the steel and road haulage industries; the Heath government denationalized Thomas Cook. And on occasion, as with the steel company, Whiteheads, in 1963 and Rolls Royce in the seventies, the Conservatives even did some nationalizing themselves. So, despite the generally poor performance of the nationalized industries, post-war Conservative governments before Mrs Thatcher's, except for issuing White Papers and stressing the need for stricter financial controls, did little either to improve or abolish them. They were usually too busy with more urgent affairs, and they were aware that denationalization would probably be followed by renationalization by a future Labour government, a cycle deeply damaging to the economy. The Conservative opposition in the late seventies, including the party leader, had much the same outlook. 'In some cases,' said the party's statement of aims, *The Right Approach*, 'it may be appropriate to sell back to private enterprise assets or activities where willing buyers can be found.'[58]

Privatization's Slow Start

The fetters on previous Conservative governments turned out to be far less of a hindrance to the Thatcher administration. Nevertheless, when privatization was launched, it was only a small vessel, and it was some time before it ventured out to sea. In the 1979 manifesto, apart from the recently nationalized aircraft and shipbuilding industries, only the National Freight Corporation was earmarked for the private sector. Like many of the moderates, Mrs Thatcher was initially, I think, influenced by the argument which Harold Macmillan later called 'selling the family silver'. Certainly at first her government showed no great disposition to decimate the public sector. Gerry Grimstone, the civil servant in charge of it, correctly called privatization 'the unexpected crusade'.[59]

For the first two or three years, as we have seen, the government's overriding objective was to make Friedmanite monetarism function in the way the master had enjoined that it did and should. Apart from the manifesto commitments the privatization measures during Mrs Thatcher's first term were relatively small, and the presence in the public sector of nearly all the concerns that were privatized was to some extent anomalous. Amersham International, for instance, manufactures medical radio-isotopes. Created by the state it worked very well as a state concern, but then even better as a private one.[60]

'In the early days,' Mr Grimstone wrote, 'sales were generally regarded within the government as a series of individual market transactions best conducted within traditional parameters that had served the city well over the years'; only later did 'a privatization programme rather than a series of ad hoc sales begin to emerge'. Obviously the earlier successes had much to do with this change, but the growth of privatization from a useful but fairly small member of the fleet to a large, imposing flagship owed less to Thatcherite conversion to its virtues than to the difficulties the government was facing elsewhere.[61]

The first important factor was the failure, except over inflation, of the government's economic policies. By 1983 output had only just recovered its 1979 level, and unemployment had more than doubled and was still rising.* The foundering of the first flagship, monetarism, produced an urgent requirement for a substitute, or at least a diversion. Secondly, the government's efforts to cut public expenditure had only resulted in increasing its ratio to GDP by some 3 per cent, and the government had failed to eliminate the massive deficits of the nationalized industries, which through Treasury accounting conventions enlarged the Public Sector

* See chapters II and IV.

Borrowing Requirement. Granted the Thatcherite 'obsession' with reducing the PSBR, those deficits provided a strong spur to drastic action. Privatization would help solve the problem. Not only would the nationalized industries' deficits no longer increase the PSBR, the proceeds of their sale – again because of the Treasury's extraordinary accounting procedures – would substantially reduce it.[62]

The third and probably most crucial development was also related to the PSBR. After British Telecom had been separated from the Post Office in 1980, British Telecom were faced with the difficulty of financing its vital investment programme of expansion. To increase the PSBR by over £1,000 million was unthinkable, yet the Treasury would not allow British Telecom to raise the money from the market on the grounds that as it was government owned it would be borrowing on privileged terms. Given Treasury obduracy, the only way out was to sell British Telecom. Finally, Labour's lunge to the left provided growing evidence that the party had become unelectable. Hence the risk of renationalization was minimal.[63]

Privatization was therefore much easier and the political need for it more acute after 1979 than it had been for previous Conservative governments. At the same time the will to embark on it was also far greater. Ideological commitment was happily joined with party advantage and governmental necessity. In consequence, during the Thatcher years, about half of the previously state-owned industries were sold to the private sector. By the time Mrs Thatcher resigned, only a few, including the railways, the London Underground, coal, atomic energy and the Post Office, remained in public ownership.

Ironically this Thatcherist flagship, the only one to be a credit to its crew, was also the only one which had not been planned and which was scarcely intended. So from one point of view privatization was a good example of old-fashioned Tory empiricism; proceeding without a pre-conceived plan or dogma, taking advantage of circumstances and building on success. Yet in another sense privatization was a triumph of ideology. Almost overnight it became the Conservative equivalent of the Labour party's Clause 4, which lays down that the party's objective is 'to secure for the workers by hand or brain the full fruits of their industry' through 'the common ownership of the means of production'. Most Thatcherites and many others in the Conservative party became as blindly dogmatic in their zeal to privatize everything in sight – even prisons – as had been the left-wing socialists of old to sweep all the major private industries into the state sector. Unlike its opposite number, moreover, the Conservative Clause 4 was largely carried into practice.[64]

Aims

The haphazard origin of the privatization programme ensured that it had several objectives. These were: improvement of the economic performances of the industries concerned; resolution of the persistent problem of management and control accruing out of the difficult relations between government and the nationalized industries; the destruction of the excessive power of the public-sector unions; the raising of revenue through the sales; and making capitalism more popular by greatly extending the ownership of shares. In addition, of course, there was the unstated but very natural objective of increasing the popularity of the Conservative party and government. The beauty of privatization was that nearly all these aims were more or less compatible.[65]

Privatization was in accord with one of Thatcherism's most basic instincts that private is good and public is bad. Neo-Liberal theology taught that privatization would *ipso facto* benefit any industry lucky enough to be subjected to it. 'Less government is good government,' proclaimed John Moore in good nineteenth-century style. 'We have . . . liberated,' he added later, 'a substantial portion of economic activity from suffocation by the state.'[66]

In fact, mere change of ownership does not make much

difference to performance. Profits of the newly privatized concerns certainly increased. But so did the profits of concerns, both private and state owned, whose ownership had not changed. Indeed the overall performance of some of the industries that were still being 'suffocated' by the state was better than that of some that had been 'liberated'. Productivity in the nationalized Post Office, for instance, grew faster than in the privatized British Telecom.[67]

Private monopolies have generally been regarded as harmful by socialists and Liberals alike. Efficiency depends much more on competition than on ownership. And when competition is impossible, public monopolies have usually been preferred to private ones which, unless the public interest is to be wholly ignored, have to be subjected to a high degree of public regulation. Hence, when in opposition in the seventies, even the most ideological Thatcherites had not advocated denationalizing the natural monopolies.[68]

However, the initial privatizations had proved of 'such major benefit', argued John Moore, one of the first to see privatization as a coherent policy, that the government decided to extend the benefit to the natural monopolies. In doing so, two of its objectives – the aim of greater efficiency and the maximization of revenue – were liable to collide. The chief benefit that privatization brought to the economy was the advent of competition, but share buyers would pay a higher price and the Treasury receive more money if the new privatized concern were to be largely free of competition. In this conflict the existing managers of the nationalized industries were strongly on the side of the Treasury. They naturally wanted things to continue in their current state except in two respects: they wanted to be free of government (especially Treasury) control and they wanted to be able to pay themselves much higher salaries. For them, therefore, a private monopoly was ideal. Who after all wants to be competed with? In theory, of course, competition is always desirable, but in practice only for other people.[69]

The cooperation of the existing management teams was

essential for the success of privatization; so normally the wishes of the industrial barons, allied to the presumed interests of the Treasury in improving its accounts, prevailed over the objective of improved efficiency by the injection of competition. Ironically, therefore, Treasury control which had done so much to wreck the nationalized industries still determined the shape of their privatized successors, and the opportunity to introduce greater competition was rejected partly to augment the Treasury's coffers.[70]

Yet often the conflict was more apparent than real. In natural monopolies, such as gas or water, genuine competition within the industry was impossible anyway. The only competition is with other utilities. To have alternative sources of water or gas supplied to households would be ridiculously wasteful. Where, therefore, the monopoly was being efficiently run as a state-owned enterprise, as was certainly true of British Gas, the right course was not to break it up (which was what the Treasury originally wanted) in the ideological pursuit of largely chimerical competition but merely to transfer it to the private sector as a proven success. So, sensibly disregarding its 1983 election manifesto which stated that 'merely to replace state monopolies by private ones would be to waste an historic opportunity', that is what the government did.[71]

Like most people I was not at all attracted to the idea of privatizing water or electricity, thinking that water above all should remain in public ownership, with more enlightened Treasury control enabling sufficient investment at last to be made. However enthusiastic the Treasury had now become for letting Adam Smith's 'invisible hand' order the economy elsewhere, it never loosened its own all-too-visible dead hand on necessary public investment. Indeed in the eighties, as in the seventies, the Treasury proved much more proficient at cutting investment than consumption. If privatization had been the only way of removing the Treasury's tight fist from public investment and reducing, say, British pollution of the rivers and the sea to tolerable levels, which was the government's only serious argument for the sale, then privatization would have been not only defensible but desirable. Yet it was not the only way. Pollution has scarcely been lessened, and powerful though the Treasury undoubtedly is, a resolute government could easily have forced it to take its attention away from the minutiae of the present and for once face the future.[72]

In some cases, the conflict between increased economic efficiency and the desire to generate revenue was real. The case for privatizing the Royal Ordnance Factories, except on 'Clause Four' grounds of dogma, was anyway so weak as to verge on the nonexistent: excess capacity is needed to cope with emergencies, and the factories were well run. And, so far from increasing competition, privatization of the ROFs actually reduced it. They were sold to their chief competitors at much less than their value.[73]

Privatization largely achieved its second aim of resolving the clash between government and management over the control of the state-owned industries. There are almost impossible difficulties in regulating private monopolies, which have certainly not been overcome by the setting-up of regulatory bodies within each of the new privatized industries instead of a general regulatory authority. BT makes enormous profits and provides a more expensive service than almost all its equivalents in other OECD countries. Yet the tensions between the government and the new privatized monopolies are less conspicuous and less damaging, politically, than the old problems of managing the nationalized industries.[74]

The Thatcher government's new trade-union legislation and the defeat of the steel workers and the miners, together with the very high unemployment of the eighties, would probably have been enough to curb union power in the nationalized industries – the third objective of the asset sales. Yet privatization certainly helped. Managements were freer to manage. No longer was the government at their backs, anxious to interfere and ready to stump up for losses. The industries were on their own.[75]

The fourth aim was also achieved. The Treasury pocketed the proceeds, though the gains brought to the revenue by privatization were chiefly useful for fooling the City and not much more. The accounting conventions governing the Treasury's computation of the Public Sector Borrowing Requirement are arbitrary and often absurd. When Peter Walker was Energy Secretary, the Treasury with its habitual short-term fixation told him to cut the capital-investment programmes of the nationalized industries. He refused, but he hit upon another way of 'saving' the Treasury money. He 'discovered,' he writes, 'that the corporation tax paid by the utilities to the Treasury counted as public expenditure. The Central Electricity Generating Board was in profit and paying large sums of corporation tax.' So he and the CEGB's accountants managed to find ways of deferring the board's payment of tax. 'This, incredibly, met the Chancellor's objective of cutting public spending. The Treasury actually got £110 million less, but Walker had cut public spending by this amount and that was all right. It was absolute nonsense of course.'[76]

Treasury accounting of the proceeds of privatization was barely more sensible. Receipts from the sales were treated as negative expenditure, an oddity which the House of Commons Treasury Committee frequently criticized as indefensible, but which the Treasury declined to alter. In consequence, asset sales counted as the equivalent of tax revenue, which they are not. They are in fact less a reduction of the PSBR than a way of financing it, like the sale of gilt-edged securities. Hence the covering of the PSBR allegedly achieved by asset sales is largely cosmetic, not real. Furthermore the sales were treated as though debt had been reduced. That was not even cosmetically true. Governments do not keep balance sheets. If they did, the balance sheet would have shown that while the government's debt had been diminished, its stock of assets had been much further reduced because the assets were sold at less than market price.[77]

Popular Capitalism

The Thatcher government encouraged share ownership in a number of ways, but by far the most successful of them was the privatization sales, whose habitual underpricing made them attractive both to the share-holding classes and to many who had never before owned shares. The most important of the big privatizations, British Telecom, 'showed what could be done and thus put into play even the largest of the nationalized industries'. British Telecom attracted two million investors, more than half of them lured into share-holding for the first time. In the eleven years after 1979 the number of individual shareholders tripled to nine million or over 21 per cent of the adult population. Of course many of the new shareholders came, and quietly went: they sold their shares almost as soon as they had gained their profit from the under-valuation of the flotation price. Furthermore many of the new shareholders invested in only one company and have only small stakes. Even so, that is still better than nothing. Although the proportion of shares owned by individuals has continued to fall, 'popular capitalism' had made considerable progress. Ordinary capitalism made no less progress; as elsewhere under Thatcherism, the rich benefited most of all. Yet the spread of shareholding and the greatly increased scale of home ownership were important steps to the attainment of Iain Macleod's ideal of a capital-owning democracy.[78]

The best and fairest way of carrying out privatization would have been that suggested by Samuel Brittan, who had advocated the same procedure for North Sea oil. His scheme was that, instead of state assets being sold to investors, shares in them would be given to all adult citizens in equal numbers. That would have had one large disadvantage: since many people would have soon sold their shares, it would have been the equivalent of a tax reduction and given a further boost to the consumption boom; taxation would have had to be increased. Yet it would have helped to mitigate probably the worst feature of Thatcherism: the treatment of the poor. It would also have been far the most ethical method. After all, in theory, the nationalized industries belonged to the nation. Therefore privatization on the Brittan plan would merely have given to the people in one form what they already owned in another. By contrast, privatization by sale deprived those not rich enough or not sharp enough to subscribe of part of their property. If the left had ever perpetrated a similar confiscation on the rich, the right would have howled with righteous rage and pain.[79]

As well as making privatization very popular Samuel Brittan's plan, which had been tried by the provincial government of British Columbia, would have made an honest woman of Thatcherite propaganda. John Moore claimed that privatization handed back industries that had no place in the public sector 'to the people of this country'. But the government did nothing of the sort. It sold the industries back only to those who could afford to buy them.[80]

Sadly the Brittan plan demanded a degree of idealism well beyond the reach of Thatcherism. By selling shares at less than their true value, the government helped shareholders and consolidated its political support. A free distribution of assets would have helped supporters and opponents alike. Those who most needed help would have gained it, and virtue might have been its own reward. But the government preferred more certain and tangible payment.[81]

One of the many follies of nationalization (from the socialist point of view) was that the previous owners of the industries were fully compensated for being dispossessed of their shares by being awarded equivalent amounts in gilt-edged stock. As a result the capitalist classes were no poorer than they had been before – in many cases they were enriched because their assets had been sunk in declining concerns. Instead therefore of furthering the socialist objective of greater equality, all that happened was that the state acquired large amounts of often run-down assets at an inflated cost. Similarly, privatization as such does not add to the wealth of the private sector. That wealth is only increased to the extent that the private sector buys the assets for less than their true value. But, unlike the earlier process of nationalization, that happened in nearly all the sales of state assets.[82]

Thus one of the objectionable features of the sales greatly enhanced their popularity. Nearly all the industries were sold off for much less than they were worth. According to Nicholas Ridley, the government found it difficult to get 'its City advisors to put high-enough flotation prices on new issues'. The City of London, which through various kinds of fees anyway made a killing out of the issues, was anxious to avoid having any of the stock left on its hands. Thus the government was a negligent guardian of public assets, failing to look after the interests of the collective public. Yet individual members of the public profited mightily from the government's lax generosity. The cut-price sales provided a considerable boost to the private wealth of those who subscribed to them.[83]

This was as good a way of bribing voters with their own money (and other people's) as has ever been invented. No 'Tammany Hall' boss in the United States ever devised anything so ingenious. Even Sir Robert Walpole, that 'tympany of corruption', as one of his opponents described him, would have acknowledged its artistry.[84]

Opinions differ as to how much electoral profit the Conservative party derived from privatization, since nearly all the new investors are thought to have been already Conservative-inclined: the government was merely rewarding its supporters. Yet the party-political advantages of privatization seem obvious enough. Nationalization had almost since its inception been unpopular, and the successive demise of the public monopolies caused few regrets. Privatization on the other hand won general approval, until dogma took control and industries (such as water), which most of the public thought naturally belonged in public hands, joined the queue for privatization. Even then there was never any shortage of subscribers for the supposedly unwanted privatization sales, and the lack of significant opposition to them testified to privatization's hold on the public. It is stretching credulity to believe that it did not materially aid Conservative fortunes.[85]

Inevitably there were some less attractive aspects of the privatization programmes, as there were in Labour's various nationalization schemes. Yet the differences between the Thatcherite Clause 4 and the Labour original were much more important than the similarities. If dogma was present in both, and if the emergence of privatization as the principal policy of the Thatcher government in 1983 was almost as fortuitous as Labour's adoption of nationalized monopolies as the vehicle of socialism in 1944, privatization was highly successful electorally for its sponsors and (though the economic gains may have been partly illusory and temporary) on balance improved the economy; nationalization damaged both the economy and the Labour party. Whereas nationalization has been widely abandoned, privatization has been adopted almost 'the world over', and like the reform of trade-union law it constituted a Thatcherite triumph.[86]

VI

Poverty

If you change the approach you really are after
the heart and soul of the nation. Economics are the
method; the object is to change the heart and soul.[1]

Mrs Thatcher, 1981

Sovereigns must take mankind as they find them,
and can not pretend to introduce any violent change
in their principles and ways of thinking.[2]

David Hume, 1742

THE CONSERVATIVE PARTY has never sought to promote equality. Quite apart from difficulties of definition,
it has always feared equality's obvious threat to both liberty
and incentives. On the other hand it has seldom gone out
of its way to heighten inequality. Conservative rhetoric that
the state is 'a partnership' and the Conservative party a
'national party' has not been mere words. Conservative
governments have usually recognized their obligation to try
to make life easier for the least fortunate members of society,
and in the first three-quarters of the twentieth century they
either accepted (eventually), or themselves took, measures to
diminish inequality.[3]

In 1830 Peel thought the great evil of the times was 'a tendency to diminish the enjoyment of the poorer classes, to lower them in the scale of society, and widen their separation from the upper classes.' Twelve years later, seeking to counter that tendency, he refused to impose more taxes on the poorer classes. Instead, he reintroduced income tax, believing that it was 'for the interest of property that property should bear the burden' of rescuing the country's finances, while he lowered the cost of living for the benefit of the poor. For Peel, social policy was at least as important as economic policy.[4]

Disraeli went further. Unlike Peel, he was opposed to the harsh new Poor Law, passed by the Whig government in 1834. In the 1840s he lamented the existence of 'two nations between whom there is no intercourse and no sympathy . . . the rich and the poor'. And some thirty years later, considering the people's health 'the most important question for a statesman', he declared 'the elevation of the condition of the people' to be a 'great object of the Tory Party', and one which was 'not inferior' to the other two: 'the maintenance of the Empire [and] the upholding of our institutions'. His subsequent government carried through more social reform than any other in the nineteenth century.[5]

Disraeli's successor, Salisbury, thought it right to be 'forward in the defence of the poor'; 'no system,' he added, 'that is not just between rich and poor can hope to survive.' His government had on occasion to make substantial if grudging payments for the support of Joseph Chamberlain and the Liberal Unionists by enacting part of the Radical programme. Yet Salisbury was much more interested in foreign policy and the Foreign Office than in social matters. And despite the Education Act of 1902 his successor, Balfour, was also largely bereft of ideas for social reform; hence Baldwin's honest admission in 1923, over the Tory objective of elevating the condition of the people, that the Conservatives 'had lagged behind since Disraeli died'. Between the wars, by contrast, considerable progress was made towards a welfare state, due largely to the efforts of

Neville Chamberlain when he was Minister of Health in Baldwin's second government; by 1939 the social services in Britain were the most advanced in the world.[6]

The governments during the thirteen Conservative years, 1951–64, reversed none of the social legislation of the Attlee administration, much of which indeed had its origins in Churchill's great wartime coalition. Successive Conservative governments expanded the social services and, though poverty was not eliminated, it was much diminished. The Heath government made vigorous and successful efforts to reduce unemployment. Much money was spent on expanding all sectors of education by the energetic Secretary of State, Margaret Thatcher; and although on the debit side some of the government's reforms created 'the poverty trap', the Health and Social Security Secretary, Sir Keith Joseph, could say with justifiable pride that he had spent on average '30 per cent more each year' on the social services than had the last Labour government.[7]

Up to 1974, then, Conservative governments made efforts to maintain national cohesion, and nearly all of them saw that the best way of protecting the social fabric was to improve the conditions of the least well-off without over-emphasis on means-tested benefits. Most of them, too, accepted both parts of Bentham's dictum: 'equality is a chimera; the only thing which can be done is to diminish inequality.' For them there were important areas of politics that could not be left to the market without unacceptable social consequences; hence the government had to intervene for the good of society as a whole.[8]

Thatcherite Neo-Liberalism

The objective of the Conservative governments from 1979 to 1990 were altogether different. Not only in economics was Thatcherism a naive return to nineteenth-century liberalism. Public provision was now frowned upon; individualism was all. Full employment became utterly unimportant, probably impossible and, perhaps, not even desirable. Leviathan was to be tamed by cutting down its functions and activities; in its blundering stead the all-seeing market (allegedly registering the rational decisions of the individual) would resume its beneficent rule. In the event government was not tamed but became more authoritarian and, so far from market forces proving benign in social matters, citizenship was devalued and society damaged.[9]

Social policy is generally supposed to be about collective action to enhance welfare and to invest in people. On that definition, Thatcherism scarcely had a social policy; to Thatcherites the means if not the end were suspect. They believed that individuals should provide their own welfare, and about investment in people they had a mental blockage. Instead of looking across the Channel, in order to emulate the success of our EC partners, they took the United States of Ronald Reagan as their model. Yet, while the primary ambition of Thatcherism was the transformation of the economy, the attempted revolution was not merely economic; it was cultural – or rather philistine – as well. Social engineering of an unusual sort was high on the Thatcherite agenda. Few, if any, aspects of the nation's life were to be permitted to escape the ideological footprints of Thatcherism. 'We offered a complete change in direction,' the Prime Minister said in 1983, 'I think we have altered the balance between the person and the state in a favourable way.'[10]

Despite its grandiloquent claims, the social policy of Thatcherism was as incoherent as its economic policy. And the two were inextricably linked. Just as the state had to abdicate control over the economy and allow the market to exercise its munificent sway, so the individual had to cease being dependent on the state and learn to behave like a good market force. Two of the main Thatcherite economic obsessions, cutting public expenditure and lowering the rate of income tax, were joined with its main social desire –

the reduction of dependency on the state. Together these obsessions permeated all aspects of social policy: from housing to social security (which was regarded as 'the main source of the dependency culture')* and from the education system to the National Health Service. And in the end it was economic failure – and the vast growth of unemployment – that frustrated Thatcherism's principal social aim; so far from being diminished, dependency on the state was increased. The number of people dependent on the main means-tested benefit rose from 4.37 million in 1979 to 8.29 million in 1986; in 1990 it was still nearly seven million – a rise of 60 per cent since 1979.[11]

On social matters the Thatcherite ideology of Manchester liberalism sometimes approached the 'social Darwinism' of

---

* Thatcherites thought that 'the dependency culture' and the welfare state were the products of modern socialism and 'quisling' consensus politicians. The civilized reforming legislation of the nineteenth and early twentieth centuries mentioned above and the measures of the pre-1914 Liberal government should by themselves be enough to rectify any such misconception. But the origins of Britain's welfare state go much further back than the nineteenth century. The Elizabethan Poor Law laid the duty of succouring the poor on the parish, which was enjoined to levy a poor rate on the better off. Drawing up his scheme of the *Income of the Several Families of England* in 1696, Gregory King divided the nation into twenty-five categories or classes and estimated that the bottom four, comprising half of the total population, 'decreased the wealth of the kingdom'. That is to say they were partially dependent on transfer payments from others. Of course the central government did not possess the means to carry out that function itself, and the Poor Law had a number of serious defects, but in the eighteenth century, at least, many parishes operated a mini welfare state. Yet, despite this lapse, eighteenth-century England palpably did not suffer from a dependency culture; whatever faults it had, lack of enterprise and vitality were not among them. What the Thatcherites regarded as a deplorable emanation of modern socialism was in reality a traditional and civilized concern for others, which had the most respectable roots deep in the history of England.[12]

Herbert Spencer; neo-Liberalism became neolithic Liberalism.* Fortunately, Thatcherites did not go as far as Spencer in believing that 'the poverty of the incapable, the disasters that come upon the imprudent, the starvation of the idle, and those shoulderings aside of the weak by the strong' are 'decrees of a larger, far-seeing benevolence'. But they did see Mrs Thatcher as 'the Joan of Arc' who had 'raised the siege of the vigorous and active elements' of Britain, a leader who had 'an intuitive sense of what the lively elements in the nation' felt and 'the energy of will as well as the serenity of mind to be able to articulate that feeling'.[13]†

Obviously the weakest – the incapable, the imprudent and the poor – could not quite be shouldered aside, or starved, by Joan of Arc and her army of the vigorous, lively and active. Yet Thatcherites abhorred the 'nanny state', which in their view molly-coddled people instead of toughening them up and forcing them to face the bracing disciplines of a market economy. Those at the bottom end of society, too weak to cope with such rigours, were Nigel Lawson's 'inescapable' casualties in the economic war: necessary sacrifices to the achievement of an enterprise society based on self-sufficiency,

---

* The word neo-Liberalism has had varied meanings. In the 1950s, for instance, it was applied to a group of thinkers who, in contrast to men such as F A Hayek and L von Mises, were not only anti-socialist but anti-capitalist as well. Disliking *laissez-faire* economics, they saw what they called 'the much-tattered flag of capitalism' as 'the distorted and soiled form' of the market economy.[14] Today (as in this book) the description is normally applied to the body of ideas particularly associated with Hayek, Milton Friedman and their followers, who are far from being anti-capitalist. These neo-Liberals whose views hark back to the nineteenth-century 'Manchester school' believe that nearly everything should be left to be determined by the market, and the market should not be distorted by government interference. They, therefore, favour minimum government and *laissez-faire* economics.

† In his defence of Thatcherism, *Modern Conservatism*, David Willetts, while questioning Spencer's targets, is 'overwhelmed by the power and coherence of his arguments'. Carlyle thought Spencer 'the most unending ass in Christendom'.[15]

thrift, entrepreneurial instincts and absence of what Mrs Thatcher called 'bourgeois guilt'.[16]

Measuring Poverty

The traditional Tory view is that 'levelling up' is a better way of dealing with poverty than 'levelling down'. Thatcherism was certainly opposed to levelling down, but it had little interest in levelling up. In so far as it admitted that there was a problem, the Thatcher government thought the solution lay simply in 'trickle down' through economic growth. Such a view was fully in tune with both its economic and its social ideas. It entailed the rich being allowed, or enabled, to grow richer and richer without government interference, a development which would ultimately also benefit the poor, who consequently would not require help from the state.

The only trouble with the trickle-down theory, beloved by the Reagan and the Thatcher administrations, is that, as both the statistical and empirical evidence clearly show, it is not true. In *The Eighties Re-Examined*, Calvin Trillin well described what happened in Reagan's United States:

> 'It will trickle down', the boomsters said.
> The eighties were when no one but a kook
> Would mention that the poorest got poorer while
> The rich lived more and more like King Farouk.
>
> Statistics now show where the boom dough went,
> The middle classes hardly gained a nickel.
> Two thirds went to the richest one per cent.
> A breakthrough: we produced an upward trickle.[17]

Levelling up is not an automatic or spontaneous process — even when the economic growth is much greater than it was during the disappointing Thatcher years. The 'trickle-down' theory does not work any better in the first world than it does in the third world. If the wealth created by economic growth is to reach down to the very poorest in society, some directing mechanism is needed. Mere trickles from the rich dry up long before they reach the poorest in the land.[18]

Such heresy was of course anathema to Thatcherism. Unlike their admission of economic losses, Thatcherites did not concede that their policies had caused any social casualties. In 1988 the Prime Minister boasted in the House of Commons that 'everyone in the nation has benefited from the increasing prosperity – everyone'.[19] The following year John Moore, Secretary of State for Health and Social Security and a devout adherent of Thatcherite values, announced 'the end of the line for poverty'. Drawing a firm distinction between 'absolute' and 'relative' poverty, John Moore used the grim language of Dickensian London to show that things were different today. 'Absolute' poverty, he averred, had been abolished by the government's 'economic success'; and while he himself offered no definition of poverty, he derided 'relative' poverty as being a mere euphemism for inequality.[20]

The New Right had long been hostile to the idea of 'relative' poverty. Confining poverty to the 'absolute' kind fitted well with Mrs Thatcher's revealing view that 'there is no such thing as society; there are only individuals and families'. After all, if society does not exist, there is nothing to be relative to. The very poor in Britain should be grateful for being better off than, say, the poor in Papua New Guinea or equatorial Africa, instead of aggrieved at being islands of misery in a sea of relative British affluence.[21]

According to John Moore, relative deprivation was 'a new kind of poverty', invented by academics in the 1960s and used by politicians since then 'to keep the fires of resentment and envy . . . forever stoked'. In fact, of course, the idea of relative poverty is not even relatively new; it has a much longer and more distinguished pedigree than academic writers in the sixties. More than two centuries ago Adam Smith, far more sensible, as usual, than his latter-day disciples, defined necessities as 'whatever the custom of the country renders it indecent for creditable people even of the lowest order to be without'.[22]

Plainly, Adam Smith realized that society does incontrovertibly exist. In consequence, poverty cannot just be assessed by absolute standards. Indeed, well before John Moore's speech, another of Mrs Thatcher's ministers had reminded her colleagues that it was the generally agreed view that 'nowadays [poverty] must be judged on relative criteria by comparison with the standards of living of other groups in the community'. The government, Lynda Chalker maintained, agreed with the Supplementary Benefits Commission that 'beneficiaries must have an income which enables them to participate in the life of the community'.[23]

Defining poverty is notoriously difficult, but at the beginning of its life the Thatcher government accepted the concept of relative poverty. Only when its policies had led to a conspicuous growth of relative poverty was the idea denounced, and the decision taken by the government, in the form of John Moore, that absolute poverty (undefined and unqualified) was the only reality. Certainly the concept of relative poverty has to be used with some caution: if Income Support allowances become more generous, they appear to increase the number of people living in 'poverty'. But very few benefits became more generous in the Thatcher era; most slightly declined in value. On relative poverty, the government's first thoughts were right. The poor are seriously affected by the customs and standard of living of the rest of society. For instance the prevalence of fridges has a considerable effect on the way food is marketed, so that the lack of one is a far greater hardship today than it was in the past. Similarly the spread of the motor car and the consequent decline or absence of public transport makes life more difficult for the elderly and families with children.[24]

In any case the distinction between absolute and relative poverty is often nebulous or even scholastic. Even 'absolute' poverty is to some extent relative. One of Boadicea's ancient Britons, accustomed to a mud hut, scanty food and at best two coatings of woad, might have found the absolute poverty of Victorian Britain – rags, insufficient food and overcrowding in garrets – relatively luxurious. Similarly the unemployed between the wars were better off than their fathers before

1914, whose poverty was in turn less grinding than that of the 'hungry forties' in the nineteenth century. Yet a quick glance at photographs of the depressed areas in the 1930s leaves no doubt that absolute poverty was widespread in the inter-war years.[25]

Equally, relative poverty is to some extent absolute. In some parts of Africa, Asia and South America some poor people die of starvation; in Britain in the 1980s poor people were far more liable to die of stress or physical ill-health than from starvation. But like their counterparts in Asia and elsewhere they died from poverty.

Experts find it difficult to agree on definitions of poverty. But a proper definition would not be confined to income. It would include Beveridge's 'five giants' – want, ignorance, squalor, idleness and disease – and it would encompass such factors as homelessness and poor education. Moreover it would be based on exhaustive research into the minimum needs and costs of the poor (which have not been properly studied since Beveridge in 1942); it would not assume that uprating benefits in line with the retail price index necessarily maintained their living standards. For one thing, not only changes in prices affect the poor; for another, as people on low incomes spend a greater portion of their income on food, housing and fuel, the RPI is an inadequate measure of inflation for them.[26]

Measuring poverty in the Thatcher era is difficult because of the inadequacy, and sometimes deliberate obfuscation, of government statistics. That in itself is revealing. Just as a government will only find it necessary to fiddle the unemployment figures when unemployment is rising fast, it will only fudge and conceal the figures on poverty when it knows that poverty is spreading; when a government is reducing poverty it will make the statistics as transparent as possible and loudly proclaim them. Thus the Thatcher government abandoned the publication of statistics of low-income families and started a series on 'Households Below Average Income', usefully (from its point of view) breaking continuity and making exact assessments and comparisons difficult.[27]

Nevertheless the statistical break could not hide a leap in the amount of relative poverty. Between 1981 and 1987 the percentage of the population living in 'Households below 50 per cent of National Income', which is where the EC draws the poverty line, more than doubled from nine to nineteen – more than 10.5 million people. The result is much the same on another determination of poverty. The level of supplementary benefit – now Income Support – is by definition the lowest income that the state is prepared to tolerate for anyone. In 1979 12 per cent of the population were living on or below the supplementary-benefit level, whereas by 1987 this figure had also risen to around 19 per cent. However the proportion of people with incomes less than half the 1979 average did not increase – nor did it decline.[28]

Thus, relative poverty grew significantly during the 1980s, encompassing nearly one tenth of the population in 1979 and nearly one fifth in 1987. Even more disturbing, children fared worse than society as a whole during this period, the proportion living in poverty doubling to reach 26 per cent in 1987. Furthermore, these statistics do not show the depth of poverty experienced (i.e. how far below these levels people fall), and they are in any case lower than the real figures, since they exclude both the homeless and those living in institutions, some of the most impoverished people in our society.[29]

This growth of relative poverty was part of the reversal of a trend which had been evident since the last war. In the 1980s, for the first time for fifty years and, possibly, for more than a century, the poorer half of the population saw its share of total national income shrink. In 1979 the poorest fifth of the population had just under 10 per cent of post-tax income and the richest fifth had 37 per cent. By 1989 the share of the poorest fifth had fallen to 7 per cent, while the share of the richest fifth had risen to 43 per cent. The rich got richer, and the poor got poorer.[30]

The Archbishop of Canterbury's 'Commission on Inner Cities' in 1985 did not need the latest figures to conclude 'that a growing number of people are excluded by poverty or powerlessness from sharing in the common life of our nation'. *Faith in the City* was self critical of the Church, but the *lèse-majesté* it committed by also criticizing the government provoked an outcry. For all their belief in the values of the market, Thatcherites never favoured a free market in criticism. Politics was their monopoly, and other institutions should not trespass. In particular the churches should confine their attention to the next world and keep out of this one. As with the Lords Report on Overseas Trade, the government tried to rubbish *Faith in the City* in advance, one cabinet source dubbing it 'Marxist', in the belief, perhaps, that concern for the poor could not possibly be Christian.[31]

Mrs Thatcher herself was 'really absolutely shocked' by the report. Its heinous offence was to suggest that the inner cities were victims of the new Conservatism, which laid too much emphasis on individualism and not enough on the collective obligations of society. The New Right has been attempting to fashion a notion of citizenship which stresses the importance of individual responsibility and of minimum government interference. That of course is valid, so far as it goes. Citizenship certainly involves obligations as well as rights, but exclusive concentration on the one is as mistaken as total absorption with the other. 'The rights and responsibilities which are supposed to unite citizens,' Professor Lister has said, can not be divorced 'from the inequalities of power and resources that divide them.'[32]

Relative poverty is real and does indeed exclude 'a growing number of people from sharing in the common life of the nation'. Unfortunately, in Thatcherite Britain, absolute poverty was also a reality. Manifestly, it no longer exists on a Victorian scale, but it has not been eradicated. Many people in Britain today (five million according to one survey) are not properly fed by today's standards; even more are without essential clothing; a rising number of people are homeless; and many families still live in appallingly cramped conditions.[33]

Whether absolute poverty grew or declined in the 1980s, and by how much, were complex questions which for long were heavily defended by statistical and other minefields. Probably only about half a dozen people were fully on top of the arguments, and I was certainly not among them. According to the Household Below Average Income figures for 1988, the _median_ income of the bottom 10 per cent after housing costs grew between 1979 and 1988 by 2 per cent; according to the same source, on the other hand, the _mean_ income of the lowest 10 per cent fell by 6.2 per cent. Another authoritative estimate was that 'the living standards of the bottom 20 per cent fell by up to 8 per cent between 1979 and 1986'. However, the latest government figures have settled the argument. They show us that, while for the population as a whole average income rose by about 30 per cent in real terms between 1979 and 1988–89, the income of the bottom 10 per cent, after housing costs, fell by 6 per cent. So while a few of the very poor saw a minuscule improvement in their deplorable conditions under Thatcherism, the overwhelming majority were substantially worse off than they had been before.[34]*

The government's figures confirm the evidence of people's eyes and also that of empirical and anecdotal evidence. After spending four years looking at acute poverty in the developing world for his book _Inside the Third World_, Paul Harrison felt compelled to write a sequel about Britain; he could no longer ignore the devastating impact of world recession and monetarism on his own doorstep.[35]

As a child before the war I remember being shaken by the sight of ex-servicemen with medals on their chests begging in

---

* The very poor were not of course the same people throughout the decade. The comparison is not between the same people but between different people at the same point on the income distribution.

the street, often playing the barrel-organ or selling matches. At the beginning of the war beggars vanished and were not seen for forty years. Then in the 1980s they reappeared on the streets of London. Those streets themselves were dirty, and even some of the main thoroughfares were so ill-kept that they often had bumps and potholes. London was almost like a third-world capital. The only things missing were the rickshaws.

The growth of poverty was blatant. Indeed there is evidence that during the Thatcher era children's diets deteriorated, their average height stopped increasing, more children were homeless, more of them were ill, and improvements in infant mortality slowed down. Mrs Thatcher's claim that '*everyone*' had benefited from the country's prosperity was palpably wrong; similarly erroneous, of course, was John Moore's claim that poverty had been eliminated. Britain had become a two- or three-tier society or, perhaps, non-society.[36]

The Upsurge in Poverty

Thatcherites felt no responsibility for the distribution of wealth, still less its redistribution, at least from rich to poor.[37] In their view, the free-market economy would produce such a vast accretion of wealth that although its benefits would be unevenly spread even the poorest would gain. As we have seen, *laissez-faire* failed to transform the economy, and the poorest failed to profit. Instead, a disturbing development of the 1980s was the emergence of an underclass: a group of people crippled by poverty to the extent that they were isolated, powerless to participate in the community and deprived of the opportunity to make choices. An 'underclass' is not an entity that can be exactly quantified, but on one careful estimate the underclass in Britain grew from just under two million in 1979 to more than four million in 1986. Very probably an underclass, whose existence is an affront to one-nation Toryism, is an inevitable accompaniment to neo-Liberalism; the USA is another case in point. In any event the new underclass was more prominent here than in much of the rest of Western Europe.[38]

Mrs Thatcher liked to claim that her policies were a role model for other countries, yet many of our EC neighbours sensibly avoided the UK's unparalleled rise in poverty. While the proportion of people with low incomes increased between 1980 and 1985 'in the Netherlands, Ireland, Italy, and above all in the UK', poverty rates in West Germany, Denmark and Portugal remained relatively constant, and in France, Belgium, Greece and Spain they declined.[39]*

Thatcherites constantly claimed that under them 'choice' in Britain had been greatly extended. Unfortunately, providing allegedly 'greater choice' does not, as Sir Ralf Dahrendorf has pointed out, 'lead to greater access'. Choice without access or entitlement is largely fraudulent. Admittedly, 'negative' freedom – 'freedom from something' – is infinitely better than tyranny. But unless something is added so that their freedom *from* something is also freedom *to* do or become something, it is of limited value or appeal to many people. As Winston Churchill wrote of the 1880s, 'conscience was free. Trade was free. But hunger and squalor and cold were also free; and the people demanded something more than liberty.' (The pre-war left-wing jibe made the same point: the unemployed are lucky because like everybody else they are perfectly free to enter the Ritz Hotel.) In the 1980s the poor may theoretically have gained in 'choice', but essentially they were perfectly free to be poor.[40]

And poor they remained. If, like their predecessors a century earlier, they 'demanded something more than liberty', they did not get it. Yet something more was certainly needed, because the multifarious causes of poverty are more structural than

* An ardently Thatcherite peer dismissed these EC figures as 'trendy liberal rubbish' on the grounds that the average British industrial wage compared favourably with other countries, a comment that combined a misunderstanding of the meaning of 'average' with ignorance of the fact that the unemployed do not receive wages, which as most people know is why they are called unemployed.[41]

personal. The sharp upturn of poverty in Britain since the late 1970s was not the product of 'a culture of dependency', a desire to opt-out or refuse work; it was the result of demographic and social changes, economic trends and economic and social policies. The last couple of decades have seen some significant changes in household patterns which have affected the prevalence of poverty, particularly concerning children. As a result of a decline in marriage and, more significantly, an escalation of divorce rates, 14 per cent of all families with dependent children were headed by lone parents in 1987, almost twice that of the proportion in 1971.[42] From the beginning of the Thatcher administration, there was, too, an increase in both self-employment and part-time labour, both of which frequently involve low-pay as well as poor working conditions. The crucial reason for the upsurge in poverty, however, was the tripling of unemployment to over three million.

The two main causes of the first great rise in unemployment under Thatcherism were the government's misjudged economic policies and the world recession;[43] a third cause was failure to help people adapt to changes in the labour market. And, contrary to the fantasies of some neo-Liberal economists, two things which did not cause that rise were a sudden attack of idleness by a large part of the workforce, or unwontedly generous treatment of the unemployed by the government.* Likewise the welcome (if belated and temporary) fall in unemployment from August 1986 to March 1990 was not caused either by a sudden rediscovery by the unemployed of the pleasures of hard work, or by the 1988 cuts in benefit. On the contrary, throughout the first rise of unemployment, its subsequent fall and its second rise,

---

* According to Soviet files, the Thatcherite Sir Alfred Sherman told the London correspondent of *Pravda* in January 1984 that 'if the unemployed get lower benefits, they will be quicker to start looking for work . . . As for the lumpen proletariat, coloured people and the Irish,' he added, 'let's face it, the only way to hold them in check is to have enough properly trained police.'[44]

benefits for the unemployed were, as the intended result of Thatcherite policy and dogma, significantly smaller in relation to net earnings than they had been in the 1970s. This produced unnecessary hardship for the unemployed without having any discernible effect on their willingness to work. OECD studied seventeen industrial countries and found no connection between a country's unemployment rate and the level of its social-security payments.[45]

The Evils of Unemployment

Certainly, a few people prefer the dole to working, but all the evidence shows that the great majority want to find jobs. People feel devalued and degraded by not being at work, and until they become discouraged and demoralized, they make great efforts to get back into employment. Yet the arch-monetarist, Professor Patrick Minford, suggested that over the three years 1982–84, real social-security benefits should be reduced by 15 per cent and the money thus saved used to cut income tax on lower-income taxpayers 'in order to reinforce the incentive effect of reducing benefit'. 'Those who remain unemployed will be worse off,' said Minford and Peel (which was obvious enough), 'but their decision to remain unemployed will be a voluntary one' (which was breathtaking). Incentives to work are of course useless unless there are opportunities to work. From his vantage point at Liverpool University, Professor Minford might have been expected to spot that for every managerial vacancy on Merseyside in 1983 there were eighteen people available and 'for every general labourer's vacancy there [were] 1,700 available'.[46] But the dogmatic assumption of right-wing economists and of Thatcherite politicians that the labour market always clears (and that therefore unemployment is voluntary) blotted out such boring facts from their sight, enabling them to go on comfortably basking in theories which blame the unemployed for not finding non-existent jobs.[47]

With well over three million people officially unemployed

(and the true figure was probably closer to four million), the annual cost to the Exchequer in lost taxes and in expenditure on unemployment benefit and supplementary benefit was estimated by an all-party Select Committee of the House of Lords in 1982 to be more than £15,000 million, or about £5,000 per person. Yet the costs of unemployment extend far beyond the direct Exchequer costs. As in previous decades, the unemployed and their children continued in the 1980s to have poorer health (physical and mental) than those in work, which leads to spiralling social costs.[48]

Mass unemployment damages the economy along with everything else. It leads to a degeneration of human 'capital', declining skills, factories that close, and sharply falling investment. Prospects are inevitably diminished. In addition, and most important, it creates misery among the workless. Economic hardship together with the loss of dignity and self-esteem lead to a progressive demoralization of the jobless and their families – a domino effect – made all the worse during the 1980s by the persistence and increase in long-term unemployment. The proportion of those who had been out of work for over five years jumped five fold between 1983 and 1988.[49]

High unemployment is also detrimental to racial harmony. And since the proportion of blacks out of work is roughly twice that of whites, racism is inevitably fostered. In 1987 the Economic and Social Research Council published a report on Britain's youth showing it to be politically illiterate, overtly racist and, if unemployed, disaffected with society. The rise in support for parties of the extreme right, it concluded, was linked to unemployment and to 'a belief that the expulsion from Britain of non-whites would lead to an increase in job vacancies'.[50]

The causes of crime which increased by 79 per cent in the Thatcher era – the fastest growth this century – are notoriously difficult to pin down. After all, crime also increased during the days of full employment. But it seems contrary to common sense to deny that there is a link between poverty, unemployment and crime, or between unemployment, the stability of society and rioting. To do so was especially implausible after the scenes of violence and disorder in Brixton in 1981, 'the like of which,' according to Lord Scarman's report, 'had not previously been seen in this century in Britain', the violence in Toxteth two months later, which Mrs Thatcher admitted was even worse, and the riots in nearly thirty other towns and cities. While the Prime Minister was right to insist that 'nothing that has happened with regard to unemployment would justify these riots', her adamant denial of a close connection between the violence and her economic policies was credible only to those Thatcherites already persuaded of the infallibility of their latter-day Joan of Arc.[51]*

Much of the ultra-high unemployment of the 1980s was attributable to Thatcherism, yet Thatcherites did not see its reduction as being something governments should directly try to accomplish; indeed they regarded it as one of their major achievements that 'figures of two and three million [unemployed] are regarded as a fact of life, unpleasant but not disastrous'.[52]

The Department of Employment's last White Paper of the Thatcher era, 'Employment for the 1990s', saw unemployment, as Keith Middlemas has reminded us, almost wholly as a matter of 'wasted resources, not as a political problem, a position which would have been regarded as inadequate if not shocking by all three contenders in the 1929 election'. Even though their antiquated economic theories prevented them from taking action to reduce unemployment, the Thatcherites might have been expected to make strenuous

---

* The link between poverty and violence was recognized centuries before the dawn of sociology or, for that matter, Thatcherism. During a rising in East Anglia against Henry VIII, 'the Duke of Norfolk met the insurgents and asked, "who is your Captain?" One John Green replied, "Forsooth his name is Poverty, for he and his cousin Necessity have brought us to this doing." '[53]

efforts to treat the unemployed with due consideration. They did, to their credit, ignore the wilder fantasies of the New Right. Even so, if their economic policies harked back to an era prior to 1929, their social policies looked back to an era far earlier than that; they treated the unemployed with a meanness that the Benthamite architects of the new Poor Law of 1834 would have recognized and applauded.[54]

The government's most scurvy act of miserliness to the unemployed was probably its treatment of unemployment benefit in the years 1980–83. In 1980 benefit was raised by 5 per cent less than the rate of inflation on the grounds that it was tax free. When, however, unemployment benefit became taxable in July 1981, that 5 per cent was not restored. Some of us revolted against such unconscionable behaviour in House of Commons votes in March and July 1982, on the second occasion reducing the government's majority to eight. But only when the 1983 General Election was imminent did the Treasury at last return the 5 per cent it had appropriated.[55]

Another minimum requirement of decent treatment was that the long-term unemployed should be entitled to the higher long-term rate of supplementary benefit, Britain's means-tested benefit of last resort. The denial of that rate to the unemployed was, as the Social Security Advisory Committee reported in 1981, 'wholly unjust'.[56] Yet the government (like its Labour predecessor) was unmoved, eventually solving its difficulty in characteristic manner by abolishing the higher rate for everyone.

Altogether the government made no fewer than thirty-eight changes to unemployment benefits between 1979 and 1988, ranging from the well-publicized abolition of earnings-related benefit to the taxation of short-term benefits. The great majority of the changes having made the system even less generous, the real value of unemployment benefit fell between 1978 and 1988 by 4 per cent and, since average earnings rose rapidly, the relative value of unemployment benefit plummeted.[57]*

The income gap between those in work and those claiming benefits thus grew wider, leaving British society increasingly divided. The UK is also geographically divided by distinctive regional patterns of unemployment and poverty, resulting in the North–South divide. In January 1988 the Prime Minister dismissed the notion of an economic and social divide between North and South as a false over-simplification. The next day a new study was published revealing 'an even clearer North–South cleavage' than in previous studies. Two years earlier, the mean price of a house in Crawley in Sussex was £56,201 and in Consett in Durham, £19,822.[58]

Naturally there are many differences within regions as well as between them. The most impoverished and deprived areas, however, were invariably those with the highest unemployment, and most of them were in the North. Yet the real divide, as Linda Christmas pointed out, is 'the divide between rich and poor'.[59]

Low Pay and Taxation

Another dire and even more widespread problem than unemployment is low pay, the incidence of which also increased dramatically in Britain during the 1980s. Between 1979 and 1991 the numbers earning less than the Council of Europe's 'Decency Threshold' (defined as below 68 per cent of average earnings) grew from 7.8 million to 10.1 million. By the early 1990s, in all regions except the south-east of England, more than 40 per cent of employees were earning below the decency threshold.[60]

* The government made almost as many changes to the counting of the unemployed as to unemployment benefit. Between 1982 and Mrs Thatcher's resignation, thirty alterations were made to the way the unemployment figures were calculated, thereby removing nearly half a million from the official count. Until August 1986, that was the only way the government could reduce the total unemployment figure. If only it had been as ingenious at reducing unemployment itself![61]

Unlike every other country in the EC except Ireland, and unlike the United States which even under President Reagan retained its federally established minimum wage (although Reagan froze it from 1981 to 1988), Britain has no minimum wage, a void of which Thatcherites were particularly proud, though as the experience of more competitive economies shows its absence is economically as well as socially regrettable.* Furthermore, in a gesture unique in the developed world, the government deregulated pay and (most of the) conditions of work for people under the age of twenty-one so that employers may now lawfully employ juveniles at any rate of pay whatever. Cobden, Bright and other Liberal ideologues who opposed the passing of the nineteenth-century Factory Acts would have heartily approved. On the other hand that exemplary Tory wet, the seventh Earl of Shaftesbury, would have been dismayed by the Thatcherite dismantling of a significant part of the social legislation which had succeeded in protecting young people from the more disagreeable manifestations of nineteenth-century capitalism.† The Thatcherite excuse for this legislative help to the strong and damage to the weak is that the free market works for the good of all, even though in such circumstances a free market does not exist, being merely a euphemism for exploitation.[62]

The government displayed a similar though in practice more cautious dogmatism towards Wages Councils, which used to give protection to roughly two million of the

---

* The 1985 government paper on wages and employment, designed to show that minimum wages cost jobs, which was often quoted by ministers, was not a Government Economic Service Working Paper, was based on very dubious assumptions and, not surprisingly, had no identifiable author.[63]

† So would Coleridge. A supporter of the Factory Children Bill of 1818, he asked a friend if he could give him 'any other instances in which the Legislature has ... interfered with what is ironically called "free labour"? (i.e. dared to prohibit soul-murder and infanticide on the part of the rich, and self-slaughter on that of the poor).'[64]

lowest-paid adults. Not all of them were abolished. Jim Prior thought we should 'not turn our back on the low-paid . . . the weakest in society do need some form of protection against exploitation'. Winston Churchill, who set up Wages Councils in 1909, thought the same:

> It is a serious national evil that any class of His Majesty's subjects should receive less than a living wage in return for their utmost exertions. It was formerly supposed that the laws of supply and demand would naturally regulate or eliminate that evil but where you have what we call sweated trades, you have no organization, no parity of bargaining, the good employer is undercut by the bad . . . where these conditions prevail, you have not a condition of progress but a condition of progressive degeneration . . . there is no power of self-cure.

There is still no 'self-cure', but the Thatcherites did not agree, believing that Wages Councils contributed to unemployment by raising wages above market levels. Once again the market was to rule, even where it worked badly or scarcely existed; in fact low pay accompanies inefficiency and makes the economy less, not more, competitive.* Elsewhere Thatcherites were relatively indifferent to the high level of unemployment – refusing to create 'false' jobs – but they were not averse to creating more low-paid employment. In the 1980s jobs at exploitative rates of pay were 'real' ones, and Britain's economic future was adjudged to lie in providing sweated labour for British and foreign employers.[65†]

Half of all women employees work part time, a figure which

---

* In 1937, the Chief Justice of the United States (a former Republican Presidential candidate) said that when there was 'exploitation of a class of workers who are in an unequal position with respect to bargaining power, the community may direct its law-making power to correct the abuse which springs from unconscionable employers' selfish disregard of the public interest'. That was the reason for Wages Councils.[66]

† Times have changed. During the last war George Orwell wrote of 'Britain with its democratic phrases and its coolie empire'. Now the phrases are commercial, and the coolies are at home.[67]

rises to two-thirds of women workers with dependent children. Part-time workers are often discriminated against over both pay and conditions; employers frequently manipulate wages and hours of work and lengths of contract to avoid social-security contributions and other obligations. Yet the draft EC directives on the social dimension of the Single Market, giving part-time and temporary workers the same rights and benefits (on a pro-rata basis) as full-time staff, were dismissed or ignored by the government when they were proposed in 1990.[68]

Tax

A further cause of poverty in Britain is tax. At the end of 1988, a remarkable two-thirds of all those with earnings below the Council of Europe's decency threshold were taxpayers. There were about 6.5 million such people and they contributed £4 billion in income tax alone. That was after the 1988 tax-cutting budget and despite many years of North Sea oil. Oil gave the Chancellor a unique opportunity to transform the taxation system for the benefit of the low paid as he did for high income-earners; it was not taken.[69]

From the start the Thatcher administration constantly spoke of the need to reduce the level of taxation, and certainly the government's popular image was that of a tax-cutting administration. In reality, however, as in other EC countries, the overall tax burden (all taxes and social-security contributions as a percentage of GNP) was higher in 1989 (43 per cent) than it was in 1979 (39 per cent). There were indeed tax cuts for the better-off, but these were paid for by increasing the tax burden on the less well-off. Income tax as a percentage of total income declined, while National Insurance contributions, domestic rates, Community Charge and VAT all increased. Between 1979 and 1990 the higher rate of income tax was slashed from 83 per cent to 40 per cent, and the 15 per cent surcharge on investment income was abolished. Overall, in comparison with other Western

OECD countries, Britain had a middling tax burden; yet, once other countries' local taxes and social-security contributions were taken into consideration, Britain's top rate of income tax was lower than anywhere else except Switzerland.[70]

Had the same been true of taxes paid by the poor, that would have been fully defensible. But while the basic rate of income tax was reduced under Thatcher governments from 33 to 25 per cent, National Insurance contributions, an equally material, although less visible, tax on earned income was sharply raised from 6.5 per cent in 1978–79 to 9 per cent in 1983–84. Because additional contributions were not payable above an upper-earnings ceiling (of £15,800 *per annum* in 1989), the tax is regressive and bears hard on many of the low paid who pay more in National Insurance contributions than they do in income tax.[71]

The last decade similarly saw a steady increase in indirect taxes such as VAT. While the yield from income tax fell from almost a third of all tax revenue in 1978–79 to under a quarter in 1988–89, indirect taxes increased by £22 billion in real terms since 1979. The overall effect of this switch during the Thatcher era was to place the heaviest burden on the poor: in 1989 the poorest fifth of the population spent 30 per cent of their disposable income in indirect taxes, while the richest fifth paid only 15.5 per cent.[72]

The 1988 budget cut income taxes by more than £6 billion, nearly half of which (£2,690 million) went to the top 5 per cent of taxpayers. As a result, the remarkable achievement of the first ten years of tax-cutting government was to increase the personal tax burden on a one-earner couple with two children earning half the average wage from 12.2 per cent of gross income in 1979 to 16 per cent in 1989, and to reduce that on a similar family earning ten times the average wage from 65.8 per cent to 37.3 per cent. The figures for all taxation are no less remarkable. In 1988 the poorest fifth paid out 40 per cent of their gross income in taxation, while the richest fifth paid out only 35 per cent. Thus the gradual shift from income tax to National Insurance contributions, local authority rates, poll tax and VAT brought massive benefits to the rich at the expense of the poor.[73]

This pattern of growing inequality between rich and poor was reinforced by the introduction of the Community Charge – an Orwellian euphemism, since the imposition had little or nothing to do with 'community' (if there is no society, can there be a community?) and, as it was compulsory, it was plainly a tax, not a charge. A comparison of the flat-rate poll tax with the domestic rates it replaced showed that although the poll tax involved extra public expenditure on rebates, only the rich gained; the poorest lost significantly, and the middle-income groups lost most of all.[74]

Blaming the Poor

During the eighties the Conservative right wing subjected the social-security system to many changes in furtherance of their belief that dependency on the state must be reduced. This campaign was closely linked with their notion of the 'deserving' and 'undeserving' poor, a distinction that was discredited nearly a hundred years ago. The notion that the poor want or choose to be poor is absurd, but the convenience of the belief ensures its survival. The undeserving poor of Thatcherite Britain were 'an underclass' which (according to *The Sunday Times*) 'spawns illegitimate children without a care for tomorrow and feeds on a crime rate which rivals the United States in property offences . . .'. In fact, while a cycle of deprivation evidently exists and individual standards of behaviour are undeniably vital, the disadvantaged and their children are trapped in their deprived circumstances less by their own personal shortcomings than by barriers of social hardship and geographic inequality and by the social-security regulations.[75]

In 1985 Nigel Lawson asked if we could 'afford a system which encourages idleness and irresponsibility'. Despite a barrage of similarly unsavoury rhetoric, the public was not impressed: in 1977, 35 per cent of voters thought that poverty was due to laziness; by 1985 only 22 per cent thought the same. At the end of 1987 13 per cent agreed and 87 per cent disagreed that the unemployed were themselves to blame for their unemployment.[76]

'Dependence on welfare benefits,' John Moore argued, 'can corrupt the human spirit' – which is undeniable, since almost anything can do so and frequently does. Still that does not make the quarter-truth a good guide to action. Thatcherites like him ignored the uncomfortable facts that it was the government's economic policy and the resulting mass unemployment which were largely responsible for the increase in dependency in the first place. The government then compounded its misjudgements by its rigid adherence to the concept of 'targeting' – in social-security matters; the idea was seldom allowed to intrude elsewhere.[77]

Mrs Thatcher upheld the right-wing belief that state-induced dependence is a temptation which may lead to people becoming 'moral cripples'. In fact state-dependence, like unemployment, is rarely a matter of choice: people who claim state benefits are normally forced to do so by their inability to find work, the dearth of adequate childcare provision and the crazy constraints of the unemployment and poverty traps. The problem is one of social organization not personal inadequacies. In any case the belief that cutting state support for the least well-off will eliminate dependency is naive, at best. Cuts in benefit merely shift the burden on to relatives and charities, or at worst result in increased debt and destitution. In addition, the stigma the government put on state-dependents was highly selective. Thatcherism castigated only those who took money from the state in the form of social-security benefits; tax subsidies such as mortgage interest and private-pension tax reliefs (the middle-class welfare state) escaped all taint of being 'undeserved' and were, evidently indeed, in some way admirable.[77]

The Fowler Reforms

Throughout the 1980s, then, the goals of social-security policy were reduced public expenditure and increased selectivity.

Prior to Norman Fowler's review and the subsequent 'reforms' of 1985–88, savings or cuts of as much as £8,000 million had already been made in social security. These were largely achieved by breaking the link between pensions and earnings (so that pensions only rose in line with prices), by ending earnings-related unemployment and sickness benefit, and by sundry other cuts. Despite these savings, however, the social-security budget, which Thatcherites had long regarded as a tempting quarry to be raided for the financing of cuts in income tax, still accounted at the beginning of Mrs Thatcher's second term for nearly a third of public spending. So, a major review of the system was undertaken by Norman Fowler, which culminated in the massive upheaval implemented under John Moore in April 1988.[78]

Over the four decades since Beveridge, Britain's social-security system had undoubtedly become unduly complex and was in need of reform and rationalization. The maze of benefits confused not only the poor but those who were trying to help them. Unfortunately, Norman Fowler's two aims of simplicity and increased targeting were incompatible. In any case the government's overriding objective was financial savings. 'For the first time in half a century,' *The Observer* complained, 'the welfare system is being overhauled with the intention of saving money rather than easing the plight of the poor [and] cuts are being made in the context of a thriving economy.'[79]

Once again the Thatcherites failed to realize that their difficulties were largely caused by their own economic policy. A government which first causes and then permits very high unemployment has too little money available to pay for everything else. And that is particularly true of a government constantly on the watch for opportunities to reduce taxes on the better off.[80]

By 1988, social-security spending had increased since 1979 in real terms by some £10 billion or by about 30 per cent. Less than a third of this (about 10 per cent), however, was due to real increases in the amounts of benefit paid (pensioners did relatively well); the rest was due to the growing number of claimants: the unemployed, invalidity and retirement pensioners and lone parents. In a few areas the increase in the level of benefit support was commendable. But it was seldom sufficient and, because of the de-indexing of long-term benefits from earnings, the living standards of those wholly dependent on social-security benefits declined relative to those in work as earnings shot ahead of prices.[81]

The 1986 Social Security Act was hailed by the government as the greatest reform since Beveridge. Income Support is less complicated than its predecessor, Supplementary Benefit, and with the new integrated means-test for housing benefit and the new Family Credit the system was made easier to administer. Claimants, however, were faced with forms for Family Credit and Income Support which were respectively sixteen and twenty pages long.

When the Act came into force in April 1988, the financial reality beneath the government's extravagant claims was an expenditure saving of over £500 million. The higher spending of £220 million on Family Credit (for families in low-paid work) and £225 million on Income Support was more than offset by a massive cut of £640 million in housing benefit, the reduction of £230 million from the replacement of single payments with the Social Fund and the saving of £120 million from not uprating child benefit in line with inflation.[82]

Help, the government maintained, was now being concentrated on those most in need. Family Credit was indeed twice as generous as its predecessor (Family Income Supplement), and entitlement was increased. That was an important improvement. Yet many of the families most in need suffered overall losses if they also claimed housing benefit (because Family Credit was taken into account when calculating housing benefit); and in addition they no longer qualified for free school meals or milk tokens. More damningly, this standard-bearer of the government's reforms which was supposed to epitomize the advantages of targeting had, a year later, a take-up rate of only 50 per cent.[83]

The Party of the Family

The trouble was that the government's doctrinaire insistence on the virtues of selectivity, or targeting via means-testing, was fundamentally flawed. That insistence led to a capricious onslaught on child benefit throughout much of the Thatcher premiership, an assault which was uneasily combined with constant claims that the Conservatives were the party of the family.[84] Characteristically, the Thatcherites' hostility to child benefit stemmed almost entirely from dogma and their ignorance of its history: their obsession with cutting public expenditure, and their belief that universal benefits are unhealthy.

The obvious truth that people with families have higher expenses and greater responsibilities than people who do not was recognized by the Younger Pitt; those who 'enriched their country with a number of children,' he said in 1796, 'have a claim upon its assistance for their support.' Child tax allowances were therefore inaugurated with the introduction of income tax in 1799. In what Castlereagh called 'an ignorant impatience of taxation', the rich 'delivered themselves from the [income] tax' after the end of the Napoleonic Wars, and when Peel bravely brought it back in 1842, he did not reintroduce child tax allowances. They had to wait until Lloyd George's 'People's Budget' of 1909. After a long struggle, family allowances – a cash benefit for each child except the first – were achieved after the Second World War. Unlike family allowances, income-tax allowances were of no value to families who were not paying tax; in the late 1970s, therefore, they were amalgamated with family allowances to form child benefit, which goes to those both above and below the tax threshold.[85]

The arguments for child benefit are compelling. It has a take-up rate of virtually 100 per cent, reaching, therefore, far more low-income families than any 'targeted' benefit; it provides security, particularly for those families whose income fluctuates; it is fully comprehensible, unlike many means-tested benefits whose low take-up is often as much due to lack of understanding as to feelings of humiliation; it provides a ladder out of the poverty and unemployment traps by reinforcing the incentive to work because it is non-withdrawable; it is administratively efficient, its overhead costs amounting to only 2.2 per cent of the expenditure, whereas a 'targeted' benefit such as Income Support costs 14.7 per cent of its budget; finally and importantly, it is paid straight to the carer who is nearly always the mother.[86]*

All in all a more desirable and cost-effective form of public expenditure would be hard to find. Its virtues were well recognized by Margaret Thatcher when she was leading the opposition. At that time she accused the Labour government of increasing the tax burden fastest on families with children. 'We are impatient,' she wrote just before the 1979 election victory, 'to implement the Child Benefit scheme fully. This measure will do more than any other benefit to help families in caring for their children.' More than a decade later the tune was still the same: 'children must come first because children are our most sacred trust.' Yet they came first only in Thatcherite rhetoric. In practice children came last. The married man's income-tax allowance, the single person's income-tax allowance, and the wife's earned-income allowance were all raised by more than the rate of inflation. In contrast, the increase in child benefit was held below the rate of inflation in 1985, and then in 1988, 1989 and 1990 it was frozen. Between April 1979 and April 1990, child benefit was cut in real terms by 21 per cent.[87]

* In 1987, 6,545,000 women received child benefit compared with 135,000 men. As means-tests are applied to *family* income, they are of no help to those mothers in families where the income is sufficient but is not fairly shared. Child benefit is therefore especially effective in providing purchasing power in favour of children because it goes to the parent directly responsible for feeding and clothing them.

By 1990 there was little doubt that child benefit was being left 'to wither on the vine'.[88] Parliamentary debates on the subject were invariably depressing. The late Brandon Rhys Williams, Tim Raison, Jim Lester, Robin Squire, myself and a few other Conservative MPs were unwavering supporters of child benefit. But the overwhelming majority of the party stayed away, only surfacing to vote as the whips directed. All good Thatcherites looked forward to child benefit's abolition. They attacked it for being poorly targeted, too expensive and unfair – a view which was endorsed at the time by the great majority of Conservative backbenchers and by virtually the whole of the right-wing press.

Showing an unusual solicitude for the least well-off, Thatcherites opposed uprating child benefit in line with inflation on the grounds that the poor did not benefit from it. Admittedly child benefit is taken into account during the assessment for income support, so that any increase in its rate is not translated into a cash increase for the poorest families. That, however, could have been easily and beneficially remedied: child benefit could have been omitted from the assessment. Leaving that aside, even if the overall cash received remains constant, it is far preferable for those on Income Support to receive a higher percentage of their income in the form of a universal benefit, which is secure and reliable, than a means-tested benefit which is neither. More importantly, many people do not take up means-tested benefits, and there are many financially hard-pressed families just above the Income Support or Family Credit levels, who are badly hit by a freeze in child benefit – to the detriment of their children.[89]

Another major criticism levelled against child benefit was its expense. Yet compared, say, with the £9 billion for the single person's income-tax allowance and the married man's £14 billion, £4.5 billion for children could be deemed exorbitant only by Malthusians or misanthropes. Once again the Thatcherites and the Treasury forgot that there are two sides to a balance sheet, and that it costs no more to pay out £4 billion in benefit than it does to forgo £4 billion by awarding a tax-free allowance.[90]

The essence of child benefit is its universality, as a result of which it embodies the basic principle that people should be taxed only on their surplus income after their unavoidable expenditure has been met. Only through such a benefit can the Treasury preserve tax equity between taxpayers with children and those without. Some 30 per cent of families with children receive more in child benefit than they pay in income tax, and most of them are out of work or not earning – e.g. lone parents. The converse is true of the remaining 70 per cent, and for them child benefit is in the nature of an income-tax allowance – with the advantage that it is not worth more to higher-rate taxpayers.*

Child benefit preserves tax fairness by horizontal redistribution between taxpayers with and without dependent children. Yet 'liberal Thatcherites', to use Norman Tebbit's description of himself, Nigel Lawson and others, attacked it for not procuring vertical redistribution – even though they are not known to have favoured any other method of securing redistribution of income from the rich to the poor.[91] Indeed they turned a dogmatically blind eye to the glaring presence of other tax benefits – mortgage-interest tax relief, private-pensions tax concessions, and tax concessions on private health insurance for the elderly – which were all universal non-means-tested benefits that subsidised the well-off far more than did child benefit. Yet only child benefit earned their puritanical disdain on the grounds, allegedly,

---

* Just why some people should feel guilty about receiving such an allowance for a deserved entitlement merely because it is paid in cash, when they feel no guilt at all about receiving other much larger sums in tax allowances by cheque or other means is a mystery. In any case, in order to remove such irrational worries, I have suggested in the past that child benefit should be renamed 'Child Credit'. At the same time the Treasury should change its accounting procedure and remove this tax allowance from the budget of the Department of Social Security.[92]

that it helped the rich. Great concern was expressed that the Duchess of Westminster should receive some £7 a week from the taxpayer, which one way and another she did not really need. These improbable levellers had of course to brush aside the awkward circumstance that at the same time as they were objecting to the Duchess receiving £7 a week from child benefit they were, by cuts in income tax, showering thousands of pounds per week on her ducal husband which he, too, did not really need. For every pound the Duchess gained in child benefit, the Duke probably gained a windfall of £1,000 in reduced tax. Yet Thatcherites favoured a means test for the Duchess but not for the Duke.[93]

The Major government's very welcome reversion to the previous Conservative position confirms the view that the enmity to child benefit stemmed largely from the previous tenant of 10 Downing Street.[94] Indeed in only three of the eleven Thatcher years did child benefit not decline in real value. Other than letting it 'wither on the vine', among the options that Mrs Thatcher apparently considered were outright abolition, taxing the benefit, and paying it only to the poor. None of these was either practicable or sensible: abolition would clearly have been catastrophic; to tax a form of tax relief would have been a palpable absurdity; and to withdraw tax-free child benefit from middle-income families would have defied the self-evident fact that children cost money and would have entailed embracing the philosophy of the radical right that children 'should be seen as a consumption good, no more meriting recognition for tax or benefit systems than a consumer durable'.[95]* Fortunately the Thatcherites did not take their general attitude that all of life's a market place quite that far. But they were a long way both from William Pitt and from putting children first.

Means-tested benefits can not successfully tackle poverty

* According to the editor of the *National Children's Directory*, children are becoming a luxury item of consumption which the poor can not afford to buy.[96]

'because they come into play too late ... claimants have to be poor in order to qualify. The safety net of means-tested benefits is one in which people get enmeshed.' In any sensible system of social security both kinds of benefit – the universal and the means-tested – are needed. Yet because child benefit is universal and not means-tested the right wing tried to smother it.[97] Just as the fixation with M3 was the most irrational and ideological feature of the Thatcher government's initial economic policy, so the attack on child benefit was the most irrational and ideological aspect of its later social objectives. On a small scale the child-benefit saga revealed the same defects in the decision-making process as did the sad tale of Friedmanite monetarism.

The Poverty and Unemployment Traps

In 1984 the Institute for Fiscal Studies said that 'any Chancellor who claims that by increasing income tax allowances he has made significant inroads in the poverty and unemployment traps ... is simply talking ill-informed nonsense.' This is precisely what the Chancellor promptly did, although on the Treasury's own calculations only 10,000 of the 850,000 lifted out of tax by the 1984 budget were also lifted out of the poverty trap. As a Treasury official explained, 'it is going to be a long hard haul to solve the poverty trap by increases in personal allowances' and 'increases in child benefit clearly are another way of improving the poverty and unemployment traps'.[98]

The government's frequent resort to the demagogic condemnation of 'slackers' and 'scroungers' was politically effective but, had reason not been annulled by dogma, the government's 'scrounger-phobia' should have led it to re-think its opposition to universal benefits. Quite apart from any moral considerations about fairness, excessive taxation of the lower paid produces tax-induced poverty and exacerbates the unemployment trap; and attempts to remedy this by resorting to means-tested benefits produces the poverty trap. During the past twenty years the long-established principle that people should be taxed according to their ability to pay has been replaced by a new-fangled delusion that tax beyond ability to pay can be rendered harmless by providing means-tested benefits for the 'really poor'. Yet since 'targeted' benefits are withdrawn as income rises, they actually set the poverty trap and inevitably penalize individual effort. So, instead of strengthening work incentives and reducing dependency, the government's policy of targeting created what it was professedly seeking to end: a dependency culture.[99]

The 1986 Social Security Act did succeed in removing the most extraordinary manifestation of the poverty trap whereby a claimant could lose more than £1 for each extra £1 of earnings. And the government's earlier cuts in unemployment benefit greatly reduced the unemployment trap without reducing unemployment. Nevertheless, partly as a result of refusing to uprate child benefit, the government managed to extend the poverty trap to more people. So much for Thatcherite imaginings that the poverty and unemployment traps were 'successfully banished from the scene'. In reality, while about 120,000 families were caught in the poverty trap in 1980, the 1988 'reforms' increased this figure to 530,000 families, in part because of the increased number of recipients of means-tested benefits but also as a direct result of the reforms. Thatcherites thought the maximum rate of tax that could safely be imposed on the rich without stifling their entrepreneurial urges was 40 per cent. Evidently, therefore, the effective imposition of a much higher rate on many of those on social security did not provide a commanding incentive to them to increase their earnings or hours of work. The oft-stated objective of the reforms – to promote self-reliance – was thus largely nullified. The new system also did nothing either to remove the trap preventing the unemployed from taking part-time work, or to encourage them to leave the unemployment register for short-term work.[100]

Not surprisingly the most ardently ideological of these

'reforms', the introduction of the Social Fund, was also the most deplorable. This replaced the single-payments scheme, which was a system of one-off grants for essential items to those claiming supplementary benefit. A reflection of how inadequate the levels of supplementary benefit had become was the increase of claims under the single-payments scheme from 37 per cent of claimants in 1979 to 87 per cent in 1985 at a cost that year of £308 million. The primary motive for launching the Social Fund was to cut public expenditure as well as, supposedly, to reduce dependency, the government's justification being that claimants and advisors were 'working the system' by making unwarranted claims. In fact, DHSS-funded research on the single payments scheme showed that 'the needs met by single-payments are genuine' and that there was actually substantial 'underclaiming' of single payments by eligible claimants.[101]

The budget for the Social Fund for 1990–91 was only £200 million and cash-limited, of which a mere £65 million was allocated for non-discretionary grants providing for maternity, funeral and cold-weather payments. One-off payments were thus limited, not by the level of need but by the level of cash available – the first time that cash limits had been introduced into social security. If people were inconsiderate enough to die towards the end of the financial year in an area where the fund had run out, that would just be too bad for their relations.[102]

The even more drastically Thatcherite aspect of the Social Fund was the allocation of most of it to loans rather than grants. This re-established local-office discretion, which is inevitably arbitrary; at the same time the right to an independent appeal was abolished. The result of this brilliant new system was that two-thirds of Social Fund payments were made in the form of repayable loans – which were then reclaimed directly from claimants' Income Support. Thus an unemployed family with children driven, for example, to ask for assistance for some necessity such as a cooker, would have up to 15 per cent deducted from their already meagre benefit for as many weeks and months as it took to repay the cost of this vital requirement. Predictably, instead of reducing dependency, this system encourages debt, revived the pawnshop and causes totally unnecessary hardship for those already on the breadline.

Even more grotesquely, the loans were only awarded to applicants who had the ability to repay them. Hence crisis payments for fire, flood, burglary or anything else were refused to the poorest if they could not afford to pay them back. This was surely taking selectivity rather far: the more destitute people became, the less likely they were to be given help.[103]

Admittedly the predecessors of the Social Fund were far from flawless. The new Fund is still at a relatively early stage and with luck it will improve. Norman Fowler even claimed that it had 'been successfully introduced'. Yet the government's watchdog, the National Audit Office, recently concluded that, while the Social Fund was achieving its main aim of saving money, growing numbers of people were becoming increasingly in debt to it. The report also revealed a quagmire of bureaucratic inefficiency and unfairness. Although the number of applications increased in 1990–91 by 30 per cent, spending was reduced by 6 per cent in real terms. Inevitably, therefore, the number of refusals had to rise to 779,000, over a third of applications. Around 23,000 applicants were rejected because they were too poor; and about 195,000 were turned down for lack of funds. In one month, only three out of forty-two offices surveyed could pay all admissible applications. At the same time the Social Fund was administratively by far the most expensive social-security benefit, costing £61 million to run, over 30 per cent of its budget, and representing a minuscule 0.5 per cent of social-security spending while monopolizing 4.2 per cent of departmental manpower – an extravagantly inefficient way, surely, of penalizing those least able to look after themselves, while allegedly attacking dependency. Of all the Thatcherites' 'acts of sanctimonious indifference' to the poor, wrote Melanie Phillips, the Social Fund was easily the worst: 'the totem of the social injustice of her years in power'.[104]

The loss of most single payments, together with the new legislation making everyone pay 20 per cent of their rates (or poll tax) and 100 per cent of their water bills, combined to make most Income-Support claimants worse off in real terms than they were before the 1988 'reforms'. John Moore's boast that 'the overwhelming majority of recipients – 88 per cent of them and that is the true figure – will receive at least as much as they did before' was more than a little disingenuous, ignoring as it did not only inflation but also the loss of single payments. Ministers made less use of the government figures which showed that when transitional cash protection was excluded only 37 per cent of recipients stood to gain, with 20 per cent experiencing no change and over 40 per cent standing to lose. The principal groups to lose on average were pensioners, who in general fared better than others during the Thatcher years, and the young unemployed. For pensioners who were reluctant to claim from the Social Fund for fear of running into debt, the erosion of housing benefit was particularly damaging; for the young unemployed at sixteen and seventeen benefit was axed completely on the grounds that a Youth Training Scheme place would be guaranteed to those unable to find jobs or other training. In fact, school leavers were often still to be found on waiting lists for YTS places several months later. Other groups – the disabled and the pregnant – also found themselves less well off than before.[105]

Families with children were expected to gain from the changes, though unfortunately the improvements which were made were effectively paid for by other families with children through the freezing of child benefit. In the event almost two-thirds of non-working families with children were losers in the long term, while lone parents were particularly badly hit: the National Council for One-Parent Families pointed out that 'the Government is worried about the high rate of benefit dependence among Britain's lone parents. Yet, paradoxically, many of the changes under the new system have actually pushed more one-parent families into poverty and long-term dependence on the state.' Barnardo's report on the 1988 benefit reforms showed 'families caught in spiralling debt and inescapable poverty'.[106]

Investigating the impact of tax and benefit changes on household incomes from 1979 to 1989 and (misleadingly) assuming a full take-up of means-tested benefits, the Institute of Fiscal Studies optimistically reported that the average weekly gain was £7 in real terms, yet the variance in gains was huge. Ranking households by their 'original' weekly income (i.e. before taxes and benefits), the poorest, with incomes of less than £10, gained only £1.65 per week, while those with incomes of between £10 and £50 gained a mere thirty-three pence. By comparison, households with incomes of between £600 and £900 a week gained £34.98, whilst those with incomes of £1,000 and above gained £286.53 each week.

The IFS analysis considerably underestimates the losses, not gains, for those on low incomes because, as has been shown, the assumption of a full take-up of means-tested benefits is unfounded. Indeed, although supplementary benefit (and its successor Income Support) are generally considered to be safety nets through which nobody should fall, the numbers of families with incomes below SB levels increased by nearly 20 per cent between 1979 and 1987 to nearly two million. Of these 1.9 million families, 800,000, were not entitled to benefit for various reasons, over half a million were entitled to housing benefit which they were not taking up, and around 600,000 were not taking up entitlements to supplementary benefit. Similar analyses of Income Support would undoubtedly produce similar findings, had they not been discontinued.[106]

Without a massive injection of extra cash, any major reform of the social-security system is bound to generate losers as well as gainers. Reform was certainly necessary, and the 1986–88 reforms achieved a certain degree of harmonization. Beyond that they failed, since they did not materially enhance the welfare of the poor; nor did they realize the government's objectives of greatly limiting public expenditure and creating incentives. Spending was reduced in some areas, but in relation to the total of public expenditure the savings were relatively insignificant, although for the recipients, of course, they were all too real. And those cuts of a few pounds a week in the income of the least well off were made to seem no less real by the Thatcherites' insensitivity in ensuring that they coincided with a fall in a £100,000-a-year executive's tax bill of £35 per day.[107]

Trying to enhance individual freedom and responsibility by constricting government intervention is in itself wholly defensible. But the rigid application of dogma with scant regard to practicalities, or to clearly foreseeable consequences, resulted in precisely the opposite of what was intended: increased dependency on state welfare benefits. In accordance with their dogma, the anti-public-expenditure brigade regarded tax allowances as benign and public spending as malignant. The consequence of this convenient differentiation was that tax and benefit changes channelled a much greater share of resources to the rich at the expense of the poor and, in particular, the near-poor. Overall, the doctrine of targeting combined with tax cuts resulted in more money for those least in want while neglecting to safeguard, let alone improve, the circumstances of many of those most in need.

Integration of the Tax and Benefit Systems

Apart from underfunding, the basic flaw of the changes lay in the government's failure to examine the benefit system together with taxation. The architect of the 1986 reforms, Norman Fowler, later attributed to the Chancellor of the Exchequer the insistence on viewing the social-security system in isolation; Nigel Lawson regarded taxation as his exclusive prerogative. If the principal objective of the review was an improvement in the conditions of the poor, the exclusion of taxation largely vitiated the whole exercise; as Norman Fowler recognized, social security and tax have to be considered together.[108] If, more probably, the government's main purpose was to cut public spending, the ban on considering taxation was useful: the gravity of the reduction in living standards faced by those at the bottom of the income scale could then be more easily disguised.

No social-security system can work effectively when as much as one seventh of the population has to rely on one single means-tested benefit, Income Support. Means-testing may cut down 'scroungers' but at the cost of increasing dependency and tightening the poverty trap. By contrast, integration of the personal income-tax and social security systems through a Basic Income (BI) scheme (sometimes also called Citizen's Income) would greatly reduce means testing. Almost all existing benefits would be abolished – from unemployment benefit and social security through to personal tax allowances and mortgage tax relief. Instead, each individual citizen would receive a basic income, either as a cash sum or as a tax credit which would be non-contributory, non-withdrawable, fully automated and tax-free. There would, therefore, be an income floor below which no one would be allowed to fall and above which all would be free to rise. Earnings would be taxed, but the poverty trap would be greatly reduced: there would be no work-tested benefits to withdraw, so the barrier to part-time work would disappear.

A full-scale Basic Income (enough to live on) would be too expensive to implement now, but the foremost exponent of BI, Mrs Hermione Parker, has proposed a more modest scheme of partial Basic Incomes. Her scheme would retain a residual, income-tested housing benefit and a reformed Social Fund, but Income Support and Family Credit would be phased out, along with National Insurance benefits and all income-tax allowances and reliefs. These changes would greatly reduce the numerous disincentive effects of the present complex system.

Removing the contributory principle would help stave off poverty, and the abolition of payroll taxes (employers' insurance contributions) would help reduce unemployment by making labour more competitive with machinery. Social insurance, introduced by Beveridge on the presupposition of full (male) employment, now works against our economic performance by encouraging the substitution of capital for labour. With Basic Income (and Citizen's Income) the basis of entitlement would be citizenship; the tax/benefit unit would be the individual (ensuring equal treatment of the sexes); all earnings rules would be abolished (decriminalizing the black economy); the availability-for-work rule would be abolished (encouraging Further Education, vocational training and re-training); and take-up would be virtually 100 per cent. The system would be easy to understand, easy to administer and easily automated; and the living standards of the poorest would be linked to those of other people.[109]

In 1973 the Heath government committed itself to a similar tax-credit scheme which would have brought together the taxation and social-security systems, but the government was defeated before it could implement the reform. For some time after it changed its leader, the Conservative party remained committed to tax credits, but unfortunately such a sensibly benevolent system as Basic Income or tax credits was too radical for the Thatcherites. They professed an interest in simplification and increased incentives, but those aims could not be reconciled with ardour for lowering the rate of income tax and their faulty notion of targeting. In consequence the poor were subjected to a relentless depression of their expectations, culminating in the 'reforms' whereby, 'at the furthest perimeter of society,' in the words of Hugo Young, 'the squeeze was now discernibly applied against a disease long identified in Thatcherite rhetoric as "the dependency culture" but hitherto thought too dangerous to try and cure by deprivation.'[110]

Conclusion

'Conviction politicians' who live by dogmas do not necessarily die by them (though some do), but they are condemned to self contradiction. The Thatcherites' social dogma decreed that the dependency culture must be destroyed: dependence on the state not only increased public expenditure, it distorted the market and offended Victorian values of thrift and self-reliance. But the greatest safeguard of independence is a job. Hence the one sure way of reducing state dependency was to reduce unemployment. Yet the government chose to maintain an unprecedentedly high level of unemployment, because Thatcherite economic dogma precluded the government from directly intervening in the economy to bring it down (though its intervention had put it up). Indeed Thatcherite economics ensured a relentless rise in unemployment from 1979 to 1986 and again from 1990. So, while Thatcherite social dogma demanded a reduction in state dependence, Thatcherite economic dogma guaranteed its increase.

Faced with such contradictions, the Thatcherites fell back on another dogma – the erroneous assumption of neo-classical economists that unemployment is voluntary. Accordingly they blamed unemployment on the unemployed; it was the unemployed who had priced themselves out of a job and had failed to mount their bicycles. The unemployed were therefore moved from the category of the deserving poor (victims of circumstance and changing economic conditions) to the ranks of the undeserving poor – the idle, the profligate and the scroungers. And they were treated accordingly. As, unfortunately, the neo-classical doctrine that unemployment is voluntary is unfounded, the attempt to cure unemployment by ill-treating the unemployed was inevitably a failure.[111]

The other sufferers from the Thatcherite regime – the rest of the poor – were the victims of that failure and of related dogmas. As we have seen, the Thatcherite articles of faith were firstly that public expenditure is a bad thing, secondly that public expenditure in Britain was abnormally high, and thirdly that lower public expenditure would rejuvenate the economy and foster the creation of a thrusting enterprise society.

The first is perhaps a matter of argument, though, as the Thatcherite case is difficult to argue, it was safer for its adherents just to assume its truth. The second was simply wrong.[112] The third is more difficult to judge (because high unemployment prevented its achievement) but its underlying assumption — which, as Professor Galbraith pointed out, is that the rich should be made richer to make them work harder and the poor made poorer to achieve the same result — seems more self-servingly convenient than factual. Certainly in the short term the assault on public expenditure was damaging, and in the long term possibly disastrous.[113]

Socially the results of the various Thatcherite articles of faith were no more encouraging. Not only did the poor not share in the limited economic growth that did take place between 1979 and 1990, the poor were relatively poorer than they had been in 1979, and many were absolutely poorer as well. Thatcherites of course were not merely not 'One-Nation Tories'; they were strongly opposed both to the idea and its advocacy. Rather than be One-Nation Tories, they preferred to be two-nation Liberals.* In consequence their policies were unrelentingly divisive and discriminatory against the poor, whose human dignity was relentlessly ignored.

'That policy is violent,' David Hume wrote 250 years ago, 'which aggrandizes the public by the poverty of individuals.'

---

* Margaret Thatcher herself was, perhaps, not a two-nation but a three-nation Liberal. 'If there is one lot of people that our leader dislikes more than the lower classes,' a senior minister said to me in 1980, 'it's the upper classes.'

Still worse is one which aggrandizes the rich by the poverty of the poor. Whether or not Thatcherite social policy added to national violence by provoking riots and increasing crime, it was, in the sense used by Hume, undoubtedly 'violent'.[114]

VII

Housing, Health and Education

> I came to office with one deliberate intent. To change Britain from a dependent to a self-reliant society – from a give-it-to-me to a do-it-yourself nation; to a get-up-and-go instead of a sit-back-and-wait-for-it Britain.
>
> Margaret Thatcher, 1984[1]

> The public provision of welfare ... remains a staple function of the nation-state in the developed economies. Indeed it is almost a definition of the nation-state that it is a form of government based on the fellow-feeling that constitutes a people or nation.
>
> Sir Henry Phelps-Brown[2]

THATCHERISM DEMONSTRATED ITS two-nation attitude and its distaste for the public sector in all fields of social policy. Fortunately, however, electoral imperatives imposed considerable restraints upon the government's capacity to translate its inclinations into its political programme.

For the vast majority of the population the strong trend towards better-quality housing continued. In the twenty years up to 1990 the proportion of households without central heating fell from nearly two-thirds to just over one-fifth, and between 1981 and 1990 the proportion of households without access to a bath or shower halved from 2 to 1 per cent. Overall housing conditions greatly improved, including those of the poorest fifth (though their position probably worsened in relation to the population as a whole), and the government's 'Right to Buy' scheme – the sale of council houses – greatly increased home ownership.[3]

The sale of council houses was not in origin a specifically Thatcherite or even a right-wing policy. In 1957 the Macmillan government gave local authorities the power to sell or lease council houses. The popularity of the policy was obvious, and many Conservative councils at the end of the sixties invited their tenants to buy their own houses – until the Labour government stamped on the idea. The Heath government revived it. Peter Walker issued a circular urging the selling of council houses and authorizing discounts of up to 20 per cent.[4]

The policy was merely permissive, however, and many councils ignored or opposed it. At the end of the Heath government about 5.5 million families still lived in council houses; nearly one British family in three was a council tenant. Accordingly, the 1974 Conservative election manifestos committed the party to giving council tenants a statutory right to buy their homes. During the years of opposition, Peter Walker wanted to go further than Mrs Thatcher, and advocated transferring the ownership of all council homes to their tenants. Mrs Thatcher feared that those on the Wates estates, the least well-off owner occupiers, whom she regarded as 'our people', would resent council house occupiers being given something for nothing (though under Walker's scheme that would have been true only of those who had been tenants for thirty years; for the rest their rent would have been treated as a mortgage repayment for the balance of the thirty years).[5]

All the same, the approach that was eventually agreed was far reaching. The 1980 Housing Act, the responsibility of Michael Heseltine, gave the great majority of those five million tenants the 'right to buy' their homes from their local authority and authorized the minister to send in commissioners should any authority refuse to cooperate. A commissioner was sent to Norwich,* and the government won a challenge in the courts mounted by that city's council. After that episode there was no more trouble, and the policy was a long-running Thatcher triumph. By the time Mrs Thatcher left office almost a million and a half families had taken advantage of the legislation, and the proportion of owner-occupied dwellings had increased from 55 per cent in 1979 to more than two-thirds in 1990. Had the sale of council houses to their tenants been combined with adequate new council building, the government's housing policy would have been both popular and an almost unqualified success.[6]

Once again, however, ideology obstructed common sense. In housing, as in health and education, the government combined increased reliance on market mechanisms with greatly increased centralization, resulting in the 'nationalization of housing policy'. Thatcherites, perennially anxious to weaken local government, to cut public expenditure and to rely on the market to conjure up what was needed, did not complement their commendable policy of giving people the opportunity to buy their homes with sufficient investment in new housing or repairs for those unable to do so. They were more concerned with diminishing the role of local authorities than with the provision of affordable homes. In consequence, so far from doing much to relieve the housing shortage which it had inherited, the government by its policies in some places drastically exacerbated it. For ideological reasons it generally preferred to rely on the market but, predictably, the market did not produce the desired outcome. Because of market failure, government intervention in housing has for a long

---

* Neville Chamberlain did much the same thing to Rotherham and Durham in 1932; and in his left-wing phase in the 1930s Clement Attlee envisaged a socialist government employing commissioners who would be 'sent down into a locality to see that the will of the central government is obeyed and its plans implemented ... He must be first and foremost a socialist.'[7]

time been seen to be necessary in most civilized countries. As usual, moreover, the Thatcherites were not consistent in their market ideology. Only the poor were its victims. While making swingeing cuts in housing benefit, which constituted a vital element of the income of the poorest, the government distorted the market by continuing to provide massive mortgage subsidies to the better off.[8]

In 1979 subsidies to owner occupiers and council tenants were roughly equal. The sale of council houses would anyway have altered the balance, but that explains only a small part of what happened. By the end of the 1980s the subsidy to council tenants had fallen to about £500 million, while the public handout to owner occupiers in the form of mortgage tax relief had risen to £5.5 billion. Government expenditure on housing benefit greatly increased, but that was the result of much higher rents and unemployment, not government largesse. During the eighties, housing benefit for those on low incomes was cut no fewer than nine times.[9]

So once again the welfare state of the poor which depended on public expenditure was cut, while the welfare state of the better-off which depended on 'tax expenditures' or allowances was sharply inflated. Looking, as was their custom, at only one side of the balance sheet, the Thatcherites played the Good Samaritan only to the better off.[10]

The number of council houses built in Great Britain fell from 85,000 in 1979 (having been sharply cut by the Callaghan government) to as few as 15,000 in 1990. Housing association output was reduced from 18,000 in 1979 to 11,000 in 1988. In housing, almost uniquely, the government achieved its objective of drastically cutting public expenditure.[11]

In their attacks on local government, however, the Thatcherites did not rest content with their benign policy of turning as many local authority tenants as possible into home owners. Nicholas Ridley, the Environment Secretary from 1986–89, was 'determined to weaken the almost incestuous relationship between some councils and their tenants'. The 1988 Housing Act therefore encouraged the transfer of tenanted council estates to other landlords. In the event, however, council tenants did not see this measure as a reasonable dilution of monopoly. Despite the blatantly rigged voting system laid down by the Act – those not bothering to vote were to be counted as voting for change – the great majority of tenants preferred to continue to live in incest. Some Conservative-controlled authorities (of which Chiltern in my constituency was the first), supported by their tenants, decided on a voluntary transfer of their council houses to another body. This had a number of advantages, while effectively preserving the council's housing stock.[12]*

Homelessness

Homelessness is far from new, but the sale of council houses, backed by financial incentives,† required a high rate of council-house building (or a far larger programme of renovating the existing stock) or some alternative provision if it was not to lead to increased homelessness. Instead, local authorities were forbidden to spend more than a quarter of the revenues generated from council house sales on new homes and renovations. In so far as the government recognized the resulting problem of homelessness, it left it to be solved by the market. Thus the placing of homeless families in temporary accommodation by local authorities owed less to bad housing management, as the Thatcherites claimed, than to the financial restrictions which they themselves imposed

* Such was the Thatcherite hostility to local government that no one connected with Chiltern Council was allowed to be chairman of the new body. After representations from the council and myself, the architect of the policy, a Conservative councillor, was allowed to be chairman, but only for the first year. His successor was therefore my Liberal opponent. He was an excellent choice and one wholly agreeable to me, but it was an odd result for a government conspicuously intent on confining patronage to Conservatives.

† Mrs Thatcher's favourite council, the Conservative-controlled Wandsworth, offered free holidays to tenants who bought their homes.[13]

on the amount of money that could be spent on repairs to make empty properties habitable.[14]

As with poverty, the statistics of homelessness are confusing. According to the statutory definitions, single people who are sleeping rough are not considered to be 'in priority need' of housing, and are therefore excluded from the figures of the homeless. On the other hand other groups can qualify as 'homeless' even though they are still housed and are merely threatened with eviction. So you can be roofless without being 'homeless', and you can be 'homeless' without being roofless – indeed the title of one category is 'homeless at home'. Yet although most of the 'homeless' were not roofless, the situation of none of them was enviable and for nearly all of them it was desperate.[15]

The number of households officially deemed homeless, which grew steadily from 56,750 in 1979 to 126,680 in 1989 (the total number over the decade comprised about three million individuals, nearly half a million in 1989 alone – half of them children), was therefore a long way below the true figure of homelessness. Local housing authorities were only required to rehouse those defined to be of priority need (such as families with children, pregnant women and those vulnerable owing to age or disability); the majority of single people and childless couples were excluded from the statistics; only half the households who applied were accepted as homeless while many homeless people did not approach their local council for help.[16]

By 1989, councils were spending only a third as much on new housing as they had done ten years earlier, yet in that year 280,000 households in England tried to register as homeless. Taking into account people in hostels, bed-and-breakfast accommodation and squats, the Salvation Army estimated that there were 75,000 overtly homeless people in the capital, 'a shanty town as large as might be expected in any Latin American city, but it is hidden'. Only 1 per cent of them – 753 people – were sleeping in the streets, though two years later the Official Census of population found almost double that number sleeping rough in London. Others thought the numbers of the homeless were even higher.[17]

Once accepted as homeless, thousands of families had no choice but to live in temporary accommodation, sometimes for several years, because of the scarcity of permanent homes. Miserable and overcrowded conditions were thus provided at enormous cost. Because local authorities were prevented by the government from providing new homes, they had 'to spend a fortune', the chairman of the Conservative-controlled London Boroughs Association pointed out, 'on [providing] temporary accommodation for the homeless. This waste of public resources,' he continued, 'completely frustrates our objective of achieving value for money and only adds to the appalling amount of human misery involved.' The number of households in temporary accommodation increased six-fold in the six years between 1982 and 1988 (from 5,000 to 30,000 households).[18]*

In 1989 the government's own figures showed that paying a bed-and-breakfast hotel bill cost £14,600 *per annum* in London whereas the first year's cost of building a home to rent in London would have been £8,000 (£5,000 elsewhere). By that year the annual cost of homelessness in London alone was £200 million. Although it was in London that homelessness caught the headlines, it increased much faster in areas such as Manchester

---

* Living in bed-and-breakfast accommodation produces a high level of stress and illness as well as a poor diet. Because they have no cooking facilities, many families buy take-away food. Hence the government's cut in the special food allowance, previously provided because of the acknowledged difficulties of such families, was not likely to improve their diet or their health. Other social-security changes had similar effects. Despite there being only paltry provision for single homeless people, the Board and Lodging Allowance was replaced in April 1989 by Income Support and housing benefit. In consequence, many single people could no longer use bed-and-breakfast accommodation for the reason that Income Support is paid in arrears which is unacceptable to most hoteliers.[19]

1. (*above*) Mrs Thatcher at the Falklands Victory Parade, 12 October 1982.

2. (*below*) Arthur Scargill with striking miners, 14 May 1984.

3. Mrs Thatcher addresses the College of Europe, Bruges, 20 September 1988.

4. March on Wapping: anniversary of the print union dispute, 24 January 1987.

5. Anti-poll tax riot in Trafalgar Square, 31 March 1989.

6. (*top left*) Nigel Lawson on his way to present the 1989 budget.

7. (*bottom left*) Mrs Thatcher with Mark Thatcher, and President and Mrs Reagan, 13 June 1988.

8. (*above*) Sir Geoffrey Howe makes his resignation statement, 13 November 1990.

9, Mrs Thatcher and the cabinet, June 1979

Back row (left to right): Michael Jopling; Norman Fowler; John Biffen; David Howell; Norman St John Stevas; Humphrey Atkins; George Younger; Michael Heseltine; Nicholas Edwards; Patrick Jenkin; John Nott; Mark Carlisle; Angus Maude; Sir John Hunt.

Front row (left to right): Sir Ian Gilmour; Lord Soames; Sir Keith Joseph; Lord Carrington; William Whitelaw; Margaret Thatcher; Lord Hailsham; Sir Geoffrey Howe; Francis Pym; James Prior; Peter Walker.

10. Mrs Thatcher and the cabinet, July 1990

Back row (left to right): Tim Renton; David Hunt; Norman Lamont; Peter Brooke; Antony Newton; John Wakeham; Cecil Parkinson; Lord Belstead; Christopher Patten; John Gummer; Michael Howard; Peter Lilley; Sir Robin Butler.

Front row (left to right): John MacGregor; Kenneth Baker; David Waddington; Douglas Hurd; Sir Geoffrey Howe; Margaret Thatcher; Lord Mackay of Clashfern; John Major; Tom King; Kenneth Clarke; Malcolm Rifkind. Only Sir Geoffrey Howe remained of the original cabinet.

11. Margaret Thatcher outside the Paris Embassy, 20 November 1990, announcing that she would fight on in the leadership contest.

where the rise in the ten years since 1978 was 325 per cent.[20]

Like the unemployed, the homeless were stigmatized by the right wing as undeserving and, just as the unemployed were blamed for not finding jobs even though there were no jobs for them to find, the homeless were blamed for not having houses, even though there were no houses available for them to live in. According to right wingers, the real cause of homelessness was moral, not economic: a 'lethal combination of progressive education, the welfare state and the permissive society has created a minority which rejects the restraints and responsibilities of the majority. True, some of the young people living rough might have fled their homes because of child abuse, although equally they might have learned that this is the fashionable reason to offer. More often, they fled because their innumeracy and illiteracy have made them unemployable in, say, the north.'[21]

That attitude might have been pardonable had it possessed even the slenderest element of supporting evidence. Homelessness rarely has anything to do with personal inadequacy; it is predominantly a result of the failures of past and present housing and family policies. Today the principal cause of homelessness is quite simple: an acute shortage of decent homes at affordable prices. Among other causes such as family break-up were the changes in social-security legislation targeted against young people – one of the few occasions that the targets were hit – notably the removal of entitlement to Income Support from the vast majority of sixteen and seventeen year olds. Despite rising unemployment, particularly amongst the young, no fewer than fourteen cuts were made in the welfare benefits available to young people, and eight of these were directly related to help with housing costs. In 1987, the Prime Minister rejected the idea of handouts for young down-and-outs, admonishing them to stand on their 'own two feet or go home to mother'. Although Thatcherism abhorred the 'Nanny-state', it seemed to glory in the governess one.[22]

In reality two-thirds of the young people taking refuge in an emergency night shelter in London, a study showed, could not return to their last settled home – less than half with their parents – even if they had nowhere else to go. Most were from areas of high unemployment looking for work, over 40 per cent had been in care in the past, and over three-quarters had had to sleep rough. Serious problems with alcohol or drug abuse were rare though growing, but a third had been approached to become involved in prostitution since they had arrived in central London. With the chances of these young people finding a job and a home being so slim, the exact manner in which the cutting of their welfare benefits was supposed to help them fend for themselves was not immediately obvious.[23]

Another major cause of increased homelessness was the Thatcher government's policy of 'Care in the Community'. Although in theory reasonable – it represented a move away from large institutions – its implementation raised the number of homeless people. Many of the mentally ill were discharged from hospital without adequate provision being made for their special needs. Thousands of people with psychiatric disorders and mental illness were effectively made homeless: they were forced into sleeping rough or using night shelters and hospitals without the resources to support themselves.[24]

The policy of government-sponsored incentives to house purchase during the Lawson boom was already rebounding on some families by the end of the Thatcher years. Those unable to keep pace as mortgage-interest rates mounted increasingly found themselves homeless towards the end of the eighties. By 1990, prolonged high interest rates were taking their toll with repossessions at record levels; as a result 44,000 families lost their homes, and the trend was still upwards.[25]

Apart from blaming poor local-authority housing management for their own mistakes, the Thatcherites cited the increased incidence of family break-up as an explanation for increased homelessness, a claim which had some justification since 40 per cent of those accepted as homeless by local authorities were one-parent families. Yet this did not justify the government's failure to remedy what it had partially explained. Nor were government ministers able to corroborate their allegations that young girls deliberately became pregnant in order to jump the housing queue.* The reality was that single-parent families tended to be far poorer than others, that not much more than a fifth of Britain's single parents were classed as 'never married' and that many of these, although technically single, were probably living as a couple.[26]

At the end of the 1980s the gravity of the homelessness problem became apparent even to the government, and money was provided for various temporary initiatives which eventually led to a considerable reduction of the cardboard-box community in the centre of London. Homelessness is, of course, a continuous flow; emergency funds assist those who are currently homeless but are unlikely to prevent people from becoming homeless in the future. So, welcome though these attempts to address the problem were, they did not come close to solving it, since the root causes of homelessness – unemployment, the dearth of affordable permanent housing and the decline of the traditional family – were ignored.[27]

Conclusion

The sale of nearly a million and a half council houses in the Thatcher era and the large rise in the percentage of home owners were considerable Thatcherite achievements. Unfortunately, they were marred by the unfair treatment meted out to the remaining third of the population which resulted in housing in Britain growing increasingly polarized. Many of the five million council-owned dwellings are in disrepair.

---

* For example Norman Tebbit's saloon-bar erudition: 'if the state advertises that young girls with children for whom no father is willing to take responsibility will be advantaged in terms of housing and income above other young unemployed . . . there is a sharp increase in the supply of single parent families'.[28]

The council house has become more and more the preserve of the very poor, with the most disadvantaged, frequently from ethnic minorities, living in the most overcrowded conditions on the worst housing estates – some of them no-go areas.[29]

The other two-thirds were much more favourably treated. The Duke of Edinburgh's inquiry into British housing recommended in 1985 that mortgage-interest relief should be phased out. Apart from its unfairness it increases home prices, which were a major factor in the unsustainable credit boom of the eighties. Four years earlier the entire Treasury team had wanted to remove the tax subsidy to home-buyers, but the Prime Minister insisted on its retention. Later in the decade Nigel Lawson tried once more; once again the Prime Minister stood in the way. To her, mortgage-interest relief was as sacred as child benefit was anathema. Even relief at the higher rate of income tax survived until after her departure.[30]

The most negative aspect of Thatcherite housing policy was the failure to increase the output of affordable homes. Ideologically inspired policies such as the social-security changes, the rises in council house rents and rates, stricter restraints on local authorities, the introduction of the poll tax and the move towards 'market rents' introduced by the 1988 Housing Act, reinforced the housing and financial pressures which generate homelessness. While the demand for housing for people on low incomes went up, the supply went down. Once again almost exclusive reliance on the market proved a profound error.[31]

Health

Health is wealth.
R A Cross, Home Secretary, 1875[32]

Within months of Mrs Thatcher's departure from Downing Street, the legacy of market-oriented policies towards health care came to dominate the political headlines. Yet, because of the widely held belief that the Prime Minister wanted to abolish the National Health Service and replace it with private health insurance, the future of the NHS had been near the top of the political agenda throughout her years at the helm.[33]

The Conservative party came into power somewhat on the defensive over health. In the 1979 election nearly 60 per cent of Conservative election addresses omitted to mention the subject, and the party manifesto, while rightly promising to devote to the armed services 'significant increases' in resources, confined itself on the health service to lavishing praise on pay beds and to giving the dynamic undertaking 'not to reduce resources going to' it.[34]

In September 1982, the government's Central Policy Review Staff circulated a paper to the cabinet on the Prime Minister's authority. Amongst radical schemes to end the public funding of higher education and slash the social-security budget was the momentous proposal to replace the NHS with personally paid-for private health insurance and to charge patients for visiting a doctor. Among the nation's institutions, only the monarchy was more popular than the National Health Service. So when the CPRS paper was leaked to *The Economist* under the heading 'Thatcher's Holocaust' and provoked a furore, Mrs Thatcher was forced reluctantly to retreat and to dissociate herself from such dangerous suggestions. The electorate was assured that the NHS was safe in the government's hands.[35]

A whiff of excessive protestation was detectable in the government's pronouncements. After all, the NHS was a monument of the welfare state, of the 'socialism' which the Prime Minister detested so vocally. As such, health in neo-liberal eyes might well seem a suitable area of life for the individual to be 'forced to be free' of the state. Hence, whatever political realities decreed, a suspicion lingered that an American-style system of privately funded care represented her ideal.[36]

'Convictions' tend to bear little relation to empirical evidence – if they did, they would be more nuanced. Yet the right-wing hankering after a system of health care

akin to that of the United States was a prime example
of its subordination of experience to ideology. Quite apart
from the overwhelming theoretical arguments against purely
private provision of health care, the land of opportunity and
free-market devotion has demonstrated that, in a system
based on private insurance, the level of insurance premium
payments is virtually prohibitive except for the young, the
healthy and the relatively well-off. In the 1980s as many as
thirty million Americans had no access to health care, because
they were not poor enough to fall within Medicaid provision
and because they were neither sufficiently well-off to afford
cover themselves, nor in jobs of sufficient status to attract cover
provided by employers; another ten million could only afford
limited cover. Not surprisingly the leading cause of personal
bankruptcy in the USA was the inability to make medical
payments.[37] Despite the vastly greater resources devoted to
health care there than here, the system in the United States
not only excludes a sizeable proportion of the population but
is administratively inefficient and ineffective as well.

The maintenance of a private sector in health care (as in
education) is vital.[38] It prevents monopoly, providing both an
invaluable safety valve and a means of satisfying demands that
cannot be met by the state service. But increased privatization
is clearly no panacea. Private health insurance schemes have
upper limits to benefits, which are often inadequate and do
not provide cover for the most expensive forms of health
care: the long-term care of the chronically sick. No private
cover exists for senility, mental handicap or most forms of
paralysis; and if, for example, your kidneys fail you cannot
get renal dialysis on private insurance. Only the NHS provides
such a service.

The entry of increasing numbers of commercial firms into
the market for the provision of hospital care during the
eighties pushed up the costs of the private sector, prompting
the memorable complaint by the Chief Executive of BUPA
that 'private medicine is threatened by commercialism'. The
cost of running the NHS rose between 1979 and 1989 by

157 per cent, but the cost of private medical insurance rose by an alarming 267 per cent despite the commercial sector's workload being largely confined to low-cost, routine procedures. Expensive services provided by the NHS such as accident and emergency treatment and intensive care are not covered by the private medical policies.[39]

Overall, the Thatcherite attitude to the National Health Service was ambivalent. Correctly discounting the right-wing goal of abolition, it regarded the NHS as deplorably socialistic and uncommercial, and it wanted to cut down public spending. Yet it gave relatively favourable treatment to health and, by substantially increasing expenditure on the Health Service, it achieved a seemingly impressive record of improvements. The number of GPs and nurses, for example, grew by over 20 per cent in the 1980s. Understandably, therefore, the government resented accusations that it was not spending enough or even had made cuts. In fact both sides were right. The government claimed to have spent 32 per cent more on health 'in real terms' during the 1980s, yet the terms were real only in part. Although the government figure was real in that it allowed for inflation, it was unreal in that it did not allow for the fact that the price of health care rose faster than the rate of inflation. This 'real price effect' is caused by the NHS being labour intensive, by expensive advances in medical knowledge, drugs and technology, and by the increasing age of the population. More has to be spent on the NHS just to preserve the status quo, let alone improve it. So while the government substantially improved its spending on health 'in real terms', its growth in expenditure failed to meet needs and demands, was smaller than that of any previous administration, and in genuine real terms amounted to a small decline. In 1988 the House of Commons Social Services Committee estimated that the NHS was underfunded by nearly £2 billion.[40]

The claims of underfunding were lent credence by a continuous stream of bed closures accompanied by unacceptably long waiting lists. Surgeons signed petitions complaining that a shortage of specialist nurses prevented them from doing their jobs properly. In 1987 the National Audit Commission produced a damaging report showing that a further 11,000 operations a year could be performed in just five health districts if scheduled operations were not so frequently cancelled because of lack of staff, and that the inefficient usage of operating theatres, some of which were in use for little more than half the week, was wasting more than £40 million a year.[41]

The crux of the problem was the heavy expense of raising nurses' salaries, which comprise about 20 per cent of the total NHS budget. Despite a welcome increase of 9 per cent in nurses' pay (and in the number of nurses), in 1987 they were earning £8,500 per annum (sisters up to £12,000) while London bus drivers had an annual salary of £10,000. The government, having only allowed 3.75 per cent for salary increases, decided quite rightly to be more generous, but jibbed at funding the full difference. Faced with a £170 million shortfall, the health authorities tried to narrow the gap by closing wards and cancelling operations.[42]

Many of the consequent allegations of ineptitude made against the NHS stemmed from government underfunding, a view which was strongly supported by public opinion. In comparison with other countries, the NHS represents excellent value for money. It is so vast – the NHS is the biggest employer in Western Europe – that there will always be inefficiences, just as there are, say, in the Ministry of Defence. But Britain spends a smaller proportion of its GNP on health than all but four of the twenty countries in the OECD. According to 1987 government figures, Britain was spending 5.9 per cent of its GDP on health care (5.3 per cent on state-funded health and 0.6 per cent on private health) while France was spending 9.1 per cent (6.5 per cent state and 2.6 per cent private), Germany 8.1 per cent (6.4 per cent and 1.7 per cent) and Italy 7.2 per cent. At the same time, health in the United Kingdom, to judge from the traditional guides of mortality and life-expectancy, is better than in the US, which spends much more, and is at least as good as in most other Western countries, though France, Germany, Switzerland and all of Scandinavia have a lower infant-mortality rate than the UK.[43]

Such comparisons are not wholly satisfactory, however, because health owes more to such factors as nutrition, sanitation, housing and environmental quality than to clinical care. In 1980, the Black Report dramatically demonstrated this, recommending in consequence: government intervention to abolish child poverty; provision of free milk and free school meals for children; investment in day-care and ante-natal facilities and higher expenditure on local-authority housing. All those proposals clashed resoundingly with Thatcherism. Hence, the government tried unsuccessfully to bury the report, the findings of which were confirmed by later evidence. The socio-economic causes of ill health are still imperfectly understood, yet it is indisputable that in every country in the world the rich are healthier than the poor.[44]

Incontestably, individual choices of life-style, particularly those concerning smoking, exercise and diet, have a vital effect on health. Yet while acknowledging the role of genetic, cultural and behavioural influences, the working group under Sir Douglas Black concluded that the predominant explanation of inequalities in health lay in material deprivation. Men in social class five, for example, die on average seven years earlier than those in class one; and infant mortality is three times as high in Wolverhampton as it is in Winchester.[45]

The link between poverty and ill-health was frequently denied under Margaret Thatcher's leadership; so the Black Report and its successor 'The Health Divide' (1987) were dubbed Marxist by a government minister, because they recorded class divisions in our society, just as the Archbishop of Canterbury's report was labelled Marxist for raising issues of poverty and deprivation. Yet the assuredly non-Marxist Mrs Edwina Currie, MP, who provoked a storm of protest for blaming Northerners' ill-health on ignorance rather than poverty, subsequently wrote that she would never 'deny the links between poverty, unemployment and ill-health . . .'[46]

Prior to 1988, the Thatcherite government was sparing in its application of drastic surgery to the health service. A business-like managerial structure was substituted for the consensus form of management adopted in 1974, thereby diminishing medical autonomy; and ancillary services were opened up to competitive tendering. These innovations produced some savings – usually gained, however, by paying the already low-paid even less – though weighed against them should be the hidden administrative costs of contracting out (such as increased monitoring) as well as the disruption and loss of morale in NHS staff and, sometimes, lower standards of cleanliness.[47]

In 1988 more politically coloured legislation abolished free eye tests for the majority of the population – the reason for this was almost purely ideological. Thatcherites did not think the taxpayer should foot the bill for something the individual could pay for. Yet almost certainly the charges, which caused a large decrease in tests, will turn out to be a false and damaging economy.[48]

Early in 1987 Mrs Thatcher had decided upon 'a reform of the public services', but she deemed 'the reform of the NHS,' Nicholas Ridley tells us, 'too sensitive a topic to expose to the electorate'. In the queue for treatment, therefore, health was behind housing and education, even though, ominously, Mrs Thatcher took 'a special interest' in the Health-Service reforms.[49] Moreover, even with a highly sycophantic press, she could not avoid damaging front-page news stories of ward closures; of children being sent home even after they had had their pre-operation medication because of lack of staff; and of sick babies being forced to transfer to private hospitals. So by the seemingly simple expedient of announcing a review of the NHS chaired by the Prime Minister herself, the clamour was stilled and a nurses' strike averted, until the White Paper edicts were published a year later in January 1989.

The review was entirely an inside job. Indeed the Thatcherite pre-legislative process often resembled the judicial procedure of the Duke of Buckingham when dealing with an alleged offence against the Game Laws in 1823. The Duke's game-keeper was the informer against Richard Deller; another of the Duke's gamekeepers was the only witness allowed; the Duke himself was the judge, and Deller was tried and convicted in the Duke's drawing room. Similarly, in the review of the Health Service, Thatcherites were the prosecutors, the Adam Smith Institute and other right-wing groups zealously promoted their nostrums, no attempt was made to gather contrary opinion, the public and the professions were largely excluded, and the proceedings took place in, as it were, the Prime Minister's drawing room. Not only the Judge, the Jury and the Court of Appeal, but even the witnesses were all Thatcherite.[50]*

Nevertheless, non-Thatcherite political imperatives could not be excluded from the court room. Furthermore, John Moore's successor as Health Secretary, Kenneth Clarke, was not a free-market ideologue. Hence the outcome was a compromise or 'a botch'.[51] On the supply side, the White Paper was relatively temperate and reaffirmed a commitment to fund the NHS from general taxation. Moreover, incentives to GPs to step up preventive work, perform minor surgery etc. were useful ideas. But their potential was largely overshadowed by the latest example of the Thatcherite infatuation with the insertion of a free-market mechanism wherever possible. Full-scale privatization was electorally impracticable; a sort of ersatz privatization was not.

On the delivery side, therefore, the Review was more extreme, introducing a market in NHS healthcare from April 1991. As was customary on such occasions, this was hailed as the most far-reaching reform in the forty-year history of the National Health Service – it was certainly far-reaching; the only doubt was whether it could properly be called reform. Whatever it was, it left intact the central principles of the NHS; that it is available to all citizens, is free at the point of

---

* The main exception to this closed secretive process of making 'policy behind closed doors' was the review of social security which consulted the public and held open hearings.[52]

use and is financed predominantly from general taxation. In this new internal market, hospitals compete with each other to sell their treatments, and health authorities or GPs buy them by making contracts with the hospitals. The larger GP practices are also allowed to manage their own budgets. Characteristically, however, devotion to the free market was combined with the imposition of unprecedented and ill-judged central controls on the daily work and priorities of individual doctors.[53]

The introduction of the internal market sparked off a storm of protest, particularly from the British Medical Association. The grave disquiet aroused in the general public was also reflected in opinion polls, by-election results and MPs' postbags. Some of it can be attributed to the government's unwillingness to consult anybody who might have given it unpalatable advice before it published its plans, but much of the concern ran far deeper than that.

The central question is the suitability of health as a target for pseudo free-market economic liberalism. There is scant analogy between the economy and the Health Service. Health care is not like any other commodity; it is not a grocery that can be neatly priced, packaged and sold. Nor as a rule are doctors, consultants and other health service professionals rapacious entrepreneurs interested only in maximizing profits. If that had been their main concern, many of them would not have chosen the medical profession in the first place. Furthermore, the government's proposals betrayed an extraordinarily narrow vision of health care since they appeared to assume that medicine is mainly concerned with short episodes of acute illness, while failing to recognize that chronic illness and groups such as the elderly, the mentally handicapped and the disabled, occupy more than half of all NHS beds.[54]

The government's analysis rests on two fundamental assumptions, neither of which is easily sustainable: that the price mechanism is an effective means of allocating resources in health care; and that cost and patient 'throughput' indicators are effective measures of healthcare performance. As to the first, the disentangling of costs and their attribution to the right places is virtually impossible; as to the second an indication of its absurdity is that in assessing the rate at which patients pass through the system, discharge and death show up in the statistics as equally 'successful'.

Another pitfall of competitive health care is the incentive to over-treat. The financial incentive to operate in the US, it has been plausibly claimed, is largely responsible for an American woman being four times as likely to have her womb removed as a British woman and for a US baby being twice as likely to be born by Caesarian section.[55]

The first wave of opting-out comprised fifty-seven self-governing trusts, with great freedom to manoeuvre whilst – contrary to the claims of the Labour party – remaining technically within the NHS. After, however, some of the newly opted-out hospitals, notably Guy's and Bradford, had made announcements within a matter of weeks of massive job cuts, the Health Secretary absolved the government from any responsibility. He thus lent some credence to the opposition's charges that these hospitals had, effectively, left the NHS.

Among the perks conferred on hospitals with trust status is that of owning their own buildings and land, as well as the right to borrow money, set their own wage rates and treat as many private patients as they wish. Trust hospitals can now sell land or build supermarkets within their grounds, and, conveniently perhaps, property development turned out to be the largest single business interest (10 per cent) of members appointed to the boards of fifty-two out of fifty-seven hospitals opting out of local health authority control. This added to fears voiced by the Association of Community Health Councils that self-governing hospitals might be asset-stripped.[56]

In the NHS the costs of administration have been exceptionally low (around 4 per cent of total healthcare expenditure in the late eighties compared with 21 per cent in America's competitive medical system). Although it is too early to be sure, the new reform may lead to spiralling costs. In a competitive system, elaborate cost-accounting arrangements are unavoidable together with previously unimaginable legal and advertising expenses. Southend district health authority made a plaintive appeal for help, saying that previously it had needed twenty accountants but that under the new proposals which required everything to be billed and costed, contracts set up and negotiated, that number would double to forty. In many hospitals, it has been noticed, departing medical staff are replaced not by doctors but by administrators. Between 1988 and 1990 clerical and administrative staff in the NHS grew by well over 10 per cent. In view of the government's normal enthusiasm for streamlining businesses and its cynicism about creating 'artificial' jobs, this result of its health policy has a certain irony.[57]

In her introduction to the White Paper entitled 'Working for Patients', Margaret Thatcher wrote, 'We aim to extend patient choice.' The DHS booklet, delivered to every household (at no small expense) stipulated that the new arrangements would not force anyone to travel further for treatment. Despite these pledges, however, patients are to be allowed to go only to those hospitals with which their district health authorities have made contracts. Since a doctor could, before the reform, refer a patient to any hospital in the country, choice was in fact reduced.[58]

Likewise the consternation over the possibility of the reforms creating a two-tier health service had some legitimate foundations. Watford General Hospital, for example, offered preferential admission schedules to two GP practices in south-west Hertfordshire.[59] While GP fund holding has been welcomed by those anxious to gain more control and to experiment with new ideas, for others, understandable anxieties have arisen about paperwork rocketing to the detriment of patient care. Despite the Thatcherite article of faith that all doctors, nurses, headmasters and members of other professions are businessmen manqué (and, even if they are not, they should be treated as such), few GPs have the time or inclination to be accountants and businessmen as well as doctors.

The House of Commons Select Committee advised that the necessary infrastructure should be established in advance of the market in healthcare and recommended careful trials. This advice was rejected as a waste of money. In September 1989, the chief architect of the government's reforms, Professor Alain Enthoven, who was responsible for the pivotal notion that money should follow patients (by means of health authorities becoming purchasers of care from competing hospitals, rather than direct providers of the service), warned that the government was trying to introduce the changes at amazing speed; he added that he found the lack of pilot studies incomprehensible.[60]

From the point of view of common sense, the government's decision 'to press ahead' before establishing the necessary infrastructure was, as the Select Committee said, 'premature', and its refusal of pilot studies was astonishing. After all, not surprisingly, running an internal market within a publicly financed health service had not been attempted anywhere before. A certain caution would therefore have been appropriate as well as in the pre-Thatcher Conservative tradition of empiricism. No legislation, as Richard Titmuss pointed out, is final, and all of it contains an element of experiment; but it is mere common prudence to do as much experimenting as possible before legislating, thus confining the risks to the laboratory, instead of making the legislation itself wholly experimental and risking unlimited damage. Dogma, however, overrides common sense, and such things as pilot studies were wholly alien to Thatcherism: they betrayed uncertainty of conviction. Moreover, in this case the Thatcherite refusal to test the plan by ordering pilot schemes was fully comprehensible; any such studies would almost certainly have shown that the reforms were undesirable. In consequence pilot schemes would have been too big a risk. The government preferred to risk the health service.[61]

Only what Patrick Wright terms 'the most ideologically impaired think-tanker'[62] from right or left could deny either the tremendous achievements of the NHS or its defects.

Clearly there were inefficiencies in Britain's largest single enterprise, not all of which could be attributed to underfunding. Under the old system, local health authorities were awarded a fixed budget for each hospital based roughly on population, but efficient hospitals (which performed a great many operations) used up their budgets part way through the year and in some cases this 'efficiency trap' forced hospitals to shut perfectly good wards. This inability to allocate resources efficiently clearly needed attention. Furthermore, any significant changes will always generate resistance; shortly before the NHS was set up in 1948, nearly 90 per cent of the doctors opposed participation in it.[63] These current changes are bound, too, to involve a period of upheaval. They will probably be made to work, at least tolerably well, not because it is sensible to try to turn a service into a market but because of the dedication of the people who work in the NHS. They will wish to ensure its success, however it is organized and whatever they think of the principles underlying the new reforms.

At the time of Mrs Thatcher's resignation, the logic of the 'reforms' pointed to the fragmentation of the health service and to an eventual reversion to something akin to the pre-war position: the poor received inferior health care free, and the rest in varying degrees and by various means paid for a better one. Yet subsequent political events, and developments in the NHS, may lead to a different outcome. In the meantime, the new market-style NHS may conceivably provide better value for money through improved resource management; or, owing to increased administration costs, it may provide the same service at greater expense. Either way the reforms, which offered no new money, may well turn out to have been an unnecessary though convenient distraction from the problem at the core of the National Health Service: persistent underinvestment.[64]

Before going on to dismiss the 'reforms' of this 'competent, inexpensive and universal health service' as quite simply 'insane', Donald Light, Professor of Social Medicine at the University of New Jersey, wondered if Mrs Thatcher, Kenneth Clarke and the Treasury knew that they were 'getting better value for money than any other health service in the industrialised world? No other system comes close in services per thousand pounds. Do they not know that experts from other systems marvel at how hard British nurses, technicians and physicians work for so little pay? Why do Britain's leaders think they can treat the nation's ills for a third less than anyone else?'[65]

The short answer to Professor Light's rhetorical question is that the Treasury and the government did not think; they just wanted to save money. The longer one is that the NHS, for all its faults, was indeed much cheaper than any alternative system, partly because its staff were prepared to accept far lower remuneration working for a service than for a quasi-business. But that was not a consideration that was dreamed of in Thatcherite philosophy. So instead of addressing the fundamental issue of chronic underfunding, the right-wing dogmatists preferred 'to force' the British public and the medical profession 'to be free' by imposing upon them a market system that would be more fragmented, less altruistic and probably more expensive than the previous National Health Service.

Higher Education

The monetarists' attack on the economy was not the only episode of its kind. The Thatcherites mounted a similar onslaught upon the universities. Once again, their ideological fixation with reducing public expenditure, regardless of the consequences, was the spur to action. In 1981 the universities were given a month's notice to plan an 18 per cent cut in three years; 3,000 academic posts were purged. This was followed by a 1983 election pledge to refrain from further cuts, which was broken within a year when further cuts of 2 per cent were exacted. Because of what they called the 'deep and systematic damage [inflicted] on the whole public education system in Britain', Oxford dons voted by an overwhelming majority in January 1985 to withhold an honorary degree from the Prime Minister. This unprecedented rebuff was fully understandable, but profoundly unwise if Oxford hoped for a less hostile government attitude to universities. Polytechnics fared far better and even prospered in the eighties. They were regarded as more efficient, more relevant to the establishment of any enterprise culture, and far less likely to oppose the government. The expansion of the polytechnics and the higher education colleges was all to the good, but did not atone for the government's treatment of the universities.[66]

When the budget cuts resulted in frozen salaries, unfilled professorial vacancies, money trimmed from libraries and the dilution of academic tenure, the brain drain of British professors flowing across the Atlantic in the early Thatcher years became a flood – over 200 between 1983 and 1988.*

In 1985 the government called for Higher Education to serve the national economy 'more effectively' – it presumably thought that slimmed-down universities, like slimmed-down manufacturing, were an active aid to economic effectiveness and efficiency. To make the universities more economically useful, the government sought to tilt the balance of higher education away from the humanities towards business and vocational studies, a policy which Enoch Powell branded

---

* Commenting on the departure of the distinguished Regius Professor of Modern History at Oxford, Sir Michael Howard, for a Professorship at Yale, Edward Luttwak wrote that had Howard been an American he would never have been allowed to translate himself to Britain 'so long as further academic honours, gold and research facilities (more gold) could keep him. For,' the American Conservative added, 'countries do not lightly surrender their natural resources – not unless they are ruled by primitives who can not tell valuable ones from mere rocks.' 'The brain drain,' wrote Harold Perkin (himself part of it), 'rivalled that from Hitler's Germany.'[67]

'barbarism'.* Mrs Thatcher deplored what she regarded as the 'anti-industrial spirit', which academics shared with the clergy. 'Nowhere,' she maintained, 'is this attitude [opposition to wealth creation] more marked than in the cloister and common room.' Worse still, the universities were not only 'anti-industrial', they were positively left wing. And, perhaps worst of all, they lacked 'conviction'; they entertained doubts. Like the civil service they were more inclined to ask questions than accept dogma, and could not be relied upon to give the government the advice it wanted. Hence the government turned to so-called independent think-tanks which like the Thatcherites themselves were not deterred by lack of knowledge or inadequate research from coming to confident conclusions. On top of all these defects, the universities, again like the civil service, were seen as absorbing too much of the country's best talent. Clearly they needed to be put in their place and brought under control.[68]

Amidst fears of universities being penalized financially for their lecturers' opinions or political orientation and for their 'anti-industrial spirit', many pressed for an amendment to the Education Reform Bill of 1988 ensuring academic intellectual freedom. But that of course would not have increased economic efficiency. The government's stance against the academics, Lady Warnock believed, stemmed less from philistinism (although that, too, was evident) than from dogmatism; dogmatists cannot tolerate high intellectual standards, which both depend upon and engender freedom of thought. In confirmation the Thatcherite militant, Paul

* In Malcolm Bradbury's 1987 novel, *Cuts*, the trendy vice-chancellor, who had recently been knighted by Mrs Thatcher, 'stirred by pressure from the government for bringing in more relevant subjects, was trying to disestablish ancient departments like classics and English altogether, and replace them by more modern ones such as a Department of Snooker Studies.' He also encouraged 'sponsored tutorials so that lecturers now discussed the poems of Catullus or mathematical equations wearing teeshirts and little caps that said on them "Boots" or "Babycham".'[69]

Johnson, attacked universities as 'the most overrated institutions of our age'.[70]

As the principal source of new knowledge, critical examination and research, universities cannot sensibly be treated like factories or evaluated by economic output indices. Free-market ideas are even less appropriate for universities than they are for health. Of course, the market and the needs of the country are bound to bring considerable influence to bear on the universities. They nearly always have: as the Robbins Report on Higher Education pointed out, 'the ancient universities of Europe were founded to promote the training of the clergy, doctors and lawyers'. And some parts of the English universities had in this century become too narrow and esoteric. Yet the universities cannot be wholly answerable to the market's immediate claims. The government's cuts in 1981 reduced the state's support for basic science by over 11 per cent. Although the government insisted that the universities tap alternative sources of private funding, sponsored research tends to be confined to issues of perceived commercial significance. 'Who would have sponsored Sir Isaac Newton,' Lord Russell enquired, 'to sit idle under an apple tree, or Archimedes to sit dreaming in a bath?'[71]

The constant battle for research funds, a Nobel prize-winning chemist maintained, sapped the energies of Britain's finest scientists and undermined the country's reputation as a world-class innovator. The government's policy towards science, it has been said, was 'characterized by a curious compound of ideology and ignorance'. With America, Germany, Holland and France spending 20 per cent more per head of population on funding science, the contention of an American institute that the quality of science in the UK declined throughout the Thatcher years, turning Britain into a third-ranking scientific nation, looked frighteningly plausible.[72]

The introduction of student loans also served neo-Liberal free-market principles, if little else. The Thatcher government froze student grants (stipulating that they were not to be increased until they formed only 50 per cent of student finance) and decreed that the shortfall would be made up by loans unless, of course, parents were rich enough to be able to prevent their offspring from beginning their working lives deeply in debt. As a further encouragement to Higher Education the government announced that the vast majority of full-time students would be excluded from social security even during the summer vacation. Except for those with dependants, students lost their entitlement to housing benefit which they were previously able to claim all the year round, and to Income Support/unemployment benefit at any time.[73]

Making Higher Education a luxury that few can afford suggested that the government hoped to diminish the number of undergraduates. However, with only 15 per cent of the age group going into Higher Education, compared to about 50 per cent in the United States and a little under 40 per cent in Japan, the government quite rightly professed a wish to double the numbers in Higher Education over the next twenty-five years. The LSE estimated that the combination of inflation and frozen grants would probably lead to the average student at the end of the century being burdened with a debt of £10,000.[74] All this seems a curious way of encouraging people to embark on Higher Education. The Thatcherite belief in incentives was here abandoned.

On top of everything else, the student-loan scheme proved to be an administrative fiasco. After the high-street banks withdrew from the scheme when threatened with a student boycott, a special company had to be set up by the government. The take-up of the loans was less than half, and the cost of running the scheme double, what was initially forecast; more than £1 was spent on distributing each £2 of loans.[75] The cost of administering each loan is some three times that of administering each student grant. Notwithstanding the £25 million hardship fund provided by the government to help students cope with the loss of benefits, students were not taking out loans because they were already deeply in debt; some had lost £400 a year in housing benefit. Government cuts in post-graduate funding contributed to the general impression that academic life was a pretty desperate career option. Even when academic salaries were unfrozen, they remained remarkably low. Not surprisingly there was not only a brain drain from British universities to universities in other countries, but an internal one as well, people leaving British universities for other jobs in Britain. In consequence there is a 'missing' generation of British academics.

Despite the systematic cuts, or possibly because of them, universities succeeded during the eighties in raising student numbers quite significantly – 45,000 more in 1990–91 than in 1984–85. The university vice-chancellors cautioned that this expansion had been achieved with continuous underinvestment which had brought the infrastructure of universities to a dangerously low level. The Public Accounts Committee had also warned that as many as forty-four universities could be operating in the red. The small but genuine efficiency gains together with damaging short-term expedients such as under-paying staff and delaying building repairs, helped to contain the loss in quality during the 1980s. Between 1980 and 1988 university spending on books and journals fell by a third in real terms – much the same happened in state schools – and in many universities library facilities and book stocks were lamentably low. The chairman of the vice-chancellors and principals, Sir Edward Parkes, predicted that the quality of university education would plummet during the 1990s unless re-investment was undertaken by the government.[76]

Yet the new Universities Funding Council said that it would only financially reward universities which expanded by taking more 'fees-only' students or extra students at marginal cost. Understandably, this prompted its former chief executive, Sir Peter Swinnerton-Dyer, to make a savage attack on the council's rigid adoption of market forces at the expense of standards. The market ruled, and the government regarded quality, Sir Peter believed, as 'an unnecessary luxury'. Earlier the responsible junior minister had privately admitted that the best universities faced the prospect of 'progressive degradation'. Quality was not the only casualty. The Thatcherite espousal of market forces (except over the salaries of university teachers which were deplorably low) was accompanied in the universities (and elsewhere) by increased state control, thereby further jeopardizing the worldwide reputation of British universities. Thus while they were privatizing water and gas, the Thatcherites were nationalizing Higher Education and housing policy.[77]

Schools

At the primary and secondary stages, British education has long been notoriously defective. Although some British schools of all types are among the best in the world, British education for more than a century has lagged well behind that of its competitors. In 1901 an educationalist ascribed governmental neglect of education to the belief of the governing class that many functions of modern life 'were best performed by people ignorant and brutish'. Rather surprisingly, in view of the treatment the poor received eighty years later, nobody seems to have made a similar allegation against the Thatcherites. Certainly many people leave school with little or nothing to show for it.[78]

The last Labour government had launched 'a great debate' on education – admittedly without much visible result – and throughout Ted Heath's government Margaret Thatcher had been a high-spending and determined Education Secretary. During that period, as she has often been reminded, she approved the abolition of more grammar schools and conversions to comprehensive schools than any other minister before or since.* But she also raised the school leaving age

---

* When Norman Tebbit complains of 'the flabby response of the Conservative establishment to the destruction of the grammar and technical schools', does he have Mrs Thatcher in his sights? In fact most shire counties went comprehensive voluntarily, often as a result of middle-class dissatisfaction with secondary-modern schools.[79]

to sixteen, set in train a large school-building programme, achieved smaller classes, and extended nursery education. In addition she issued a major White Paper which envisaged expansion in almost every field of the education service.[80]

The reform of school education might have been expected, therefore, to be an urgent priority of the new Thatcher government. In fact its urgent priority, as in all areas, was to save money. Its 1979 White Paper on education aimed for a cut in real terms of 7 per cent over the next three years – an aim which was largely frustrated. The Labour government's legislation compelling local authorities to go comprehensive was immediately repealed, and later an important step forward was taken with the introduction of GCSE courses to replace O-levels and CSEs, a reform generally thought to have raised standards and led to a higher proportion of pupils staying on at school for A-levels.[81]

The 1980 Education Act sought to promote parental choice of schools by laying down that Local Education Authorities must in principle comply with parental preference; appeals committees were established. It also limited LEAs powers to reduce admissions to any school, and it set up the assisted-places scheme. The 1986 Act established new governing bodies for schools, and it gave them new responsibilities and powers, bringing more autonomy to each school. It also abolished corporal punishment. These were far from negligible reforms, yet between 1983 and 1987 school education was largely spared the tuition of Thatcherism and did not in the end suffer the savage expenditure cuts that were inflicted on the universities.[82]

In the end, however, the schools could not escape the full Thatcherite ordeal. The last thing education needed after Labour's attacks on the grammar schools, Chris Patten wrote in 1983, was 'the shock of another "political impulse", another surging political advance'. But before long that was what it got. According to Nicholas Ridley, the Prime Minister believed that schools 'should be encouraging the enterprise culture and not the dependency culture . . . and she was determined to achieve more choice for parents and higher standards for all'. Unfortunately, when Mrs Thatcher decided to 'take a special interest in the problem', there were no plans for change in education before her; yet the education reforms were 'hammered out in . . . no more than a month'. In addition, once action had been decided upon, consultation was as usual inadequate, and the bill was rushed. During 1987 a new charter for education was conceived and so speedily encapsulated in the Education Reform Bill of 1988 that it required hundreds of amendments. Yet again the Thatcher government legislated on the hoof.[83]

This important act established a national curriculum, local management of schools and grant-maintained schools; it also sought to maximize parental choice of schools. The principle behind central government outlining a national core curriculum has been widely supported by politicians, academics and teachers, marking a milestone in educational reform. Unfortunately, the milestone initially gave faulty directions, largely because the curriculum was implemented with undue haste and without consulting the teachers. As a result there was a series of ministerial retreats from the full curriculum originally promised by Kenneth Baker.

The rest of the measures owed at least as much to free-market dogma as to educational considerations. As in other fields of social policy, Thatcherism was seeking to substitute competitive consumerism for state provision. This was to be achieved by allowing schools to opt out of local authority control and to become grant maintained; by making schools manage their own budgets; and by removing the right of local authorities to ordain the number of children at each school.

In 1980 the government had changed the rules to allow schools to take in as many pupils as they can safely cater for in order to give parents increased choice. The introduction of more 'open enrolment' following the 1988 Act seems superficially to have everything to be said for it: greater parental choice is obviously desirable and good schools will now contain more pupils. Yet much of the benefit is illusory.

Parental choice is really a misnomer. Parents can express their preference for a particular school, but that is what they could, and did, do before. Unlike chocolate manufacturers, schools cannot hugely expand their production – they are constrained by the size of their buildings etc. If chocolate manufacturers step up their production, there is no reason why the quality of their chocolate should deteriorate. But if a school becomes larger or more overcrowded, its quality may well decline. It may have been successful and popular precisely because it was quite small and uncrowded.

And parents who are denied their first choice, which they think that 'parental choice' has promised them, feel short-changed. That has been made more likely by the High Court judgement in the Greenwich case which made it impossible for a local authority or a governing body to give any priority to their 'own' applicants over applicants from neighbouring LEAs. For a great many parents, therefore, it is now more difficult to achieve their first preference than it was before. Moreover, if one school crams in many more pupils, other less popular schools may have too few to be viable. At the very least there will be a very wasteful use of school buildings. Even Nicholas Ridley recognized this problem, though he thought it could be overcome.[84]

The whole problem has been made more difficult by the most contentious provision of the 1988 Act, which gives schools freedom to opt out from control of their local education authority if they so wish, and indeed bribes them to become grant-maintained with additional funds. This means that there will be increasing numbers of areas in which there are no schools where the local authority is in a position to exercise both its planning function and its control over admission. This will make life more difficult for many parents without giving them greater choice. They may be subjected to marketing techniques by the opted-out schools, but when a school is over-subscribed, it is the school that chooses its pupils not the parents that choose the school. This re-introduces the principle of selection, for which there is something to be said: it works well in Buckinghamshire (although in neighbouring Hertfordshire the comprehensive system works equally well). But if there is to be selection, it should surely be operated in an orderly way, not by fragmenting planned educational provision and establishing a mini-market with attendant chaos. Furthermore there is the problem of the unpopular or unfashionable schools, mentioned earlier. 'We do need,' Cardinal Hume has said, 'to be aware that competitive markets always create losers and as a society we cannot afford to allow any schools which meet local needs to lose out.'[85]

The reasons for the introduction of opting-out were both political and ideological. The political inducement was to curb the power of Labour-controlled councils. The ideological commitment was to inject an element of market competition into the delivery of state-funded education. Nicholas Ridley has said that he produced the opting-out idea; it is unlikely that anyone will wish to dispute his claim.[86]*

There is something to be said for opting-out in places where the local authority is either massively incompetent or so politically actuated that it is damaging its pupils' education. But that applies to very few authorities, and could be fairly easily remedied† without throwing a large ideological spanner into the educational system of the entire country. If schools opt out on anything approaching the scale hoped for by the government, local authorities will be quite unable to plan the educational system for their areas. The idea that the market is a satisfactory substitute is dogmatic fantasy. The classical economists – the mentors of our neo-Liberals – did not believe that education should

---

* 'The language,' Patrick Wright points out, 'has undergone striking transformations. It really was not very long ago that the term "opting out" implied deluded irresponsibility; people who proposed it were derided as "drop-outs" and subjected to firm lectures in the quality papers ... Nowadays, of course, "opting out" is government policy.'[87]

† See chapter VIII below.

be left to the consumer. They advocated state intervention in education, though certainly not a state monopoly. Adam Smith favoured state education, and John Stuart Mill thought that on education the *laissez-faire* principle entirely broke down; 'the person most interested is not the best judge of the matter, not a competent judge at all.' Earlier, Nassau Senior had laid down that it was 'as much the duty of the community to see that the child is educated as to see that it is fed.'[88]

Of course the market has great appeal as well as great uses. Those who do not bow down before it can always be derided as authoritarian or paternalistic and as seeking to put their preferences before those of the public. Unfortunately, the market often has unacceptable social consequences. And just as largely unregulated market forces in the economic system often do not produce the most desirable outcome, so elsewhere there is no reason why the mere counting of preferences should produce the best, or even a particularly sensible result.

Forty years ago Lord Radcliffe deplored 'a theory of democracy in which the leaders recognise no higher duty than to try to find out what the public wants and then to see that it gets it — a sort of bungalow *populi*, bungalow *dei* theory.' He could not imagine 'any conception of society more weak-minded or more destructive'. There is such a thing as the public good of the country, and no amount of 'freedom', 'choice', populism or neo-Liberal rhetoric can deny it or, by themselves, achieve it. The community and society do exist, and they are not the mere aggregation of individual wishes. 'If government were a matter of will upon any side,' Burke told his constituents at Bristol, 'yours, without question, ought to be superior. But government and legislation are matters of reason and judgement, and not of inclination.' How much should be spent on education, housing or health cannot be decided by the market. They are matters of reason and judgement, not just of consumers' inclination.[89]

Thatcherites see the world as a prolonged pursuit of

groceries whereby people choose education from Tesco and local government from Sainsburys. To them, there is no essential difference between a school or university and a supermarket. But this view is fallacious. Education is not a simple commodity; unlike the purchase of vegetables or a packet of cigarettes it involves a number of relationships.* And, fortunately or unfortunately, schools cannot be bought and sold like sausages or children's clothes. Some authority has to decide what schools there are going to be and their size and place. And if local authorities are to be prevented from performing those essential functions, central government will have to do it. Alleged choice by the consumer leads in the end to government control. Yet central government is in no position to assess local needs.[90]

The ostensible reason given for lessening the role of local government was to give power to parents. The reality is that it is the most affluent and astute middle-class parents who will exercise their right to opt out, and their schools will pocket the government's *douceur*; schools in deprived areas of unemployment will not feel able to enter 'the market' and compete for pupils. This is bound to result in a sought-after sector of grant-maintained schools and a poorer sector of lesser-quality schools under local authority control – another example of the middle-class welfare state.[91]

That would be the logical outcome of consumerism. Just as the richer classes can afford better groceries, so they will be able to get better education through some voluntary funding. In a sense this happens in the independent sector, but all the costs of the public schools are borne by the parents. Opting-out is likely to lead to a three-tier system: the independent sector, the well-off opted-out state schools

---

* In a ballot on whether a school should opt out, only the current parents are allowed to vote. This has been likened to seeking a poll of customers who happen to be in a Marks and Spencer store as to whether they would like that branch to separate itself from head office in Baker Street.

and a rump of underfunded local authority schools which in many areas will be largely confined to the poorer classes. That would indeed be a Thatcherite throwback to pre-1870, before there was a national system of education; its chief effect would be social divisiveness and perpetuation of the 'underclass'. In any case, freedom to choose schools should not mask the necessity of improving schools which are of lower quality.[92]

Even supporters of grant-maintained schools condemned the attempt to detach schools from local-authority control before completing the process of devolving budgetary and managerial control to school level. To rush such changes seemed mere pandering to the ideological fervour of Thatcherism. The devolution of financial responsibility to the schools is on the whole welcome. Many head teachers, however, do not wish to become entrepreneurs and find the extra administrative burden heavy, if not intolerable. A few, too, have been compelled to turn down or get rid of experienced teachers in favour of probationers because they cost less. In addition, with pupil-based funding, the Local Management of Schools scheme seems to have an in-built and wholly undesirable bias against small schools and schools in the inner cities.[93]

The promotion of parental choice and the devolution of power have been much emphasized, helping to obscure the realities that an important aim of the reform was to cripple the power of local government and that the end result will, by default, be transfer of power to Whitehall. Conservatives have always favoured the dispersal of power, and so (in theory) do most neo-Liberals. Nevertheless from the days of the Physiocrats in eighteenth-century France, *laissez-faire* ideas and absolutism have often comfortably cohabited. Graham Wallas wrote of the laws of political economy standing from 1815 to 1870, 'like gigantic stuffed policemen, on guard over rent and profits'.[94] Yet, both then and later, *laissez-faire* required real as well as stuffed policemen to guard it.

The imposition of an often inappropriate quasi-market

system demands over-weening government, and the Thatcher years saw galloping centralization. An administration which in theory favoured less executive power was in practice greedy to extend it. The 1988 Act gave more than 400 new powers to the Secretary of State for Education and Science.[95]

Schools suffered a further intrusion of market-forces with the government's compulsory-tendering legislation. Remarkably, this does not apply to grant-maintained schools; and less remarkably, it has already had to be modified in relation to small schools as it was found to be unworkable. In education, as elsewhere, Thatcherism signified hasty legislation followed by a lengthy and more leisurely process of trying to repair the damage. Much repair work still needs to be done. In the meantime, a letter from Dr Adrian Elliot, Copmanthorpe, York, summed up the situation shortly after Mrs Thatcher's resignation.

> In the comprehensive school of which I am Head, weeks and weeks of staff time have been spent . . . on introducing an unfair and complex system of financial management with inadequate training and faulty information technology; absorbing an overweight national curriculum accompanied by massive documentation, much of which has been later withdrawn or fundamentally revised; struggling to keep open an often filthy and unhygienic school, conditions created as a result of Nicholas Ridley's privatisation of council services. While I do not subscribe to the view that the Government has been deliberately attempting to undermine State education over the past three years, its actions, whether through incompetence or neglect, have certainly had such an effect.[96]

Contrary to popular perceptions, overall standards in the state education system have almost certainly improved since the 1940s. The trouble is that we have lagged behind our competitors abroad. The glaring deficiencies that remain led to the Prince of Wales inveighing against the prospect of 'an entire generation of culturally disinherited young people' and to Sir Claus Moser warning that Britain 'is now in danger of becoming one of the least adequately educated of all the advanced nations – with serious consequences for its future socially, economically, technologically and culturally'.[97]

Exam performance has improved substantially, if we can assume that the required standards remained the same: in 1964–65, 64 per cent of all pupils left school without any graded examination passes but only 9 per cent did so in 1984–85, a significant improvement. Yet fewer teenagers continue their education after sixteen in Britain than in any other EC country except Greece. In the United States and Japan about twice as many children stay at school or college beyond sixteen as they do in Britain. Also standards in maths, science and languages are woefully inadequate, and in 1990 the HMI reported that one third of all pupils were getting a 'raw deal'. As in the past, Britain successfully educates the most academically bright pupils, but schools provide only a middling standard for the average and fail to raise the sights of those who fall in the lowest band of academic attainment. That of course is not all the fault of the education system. The issue of poverty is intertwined with education, as it is with every other aspect of social policy; social factors account for most of the differences in achievement levels between different areas. What a child brings to school is more important than what goes on in the school itself.[98]

Ultimately, the success or failure of the education system largely depends on the level of government funding. The Thatcher government claimed to have increased spending by 14 per cent more 'in real terms', but once again the terms were only partly 'real'. Because of the 'real-price effect' – that is to say, the high labour content of education and the limited scope for productivity gains push up education costs faster than the retail price index – there was no real increase in expenditure on education. Indeed, according to OECD figures there was a fall.[99]

The level of capital investment was threateningly low; unfortunately successive governments have lamentably under-estimated the need for capital investment in schools – it is now less than a third of what it was in 1973. As a result, according to a recent survey, 44 per cent of schools had defects in at least one roof, leading to leaks, collapsing ceilings and water running into electrical fittings. In 1987, the government held back the chief inspector's report until after the general election because of its embarrassing evidence of crumbling classrooms, unfilled teacher vacancies and the great divide between schools whose parents could afford to buy textbooks and those who could not.[100]

Many school buildings, therefore, if not their values, were 'Victorian'. Yet, even while boasting of general economic prosperity, the Thatcher government decreased the proportion of GDP spent on education from 5.3 per cent in 1980–81 to 4.9 per cent in 1988–89. In contrast, the USA devoted 6.7 per cent of its GDP to education, Sweden 7.2 per cent and Denmark 7.9 per cent. Subsequent increases in the education budget represented cuts in real terms.[101]

To precipitate a massive upheaval in the structure of education while providing less, not more, money to finance the changes was yet another bizarre false economy.

Apart from chronic underfunding by international standards, the major problem bedevilling the state education system was the demoralization of the teaching profession. Thatcherites seemed incapable of understanding that good teachers are the key to a well-educated nation. After the strikes of the mid-eighties, the government and the Thatcher-worshipping press vilified the teachers and blamed their so-called trendy teaching methods for inadequate standards in the classroom. Whether or not some of the methods were misguided, they had not been dreamed up by the teachers. The militancy of teachers' unions certainly did not help their pupils or their own image, but the majority of teachers remain modest and dedicated. Thatcherites never had much respect for public servants outside the police and the armed forces, but the teaching profession seemed to excite their particular contempt. Under Mrs Thatcher, teachers became progressively demoralized, confused and underpaid, with the inevitable consequence in some areas of a critical shortage of teachers.[102]

In 1975, teachers' salaries were nearly 40 per cent above the white-collar average; by 1990 that had fallen to 5 per cent. Between 1981 and 1990 the real earnings of the average non-manual worker rose by 26 per cent; those of teachers rose by only 12 per cent. Hence teaching was no longer competitive with other graduate professions. And whatever else they do, student loans will not improve the supply or quality of teachers. Large numbers of graduates are unlikely to hurry into a poorly paid profession when they are already burdened by debt. Perhaps more serious than their material rewards is the teachers' diminishing status in society. (Much the same is true of engineers.) Teaching used to be a profession that enjoyed prestige – as it still does in other countries like Germany where teachers are accorded the same respect as family doctors.[103]

The teachers were not of course the only people who were excluded from consultations during the usually secretive, rushed and highly partisan preparation of legislation during the Thatcher era. (The same thing happened to the Local Authority Associations with damaging consequences.) But it was needlessly provocative and improvident to alienate the teachers by not consulting them over the 1988 reforms, and then to expect them to implement the changes at break-neck speed. Overloading them with confused curricular changes and time-consuming tests on top of low pay and already low morale caused at one moment nearly a third of teachers to wish to leave their profession. That extreme exasperation did not last long, but morale remained low.[104]

Conclusion

The Thatcher government was unable to understand the concept of intellectual investment, because it does not produce immediate cash returns. An under-educated society will in due course become socially unstable and economically inefficient, but Thatcherites were too blinkered to appreciate that simple point. For them, immediate economies and tax cuts were far more important than the long-term future of the country.

Despite eleven years of relentless hectoring, the British remained relatively impervious to Thatcherite values. Unfettered individualism made little or no headway, and the collective provision of health, education and (to a lesser extent) housing remained at least as popular as before 1979. The great majority of people evidently wanted greater spending to achieve higher standards in the public services for which they were prepared to forgo lower taxes – even if they preferred not to vote for substantial tax increases by voting Labour.[105]

The market was God to Thatcherites except when the consumers wanted a non-Thatcherite product. Then, provided the electoral dangers could be contained, their wants were ignored. They might want improved social services; what they were going to get was more tax cuts (at least if they were quite well-off), since that was what was better for them. Thus Thatcherites happily distorted the market by subsidizing people to buy shares in the new private monopolies, yet refused to realize market demands for better education and health provision as these would entail expansion of the public sector.

Dogmatic Thatcherism was largely responsible for the deterioration of the social-security system, for inadequate investment in housing, education and the NHS, and for aggravating the difficulties suffered by the near poor as well as the poorest in our society. Yet although the Labour party was never remotely electable until well after the 1987 election, the Thatcherites were fenced in by political constraints. Because they could not change public attitudes to the welfare state, or to fairness, or to poverty (except over acceptance of high unemployment) – indeed opinion moved the other way during the eighties – they had to eschew the most radical (or reactionary) New-Right policies. Although the measures they took may in the end lead to both, they could not secure abolition of the NHS nor inflict education vouchers on a hostile public opinion.[106]

Even their war against public expenditure, though it produced highly detrimental cuts in some areas, was by their criteria unsuccessful. In real terms public expenditure never rose by less than 1 per cent a year between 1979 and 1990, and at election times it rose by over 4 per cent. Thus despite cumulative underfunding, the structure of the welfare state remained largely intact. That, though, was of little comfort to those at the bottom of the heap.[107]

The term 'poverty' may have been banished from government documents and replaced with such bland euphemisms as 'low income', but with the Thatcherites' economic achievements now looking distinctly ragged, the widening inequalities they fostered in our society will be less easily eradicated. Sooner or later, the series of misguided social policy decisions, justified by faith not reason, will have to be remedied. Dogma and ideology divide society; a sense of 'social citizenship' unites it. The threat of economic insecurity is more likely to induce resistance to change than to encourage economic adaptation. So, for the sake of economic efficiency, as well as social equity, progress towards higher employment, and an enduring commitment to social well being and to the dignity of the individual, are essential.

VIII

Means and Ends

> I cut back the powers of government . . . just look at
> the many people who voted for me.
> Margaret Thatcher, 1992[1]

> Man, always avid for power through having more,
> desirous of having all only because he possesses much.
> Montesquieu, *Grandeur et Décadence*[2]

A FTER MRS THATCHER had won her third election
victory and had expressed her intention 'to go on and
on', at least, it seemed, to the millennium and perhaps beyond,
Julian Critchley began to talk of 'the thousand-year Reich'.
He was joking, of course, though the Prime Minister's boast
that 'Thatcherism is for centuries', soon provided another
instance of nature copying art.[3] Margaret Thatcher's over-
throw brought to many in the Conservative parliamentary
party a feeling of liberation: the occupation had at last ended,
and after being for so long, as it were, part of Eastern Europe
we had rejoined the West. Although the deThatcherization of
the parliamentary party undoubtedly transformed its atmosphere, talk of an occupation was also a satirical extravagance.
Both exaggerations were built, however, on an important

substratum of truth: almost as much as dogmatic individualism or the dislike of state help, the will to extend the power of the Prime Minister herself, in President de Gaulle's phrase, *à tous les azimuts*, if not for centuries, for as long as possible, lay at the heart of Thatcherism. For all her seemingly endless talk of 'freedom' and her claim to have 'cut back the powers of government', Mrs Thatcher's administration did more to amass and centralize power than any peacetime British government in this century.[4]

Thatcherites were at best not interested in, at worst positively opposed to, constitutional reform. That became clear in the opposition years over the future of the House of Lords. All the leading Conservatives who possessed what Roger Scruton calls 'the "inward" knowledge that a great institution demands' – Lords Home, Hailsham and Carrington – were in no doubt that the second chamber needed reform. Yet Mrs Thatcher and the right wing of the shadow cabinet, none of whom had any such 'inward' knowledge, obstructed the reform proposal, evidently agreeing with Mr Scruton that the House of Lords should be protected from 'the contagion of democracy'.[5]

The year before the 1979 election Quintin Hailsham published an impressive and prophetic book, *The Dilemma of Democracy*. In it he warned of the danger of what he called 'elective dictatorship' and averred that our traditional constitution was breaking down and could not be remedied by any *ad hoc* tinkering. While Hailsham was 'agnostic' about proportional representation for the House of Commons (though the logic of his argument seemed to point to it fairly strongly), his book put forward a radical programme of constitutional reform. Yet when he became Lord Chancellor in Mrs Thatcher's government, he 'was given no remit to carry through constitutional changes of any kind, and no proposals for constitutional change formed any part of the election manifesto'. Lord Hailsham was disappointed by Mrs Thatcher's shunning of constitutional reform, but defended it on the grounds that the Prime Minister was right to give priority to her economic reforms. We have seen what those did to the economy.[6]

The Conservative monetarist right fundamentally disagreed with Hailsham's diagnosis. They believed that Britain's relative failure since the war was due to all previous British governments having followed the erroneous prescriptions of John Maynard Keynes and other heretics. In their view there was nothing wrong with Britain that could not be cured by a stiff dose of Hayek and Friedman. Hence their neglect of constitutional reform, although here they were not so different from their predecessors.

Promising a measure of parliamentary reform acceptable to all 'moderate, impartial and well educated men,' the Prime Minister, Lord Derby, said in 1858 that 'it was necessary to adapt our institutions to the altered purposes they are intended to serve, and by judicious changes [meet] the demands of society.' Yet at least since 1945 British governments seem to have lost the capacity to adapt our institutions. There have been some constitutional reforms: Harold Macmillan's introduction of life peers into the House of Lords was useful but a long way from being an adequate reform of the upper House; the setting up of the National Economic Development Council; the creation of Ombudsmen; and the House of Commons Select Committees. That is about all. Constitutionally, British governments since the war have been largely sterile.[7]

The Thatcher governments, therefore, can not be fairly criticized for being less creative, constitutionally, than their predecessors. Yet even if governments do not improve the constitution, they should at least prevent its deterioration. The first of the three great objects of the Tory party, laid down by Disraeli, 'is to maintain the institutions of the country'.[8] Did the Thatcherites carefully preserve British institutions? Constitutional issues, Thatcherism's treatment of the national institutions and its running of the political system can conveniently be considered together.

The Legislative Process

Much as Downing Street ceased in the Thatcher era to be like 'a transport café' for trade-union leaders, Whitehall became unfamiliar territory to 'the great and the good'. In more than eleven years Mrs Thatcher failed to provide them with a single Royal Commission. Arguably that omission prevented postponement of necessary action, yet Conservative governments have not normally wished to be judged by the speed and quantity of the laws they pass. The Thatcher government forced through almost forty statutes with the aim of reducing the independence of local government, most of them ill-prepared and ill-considered. Faced in 1812 with one similarly hasty and imprudent measure, Byron told the government front bench in the Lords that he thought 'a little investigation, some previous enquiry would induce even them to change their purpose'. Some previous enquiry, even if not a Royal Commission, would have prevented at least thirty of those local government bills.[9]

Thatcherite legislation seldom emanated from investigation. After the Falklands victory the Conservatives could feel confident of their electoral prospects for most of the eighties, confidence that hardened into certainty after the victory of 1987. That assumption fostered the conviction that within certain (fairly wide) limits the government could do what it liked in the way it liked. Therefore no special efforts to gain consent for its measures were needed; consent was bound in the end to be forthcoming, since the voters had no real choice.

In relying upon the traditional patience of the British people, the Thatcherites were taking a bigger risk than they realized. The gaining and giving of consent is a complex business which is cumulative over generations. A prudent government should nurture that process, not weaken it by giving the impression that once the voters have returned a Conservative government to power their sole remaining function is to obey the law.[10]

The government came into office in 1983 and 1987, having won about 43 per cent of the popular vote. While that was enough to give it an enormous majority in parliament, 43 per cent is very far from being a majority of those voting, let alone a majority of the country. When the main parties are far apart, as they were till well after the 1987 election, an incoming government cannot strike some compromise between its policies and those of the opposition. Yet its awareness that it represents at most only half the country traditionally persuades a British government to pay some attention at some stage to the views of the half which did not vote for it. It listens; it does not govern by diktat and dogma. That convention was one of the many which Thatcherism flouted.

The views of the public were of little consequence during the legislative process. Disliking public inquiry, despising opposition and believing in Thatcherite infallibility, the government customarily kept all the preliminaries to legislation in its own hands, only listening in private to groups and individuals who would give it the advice it wanted. As a result, the government, especially in its third term, produced a mass of legislation – the poll tax, water privatization, the Health Service changes, football identity cards – strongly opposed by a large majority of the country.

The House of Commons

Given their partisan and secretive origins, which were not subsequently offset by much in the way of good sense and fairness, the government's proposals required genuine discussion in both Houses of Parliament, if full legitimacy and consent were to be gained, and if the phrase 'parliamentary democracy' were to have more than a formal meaning. Genuine discussion presupposed, in turn, the government's willingness to listen to conflicting views and on occasion to modify its own programmes. Unfortunately, though, the Thatcherites rarely paid much attention to the argument and, whenever they could, they truncated parliamentary discussion, guillotining more bills than any previous administration. 'The subtle machinery of the Committee and Report stages of Bills' has become, as Mr Mount writes, merely 'a mockery'. The government relied on an extreme use of the doctrine of the mandate, executed by its automatic, whipped majority, to put its proposals on the statute book, and on support from the press to provide the appearance (and often the reality) of consent.[11]

According to the mandate doctrine, a government has the right or the duty to turn into law any proposal that it happened to mention in its election manifesto. Certainly a government should try to keep faith with the electorate by sticking to the general lines of the programme that it put before the country at the previous election, but that is as far as the doctrine can reasonably be taken.

We know that parts of both Conservative and Labour manifestos are often thrown in without much careful thought – for example the insertion of the provisions to abolish the GLC and to introduce rate-capping into the 1983 manifesto was not the result of informed discussion but of prime ministerial insistence. In any case the electorate tends to decide its vote on general issues and impressions. Most voters are not concerned with the detailed policies on offer; many are not even aware of them. Long before she became prime minister, Margaret Thatcher herself expressed 'doubt whether the voters really are endorsing each and every particular when they return a government to power'. Besides, the vote is not subject to nuances. The citizen cannot vote 'Conservative but . . .', or 'Labour, provided that . . .'. He has to buy all or nothing. Finally nobody can be sure whether the voters voted primarily on the parties' previous record or on their future proposals. So even at the best of times the doctrine of the mandate is largely fictitious. But when it is invoked by a government which has gained only 43 per cent of the popular vote, fiction becomes farce.[12]

However farcical in theory, the mandate doctrine was

a useful weapon for the whips, helping them to ensure the obedience of Conservative backbenchers and win large majorities in almost all votes. I myself had no cause for complaint. The whips always treated me with complete and friendly civility. They never remonstrated at what I had said or done, and seldom made much effort to influence my vote. I was, however, to some extent exceptional. I had been through the patronage system and out on the other side. I never sought accommodation with the regime, did not want to go on parliamentary trips abroad, and, as the possessor of a minor hereditary title, had no desire for a knighthood; finally, if the chief whip had complained to the chairman of my constituency association, he would have been politely rebuffed. There was, therefore, nothing the whips could do, and indeed I think they were too civilized even to consider trying.

Of course things were different for those who still had their political career before them. Younger potential rebels did have their arms twisted and were made aware that their future ministerial prospects were in jeopardy. Still the methods used were, I think, no rougher than those employed by, say, Captain Margesson in the thirties against the opponents of Chamberlain's 'appeasement' policy, or by other post-war whips' offices. The Conservative party is conformist by nature when in power and, in the eighties with the added element of ideology, was even more conformist than usual. Like most people outside Westminster, the parliamentary party was carried along by the strong current of fashionable opinion. Many MPs were time-servers, but many were true-believers.

Michael Latham (who was never a true-believer or a time-server) asked in some wonderment, 'why did the party, including myself, go on backing them?' He was talking of the 1988 social-security reforms, but the same question could have been asked about many other policies. Whatever their motives, the overwhelming majority of the party always did exactly what it was told. Hence, for many MPs, the occasional absence of precise instructions from the government caused much 'doubt, hesitation and pain'.[13] The last time the televising of the Commons was defeated, unnerving uncertainty existed as to the Prime Minister's current attitude. She had long been strongly opposed to the entry of television cameras into the chamber, then she was said to have been converted to their advantages, but finally, it was rumoured, she had been deconverted. The vote on the issue was a free one, so the guidance of those useful shepherds, the whips, could not be sought, and when the vote was called many sheep did not know which way to scurry. The spectacle of a number of colleagues caught in the usual melée at the bar of the House trying desperately to see which way Mrs Thatcher was going, so that they could speedily follow her, provided some innocent merriment.[14]

Television later provided a striking demonstration of the parliamentary party's almost limitless capacity to concur and comply. At the time of its second reading the 1990 Broadcasting Bill, proposing amongst other things auctions for the Independent Television franchises, was one of the least-easily defended pieces of legislation (it was still thoroughly undesirable when it was finally passed, but David Mellor improved it during the committee stage). Yet on the second reading only three Tory MPs voted against it.*

A year later Mrs Thatcher expressed herself 'heartbroken' by some of the results of the Bill, adding that she was 'only too painfully aware that I was responsible for the legislation'. That was handsomely said, but if the main responsibility was hers she was not the only person at fault. Shortly after Munich, Winston Churchill warned 'Honourable Gentlemen above the gangway – pledged, loyal, faithful supporters on all occasions of His Majesty's government' – that they too had 'a great responsibility'. They 'must not imagine,' said Churchill, that they could 'throw their burden wholly on the Ministers of the

---

* George Walden, who also spoke against it, Bill Benyon and myself.

Crown.' Much power rested with them. 'One healthy growl' a few years ago, Churchill added, would have made a great difference; a sizeable rebellion that night 'would not affect the life of the government, but it would make them act'.[15]

In the eighties the Conservative backbenchers seldom managed a 'healthy growl', and only once did they make the government act, or rather stop it from legislating. Unfortunately that exceptional rebellion defeated what was probably the government's best economic measure of the decade: the Sunday Trading Bill. Like the Sabbatarians, the Falkland Islands lobby produced an unhealthy growl that did much damage. Otherwise, 'the honourable gentlemen above the gangway' behaved precisely as their predecessors in the thirties had done, the only difference being that they were submissive for a much longer period. Hence Conservative backbenchers – what Churchill privately called 'this over-whipped crowd of "poor whites" ' – provided no curb on Thatcherism; if anything they were more a spur than a bridle.[16]

The Cabinet

Bridles were everywhere scarce. Of the ministers outside the cabinet, Ian Gow and Nicholas Budgen resigned, and the Law Officers, Michael Havers and Patrick Mayhew, firmly insisted on an enquiry into the leak of the latter's letter on Westland. But such independence was rare. And if the poll tax and the Broadcasting Act (as well as much else) demonstrated the desire of backbenchers to please their leader, they also revealed the subservience of the cabinet. As was indicated earlier, Margaret Thatcher's later cabinet was chiefly a formal body; major issues were rarely discussed there. The one point of agreement between Mrs Thatcher, Geoffrey Howe and Nigel Lawson on the ERM was that the issue should be kept well away from the cabinet. When President Reagan decided to bomb Libya and wished to use

British bases, the Prime Minister in conjunction with three senior ministers (none of whom favoured the idea) granted permission. Not unreasonably in the view of the need for security, the cabinet was not informed until the night of the bombing, when it was strongly in favour of Britain distancing itself as far as possible from the American action. Yet, in her statement in the Commons the next day, Mrs Thatcher completely disregarded the cabinet's views. Meetings of the cabinet gave the appearance of collective decision making, but seldom provided the reality.[17]

The Prime Minister's downgrading and bypassing of the cabinet caused resentment among some of those excluded from 'one of us' circles and sometimes produced serious trouble. Not all members were mere Thatcher-fodder. Michael Heseltine's defiance of the Prime Minister (followed by his resignation) was probably the most spectacular of the century. Peter Walker went his own way in Wales – he had made the promise of a free hand a condition for his accepting the job. Geoffrey Howe and Nigel Lawson opposed the Prime Minister over Europe, and both eventually resigned. In general, however, the cabinet, like the backbenchers, did what it was told.[18]

Towards the end of the era the cabinet was sometimes exhorted by commentators to end its 'servility'. After Geoffrey Howe's removal from the Foreign Office and again after Nigel Lawson's resignation from the Treasury, an abridgement of prime ministerial domination and a reversion to cabinet government were urged by many – and expected by the naive. In the event, of course, Mrs Thatcher was only chastened for a few days at the most. As Carlyle wrote of Louis XVI's situation after the fall of the Bastille, 'a quite untenable position, that of Majesty put on its good behaviour!'[19]

The Civil Service

More excusably the civil service, too, was no barrier to Thatcherocracy. With the possible exception of the French, the British civil service is almost certainly the best in the world. Traditionally one of its principal functions is to draw attention from long experience to the flaws in the instant panaceas enthusiastically adopted by its ministerial masters in opposition or, when in government, from think-tanks or seminars at Chequers. Mrs Thatcher, however, had no great admiration for public servants in general – much preferring businessmen, sometimes rather dodgy ones – or for civil servants in particular, perhaps thinking that if they had been any good they would have been in the City making money. And she favoured people who provided her with solutions, even if they were not fully aware of the problems, over those who knowledgeably pointed to difficulties. In consequence almost unanimous official advice against the poll tax counted for nothing. The Prime Minister wanted civil servants to implement dogma, not to expose its errors.[20]

Most civil servants soon saw that the way to live with ideology was to appear to share it. Some at the Department of Industry, anxious to seem cooperative, asked Keith Joseph for a reading list to brief themselves on free-market principles; he obliged with twenty-nine titles, ranging from Adam Smith to eight of his own pamphlets. Mrs Thatcher played a much greater part in the appointment of top civil servants than any of her predecessors. The charge that she politicized the civil service is overstated, but the careers of those who crossed her seldom prospered, and the enthusiastic championing of neo-Liberal ideas was an aid to advancement.[21]

'The soul of our service,' wrote Robert Vansittart, who was private secretary at No 10 to both MacDonald and Baldwin before becoming head of the Foreign Office, 'is the loyalty with which it executes ordained error.' That has been true for a long time, though Vansittart's own loyalty to error had narrow bounds. (At the Foreign Office in the thirties he gave information about developments in Germany to Churchill, the government's leading opponent, and at the San Remo Conference in 1920 he advised the French and the Italians to stand up to Lloyd George.) In the eighties, except for fairly junior figures like Clive Ponting, civil servants executed ordained error without demur. As was its duty, Whitehall supplied the baggage train for the Thatcherite crusaders, though that description perhaps flatters the status of officials; often they were more like prisoners. In an attempt to bolster the government's failing legal case against *Spycatcher*, the head of the civil service to his dismay found himself transported, like a convict of old, to Australia.[22]

The House of Lords

If the House of Lords was far from being the watchdog of the constitution, it was much less Mrs Thatcher's poodle than was the House of Commons.[23] It did quite often defeat the government on relatively minor matters. But when the government was defeated, it reversed the Lords vote by using its automatic majority of 'poor whites' in the Commons. And, when the War Crimes Bill, which had not been mentioned at the 1987 election and on which the expertise of the Lords was vastly greater than that of the Commons, had been annihilated in the Lords even more in argument than in votes, the government insisted on reintroducing it – a clear abuse of the Parliament Act.[24]

Because of the large Conservative majority among the backwoods peers, the government was never in serious danger on major issues. On such occasions it could always ship in from the shires a hundred or so peers who never normally attended and who usually knew little of the matter in question. This was at some public expense in transport fees and attendance allowances and also, no doubt, at some personal expense to the chief whip, in dispensing whiskies and sodas to some of the bewildered gentlemen he had summoned from their harmless pursuits in distant parts of the country to do their duty by swamping the votes of the rather better-informed working peers. The most notorious of those occasions was when the Lords voted down the introduction of a progressive element into the poll tax. Such a phalanx of backwoodsmen was then mustered that the second largest turnout in the history of the House of Lords was recorded. Since the passage of the amendment would have cost most of them hundreds of pounds a year, their visit to London was undoubtedly, as the Michelin guide has it, *vaut le voyage*.

Despite possessing this ultimate weapon, Mrs Thatcher was irritated by the occasional insubordination of other peers. When learning that some of the people she had ennobled had voted against the government, she said, 'I sent them there to support me: they ought to know better.' So resentful did she become of the indiscipline of the House of Lords that before the 1987 election she considered reducing its powers. Thus the Prime Minister, who considered that 'our present constitutional arrangements continue to serve us well and that the citizens of this country enjoy the greatest degree of liberty that is compatible with the rights of others and the vital interest of the state', did find them in one respect inadequate: the weakest second chamber in the world had too much power.[25]

Plebiscitary Democracy

The government and its followers in parliament customarily behave as though Britain has a system of plebiscitary government. Because it won the last election, a British government thinks it has the right to force all its legislative proposals through parliament on to the statute book, no matter how furtive and inadequate their preparation, nor how conclusively it loses the argument on the floor of the House. Its backbenchers almost invariably support the government in the division lobby, not because all of them agree with what the government is doing, but because they do not want to precipitate another election – they would be in trouble both with the party's leadership and their constituency association if they did. Hence much of the proceedings of the House of Commons is mere ritual. The result of the previous general election is what matters.

The Thatcher government's treatment of parliament was in no sense revolutionary. Books with titles such as *The Passing of Parliament* and *Can Parliament Survive?* appeared shortly after the war; as long ago as the 1920s Lord Robert Cecil said that the real principle of British government was purely 'plebiscital'. The Thatcher era merely saw a ruthless intensification of a trend which had long been apparent. For instance the number of parliamentary private secretaries (MPs who assist ministers) increased to fifty-one and discipline over them was strengthened. When I was PPS to Quintin Hogg in 1963–64, I voted against the government without receiving even a mild complaint from the whips; in the eighties a PPS who signed an early-day motion (a fairly unimportant parliamentary device – Iain Macleod used to call EDMs 'graffiti') even slightly hostile to government policy faced immediate dismissal. Thus the government's effective 'payroll vote' was about 130 – a substantial segment of the parliamentary party.[26]

Once a constitutional development has become so pronounced that it is virtually undeniable, one of two things should follow: either reform should be introduced to counteract it, or if the development is desirable or irrevocable it should be recognized and the constitutional rhetoric adjusted. In other words either our system should be made more parliamentary or its plebiscitary nature should be acknowledged. Yet neither has happened. When a referendum is suggested, the government of the day normally responds that such a device would be inappropriate, since we are a parliamentary not a plebiscitary democracy. At the same time it does nothing to strengthen parliament. This situation is of course ideal for the government: as Britain is in theory a parliamentary democracy, referendums are held at bay and the voters kept in their place; and as Britain is in reality a plebiscitary democracy, the government controls parliament and does not reform it. So we remain a plebiscitary democracy – without plebiscites.

Shortly before the 1970 election I wrote to Ted Heath

suggesting that the Conservative manifesto should say that once the Tory government had agreed terms with the EEC it would hold a referendum before joining. I received a friendly but emphatically non-committal reply. Admittedly my argument was mainly electoral: since Harold Wilson and his party were known to be reluctant Europeans, they could always convey the impression to the voters that they would stand out for better terms than Ted Heath would; the best way to outflank Wilson, therefore, was to promise a referendum. But my plea was also based on the idea that unless public opinion favoured entry, any government would have difficulty in taking the country into Europe and keeping it there.

Like Ted Heath, Margaret Thatcher opposed referendums – until she had been deposed. Nevertheless significant constitutional changes should, in my view, be ratified by a referendum. (I think a referendum should probably have been held after Britain signed the Single European Act in 1986.) The point is that either we should take steps to make ourselves more of a parliamentary democracy, which effectively means introducing proportional representation, or we should have more referenda. We could of course have both. Yet no party which does as well as the Conservatives do under the present electoral system can be expected to change it. So that is not, for the present at least, an option.

News Management

What happens in parliament and elsewhere is often less significant than what people think has happened, and their impressions are usually derived from the mass media. Hence the Prime Minister's press secretary is a figure of considerable importance, since he does much to set the tone of the government. Precisely how far, if at all, Britain travelled under Mrs Thatcher towards a presidential form of government is debatable, but Mr (now Sir) Bernard Ingham, who except for the first five months was Mrs Thatcher's press secretary throughout her term, gave the impression that he, at least, thought he was serving in a presidential government. In so doing, he was of course acting fully in accordance with the Prime Minister's desires; otherwise he would not have held his office so long, nor would Mrs Thatcher have been so unstinting in her praise of him.[27]

'I must tell you,' Mr Ingham informed a private IBA dinner, 'that I ... have never regarded the Official Secrets Act as a constraint on my operations. Indeed I regard myself as licensed to break that law as and when I judge it necessary.' The Official Secrets Act of 1911 was so widely drawn that no doubt any press secretary had to break it, but probably none of Ingham's predecessors would have expressed themselves with quite such arrogance, and certainly none of them was given such a wide licence to leak as Mrs Thatcher gave Mr Ingham.[28]

Ingham was permitted to leak differences of opinion that arose in cabinet, and particularly in Mrs Thatcher's first two years he told lobby correspondents (on an unattributable basis of course) stories of the Prime Minister's smashing victories, some of them mythical, over her cabinet colleagues. Through his 'leaks' Ingham played a leading role in Mrs Thatcher's quarrels with her cabinet colleagues.[29]

Thus while Mrs Thatcher was ostensibly defending a colleague on the floor of the House of Commons, Mr Ingham, speaking to lobby correspondents upstairs, might be gloatingly putting the boot into the same man under the protective cloak of anonymity. (Experienced lobby correspondents were well aware that on these occasions it was the monkey not the organ grinder who was expressing the organ grinder's real view.) Francis Pym, John Biffen and Geoffrey Howe, among others, were the targets of this ingenious if unattractive double act. In behaving as he did, the press secretary was not exceeding his brief – if he had done so, he would have been sacked. In short, Ingham, in John Biffen's memorable words, was 'the sewer not the sewage'.[30]

Not surprisingly this peculiar use of the lobby system

offended many members of the lobby – the *Guardian*, the *Independent*, and the *Scotsman* withdrew from Ingham's unattributable briefings – and probably the whole system would have been changed by a lobby vote had not Mrs Thatcher's press-baron allies ordered their employees to support a system which so well suited both them and her.[31]

The Thatcher-and-Ingham act also drew much outside criticism. The Prime Minister's former Lord Chancellor, Lord Hailsham, said that for her to use Bernard Ingham to undermine her colleagues was 'dishonourable conduct towards ministers'. Her former Defence Secretary, Sir John Nott, called Ingham's use of the lobby 'sickening, deplorable and malicious'. Her predecessor as Conservative leader, Ted Heath (whose press secretary had been Sir Donald Maitland, a most distinguished diplomat respected by all journalists) said that the press office at No 10 had been used 'in a way which can be described as corrupt – in a way which went far beyond not only the achievements but even the aspirations of any previous government'.[32]

It was corrupt, not of course in the financial sense but in a more important one. The government news service was subordinated not just to party but to personal advantage. By the abuse of the lobby system which shields the identity of the briefer, the 'news' was being managed and massaged for the benefit of the Prime Minister. Mr Ingham could spread as much poison as she wanted without either ever being called to account for his words.[33]

The Westland crisis nearly brought long overdue nemesis to this double act. Indeed, it would probably have done so if Neil Kinnock, instead of making a long partisan speech, had limited himself to a few straight questions. Mrs Thatcher would then have had no answer, and the downfall that she seems to have more than half expected would probably have followed.[34]

On 3 January 1986 Mrs Thatcher and her staff, annoyed by a provocative letter Michael Heseltine had written to the European Consortium he was assembling to rescue the

Westland Company, and believing it contained inaccuracies, conceived the idea of getting the Solicitor-General, Sir Patrick Mayhew, to study the letter. If he shared their view, he would be invited to write a letter of his own to Heseltine correcting him. The crucial fact about such a letter is that, had it been written and remained private within Whitehall, it would have been useless. Michael Heseltine would have slightly amended his original letter, and that would have been that. In other words, the only point of asking the Solicitor-General to write his letter was so that it could be leaked.[35]

Over the weekend the Solicitor-General studied Heseltine's letter and decided that, on the limited information available to him, one sentence in it did contain 'material inaccuracies'. His letter expressing that view arrived at Heseltine's office on Monday just before lunch. At the same time copies arrived at No 10 and at the office of Leon Brittan, the Trade and Industry Secretary and Heseltine's chief opponent. The letter was received calmly at the Ministry of Defence. Michael Heseltine telephoned Patrick Mayhew saying he would give a detailed response later in the day; when he did so, Mayhew raised no further objections.[36]

In Downing Street and the DTI, however, the letter caused excitement. It was seen as a fine opportunity to discredit Heseltine – but only of course if it was leaked. And the difficulty about leaking it was that there is a firm convention that advice from the law officers to ministers is confidential. All the same the letter was very selectively leaked to the Press Association – only the two words 'material inaccuracies' were quoted – and immediately created a storm. Mrs Thatcher said later that, while she regretted the leak, the letter had to be got into the public domain before Westland held an important press conference at 4.00 pm. But that provided little excuse. Apart from the fact that the letter, if not selectively leaked, was of little importance, the chairman of Westland was in close touch with both the Prime Minister and Leon Brittan throughout the row; Downing Street had no need to use the Press Association to communicate with him.[37]

Furious at the disclosure of their confidential advice, the law officers demanded an inquiry. The Prime Minister had no alternative but to accede, and poor Sir Robert Armstrong, the secretary to the cabinet, had to go through the charade of taking nine days to inquire into a matter which could have been cleared up in less than an hour at Downing Street.[38]

That the information officer at the DTI, Colette Bowe, leaked the Solicitor-General's letter is not at issue. The dispute is over what happened before she called the indispensable Chris Moncreiff at the Press Association. There are three versions. The Ingham version is that Colette Bowe told him on the telephone that 'she had been given ministerial permission to "leak" the Solicitor-General's letter' and that he 'expressed grave reservations' about her doing so. When asked to do the leaking, he refused 'point blank' and told Colette Bowe that he 'had to keep the Prime Minister above that sort of thing'. (In view of what had been going on over the last few years, surely a remarkable claim.) Ingham now regrets, he tells us, that he did not advise Colette Bowe 'to have nothing to do with the ploy itself'. Finally, Ingham says he did not inform Mrs Thatcher 'about the circumstances' (which, in view of their very close relationship, is also surprising).[39]

The second version is that of the Armstrong inquiry, whose verdict was that there was a 'misunderstanding' between the civil servants involved. Sir Robert had a duty to get his ministerial masters out of the nasty hole they had dug for themselves, and 'a misunderstanding' was the only way of avoiding severe censure of either No 10 or the DTI. The solution was therefore as convenient as it was implausible and need not be further considered.[40]

The DTI version is that Bernard Ingham telephoned Colette Bowe, told her that he did not want the leak to come from Downing Street, and ordered her to do it herself by calling Chris Moncreiff. She refused three times, after which, according to one account, Ingham said: 'You will . . . do as you are . . . well told.' (Ingham says that is 'a plain straightforward lie'.) Miss Bowe was still deeply unhappy, and according to the Armstrong Report she 'shared her burden' with Leon Brittan's private secretary. Still unhappy, she then tried to refer the matter to the principal personnel officer and the permanent secretary, but both had gone to lunch. Eventually she rang Chris Moncreiff.[41]

No outside observer can now be certain which version is correct, but the DTI's is overwhelmingly the more probable, since the initiative from No 10 to persuade the Solicitor-General to write his letter must have envisaged a leak, without which the whole exercise was pointless. Secondly, Ingham was closely involved in the Prime Minister's disputes with her colleagues, and to leak a law officer's letter does not appear to be going significantly further than he went in other quarrels. In addition we have Leon Brittan's categorical testimony three years later that the leak was 'approved by Mr Charles Powell, the relevant Private Secretary at Number 10, and it was approved by Mr Bernard Ingham, the Prime Minister's Press Secretary . . . there would have been no question of the leaking of that document without that express approval from Number 10'. That seems conclusive; conversely, while Sir Bernard still sincerely believes that he is in the right, his attempt to blame Colette Bowe seems neither credible nor creditable.[42]

Whatever the truth of the matter, the whole Westland imbroglio was murky and ignominious, and it revealed a remarkable lack of scruple in the conduct of government. Fortunately it marked, as far as we know, the low sleaze mark of the Thatcher administration.[43]

The Press

Bernard Ingham's dealings with the mass media were normally more humdrum. The Thatcherites found most of the Conservative press as easy to control as Conservative backbenchers; their attempts to control the rest of the media were the most conspicuous demonstration of Thatcherism's urge for power, not unmixed with paranoia.

When Mrs Thatcher came into office, Britain had probably the best television in the world and at the popular end of the market probably the worst newspapers. There was nothing outstandingly new about that of course. George Orwell thought 'the English press at normal times [was] deeply dishonest'. He believed the immediate enemies of truthfulness and freedom of thought were the press lords (though he thought the intellectuals' disregard for freedom still more dangerous) and wrote of 'the crooks and charlatans' who owned and ran the press. A little later, at Labour's conference in 1948, Aneurin Bevan said the British was 'the most prostituted press in the world ... pumping a deadly poison into the public mind week by week'.[44]

Yet, compared with what it has been like in recent years, the British press in Orwell's and Bevan's day was virtuous if not quite virginal.[45] The only crook or charlatan to own or run newspapers in the Thatcher era was Robert Maxwell. Unfortunately the papers of his honest and honourable competitors were no better than his; some indeed were worse – notably Lord Stevens's *Star* and Mr Murdoch's *Sun* and *News of the World*. Much of the blame for the plunge in press behaviour (which had tended to improve a little in the fifties and sixties) is usually ascribed to Rupert Murdoch's arrival in Fleet Street, and there seems no reason to dissent from that judgement.*

Yet, whatever damage he did to journalistic standards and to the tone of political debate, Rupert Murdoch did the press and the country a signal service by breaking the monopoly power of the print unions. Union behaviour (abetted by abysmally bad management) in Fleet Street had long epitomized what was worst in British trade unionism:

---

* Other countries were also affected but seem to have been more successful in avoiding infection. In the United States the *Columbia Journalism Review* claimed in 1980 that Murdoch's *New York Post* was 'no longer merely a journalistic problem [but] a social problem – a force for evil'. And Murdoch was stigmatized by the editor of the *New York Times* as 'a bad element practising mean, ugly, violent journalism'.[46]

abuse of power, bloodymindedness, overmanning, corruption, inefficiency and idleness. The print unions had learned nothing from the winter of discontent or the government's trade-union legislation, or even from the recently defeated miners' strike. In Eric Hammond's words 'they believed they were invincible'. Too late, they discovered they were not. Outmanoeuvred by Rupert Murdoch's transfer of his newspapers to Wapping, they still insisted on the sort of deal which they should have known Murdoch would never accept. And when he did not, they resorted to violent picketing to which the police sometimes overreacted. (Eric Hammond was badly kicked by angry printers.) Although many suffered the loss of their job and hardship they did not merit, most of the rank and file of the print workers differed from the miners. They were not 'lions led by donkeys'; they were even greater donkeys than their leaders. The two trade-union leaders most involved saw what was needed but could not persuade their troops.[47]

The result of Murdoch's successful battle of Wapping was that the barriers the print unions had erected against new technology and efficient methods of work were smashed; Murdoch's production costs were halved. Other newspapers followed Murdoch as quickly as their proprietors' less brutal measures allowed, and the successful launch of the *Independent* was made possible.[48]

Murdoch's pop formula differs more in degree than in kind from other bottom-grade tabloids: his papers are cruder, nastier and show even less devotion to the truth than their rivals. The formula is based on what A J Liebling called 'the classic trichotomy — blood, money and the female organ of sex — that made good papyrus copy in Cleopatra's time'; to those ingredients were added, in our time, the royal family, well-rewarded adulation of Mrs Thatcher and jingoism. Thus the Murdoch papers are saturated with sex and sex scandals (true or false) — Murdoch professes himself to be shocked by what he regards as the British obsession with sex compared with puritanical America; but he is evidently not disturbed by his papers ministering to that alleged obsession. An even more important component of the Murdoch formula is the royal family. Rupert Murdoch is a republican, and to see a very rich man making himself even richer by retailing his minions' (often false) stories about the royal family, usually based on fabricated sources ('a close friend of the Royals' etc.), in the confident knowledge that the royal family will not sue for libel, while at the same time some of his papers are seeking to weaken if not destroy the monarchy, makes an arresting if scarcely wholesome spectacle. Extreme right-wing politics naturally gratified the Thatcher regime and was likely to lead to lower taxes which would make Murdoch richer still. The last ingredient of the successful formula – ultra-nationalism – will be familiar to readers of Evelyn Waugh's *Scoop* and is readily defended by Rupert Murdoch: that Britain does not have 'enough bloody pride' is the firmly held view of the patriotic Australian who became an American citizen to enlarge his business empire.[49]

While the British serious papers remained as good as anywhere, the general state of the so-called popular press in the Murdoch and Thatcher era can be gauged from the considered opinion of four people: two newspaper proprietors, an American pop star and a right-wing commentator – not a tribunal that can be said to be stacked against the tabloids. The owner of the *Daily Telegraph*, Conrad Black, one of the big five who controlled 90 per cent of national newspaper circulation in the eighties – the other four being Murdoch, Maxwell and Lords Rothermere and Stevens – thinks 'the London tabloid journalism ranges from the saucy to the completely, dangerously scurrilous, and frankly, far worse than anything I've seen in any other English-speaking place'.[50]

As the only member of the big five with clean hands (he does not own a tabloid), Mr Black had nothing to conceal. Yet the owner of the *Daily Mail*, Lord Rothermere, was no less outspoken. In a bizarre correspondence in the *Financial Times* with one of his own editors who had defended press intrusion into the private lives of the rich and famous, Rothermere pointed out that the logic of his editor's policy was that 'as citizens succeed in this material world, they would be increasingly subject to the obscene inquisition of the currently hypocritical journalism of the sensational press'.[51]

Next, the testimony of a victim of that 'obscene inquisition'. 'Why,' asked Madonna, 'are [the British tabloids] so awful? ... If I talk to them, they twist the words; if I don't, they get me for not doing so. You can't believe to what lengths they go. But what I want to know is – do they believe what they're writing themselves, or do they just have to write it?'[52]

Finally, Mr Paul Johnson maintained in 1991 that standards had continued to fall, trenchantly denounced 'prurient tabloid entertainment', pointed to the need to make 'invasions of privacy liable to civil damages, and, in the worst cases, criminal prosecution' and asked when MPs were going to 'pluck up a bit of courage and end this glaring abuse?'[53]

That very fair question would have been even better addressed to the press lords themselves or to the government. Public distaste, parliamentary clamour and the fear of legislation persuaded the government to set up the Calcutt Committee in 1989. That recommended the appointment of a press complaints commission to give the press one more chance to clean itself up by self-regulation. On top of some very expensive libel actions, the Commission scared the press proprietors into a tactical withdrawal, and some of the tabloids' excesses were curtailed for the time being. But as two tabloid editors sat on the Commission – which was like recruiting the Metropolitan Police from Wormwood Scrubs – it was not an effective body and, as Mr Johnson maintained, press standards did not improve for more than a few months. In general, therefore, those whom Peter Jenkins called 'the lords of the gutter press' did nothing. Self-regulation meant non-regulation. 'As long as people are making very large sums of money out of peddling rubbish,' the editor of the *Daily Telegraph*, Max Hastings, pointed out, 'it seems reasonable to assume that they will go on peddling rubbish as long as they are allowed to.'[54]

The press barons' failure to act was therefore as predictable as it was inexcusable. But what of the government? Mrs Thatcher's ambition was to 'change hearts and minds';* only by doing so could she achieve the country's transformation that she saw as her mission. She was determined that the nation's children should be taught what she regarded as the proper things. She was similarly determined that television should not debase young, or even old, minds by the exhibition of violence and other undesirable traits. She even (very mis-guidedly) intervened to stop government funding of a national study of sexual behaviour – badly needed because of AIDS – on the grounds that it would be too intrusive. Yet not only did she take no action to improve some of the worst and most intrusive newspapers in the world, she remained silent on the subject; and silence was for the Prime Minister not a normal condition.[55]

The solution to the problem of why Mrs Thatcher's reforming zeal was directed against virtually every facet of British life, save the part most in need of it, is simple. Except those of Robert Maxwell, all the papers that most offended truth and decency were owned by her vehement admirers and consistently gave her strident support. The sins of the Murdoch, Stevens and Rothermere press were thus more than atoned for by the cleansing fact that they were all 'one of us'. They were

> Born to be sav'd, even in their own despight;
> Because they could not help believing right![56]

Their Thatcherite zeal not only exempted the tabloids from reform or punishment, it made them eligible for rewards. When in 1980 Rupert Murdoch wanted to buy *The Times* and *The Sunday Times* his bid (because *The Sunday Times* was 'a highly profitable newspaper') should have been referred

* See chapter VII above.

to the Monopolies Commission. It was not, with the result that Murdoch gained control of more than a third of the circulation of British national newspapers – an unhealthily high proportion even if he had been likely to exert a benign influence on British journalism and politics.[57]

What should be done about the British press? A law giving a right to privacy is perfectly feasible and long overdue; a right of reply is more debatable, though France and Germany have operated one for many years without great difficulty.[58] For both libel and privacy cases it should be possible to lay down that, provided the judge ruled that the action was a serious one, press proprietors as well as editors had to submit themselves to cross examination by the plaintiff. That would probably do more than anything else to clean up the press.*

Other countries restrict the ownership of newspapers to citizens and residents of their own country. Such a requirement (which has been advocated by, among others, Auberon Waugh and the avidly Thatcherite columnist, Sir John Junor) should be introduced here. After all we do not allow foreign citizens or residents of other countries to sit in parliament; similarly there is no reason why we should allow far more powerful men whose primary interest is in the affairs of other countries to wield power and influence in Britain. Finally there should be stronger restrictions on cross-ownership of

---

* As owner and editor of the *Spectator* I had to give evidence in the libel action that Aneurin Bevan, R H S Crossman and Morgan Phillips brought against the paper in 1957. It was an unpleasant experience, though untypical of such cases in two respects. Firstly the Lord Chief Justice, who disliked the *Spectator*'s opposition to capital punishment, displayed blatant bias. More importantly, the behaviour of the plaintiffs, whose perjury was later admitted, was also, one hopes, unusual. In a much earlier case, an English judge, exasperated by an Irish witness, who was clearly perjuring himself, asked him, 'what happens in your country when witnesses commit perjury?' 'Well, my Lord,' replied the Irishman, 'I think their side usually wins.' In the *Spectator* case their side did indeed win.[60]

television and newspapers; in the US the rules are stricter than here.[59]

Even an admirer of our popular papers, if such an improbable figure can be imagined, could scarcely be proud of their performance in election campaigns. David Butler was 'appalled, when as a matter of duty' he read all the popular papers during the 1987 election. Writing of the 1992 election in the *New York Times* Anthony Lewis, one of the most respected columnists, wrote that British journalism was 'of a kind now hardly known in the United States: grotesquely partisan, shamelessly advancing one party's cause. And almost all of it is pro-Conservative.'[61] Indeed, many of the so-called news stories in the tabloids during the election would still have been considered 'grotesquely partisan' if they had been printed as leading articles.

The extent to which newspapers in general and the tabloids in particular influence their readers at election and other times is problematic. Certainly the press is widely distrusted, and most people take their news from television. Nevertheless it seems unlikely that the incessant Thatcherite propaganda of the tabloid press did not have considerable effect, especially on the minds of people who read only one paper. When he was British ambassador in Franco's Spain during the war, Lord Templewood noticed even on himself the effect of press 'propaganda . . . the unchecked stream of violent abuse and tendentious lies' although he knew all of it to be untrue. Certainly the controllers of the tabloids must believe that what they say affects their readers' opinions and votes. Otherwise, presumably, they would find it less trouble to tell the truth.[62]

The Attack on the Intermediate Institutions

Guided by much its most important element – the Prime Minister herself – this was the apparatus for the achievement of Thatcherite objectives, most of which have been considered earlier in this book. If, as has just been seen, there was little that was liberal about Thatcherite means, there was less that was Conservative about Thatcherite ends. In practice, of course, means and ends were intermingled. Of the two grand Thatcherite objectives, the continuance of Thatcherite rule was at the same time both an end in itself and a means to the second objective: the extension of 'freedom' by the creation of an enterprise culture and a free-market state.

Although this second objective was certainly an aspiration and was a major element in Thatcherite ideology, there was no overall strategy to achieve it. Instead of a pre-meditated war, there was a series of tactical battles. No master plan was drawn up to wreck Britain's intermediate institutions; the various attacks on them were usually the result of their opposition either to Thatcherism in general or to some particular Thatcherite aim. The offensive against the professions – a vital element in a modern civilized state – was more ideological, but in its implementation it, too, was often more tactical than strategic.[63]

Montesquieu was probably the first modern writer to stress the importance of intermediate bodies between rulers and ruled. Burke soon followed. 'The perennial existence of bodies corporate and their fortunes,' he wrote in 1790, 'are things particularly suited to a man who has long views. Liberty was what distinguished the British constitution, but liberty must "be ascertained by wise laws, and secured by well constructed institutions".'[64]

There is nothing simple, Burke stressed, about the foundations of liberty. They are not to be found merely in the individual or in the state, but in a complex assortment of historic rights, laws, traditions, political institutions and corporations. It is these buffers between the individual and the state which preserve liberty by preventing a direct confrontation between them. When they are swept away, tyranny or anarchy follows. Conservative writers from Burke and de Tocqueville to Oakeshott have stressed the vital importance of barriers between state and citizens. So Thatcherism's frank hostility to intermediate institutions was another deep break with the Conservative tradition.[65]

Some advocates of 'pluralism' merely assume that the widest distribution of power enhances the democratic nature of the state. The Conservative attachment to intermediate institutions is more selective. Conservatives recognize that such bodies should not necessarily be applauded regardless of their intentions and activities. As in the case of the trade unions, they are capable of growing too powerful, and when this happens they need to be curbed, as they were by Mrs Thatcher. Yet when a government endangers the freedom of the individual, such collective groupings provide an essential first line of resistance.

The Monarchy and the Church

The monarchy's position above politics usually kept it out of the firing line. True, the Duke of Edinburgh chaired a committee which recommended the abolition of mortgage income-tax relief, and the Queen's view of the Commonwealth was plainly very different from the Prime Minister's.* Occasionally the Thatcherite press tried to make trouble between Buckingham Palace and Downing Street. Some of the New Right waged 'a deliberate campaign,' wrote Peregrine Worsthorne, 'to disparage all the institutions of Britain that pre-date the ascendancy of the new entrepreneurs'. No doubt many of the New Right dreamed of the day when Great Britain plc was presided over by Lord Chalfont or Lord Wyatt of Weeford, not the House of Windsor. But although

---

* Mrs Thatcher herself sometimes betrayed monarchical tendencies: her haste to arrive at the scene of disasters and convey her sympathy to the victims suggested some confusion of roles. That confusion was not always limited to what was irreverently called her 'ambulance-chasing'. The Prime Minister's taking of the salute at the victory parade after the Falklands war was monarchical, and the late David Watt wrote in *The Times* of her journey to the Falkland Islands that 'the constant references to her troops . . . proclaim this is a royal visit'.[68]

the Prime Minister may have regarded her visits to the Queen as 'largely a waste of time', the proprieties were preserved, except by the press, and Mrs Thatcher herself was said to be a fervent monarchist.[66]

The Church of England enjoyed no such immunity from attack. Ever since 1980, when Dr Runcie's enthronement sermon as Archbishop of Canterbury showed him to be a humane moderate, he was suspect to the right. The Falklands Thanksgiving Service changed suspicion into hostility. Instead of giving a jingoistic address suitable for quotation on political platforms or at regimental dinners, the Archbishop went so far as to treat the service as a religious occasion, preaching on the need for reconciliation and peace. That affront was then aggravated by the Church's report on the inner cities, which suggested that the government was neglecting the problem. As Thatcherism divided the country, the Church tried to hold it together.[67]

Clearly the Church, indeed all the churches, had to be put in their place, which was one of junior subaltern to the central government. That was not all. Like so many people who found Thatcherism uncongenial, the churches were evidently in a state of invincible ignorance; to remedy it, in an era of large take-over bids, the most spectacular bid of the lot was the attempted Thatcherite take-over of Christianity. Both to ensure the churches' due subordination and to ensure the supremacy of the new cultural values, Christianity had to be remoulded. The churches, it turned out, had for centuries been in fundamental error, failing to realize that instead of Christianity being about helping sinners, the poor, the weak, the old and the infirm, it was about capitalism and the creation of wealth. Almost the only biblical quotation in Mrs Thatcher's celebrated 'Sermon on the Mound' at Edinburgh to the General Assembly of the Church of Scotland was St Paul's remark that 'if a man will not work he shall not eat'.* The Parable of the Good Samaritan

---

* In the next verse St Paul goes on to complain of 'busybodies'.

had been widely misunderstood; its point was not that the Samaritan had charitably helped the needy but that if he had not been a successful entrepreneur he would not have had the two pence in his pocket that enabled him to do so.[69]

John Wesley was the Thatcherite model. That good high Tory, said Mrs Thatcher, 'inculcated the work ethic and duty. You got on by your own efforts.' As a former Methodist, Mrs Thatcher might have known better. Wesley was far from being a prophet of capitalism. Having provided things 'needful for yourself and your household', you should, he thought, give away the rest to the poor, which he himself did; burying your money in the Bank of England was like throwing it out to sea. Wesley also firmly believed that the burden of taxation should be borne by the rich not the poor. Worse still, he would endeavour 'to show,' he said, 'that Christianity is essentially a social religion; and that to turn it into a solitary religion is indeed to destroy it'. Finally – horror of horrors – Wesley in the 1740s was not only what Norman Tebbit calls a pinko, but a red: he wanted to establish a kind of religious communism.[70]

None of that signified, however. Ignorance is an aid to dogma, and Wesley was enlisted as a proto-Thatcherite. Much as the Queen is the Supreme Governor of the Church of England, Mrs Thatcher was the Supreme Head of the Free-Market Church Militant, and the Christian sects had no business meddling in its affairs. Despite John Wesley, Christianity was essentially a solitary religion. So, along with much else, religion was privatized. Morals and the next world were the churches' only legitimate business – and even in that limited sphere they were, in the Thatcherite view, highly inefficient.[71]

Like the churches the universities were heretics to Thatcherism, and like them they interfered with matters well beyond their proper concern. Whatever the universities might have the presumption to think, they were not there to provide a cool critique of society nor to decide what is knowledge and how it should be extended. That was the job of the state and the market. Hence a pretentious élite like university teachers needed to be cut down to size; even more than the churches, the universities were attacked with the results that we have seen. In the thirties Ortega y Gasset wrote that if the universities gave up or were crippled, their role would be taken up by the media. That would have been an outcome fully agreeable to Thatcherism.[72]

The Judiciary and the Law

The Thatcherites made no attack on the judiciary; they had no need to. The judges were lambs under the throne. The Law Lords eventually came to the right decision on the *Spycatcher* case, but only after it had become clear to virtually everybody except the government that the government's case was untenable.[73]

Most people agreed that the secret services should be kept secret, that *Spycatcher* was a shocking book, written out of greed and malice, and that the government was fully justified in its original attempts in the early eighties to prevent Peter Wright from publishing it, even though it had not tried to stop the publication of a similar book by Chapman Pincher whose main source was Peter Wright. Yet the people the British government should be primarily concerned to keep in the dark about the secrets of the secret service are not the British but the nation's enemies (who in the years 1986 to 1988 were still thought to be chiefly the Soviet Union); and long after the Soviet secret service had learned everything it wanted from *Spycatcher* by reading the Australian newspapers or buying the book in America, the government continued to try to stop anything about it being published in this country.[74]

For a long time it succeeded in doing so through the co-operation of the judges. The government resorted to an indiscriminate use of injunctions to stop newspapers publishing what the government did not want them to. This was a reversion to the position that prevailed before the Licensing Act came to an end in 1695: prior restraints on publication, something which is quite unacceptable in a free society, at least in peacetime.[75]

As late as July 1987 a majority of the Law Lords upheld the government's case and allowed the continuance of the injunctions. 'I can see nothing whatever,' Lord Bridge of Harwich said in his powerful dissenting judgment, 'either in law or on the merits, to be said for the maintenance of a total ban on discussion in the press of this country of matters of considerable public interest and concern which the rest of the world now knows all about and can discuss freely.' Lord Bridge went on to express the hope that the government would recognize that its 'wafer-thin victory' had been gained at a price which 'no government committed to upholding the values of a free society [could] afford to pay'.[76]

Yet why did it ever get even a wafer-thin victory? The government could fairly say that it had only asked for injunctions; the courts had granted them. And even if it should be no part of a government's job to persuade the judiciary to make asses of themselves, the judges did not have to comply. Writing in *The Times*, Lord Scarman pointed out that Lord Oliver (the other dissentient) had convincingly shown that there was in law 'no arguable case at all' for a continuance of the injunctions.[77]

In a still more famous dissenting judgment – in the case of Liversidge v Anderson in 1941 – Lord Atkin said he had 'listened to arguments which might have been addressed acceptably to the Court of King's Bench in the time of Charles I', and he complained of judges showing themselves 'more executive minded than the executive'. In the many *Spycatcher* hearings the judges, with some glittering exceptions, cravenly accepted similar arguments.[78]

Only in October 1988 did the House of Lords finally decide, in the words of Lord Griffiths, that if the law was what the government said it was, 'then the law would indeed be an ass, for it would seek to deny to our own citizens the right to be informed of matters which are freely available throughout the rest of the world and would in fact be seeking in vain because anyone who really wished to read *Spycatcher* can lay his hands on a copy in this country'. At last the law had caught up with life.[79]

The judges' sorry performance over *Spycatcher* lowered the prestige of the legal profession, as did the Court of Appeal's inexplicable reluctance to put right a series of miscarriages of justice which were widely recognized as such, long before the Court of Appeal was prepared to agree. As a result, people were less ready to listen to the bar and the judges when they objected in 1989 to the government's Green Paper on proposals for law reform, especially as the language and complaints of the Lord Chief Justice and others were grotesquely overblown.

That was a pity, because the Green Paper represented, as Lord Beloff and Michael Beloff QC pointed out, 'a new twist in the attempt by Whitehall departments to control the independent and corporate bodies which have been the foundation of English liberties'. It was, they added, the same sort of thing that was being done to the universities.[80]

Of course the professions can not be immune to democratic or governmental scrutiny. (The legal profession had recently been the subject of a Royal Commission.) All the same 'the existence of independent and learned professions,' wrote Lord Hailsham of an earlier Green Paper, 'is one of the hallmarks and glories of a free society.' Certainly the professions have played a vital role in the development of a free British society over the last three centuries. And self-government has been their hallmark – something that has historically appealed to Conservatives. Yet to Thatcherism the learned professions were just another bunch of small businesses – and if they were not, they should be forced to conform to that stereotype, however inappropriate an injection of Manchester or Grantham liberalism might be for their particular conditions of work. For the Thatcherites to think that the learned professions were uncompetitive showed an extraordinary misunderstanding – the English bar is probably one of the most competitive arenas in the world.[81]

The government's proposals to increase 'competition' in the law would merely make litigation more expensive, while the introduction of American-style contingency fees (i.e. a litigant pays his lawyer only if he wins), would be an invitation to corruption. On what was most needed, which was properly within the government's power – the improvement of legal aid – there was, as Lord Alexander QC pointed out, 'a deafening silence'. But that of course would have cost the government money, which was needed for cuts in income tax.[82]

The professions, as Lord Hailsham wrote, are 'an essential but separate component of contemporary Western and democratic culture', and any attempt to impose upon them 'a crude and ideological framework in the interests of competition [would] undermine the independence and vigour of a particularly valuable element in a free society'. The government's attitude to the professions exhibited yet again the centralizing tendencies of Thatcherism. Nevertheless, partly because, after initial mistakes, they were intelligently defended, the learned professions got off more lightly than the broadcasting organizations.[83]*

Television

Any charitable suspicion that the Thatcherite refusal to civilize the tabloid press might have sprung from a reluctance to interfere with freedom of speech was dispelled by the government's treatment of broadcasting. Whether its attack on British institutions and the professions was more the result of Thatcherite ideology or of its appetite for power is impossible to determine. The two overlapped, and the BBC stood in the way of both. As a public body the BBC was not properly subject to the market and was a 'socialist' institution, believed

---

* The French revolutionary constitution of 1791 decreed the abolition of every kind of corporation: 'The national Assembly abolishes irrevocably all institutions which have been injurious to liberty and equality of rights . . . There are no longer any guilds, or corporations of professions, of arts or of trades.'[84]

to be unreceptive to Thatcherism. Not surprisingly therefore, Thatcherites from the start regarded it with deep hostility and suspicion. Norman Tebbit later described the corporation as 'a sunset home for the insufferable, smug, sanctimonious, naive, guilt-ridden, weak and pink'.[85]*

Yet during the first Thatcher government the BBC was fairly well protected by the Home Secretary, William Whitelaw. Having dealt with broadcasting matters when opposition chief whip in the 1960s, he had found himself treated fairly by the BBC and 'could never agree with those, certainly a majority in my own party, who consistently believed that the BBC was wholly biased against Conservative governments'. In consequence he sought 'the maximum independence of the BBC from government and party political interference' – a very unThatcherite attitude, but then, for all his unswerving loyalty to the Prime Minister, Willie Whitelaw was never a Thatcherite.[86]

Whitelaw's recollections of his years in opposition were especially relevant, since the attitudes of Mrs Thatcher and her court and those of Harold Wilson and his retinue were almost identical. Paranoia about the BBC was rampant in Downing Street in both the sixties and the eighties.† Just as

---

* This was the sort of thing Senator Joe McCarthy used to say about the US State Department and exhibits the same kind of intellectual Poujadism. Intellectual Poujadism I take to mean right-wing envy and scorn of intellectuals and institutions whose primary purpose is not the making of money. Hence the Thatcherite dislike of the universities.

† To be fair, the paranoia in the sixties was not confined to Downing Street. It infected both Conservative leaders and fairly obscure backbenchers. In the six months before the 1970 election Iain Macleod refused to appear on the BBC 'because of its sustained hostility to the Conservative Party', though that may have been a pre-emptive strike. And I apparently – I say 'apparently' because the useful censorship of selective memory has obliterated any recollection of the incident from my mind – made an utterly moronic speech, claiming that Wilson's anger with the BBC was really a smokescreen to hide the Corporation's left-wing leanings. No wonder H L Mencken thought that 'honest autobiography is a contradiction in terms'.[87]

(the later very left-wing) Tony Benn in the sixties favoured the BBC being forced to take advertising, so in the eighties that was a Thatcherite article of faith. Mrs Thatcher's mouthpiece, Bernard Ingham, told the BBC's Director General with his usual courtesy, 'Just take advertising on Radios One and Two, and don't argue.' In 1984 the government set up the Peacock Committee to stop the BBC arguing, but guided by the weight of evidence the Committee, like the BBC, rejected the idea.[88]

In the sixties Benn thought broadcasting was 'really too important to be left to the broadcasters'; in the eighties it never occurred to Mrs Thatcher to leave it to them. Harold Wilson held up ITV to the BBC as a model of impartiality, so – initially – did the Thatcherites. Both the Wilson and the Thatcher governments used the threat of reduced revenue to try to bring the BBC into line. Just as Wilson politicized the BBC's Board of Governors, so did Mrs Thatcher – only more so. Just as Harold Wilson set up a unit to monitor the BBC's political coverage and to detect anti-Labour bias, so Norman Tebbit set up a unit to monitor the BBC's pro-Labour bias.[89]

In one respect Tebbbit's campaign against the BBC went further than Harold Wilson's ever did. He submitted a dossier of complaints about the BBC's 'misleading and unbalanced' coverage of the American bombing of Libya. Unfortunately the 'analysis' was an inaccurate and trivial propagandist compilation which identified impartiality with what Conservative central office would like the BBC to have said. Not surprisingly, though to the disappointment of Norman Tebbit, those who had compiled and vouched for the dossier preferred to remain anonymous. Even Bernard Ingham, seeing the weakness of the complaint, distanced the government from it. The BBC had no difficulty in shooting it to pieces.[90]

The crucial difference between the position in the sixties and the eighties was that Mr Wilson had some slight excuse for his paranoia, in that after his first few months he had most of the press strongly against him, whereas Mrs Thatcher always had the press predominantly and aggressively on her side. The managing director of BBC Television put it well: 'It was President de Gaulle who said: "They have the newspapers. I have television." Why should Mrs Thatcher have both Fleet Street and the BBC?' Montesquieu could have given him the answer: the possession of great power does not satisfy; it merely whets the appetite for more.[91]

Yet if Norman Tebbit's attack on the BBC over the Libyan bombing was a failure, his general campaign of intimidation was, as he well realized, more successful. The government's softening-up of the BBC had of course begun well before Tebbit's arrival at central office; indeed the BBC was under pressure even when it was still being largely protected by Willie Whitelaw. As early as 1979 Mrs Thatcher had grimly pronounced that 'the Home Secretary and I think it is time the BBC put its own house in order' – which meant doing what it was told by the government. In some of the rows the BBC was at fault, but the main difficulty was that the Prime Minister and Bernard Ingham regarded themselves as the BBC's absentee editors-in-chief who had a far better understanding of what should and should not be broadcast than did the wets, pinkos and socialists who actually ran the Corporation.[92]

Both Northern Ireland and the Falkland campaign caused trouble between the BBC and the government, but it was only in her second term, when Leon Brittan had succeeded Whitelaw, that Mrs Thatcher went far beyond any of her predecessors in the war that she waged against Britain's supposedly independent television authorities. Soon after the defeat of the miners, the BBC became the chief 'enemy within'. War was declared over a BBC film about Northern Ireland, *Real Lives*. Normally the Thatcherite press danced to the tune of the government; this time the government danced to the tune of its press. After a *Sunday Times* question to the Prime Minister and the subsequent story, Leon Brittan, acting on what he assumed were Mrs Thatcher's wishes, wrote a public letter to the chairman of the Corporation asking him to prevent the programme being broadcast. (Noel Annan, who had chaired a commission on broadcasting, compared the Home Secretary to both 'a demented poodle' and 'a charging rhinoceros'; presumably he meant Leon Brittan was being a poodle to Mrs Thatcher and a rhinoceros to the BBC.) Most unusually the BBC's governors – by that time a body that had been heavily packed politically (nominees likely to show independence were rejected) – decided to watch the programme and, against the advice of their managers, prohibited it. In other words the governors acted as the government's censors. The full extent of their unbecoming docility was unkindly revealed a few months later when the programme was broadcast, with only one cosmetic change, and shown to be innocuous.[93]

In 1987 the Ministry of Defence prevented the screening of a film about the second Zircon spy-satellite project on security grounds. That may well have been defensible. What followed, however, was not. The flat of the left-wing journalist who had made the programme was searched together with the offices of the *New Statesman*. This Soviet-style behaviour was followed by a similar descent on the Scottish office of the BBC. The first two search warrants were successfully challenged by the Corporation; the third was allowed though it, too, was probably invalid. To the benefit of Glasgow's criminals, the CID was diverted to stripping the BBC's offices and taking away three vanloads of filing cabinets, including documents to which they were not entitled. This sinister incident was described, not unfairly, by the BBC's assistant director general as 'a shabby, shameful state-sponsored incursion into a journalistic establishment'. The former Home Secretary, Roy Jenkins, wondered 'for what supremely important reason the government was prepared to look as though they were running a second-rate police state, infused equally with illiberalism and incompetence'. That there were no reasons other than pique and the corruption of power was demonstrated by subsequent events. No charges were ever brought, and the film was shown two years later with no damage to the state's security.[94]

The government claimed that the police's entry into the furniture-removal business had had nothing to do with any minister. Even if that claim were true, it was barely relevant. The police would never have behaved in such an overbearing manner had they not known that they were acting on behalf of a notably illiberal government which would certainly approve. Meanwhile the chairman and the deputy chairman of the BBC had similarly responded to the government's hopes, though not its orders, by dismissing Alasdair Milne, the director general; he had never been 'one of us'. This was the first (and we must hope the last) time the BBC's director general had been dismissed in such a way.[95]

All this had, as was intended, a considerable effect on the BBC. Morale crumbled, and the BBC became more cowed. I have never been among the Corporation's warmest admirers, and it makes a large number of avoidable mistakes. But like it or not, the BBC as an independent body has enormous prestige abroad for the very reason that it is believed to be independent, and to anybody who favours a plural society it is of immense value at home. The government's attempt to destroy the BBC's independence therefore was, like the Thatcherite attack on the universities, sheer vandalism.[96]

Like Harold Wilson, Mrs Thatcher long upheld ITV as a model of objectivity (i.e. cooperation) that the BBC should follow. But then, unaccountably, instead of the BBC becoming like ITV, ITV became like the BBC: it started to broadcast programmes inconvenient to the government. In the light of what had happened to the BBC, that was an admirable but, like Oxford University's refusal of a degree to Mrs Thatcher, a foolhardy decision.

The main cause of the transformation of ITV from 'one of us' to yet another 'enemy within' was *Death on the Rock*, Thames Television's programme about the SAS's shooting of three IRA terrorists in Gibraltar on 6 March 1988. True to form, the Thatcherites tried to prevent the programme being shown. Mrs Thatcher alleged that it prejudiced 'the rule of law', a claim ridiculed by Lord Scarman who pointed out that there was not going to be even a public inquiry, let alone a trial, in Britain. And Conservative backbenchers provided their customary rhubarb about the media 'providing gratuitous support for acts of terrorism' and the programme being a 'stab in the back for the nation'.[97]

In view of the outcry by the government and the government press, followed by the verdict of the inquest in Gibraltar that the killings had been lawful, Thames Television set up an inquiry under Lord Windlesham, a former leader of the House of Lords, assisted by Richard Rampton QC. After months of careful investigation, they vindicated the programme. It had not violated the due impartiality requirement of the 1981 Broadcasting Act, and it was 'trenchant and avoided triviality', a view that was widely held elsewhere, the film winning the BAFTA and Broadcasting Press Guild awards for the best single documentary. David Windlesham and Mr Rampton were men of unquestionable integrity, which after Westland was rather more than could be said for some of the programme's traducers. Yet Mrs Thatcher summarily dismissed such an inconvenient expert judgement, clinging to her own view, in defiance of the evidence, that the programme's many 'inaccuracies' demonstrated a conscious failure 'to pursue the truth'.[98]

That effectively was the end of ITV as it had been known since its inception in 1955. If Independent Television was not going to do what it was told, it had to be changed to make it amenable. In a speech to the Press Association in June 1988, the Prime Minister had announced that the way forward was more channels because 'the free movement and expression of ideas is guaranteed far better by numbers and variety than it ever can be by charters and specific statutes'. Superficially that was odd, since the objective of the government had been to inhibit the free expression of ideas on television, while the charters and statutes to which Mrs Thatcher objected sought to preserve free expression. But the oddness was only superficial. A multiplicity of channels as in America, allegedly providing choice but in reality providing fifty-seven varieties of the same trivia, would achieve the Thatcherite objective: the neutering of television as a forum for political ideas independent of the agenda set by Downing Street.[99]

The ensuing White Paper duly extended the Thatcherite supermarket philosophy to television. The ITV franchises for 1992 would be awarded to the highest bidder; there was to be no requirement of quality; money was all. Nor was the BBC forgotten. The licence fee was to be frozen or reduced from 1991, and the night hours on one BBC channel were to be 'sold for use to provide new services by the highest bidder'.[100]

Seldom has a government document been received with such dismissive scorn. Writing in *The Sunday Times*, Simon Jenkins, a member of the Peacock Committee and the future editor of *The Times*, assumed that its title *Competition, Choice and Quality* was 'satirically' intended and designated the White Paper 'a monument to political revenge'. In the *Independent* Peter Jenkins thought the White Paper revealed 'no vision capable of rising above the privatised gasometer'; it was 'a fourth form answer'. George Walden MP thought every word of the title was 'palpably false' and almost everything about its contents was 'bogus'. How had such an absurdity been inflicted on the government and, more important, upon television and the country? 'Ministers, baffled at how to assuage Margaret Thatcher's rage,' wrote Simon Jenkins, had 'simply unleashed the Treasury to tax television into the oblivion of pap.'[101]

The television authorities took no comfort, however, from this derision, realizing correctly that absurdity was no longer an obstacle to proposals becoming law. Hence the immediate results were all that Mrs Thatcher could have hoped for. Faced with the prospect of an auction for their franchise, ITV companies naturally stopped spending money on the more expensive programmes. That was all to the good, since it was expensive documentaries that were likely to put forward views not wholly in accordance with Thatcherite orthodoxy. More generally, both ITV and the BBC became more concerned to keep their heads down and to do nothing to offend the great editor-in-chief in Downing Street.[102]

The ensuing Television Act, like the White Paper, was, as she later admitted, very much Mrs Thatcher's baby. As was mentioned earlier, the original bill was made rather better by David Mellor (and by pressure from the future head of the new body, George Russel) at the committee stage, but the results of the bill were still woeful. Central Television and Scotland got their franchises renewed for £2,000 each, while Yorkshire had to pay £37 million. The Treasury ended up very little richer. Thames Television, the primary target, lost its franchise.[103]

Such was the outcome of the politics of revenge and reward. The BBC and Independent Television were both maimed. On the other hand the gutter press prospered. Mrs Thatcher said she would 'strain everything to prevent our young people from some of the violence and pornography that they would otherwise see'. As we have seen, however, her straining was confined to television. The only straining over the tabloid press was to do their owners favours. The owner of Sky (Murdoch) and other satellite channels were absolved from rules against cross-ownership with newspapers. Further, the prohibition against a television organization being allowed to buy exclusive rights to show certain major sporting events was relaxed. The way was opened for Sky Television to buy up such events, make people buy an ugly and expensive satellite dish for the privilege of seeing them, and later, no doubt, charge them for doing so. To non-Thatcherites that was just another benefaction to Rupert Murdoch, enabling him or some other tycoon to acquire monopoly rights and hold up everybody else for ransom; to Thatcherites, on the other hand, it was a model of how to 'roll back the frontiers of socialism [and] roll forward the frontiers of freedom'.[104]

Since no money changed hands, there was nothing strictly corrupt in any of this. The situation was not the same as in the days of Sir Robert Walpole, of which Swift wrote,

> A Pamphlet in Sir Bob's Defence
> Will never fail to bring in pence;
> Nor be concerned about the Sale,
> He pays his Workmen on the Nail.

Yet we may well doubt if any of it would have happened if Mr Murdoch and his confrères had been leading the Hallelujah Chorus for Neil Kinnock. As Swift put it,

> From Party-Merit seek Support;
> The Vilest Verse thrives best at Court.[105]

Local Government

The most damaging of the Thatcherite offensives against what de Tocqueville called 'secondary powers' was the relentless campaign against local government. Since Conservatives naturally savour a diffusion of power – an old idea, now fashionable under the name of subsidiarity – and oppose its concentration at the centre (hence their hostility to socialism), they have traditionally believed, with Salisbury, that local government is 'a very good thing ... it gets rid of the harshness and unbending woodenness which is the character of all governments which are directed exclusively from the centre'. Earlier, in the same vein, Disraeli had said that 'centralization [was] the death blow of public freedom'.[106]

Here, as so often elsewhere, Thatcherism was at direct variance with the Conservative tradition and also, more unusually, with the Liberal tradition. John Stuart Mill favoured local government; Hayek, too, agreed with Disraeli that decentralization was an aid to liberty and with Salisbury that – where private initiative could not be relied upon – action by local government was likely to be less coercive than action from the centre; he thought the possibility that people might change their residences made it necessary for 'local authorities to provide as good services at as reasonable costs as their competitors'.[107]*

---

* Giving a socialist view, Sidney Webb welcomed local diversity because 'those who did not like the arrangements of Hampstead would always be able to move to Highgate'.[108]

The assault on local government had diverse origins. The Conservative manifesto for the second 1974 election promised to 'abolish the domestic rating system and replace it by taxes more broadly based and related to people's ability to pay'. It also promised to reduce the mortgage-interest rate to 9.5 per cent and to keep it there. These proposals emanated from Ted Heath, who had been urged by the Canadian prime minister to embrace more popular policies, and from the Conservative research department of which I was then chairman.[109]

They prompted Paul Johnson – shortly to embark on his startlingly speedy voyage from the far barmy left to the far splenetic right – to accuse Mrs Thatcher, the shadow Environment Minister, of making 'cavalier spending promises' in contrast to 'the austere Powellism of Keith Joseph'. In fact, far from their being Mrs Thatcher's own promises, she disliked them and made a well-justified complaint to me that she had not been adequately consulted. Nevertheless she propounded them in public with great spirit and skill. I wrote to congratulate her on a superb election broadcast on the subject – something I have never done to anybody else before or since.[110]

Evidently, indeed, her advocacy was so persuasive that she convinced herself. 'Hailsham's law' lays down that a defeated party is not bound to stick to policies which the electorate has (notionally) rejected. That, after all, is common sense, and it seems all the more appropriate when a party changes its leader. Over mortgage interest Hailsham's law was quickly applied, but over rates it was spectacularly overthrown. Despite having been strongly opposed to the policy, Margaret Thatcher was not only converted to it, but abolition of the rates became one of her most pressing ambitions – a massive misfortune for local authorities. Local-government finance became a matter of considerable interest to the party leader, and if she could not immediately abolish the rates – the 1979 manifesto said that reduction in income tax must have priority – she continually sought ways of bullying local authorities into limiting them.

The second major cause of the attack on local government

Dancing With Dogma

similarly dated from before 1979 and was not derived from Thatcherism. It had become a firmly held Treasury view that the control of local government spending was necessary to achieve macroeconomic balance and stability; otherwise, excessive local authority spending, the Treasury maintained, would cause inflation, crowd out private investment and damage the government's monetary policy. Thatcherites embraced this Treasury view with as much alacrity as they had adopted the Conservative research department's project of abolishing the rates. Unfortunately, like the famous inter-war 'Treasury view' that no additional employment could be created by state borrowing since such public investment would crowd out private investment, the new Treasury view of the need for strict control of local-government spending to preserve economic stability was largely erroneous.[111]

The third major reason was the Thatcherite dislike of opposition. As we have seen, intermediate institutions were despised and disliked because they got in the way of 'free-market forces', interposed themselves between the electorate and the government and were liable to disagree with Thatcherite policies. These objections were particularly applicable to local government, much of which, as usually happens in Britain, was controlled by the opposition party. Since Labour's heavy defeats in 1968 and 1969, the party had become much more left wing in London and most big cities; and it was a major part of the Thatcherite mission to bury 'socialism' locally as well as nationally.[112]

A fourth reason arose from the unsettled state of local government. As long ago as 1963 Professor William Robson wrote a book entitled *Local Government in Crisis*, and six years later an observer described local government as 'the sick man of England', while conceding that the sickness was not specifically British – there were few countries whose system of local government was not markedly inferior to their central political system. In 1979 British local government was healthier, but through no fault of its own it was far from being a well-designed system in perfect working order. Hence the

Thatcherites could legitimately think that they should improve it. And, rather like their treatment of the economy, their very hostility to local government, while inflicting much damage, did make many local authorities more efficient, and also more considerate of their electorates. Their drastic shake-up of the local-government bureaucracy was in many places valuable and badly needed.[113]

The initial Thatcherite assault on local government spending stemmed, however, from the government's obsession with reducing public expenditure. Contrary to the Thatcherite myth, local authority spending, like the rest of government spending, was not out of control in 1979, having in the four previous years twice fallen below Whitehall's target; in the other two years it had been 0.3 and 1.7 per cent above it. There was a complicated relationship between Whitehall and local authorities, and the government had various means of controlling public spending. The government set the level of rate support grant which in 1979 accounted for well over half of local authority revenues. Local authorities are not allowed to borrow to meet current expenditure, and their capital expenditure is controlled. In addition the Callaghan government had set up a consultative council on local government finance, where the Treasury could meet representatives of local authorities and seek to influence their expenditure.[114]

Yet for the new government these weapons were either distasteful or inadequate. Consultation was never a favoured Thatcherite activity, and as with trade unionists, the government preferred to shout at local authorities than to consult them. It was not only against foreign countries that the megaphone was used as a non-diplomatic tool. Instead of seeking like its predecessors to influence the total level of local government expenditure, the government aimed to control the expenditure of each local authority, using the quasi-norms that Whitehall calculated for the distribution of the RSG as a method of control. However badly central government failed to cut its own expenditure, no such latitude was to be allowed to local authorities.[115]

In consequence local government was subjected to seven different grant systems in three years, none of them an improvement on its predecessor. How local authorities were expected to plan their expenditure when the government was constantly changing the system was not explained. Ironically the government's then prevailing doctrine – monetarism – should have saved it from this folly. 'By all means limit Exchequer grants and government loans,' wrote Enoch Powell, 'but every monetarist knows that the rates cannot cause inflation and councils cannot print money. So why set every elected council by the ears from one end of Britain to the other? It doesn't add up.'[116]

The opponents of the government's many assaults on the autonomy of local government fully agreed with the repeated Thatcherite contention that Britain is a unitary not a federal state. (They would also have conceded, if pressed, that Britain is an island and the world is round.) However, they also believed – for the very reason that Britain is a unitary state, lacking the protection of a federal constitution – that the central government should be all the more careful to preserve local democracy. That was a vain hope.[117]

Well before the 1983 election it was clear that the government's domineering approach to local government produced much activity but little profitable result. Attempted direct control did not work. Yet in true Thatcherite style the government decided to reinforce failure. Almost the only part of local-government finance that the Thatcherites had not tried to control directly was the rates. Now even that last vestige of governmental self-control was abandoned. The cabinet had already rejected the idea of limiting rate increases, but, despite Michael Heseltine's strong opposition, rate-capping, together with the abolition of the Greater London Council and the Metropolitan Counties, were at the Prime Minister's insistence inserted into the 1983 election manifesto.[118]

Thus for local government 'the Maoist era of permanent revolution', as Dr Ramsden put it, continued in Mrs Thatcher's second term – and in her third. Because of the antics of Mr Ken Livingstone and others, the GLC and the Metropolitan Counties did not have many friends.* Yet the abolition of properly elected bodies because their politics and policies were opposed to Thatcherism was at the very least a little lacking in subtlety. That these bodies had been sentenced to death because they were socialist controlled was never in serious doubt, but in his rough, honest way Norman Tebbit made the government's political motivation explicit. The GLC was being abolished, he said, because it was 'Labour-dominated, high-spending and at odds with the government's view of the world' – plainly a capital offence.[119]

The government's new barrage against local government was no better prepared or more carefully thought out than its previous one. The original proposals for abolishing the GLC involved a blatant 'gerrymander': removing an elected majority of one party and substituting a nominated majority of another (the government's) was a novel form of democracy. The final proposals were only a little better. London was left without a directly elected representative assembly; the GLC was succeeded by quantities of quangos, which led to no reduction in expenditure.[120]

The government's Rates Act of 1984, which removed the power of local authorities to determine their rate level, was a more serious blow against local democracy. Until the eighties local government possessed autonomous powers, which depended on two important principles. Firstly, local government was able to raise its own revenue on whatever scale it wished (subject to the constraint of the ballot box)

* Except among the voters, of course. In BBC Radio's Man of the Year Poll in 1982 Ken Livingstone came second only to the Pope, a success which possibly contributed to the government's decision to abolish the GLC.[121]

simply by changing the rate poundages that it levied. Secondly, although about half of local government expenditure was funded from the centre by means of the rate support grant, local authorities were financially accountable to the rate payers for the way they spent their money. Both these principles – and therefore the autonomy of local government – were destroyed by the Thatcher government, whose rate capping did not even 'have the intended effect' of reducing expenditure.[122]

By the beginning of 1986, local government had been subjected to ten different finance systems – no longer, admittedly, a different one every six months but still well over one a year. The frequency of the changes was proof in itself of the ineptitude of the legislation. The later systems involved Whitehall laying down exactly what each local authority should spend. This was central government arrogance at its worst. Every local authority had different needs and different resources, and a few civil servants in the Department of the Environment had far too little knowledge to make final decisions about local authority expenditure – as, to give them their due, most of them well realized. Inevitably these Whitehall edicts were very much a hit-and-miss affair, often producing idiotic results, as they did in Buckinghamshire.[123]

There were at least three ironies about all this frenzied legislation and executive commandments: the patient was scarcely suffering from the illness the government diagnosed and did not require the medicine that the government forced down its throat; the medicine made the patient worse; and there were two good remedies that could easily have been prescribed and administered.

The local-government spending problem was largely illusory. Local-government expenditure was not spinning out of control. In fact central government showed less restraint in its expenditure than did local government. Indeed the problem chiefly arose from government ministers seeking to impose on local authorities cuts in spending which they would never have dreamed of imposing on themselves. They seemed to forget that local authorities had statutory responsibilities to provide certain services. As ministers did not have to provide those services themselves, they found it easier to cut the money for local authorities (and let them solve the problem as best they could) than cut money in areas where they themselves had the statutory duty to provide services.[124]

Ministers exercised pressure on local authorities by cutting the rate support grant – from 61 per cent of total expenditure in 1979 to 39 per cent in 1990. But they were not content to rely on that weapon alone partly because it wounded nearly all authorities fairly equally, whereas they wanted to maim only the left-wing ones, and partly because it led to an increase in rates. Hence all their ineffective attempts at direct control. But there was yet another irony. Because they did not want to inflict greater damage on Conservative councils than they already had (which was a lot), they did not always exert sufficient pressure on local-authority spending via the rate support grant. Thus while they used a whole range of dud guns to try to shoot local-authority spending, they did not consistently use the only weapon that really worked, and consequently failed in their objective of reducing local council expenditure.[125]

The final irony was that the government could easily have solved the problem of 'loony-left councils' by two simple measures. At the last GLC election in 1981 Labour won less than 42 per cent of the vote (only 2 per cent more than the Conservatives) yet won a majority of the seats. Much the same thing happened in the Metropolitan Counties. In 1983 in Liverpool (where only one-third of the council was up for election) Labour gained only 47 per cent of the vote yet won two-thirds of the seats. With proportional representation most of those councils would not have had Labour majorities, and extreme left-wing policies would have been out of the question. The chief objection to PR for national elections – that it would produce weak government – whether justified or not is not applicable to local elections.[126]

The second necessary and easy reform was to abolish the levying of non-domestic rates by local authorities. Since non-domestic rates were not paid directly by local voters, accountability was lacking and the tax was not a suitable local tax. It needed to be nationalized – a justified piece of centralization.[127]

Unlike proportional representation for local government, the reform of non-domestic rates was eventually undertaken by Margaret Thatcher, at the same time as she introduced the poll tax. With the so-called Community Charge, or poll tax, the Prime Minister achieved her great if rather mysterious ambition – mysterious in view of her attitude in 1974 – of abolishing the rates. The poll tax was in many ways the epitome, if not the apotheosis, of Thatchocratic rule; it was also in large part its nemesis.

The poll tax epitomized personal rule both in its own features and in the way it became Conservative policy and the law of the land. It was devised to meet what was thought to be a crisis for the Conservative party in Scotland, which was then wrongly used as a guinea pig for England.* Despite the obvious signs that the Scottish guinea pig was suffering, the poll tax was then extended to England and Wales. Nearly all official advice was against it. Yet apart from Walker and Lawson, the cabinet was supine and the overwhelming majority of the parliamentary party innocently obedient.[128]

As was obvious at the time as well as later, the Community Charge embodied every known feature of a bad tax. It was wholly unfair: 'the not-quite poor' paid as much as the rich; it was expensive; it was difficult to collect; and because of

---

* Having described the poll tax in January 1986 as 'a distinctly unappetizing prospect', I disapproved of its imposition on Scotland and abstained in the divisions on it; I should have voted against, but the temptation to take the opportunity of staying away from the Scotland debates was too strong. In my 1987 election address I said: 'We should wait to be sure that the Community Charge is a success in Scotland before introducing it here.' That would have been enough to ensure that England never had to endure it.[129]

its palpable unfairness many would inevitably refuse to pay it. That staid body, the Rating and Valuation Association, thought there would be five million summonses a year.[130]

The poll tax was also the culmination of the Thatcherite market or rather supermarket philosophy. It graphically illustrated the Thatcherite attitude to institutions and their wish to give the market a monopoly. Yet while the market may satisfy demands, it does not deal with needs or equity, which require institutions. But in the Thatcherite philosophy the people of this country were not so much citizens as consumers. Hence demand was all that mattered. Much was made of more choice being provided, but the alleged choice was very much circumscribed by the government. People could not choose to be citizens rather than consumers, they could not choose to make collective choices, they could not choose more education or more health rather than more private spending. They could only choose to be consumers. Institutions such as local government could not be allowed to stand in the consumers' way; they were therefore downgraded and their independence was diminished. The only institution of course that was not weakened was central government which was made more unchallengeable by the undermining of the others.[131]

While Britain was becoming ever more centralized and was fragmenting and weakening local government, the rest of Western Europe was moving in the opposite direction. Both in traditionally decentralized states like the Scandinavian ones and in traditionally centralized ones like France, Italy and Spain, decentralization was greatly extended. Similarly the United States, Canada and Australia, as well as Continental Europe, did not share the Thatcherite obsession with centralizing all decisions on public expenditure and waging fiscal war on the localities. Italy's expanding economy owed much to the initiatives taken by local and regional authorities.[132]

So not only the churches, the professions, the universities, the broadcasting organizations and the local authorities were out of step with Thatcherism, but nearly every other Western country as well. Despite this, as was pointed out earlier, the British government by enforcing more competition improved in some ways some of the services provided by local authorities. Yet the overall verdict must be heavily adverse. What Ferdinand Mount calls 'the frenetic and mostly futile legislative activity' of Thatcherism wrecked the morale of local government, destroyed its autonomy and left both its structure and its finances in chaos.[133]

Scotland

While Scotland of course is not an intermediate institution, it was treated rather like one, suffering from the centralizing urge of Thatcherism. So it seems logical to mention it here.

In May 1968 the party leader, Ted Heath, proposed an elected Scottish assembly. Two years later the party's Scottish constitution committee, chaired by Sir Alec Douglas Home, also proposed an elected Scottish assembly. Nothing was done during the Heath government because a royal commission set up by the Labour government was still sitting. In October 1973 the royal commission also favoured an elected assembly, though left its exact form open for discussion. At both the 1974 elections the Conservative party promised Scotland devolution. Finally in May 1976 William Whitelaw, Mrs Thatcher's deputy, 'restated our commitment to a directly elected assembly in Scotland'.[184]

But then things began to go backwards. Although she reiterated the Conservative commitment at the same time as her deputy, Margaret Thatcher was probably never much in favour of an assembly. In any case the shadow cabinet decided to oppose the Labour government's Scottish Bill of 1977 with a reasoned amendment. Having long favoured devolution for Scotland and given my reasons in a couple of books, and thinking the reversal of the party's position for short-term gain uncomfortably reminiscent of Harold Wilson, I told the party leader that as I could not vote against the Scottish Bill I would resign from the shadow cabinet. At her most charming,

Margaret Thatcher would have none of it, saying that the chief whip would have to arrange for me to be away. So, rightly or wrongly, I stayed.[135]

The result of the 1979 referendum in Scotland (a very small majority in favour, but well short of the necessary 40 per cent of the electorate) killed devolution – for the time being – as well as the Labour government. Yet the issue was not going to disappear, and the incoming Conservative government should have treated Scotland, which was far from holding Thatcherite views and elected a dwindling number of Conservative MPs, with some care. Such sensitivity was aggressively absent, however, and the imposition of the poll tax confirmed the Scottish conviction that the British Conservative government regarded Scotland not as a proud nation but as a small and tiresome province which needed bringing up to scratch by a sharp course of Thatcherism. In consequence the desire for devolution and a Scottish assembly was strongly revived.[136]

If a large majority of Scots want a Scottish parliament (which most of the time they do) I have never been able to understand why the great majority of the Conservative party should nowadays be so determined to frustrate them. Some right-wing Conservative MPs do not like Scotland – largely because it returns so many Labour ones – and would be content for it to become independent. But most, I think, are genuinely mistaken about the British constitution and its history. They seem to be under the misapprehension that the Act of 1707 was an Act of annexation by England not an Act of Union between the two countries.

Thatcherism, right wing though it was, had some of the characteristics of Jacobinism – a Jacobin, said Hazlitt, 'is one who would have his single opinion govern the world, and overturn every thing in it'. Similarly many Conservatives have come to hold the kind of opinion of the British constitution that Burke described as Jacobinical: the idea that constitutional arrangements should be simple and tidy and uniform. In fact, as Ferdinand Mount has eloquently argued, there is no reason why constitutional arrangements should be symmetrical, and the British constitution never has been tidy – something which both Burke and Disraeli regarded as one of its principal virtues. At no time in our history has every citizen or every part of the United Kingdom had exactly the same rights and obligations. To make, therefore, constitutional arrangements for Scotland, or for that matter Wales (as has long been done for Northern Ireland), which did not extend to the rest of the United Kingdom, would be neither inconsistent with British history nor inimical to Tory attitudes. Such arrangements would merely reflect the obvious fact that circumstances vary in different parts of the United Kingdom.[137]

Many Conservatives are impressed by the so-called 'West Lothian question', which Tam Dalyell persistently asked Labour ministers in the seventies: why should Scottish MPs be allowed to vote on, say, education and housing at Westminster, if English MPs (and also Scottish MPs) are to have no control over those subjects in Scotland? Mr Dalyell is a doughty crusader, but there he and those who agree with him are being legalistic if not Jacobinical. What happened in England would have great influence on what was done in Scotland, since great disparities between England and the rest would not be tolerated by the electorates of the devolved areas. So while the number of Scottish MPs at Westminster would have to be cut back so that the ratio of Scottish MPs to their electors was no higher than in England, to allow the Scots some influence on decisions made for England at Westminster would not be unreasonable.[138]

Such a concession should not be too high a price to pay for the maintenance of the union. Many right-wing Conservatives, as has been said, are not prepared to pay any price at all, since they would be pleased if Scotland left the UK. Many of the people who hold such a view are also 'anti-Europe' and would themselves like to leave the European Community. Thus if they had their way, Scotland would become a Belgium to England's Holland, though with Scotland in the EC and England out of it. That surely would be the ultimate in 'little Englandism'.

Conclusion

The Thatcherite attitude to intermediate institutions was well summarized by Norman Tebbit after Mrs Thatcher's fall. When Michael Heseltine remarked that we needed 'responsibly elected local authorities . . . to provide a check and balance to Westminster', he had 'made up', according to Tebbit, 'an entirely new and quite false constitutional theory'. (In fact it is a well-established and quite true constitutional theory.) Revealingly, Tebbit went on to say that 'local government is not to be used or seen as a way of frustrating the outcome of general elections.'[139] Rarely has the Thatcherite dislike of pluralism and its adherence to plebiscitary democracy been better expressed.

The Thatcherite devotion to both the free market and a strong state is sometimes described as paradoxical. Yet there was no paradox in rhetoric about 'liberty' and the rolling back of the state being combined in practice with centralization and the expansion of the state's frontiers. The establishment of individualism and a free-market state is an unbending if not dictatorial venture which demands the prevention of collective action and the submission of dissenting institutions and individuals.[140]

Hayek's famous book, *The Road to Serfdom*, which was published in 1944, is instructive here. (Interestingly Hayek was primarily arguing that central planning would eventually lead to Nazism – Stalinist Communism was scarcely mentioned.) As Herman Finer pointed out in his *Road to Reaction*, Hayek allows no compromise or moderation; his book is an anti-democratic, quasi-dictatorial tract, intolerant of countervailing institutions. Nothing is to stand in the way of the free market, and no such fripperies as democratic votes are to be allowed to upset it. The unadulterated free market is unalterable, and those who dislike it or suffer from it must learn to put up with it. In Rousseau's language, they must be forced to be free.[141]

Thatcherism is in that tradition. While genuinely devoted to nineteenth-century free-market principles and the economic ideas of Ricardo and other classical economists, the Thatcherites, in pursuit of their utopia, sought a virtual monopoly of power and opinion. The need to impose a 'free economy' easily overrode the desirability of nurturing a plural society. Furthermore, Thatcherite adherence to free-market dogma was itself subordinate to the imperative of keeping Margaret Thatcher in office. Hence British institutions were a casualty both of Thatcherite dogma and of its hunger for power. Instead of seeking like good Tories, as Disraeli adjured, 'to maintain the institutions of the country', Thatcherites were indifferent or hostile to them. They behaved, indeed, like some unscrupulous property developer bulldozing listed buildings that stood in the way of a quick profit.

'Our freedom,' wrote Michael Oakeshott, 'depends as much upon the moderation of the power exercised by government as upon the proper and courageous use of that power when necessity arrives.' Thatcherism could not be faulted on the second part of that dictum, but it ignored (or would have deprecated) the first part. It was able to do so because of the peculiar nature of the British constitution. A constitution is a device for limiting the power of the executive. The singularity of the British one – an instrument that used to be widely venerated: George III once wrote of its 'beauty, excellence and perfection' – lies in it never having been reduced to a single document or even a collection of documents. In consequence much of it is a matter of convention not law. Thus many of the limits that are placed on executive power are informal. 'It is,' Burke wrote, 'the spirit of the English constitution' which gives it life. More recently an acute French observer thought that 'the true secret' of our constitution was a 'state of mind'.[142]

Thatcherism laid bare the fragility of the British constitution. The attributes which had previously been considered virtues turned out, under stress, to be liabilities. Unlike a law, a convention can be broken almost as easily as a state of mind can be changed. Thatcherites disregarded (or were unaware of) the spirit of the British constitution; they observed only its insubstantial letter. 'Moderation' in the exercise of power, whose crucial importance was emphasized by Burke, Oakeshott and many others, was despised, if it was ever contemplated; the word itself because a dirty one like compromise, the badge of shame worn by believers in consensus politics.[143]

No wonder Mrs Thatcher had no inclination to reform the constitution. By providing practically no obstacles to the exercise and accretion of executive power, it suited her perfectly. Even though under her leadership the Conservative party never won as much as 44 per cent of the vote, virtually nothing stood in the path of plebiscitary democracy. The only restraints lay overseas.

IX

Foreign Policy

MS WALTERS: How do you feel when they call you the Iron Lady?

MRS THATCHER: I think that they are right. You have to have firmness in decision. You have to have firmness. You'd be no good if you didn't. Frequently, the decisions you have to take are those which are right for the long term of your country, of your beliefs. But in the short term, they're tough . . . And people say, well we may not agree with everything she does, she's tough, but we know she's strong. We know she'll stand up for our interests abroad. We know she'll do the right thing at home. We respect her, and we feel secure.

March 1991[1]

I divined the fundamental traits in her character: for her, her interlocutor had no dialectical existence. She was prepared to meet him only on condition that he accepted her point of view in its totality. If he expressed even a slight reservation she would fight him until he gave in.

Valéry Giscard d'Estaing on Mrs Thatcher at breakfast at the Venice Summit in 1980[2]

UNDER THE WILSON and Callaghan governments, Britain counted for little in international affairs. 'Our decline in relation to our European partners', wrote Sir Nicholas Henderson, the British Ambassador to France, in his farewell dispatch in June 1979, 'has been so marked that today we are not only no longer a world power, but we are not in the first rank even as a European one.' Margaret Thatcher did little to change Britain's power, but she greatly enhanced British prestige. Much of her international reputation was gained in the Falklands War but, leaving that aside, Mrs Thatcher's insistence on playing a conspicuous role in every available international controversy made Britain once again a country to be reckoned with. Whether her belligerent style and outlook always furthered British national interests, as opposed to her own political and personal ones, is debatable, but Britain's renewed prominence on the international stage was undoubted.[3]

The Prime Minister made Peter Carrington Foreign Secretary; I became Lord Privy Seal, Government Spokesman on Foreign Affairs in the Commons and, effectively, his deputy.* The other four ministers in the Foreign and Commonwealth Office – Douglas Hurd, Peter Blaker, Nicholas Ridley and Richard Luce – were an exceptionally strong team. As Nick Ridley correctly wrote, he was the only Thatcherite amongst us, adding less correctly that there was nothing he could do 'either to hold the department's budget under control or

---

* In the entry for 30 April 1979 in his *European Diary 1977–1981*, Roy Jenkins describes how this came about: During the election campaign Ian Gilmour told me 'that he was pretty committed to accept the number two job at the Foreign Office, under Carrington. The night they had won the no-confidence vote in the House of Commons, he had rashly agreed over a late-night drink with Carrington that he would do this, which greatly strengthened Carrington's claims to the Foreign Office, which now seem fairly clearly established.' I told Peter Carrington that I would not be anybody else's deputy but would be glad to be his. Although Peter had said it would be a partnership, I rather regretted my commitment the next day. After a few weeks of the new government, however, I was delighted to be in the Foreign Office and mightily relieved not to be anywhere else.[4]

to implant different policies'. He had no need to hold the FCO's budget under control: it was small and never out of control, though what he calls the Thatcherite 'faithful' in the Treasury did insist upon unnecessary and damaging cuts. The inclination, he now claims, 'to implant different policies' was news to Peter Carrington and me. At the time, safely isolated in the Foreign Office from Thatcherite dogma, Nicholas Ridley was an excellent minister.[5]

Its scarcity of Thatcherite ministers presumably fostered the Prime Minister's distaste for the Foreign Office, yet her anti-Foreign Office prejudices, which far exceeded her animosity to the rest of the civil service, did not decline when the FCO was no longer a largely Thatcherite-free zone. She took her hostility to the length of abandoning the practice of conferring a peerage on the retiring Permanent Secretary and other particularly distinguished diplomats, even though Sir Michael Palliser (her chief of staff at No 10), Sir Nicholas Henderson and Sir Anthony Parsons all performed brilliantly during the Falklands War.* The Foreign Office was yet another intermediate institution which impeded the Prime Minister's dominance, and its independence of view and its ingrained conviction that rudeness to foreign governments was not necessarily the best way of furthering British interests put it irredeemably in the ranks of 'one of them'. The level of ability in the Foreign Office is astonishingly high – as with the home civil service, its only rival is the *Quai d'Orsay* – and Mrs Thatcher's resentment and antagonism are more revealing of her own limitations than of those of the FCO.[6]

The most pressing issue facing us when we came into office was Rhodesia. The month before the British went to the polls, an election in Rhodesia had resulted in a victory for Bishop Muzorewa and a black majority, based

---

* They were also well qualified to make outstanding contributions to debates in the Lords, whereas the talents of some of the businessmen Mrs Thatcher preferred to ennoble perhaps lay more in making outstanding contributions to party funds.

on 64 per cent of the electorate, in place of the previous white regime led by Ian Smith based on 3 per cent of the population.[7] While still leader of the opposition, Mrs Thatcher had sent out Lord Boyd and other observers to report on whether the elections had been free and fair; and the Conservative government came into office here with an only slightly hedged commitment to recognize Muzorewa (as soon as he had formed a government), to return Rhodesia to legitimacy, and to lift sanctions. Shortly after the British election, Alan Boyd reported that the Rhodesian election had indeed been free and fair; and Mrs Thatcher was eager to recognize Muzorewa straight away.

The trouble was that although the leaders of the Patriotic Front, Joshua Nkomo and Robert Mugabe, had been released from prison, they had not been allowed to play any part in the election, which on the face of it did somewhat limit its freedom and fairness. Certainly the 'internal settlement' (which had made the election possible) and apparent black majority rule were an enormous improvement on what had gone before, but the whole of Black Africa and most of the rest of the world regarded the new regime in Salisbury, with much justification, as camouflage for the continuation of white rule by Ian Smith. To have recognized the Muzorewa government would have embroiled us, therefore, with most of the rest of Africa and many other countries too, endangered the future of the Commonwealth and damaged British economic interests – without conferring much benefit on the regime in Salisbury. The civil war, which had already claimed 20,000 lives, would have continued; and nobody else except South Africa would have joined us in recognition. The Rhodesian problem would have gone on festering.[8]

At that stage we had little idea of how to extricate ourselves from the difficulty caused by an ill-judged election commitment and the post-imperial prejudices of a large section of our supporters. Their clamour for immediate recognition of Salisbury was fuelled by our precipitate recognition of a new government in Ghana after a coup; unfortunately the day after we recognized it, the military junta started executing generals in public.*

To avoid or at least postpone the recognition of Bishop Muzorewa that was fully expected by Mrs Thatcher and most of the party, we decided to engage in an orgy of consultations: with the Salisbury regime itself, with the 'Front-Line States' surrounding it, with the Patriotic Front, with Nigeria, with the Commonwealth, with our European partners, and with anybody else we could think of. We knew in advance what the results of these consultations would be. Everybody would concede that much progress had been made in Rhodesia, but everybody (except South Africa) would be insistent that the new Rhodesian constitution was highly defective, as indeed it was, and that on no account should we recognize the regime or lift sanctions. Yet the consultations bought time, and time was all the more necessary because the most important part of our 'consultations' was at home.

Somehow Margaret Thatcher had to be weaned from her fiercely held view, shared by a large segment of the Conservative party at Westminster and in the country, that we should unilaterally and immediately recognize the Salisbury regime. Apart from anything else, damage limitation demanded that there should not be a bruising row at the Commonwealth Conference at Lusaka in August, still less a break up of the conference. Unfortunately, the Prime Minister at this point seemed determined to jeopardize the prospects of getting through Lusaka unscathed. On her way back from an economic summit in Tokyo, where she had been a success, she said in Australia that British sanctions would end in

* After a lengthy struggle with the Foreign Office legal advisers, I did eventually succeed in changing its long-cherished practice of recognizing 'governments', which was liable to land us in this sort of embarrassment, to the one followed by most other countries of recognizing 'states', which largely avoids it.

November and doubted very much whether a renewal would go through the British parliament. This aroused everybody's suspicions that all we were engaged in doing was playing the issue along with the object of keeping the Lusaka Conference quiet, and then recognizing the Salisbury regime sometime in the autumn.

'Consulting' and converting the Prime Minister was an arduous process. She still regretted that we had not recognized Muzorewa immediately, and at some angry and tedious meetings her only concern appeared to be to help the Bishop. She never seemed to realize that British interests were heavily involved and should not be ignored by any British government, let alone a Conservative one. The Foreign Office was frequently accused of being wet and unscrupulous, but that did not disturb us. At one of the meetings a senior minister (not in the Foreign Office) passed me a note saying 'we seem to be getting somewhere millimetre by millimetre'. It was indeed hard pounding; millimetres gained at one meeting might be lost, with other ground, at another. Eventually some sort of reluctant conversion did occur, largely brought about, I am pretty sure, not by the meetings but by Peter Carrington's private persuasion. The conversion remained fragile.

The next important step was the debate on 25 July, the opposition having demanded that Rhodesia should be discussed before the Prime Minister and Foreign Secretary departed for Lusaka. Since James Callaghan had announced his intention of taking part, Margaret Thatcher clearly had to make the opening speech. She sent back the Foreign Office draft certainly once and I think twice, but despite some protests she eventually agreed to say everything that was asked of her. Her answers to interruptions, therefore, were all that we had to worry about.

Her speech showed once again that both MPs and the press seldom listen to what is actually said. They hear what they want, or what they expect, to hear. The speech contained this key passage:

The Commonwealth Heads of Government meeting in Lusaka will be an important stage in these consultations. Subsequently, the British Government will put forward firm proposals on the constitutional arrangements to achieve a proper basis for legal independence for Rhodesia ... We should aim to make the proposals comparable to the basis on which we granted independence to other former British territories in Africa. They will be addressed to all the parties to the conflict.

The Government's purpose will be to help those who wish to resolve their political problems by democratic and peaceful means. We cannot subscribe to a solution which seeks to substitute the bullet for the ballot box.[9]

This clearly signalled a switch from her previous stance of wanting to recognize the government in Salisbury; it presaged the agreement later reached at Lusaka and a subsequent constitutional conference. But while one or two people touched on it, the significance of what the Prime Minister had said was not understood by the House or by the press. This was probably due in part to her having read out her speech with much less than her usual conviction, except when she inserted some of her own views. She continued to sit beside me for almost the entire debate, and from her comments to me it was not entirely clear that even she realized the importance of her speech. Whenever somebody criticized the Foreign Office line (then or later), she would quickly agree with him while I pretended not to hear. In general her attitude while sitting down – in stark contrast to her speech – was of somebody who wanted to recognize Muzorewa immediately and who profoundly distrusted the Foreign Office.[10]

I had a very easy ride when winding up (despite having been adjured by the Prime Minister not to say anything which would preclude early recognition of Salisbury even without constitutional changes). I said some things which showed which way the wind was blowing: 'We recognize the importance of the Patriotic Front and we have included it in our consultations. When our consultations are complete we shall be making proposals for a settlement which we believe will be seen to be fair and reasonable.' But naturally nobody paid any attention.[11]

The Prime Minister's conversion prevented trouble at Lusaka. Characteristically unaffected – except to the extent of wearing dark glasses – by her belief that acid would be thrown at her when she arrived, Mrs Thatcher enjoyed a triumph at the conference. So did the FCO: she was so impressed by Michael Palliser, the Permanent Under-Secretary, and Tony Duff, his Deputy, that she became a convert to the Foreign Office. Unfortunately the conversion was only temporary.[12]

In their communiqué the Heads of Government agreed that before independence Zimbabwe should adopt a democratic constitution including appropriate safeguards for minorities; that free and fair elections should be supervised under British government authority; and that the British government should call a constitutional conference to which all the parties would be invited.

Fortunately the Prime Minister's conversion to these ideas lasted longer than her new-found admiration of the Foreign Office. The external conditions were propitious for a settlement of the Rhodesian question. The Front-line states were anxious for the war to end. The Patriotic Front, too, was war weary like the whites, and did not want to have to go back to the bush. The whites knew that they needed to get the backing of the international community for removal of sanctions.

Lusaka led naturally to the Lancaster House Conference. I wrote a full account of it at the time, but for a variety of reasons it is too soon to tell the intricate story now. In any case Lancaster House had little to do with Thatcherism, although the Prime Minister once visited Lancaster House during a break in a plenary session and performed brilliantly.

Considering the civil war, the many atrocities and the oppression, all of which were longstanding, the atmosphere of the conference was surprisingly good. Unfortunately, Bishop Muzorewa decided that the former prime minister, Ian Smith, would do less harm in London than in Rhodesia. To begin with, Smith was something of a folk hero in Britain and was cheered wherever he went. At one party given by a right-wing peer (which was described by Willie Whitelaw as the nastiest party he had ever attended) Ian Smith was mobbed and poor Bishop Muzorewa was ignored. As a result, the Bishop apparently drank rather more than he usually did; perhaps as a penance, the next day for the first time he came to the conference in entirely secular clothes.

The adulation Ian Smith received outside did nothing to lessen his arrogance inside Lancaster House. He was the only man who unfailingly raised virtually everybody's hackles, not least those of the black members of his delegation. In a remark not made in plenary session, fortunately, but which was widely reported, he said that 'our blacks' are no good; 'their blacks' are much better. He seemed to have no conception of his responsibility for the Rhodesian tragedy. He was almost always rude and obtuse, and both Peter Carrington and I found him infuriating. He came to the conclusion that we were both racialists who did not like whites. In fact we just did not like him.

The Foreign Office team, which ran the conference and briefed Peter Carrington, Richard Luce and myself, worked a seven-day and, seemingly, a seven-night week. I did not always agree with them, but they were superb throughout, never negative and never non-plussed by unexpected turns of events. I was also well briefed by my very knowledgeable joint private secretary, Stephen Gomersall, and within the Foreign Office I was dubbed the member for the Patriotic Front. Such a stance seemed to me necessary to offset the pro-Salisbury bias of a number of officials.

In the end, an agreement was reached by one means or another. Elections were held, and under the capable guidance of Christopher Soames, the governor, Zimbabwe became independent with Robert Mugabe as its first, and so far only, prime minister.

The British prime minister could have insisted upon immediate recognition of Bishop Muzorewa's government. She could have refused to change her attitude before the Lusaka Conference. She could have refused to allow Nkomo and Mugabe to attend Lancaster House, and she could have wrecked the negotiations there in any number of ways which would have received some Foreign Office support. She nearly did all those things, but in the end never quite did. Her restraint and her readiness to be persuaded may have been due to her realizing that she was a novice in foreign affairs. That, however, is unlikely, since her inexperience did not prevent her charging all round the EEC china shop over the British budget contribution. Maybe her moderation was due to her occasionally allowing, as Peter Carrington and others have suggested, her head to rule her heart (though I was never sure that, admirable as both those organs were, there was in her case much of a distinction between them). But whatever the cause, dogma did not rule, and Mrs Thatcher deserves every credit for presiding over the first diplomatic success of her administration.

Britain's Contribution to the EEC Budget

The original plan was for Peter Carrington to stay in London for the last stages of the Lancaster House negotiations and for me to accompany Mrs Thatcher to the EEC summit meeting in Dublin. But when Peter discovered how the Prime Minister intended to handle the question of the British budgetary contribution at the summit, he rightly decided that we should change places, though in the end he was able to do little to restrain her.

Britain's refusal to take part in the formation of the EEC and President de Gaulle's vetoes of our subsequent applications had had the inevitable result of many of the Community's arrangements not suiting our interests. That was especially true of the way the Community was financed. Much of the EEC's revenue was raised from customs duties and import levies on trade with countries outside the EEC; at the same time most of the Community's budget was spent on agriculture. In consequence Britain was in a doubly adverse position: since we imported more goods from the outside world than did our partners, we paid a disproportionate amount into the community coffers; and since our agricultural sector was smaller than our partners', we received a disproportionately small amount out of those coffers.[13]

The problem had been recognized in 1970 during Ted Heath's accession negotiations, and the Commission had then given an important and, subsequently very useful, assurance: 'Should unacceptable situations arise within the present Community or an enlarged Community, the very survival of the Community would demand that the Institutions find equitable solutions.' Transitional arrangements were then negotiated, which, it was believed, would keep the problem within bounds until Britain's pattern of trade altered and the EEC's expenditure became less overwhelmingly agricultural.

The succeeding Wilson government was pledged to improve the transitional arrangements in its renegotiations, but the elaborate mechanism that was established to deal with the problem had so many conditions attached to it that it never came into operation and did not produce a single pound of refund throughout the life of the Labour government. Nevertheless not until 1978 when James Callaghan expressed his concern to the president of the commission, Roy Jenkins, was the problem about to become acute. Britain had by then sunk to being one of the poorest members of the Community – yet by 1980 she would be the largest contributor to the Community's budget.[14]

If the EEC's financial arrangements were ill-suited for Britain's needs, the row over them was perfectly adapted to the temperament and opinions of the incoming Conservative prime minister, who looked forward to the prospect with relish. Margaret Thatcher had never been an enthusiastic European. Except for denouncing the referendum as a device for dictators, she had played a minor part in the referendum campaign in the mid-seventies. She regarded the Community's chief use as a back-up to NATO in the struggle against

Communism. Leading a crusade against public spending at home, she could conceive no less desirable item of expenditure than payments to foreigners. A crusade against our partners in the EEC over our budget contributions was thus an ideal complement to her monetarist crusade.[15]

Mrs Thatcher's strength – and weakness – as a controversialist was that she could rarely see that her adversaries often had an arguable case. Like Giscard, Helmut Schmidt was struck by her inability to understand any point of view but her own, likening her in that respect, and in her urge to see the Community as a battleground in which she should always be seen as the victor, to Harold Wilson.[16] Had France, say, been in Britain's position in 1979, one can readily imagine Mrs Thatcher arguing with passionate conviction that France had signed the accession treaty, knowing full well what it entailed, had then renegotiated the terms, and had therefore twice agreed to the financial arrangements. What, she would have crushingly enquired, was the point of nations signing treaties and agreements, if they refused to abide by them the moment they became inconvenient? In any case, she would have continued, France's problem mainly stemmed from its failure to adapt its balance of trade and to give sufficient weight to Community preference. She would have concluded with some scathing words about the absurdity of France pleading poverty when the large windfall of North Sea oil was about to give it an enormous advantage over all her Community partners and make it once more a very rich country.

Initially our partners in the Community were reluctant to recognize the extent of the problem or the strength of the British case. The Prime Minister raised it with the French president and the Italian prime minister, Peter Carrington discussed it with the Germans and the Danes, and I went to the Hague, Brussels and Luxembourg. None of us got very far. At the Strasbourg summit in June, according to Roy Jenkins, Mrs Thatcher 'performed the considerable feat of unnecessarily irritating two big countries, three small ones and the Commission with her opening performance at a European Council'.[17]

By the autumn our partners were more ready to concede the existence of a serious problem – in 1980 our payments to the EEC would exceed our receipts by more than £1,000 million. Not surprisingly, however, they were not prepared to accept our over-ambitious contention (thought up by the Prime Minister and the Treasury) that we should be in 'broad balance', that is to say that, though not necessarily in each individual year, our contributions to the Community budget should be roughly equivalent to what was received from it. The Commission's paper that the Strasbourg Council had requested was helpful to the case, and pointed the way to a reasonable solution.

At the Dublin summit, however, the Prime Minister lived down to all Peter Carrington's worst fears. After giving a shrill exposition of the British case – I am not asking for anybody else's money, I just want 'my money back' – at the first afternoon session of the Council, she again harangued her colleagues for almost the whole of a working dinner which took some four hours. Schmidt feigned sleep, Giscard sat back contentedly watching her weaken her own position, and the others became increasingly unconvinced of the validity of the British case.[18]

Mrs Thatcher was treating the European heads of government as though they were members of her own cabinet. In some ways indeed their position was even less enviable than ours. While they had the advantage of being solaced by food and drink, which we never were, their ordeal was far longer than ours. Furthermore while we almost never had more than one cabinet meeting a week, they had three (far longer) sessions in two days. Arguably, of course, the Prime Minister's treatment of her colleagues on the Council was an effective means of getting her own way. They might have been so appalled by the experience that they determined never to repeat it, even if that meant giving in to the British demands. Yet while her performance should have had some deterrent value, the European leaders proved ready to subject themselves to more punishment. Indeed Schmidt hardened the German position after Dublin.[19] Mrs Thatcher never realized that after the very negative conduct of the Labour government and then her own flouting of the customary conventions of tolerable behaviour, most of our partners were beginning to question whether they wanted us to stay in the Community.

At Dublin Mrs Thatcher was offered a refund of some £350 million – 'a third of a loaf' as she called it – which was nowhere near enough. In the Foreign Office we always aimed to bring back two-thirds of the loaf, though the Prime Minister may still have been hoping for the whole £1,000 million; Dublin necessitated a review of our tactics. In one way we decided to get rougher: we would refuse to agree to any decision being taken on any matter which any of our partners might link to the budget question. That decision was to some extent balanced by our abandonment of the phrase, a 'broad balance'; we were now seeking 'a genuine compromise'.

With Lancaster House at last concluded, I was a freer man and was put in charge of exploring the possibility of a European agreement. The exploration took the form of a visit with my 'European' joint private secretary Michael Richardson, who was very well versed in Community affairs, to all the Community capitals. The first one was Rome where I saw Cossiga, the Italian prime minister. That visit, Roy Jenkins told me shortly afterwards, had not gone particularly well. The difficulty was that I was not allowed to mention the sort of figure we might find acceptable. This was not surprising since the Prime Minister, the Treasury and the Foreign Office did not agree. But the Italians held the presidency, and they wanted to learn our figure.[19a]

My other visits were, I think, quite useful – indeed something was achieved even in Rome where the Bank of Italy and the Foreign Minister accepted that we had a considerable problem. Obviously I put the argument less abrasively than the Prime Minister, but it was of some value to demonstrate to our partners that even in strict Community terms we had an unanswerable case. The most important outcome, however, was that my opposite number in Germany, Klaus von Dohnanyi, whom I saw both here and in Bonn, became engaged in the search for a solution.

At the Luxembourg summit Schmidt proposed that the British contribution for 1980 should be based on the average of 1978 and 1979, which was a good offer. Giscard then proposed that the refund (but not the contribution) should be the same in 1981 as 1980, which meant that the risk of an increase in the budget would be wholly borne by the British. Nevertheless, the offer amounted to a substantial refund, and virtually everybody on the British side was strongly in favour of accepting it. But the key exception was Mrs Thatcher, so the conference broke up in disarray, and the crisis in the Community deepened.[20]

Schmidt and Giscard had had enough of the problem and of the Prime Minister. They withdrew the offer they had made and said they would not take part in a similar discussion at the next European summit. It was therefore left to the Foreign Affairs Council to try to pick up the pieces.

My wife and I went to Italy for the Whitsun recess where we were joined by the Jenkinses and other guests. However, Roy and I only lasted the weekend there. Michael Richardson telephoned to tell me that Dohnanyi wanted to see me in Bonn, while Roy had to return to Brussels for a meeting of the Commission. I dined alone with Dohnanyi in his flat. Klaus von Dohnanyi, who had the most fertile mind of any minister involved in the negotiations, thought the only way out of the impasse was for the refund offered to us by our partners in the second year to be increased and for some safeguard to be provided for the third year; at the same time a different basis of calculation had to be used so that everybody could feel the agreement was an improvement on Luxembourg. Our official negotiating stance was for a solution 'to last as long as the problem', which was usually taken to mean about six years, but three years seemed to me to be acceptable; if we insisted on a longer period, we would get lower refunds. I think this meeting was useful; it may even have been crucially so, for it was Dohnanyi who essentially provided the solution which was adopted in Brussels forty-eight hours later. I then went on to the Hague, where the Dutch were by then allies.

Neither the German nor the French foreign ministers – Genscher and François-Poncet – attended the Foreign Affairs Council later that week, evidently believing that nothing important was going to happen. That was all to the good. Dohnanyi was more anxious for a settlement than his chief, and Bernard-Reymond was rather easier to handle than his. Peter Carrington arrived not in the best of tempers, having endured, I think, a particularly trying meeting on the subject with the Prime Minister. The first session got nowhere, and then at the working dinner Bernard-Reymond announced that he could not stay for the continuation of the Council the next day, though he was unable to give any remotely convincing reason why he had to be in Paris. Peter Carrington became increasingly irritated and threatened to break off the negotiations. In view of Klaus Dohnanyi's helpful attitude, that would have been decidedly inopportune, and I prevailed on him to stay.[21]

Colombo, the Italian foreign minister and the president of the Council, who was very good at keeping the peace – appropriately so, as his name is the Italian word for 'dove' – eventually got everyone to agree to remain and to hold a series of bilateral meetings throughout the night. Most of the meetings were between Colombo and Roy Jenkins and individual delegations, though the delegations also met each other from time to time. The negotiations were largely based on Dohnanyi's plan. The French were less difficult than we expected, probably because they had made their own position weaker by insisting on linking agriculture prices to our problem. At one moment when the negotiations appeared to be bogged down, I would have taken the risk of making a concession to them, but Peter Carrington, quite rightly as it turned out, refused. He negotiated with his usual skill, though the chief credit for the agreement which was eventually reached at about 9.00 am went, above all, to Klaus von Dohnanyi and then to Emilio Colombo and Roy Jenkins.

By the agreement we got our contribution for the first two years reduced by two-thirds and an undertaking for the third year that, if structural changes in the budget had not solved the problem, there would be a similar refund. In return we lifted the reserve we had placed on the increase in CAP prices and on the sheepmeat regime which all our partners favoured (and which brought great benefit to British sheep farmers), and committed ourselves to reaching agreement on a common fisheries policy by the end of the year.

We were pleased by the result of a hard night's work and on the flight back had champagne for breakfast both to recuperate and to celebrate. The agreement however was not a binding one. It was *ad referendum* to all the governments, and we knew our leader too well to think that she, too, would be opening champagne. We believed, however, that she would be able to recognize the benefits of the agreement.

Meeting at Chequers

We landed at Northolt and drove straight to Chequers, where Mrs Thatcher was holding a seminar on the Middle East. She had been sent a flash telegram telling her what had been provisionally agreed in Brussels, and she came out to the front door to meet us. Had we been bailiffs arriving to take possession of the furniture, or even Ted Heath paying a social call in company with Jacques Delors, we would probably have been more cordially received. The Prime Minister was like a firework whose fuse had been already lit; we could almost hear the sizzling.

After this unpromising beginning, we were ushered into a large and comfortable room. The atmosphere did not improve. Mrs Thatcher began by saying that we could not possibly afford it though she did not explain why.

We continued with competitive resignations: we had sold the country down the river, said the Prime Minister, she would resign. No, no, said Peter Carrington, we'll resign. (And at that stage we would have been very happy to do so.) No, said Mrs Thatcher, she would resign. And so on. When that unproductive exchange could be continued no longer, the meeting moved a little closer to the point.

The Prime Minister no longer seemed as though she would actually explode, but she was still strikingly *flambé*. So it was difficult to discern the exact structure of her argument, but it was tolerably clear that she thought the agreement lousy. We had not achieved, she said, everything that we had sought. (That, of course, was true, and has probably been true of every single successful diplomatic negotiation.) Worse than that, we had accepted terms worse than those she had refused at the Luxembourg summit a few weeks previously. (That was not true.) Moreover, it would put up the retail price index (true, but only infinitesimally, and a bit rich coming from somebody whose economic policies had in the last year propelled the RPI up from 10 to 20 per cent). All in all, we had let the country down and had behaved just as any good Thatcherite expected the Foreign Office to behave, especially when it was headed by two such notorious wets. Those expectations were encapsulated in two of the refrains of her press secretary, Bernard Ingham: 'Typical bloody Foreign Office' and we've 'got to screw the Foreign Office'.[22]

Few civil servants were in the room. But to my surprise a beautiful lady from the Treasury, Mrs Rachel Lomax, was present. I had no idea why, but presumed that it was to ensure that the wet Foreign Office was seen off by the dry Thatcherites of 10 Downing Street and the Treasury. If that was the idea, it miscarried. The Treasury lady turned out to be far more effective at controlling the Prime Minister than two rather jaded cabinet ministers. The effects of the champagne had long since worn off.

For a number of years I had regarded Mrs Thatcher as the mistress of irrelevant detail. For most of a meeting she would fasten onto some largely peripheral point and ignore all the matters of importance, but that morning she excelled herself. She chose to concentrate on the agreement's effect on foreign aid. As the agreement had nothing to do with foreign aid, we found this difficult to deal with. We felt like goalkeepers being asked to save shots that were going into the crowd miles wide of the goal. The most we could manage were despairing dives.

Mrs Lomax, however, proved well able to deal with these ill-directed balls. 'No, Prime Minister,' she would say sweetly if a little wearily, 'you have not got that quite right. The point is . . .', and then she would go on to deliver a comprehensive rebuttal. Or, 'No, Prime Minister,' she would say patiently, 'I think you must be looking at the wrong page. If you look at page 297, you will see . . .' It was beautifully done. What a pity, I thought, that Mrs Lomax is not in charge of the economy.

After what seemed like an interminable barrage of irrelevance (I think it was between two and two-and-a-half hours), Peter Carrington could stand it no longer. He said: 'Prime Minister, we have been up all night, we have not had one moment's sleep, we have been here for hours. Could we please have a drink?' Mrs Thatcher's naturally good (social) manners immediately asserted themselves, and drinks were brought. But the improved atmosphere lasted only a short time, and lunch was barely a truce. The Prime Minister talked mostly to her Middle East seminarians but found time to toss a few jibes at us. I swallowed them easily with the food and drink.

To my mind there was only one explanation for the Prime Minister's attitude. Her objection was to the fact of the agreement, not to its terms. That was not because we had succeeded where she had failed. It was because, to her, the grievance was more valuable than its removal. Not for the last time during her term of office, foreign policy was a tool of party or personal politics. However badly things were going in Britain, Mrs Thatcher could at least win some kudos and popularity as the defender of the British people against the foreigner. Hence a running row with our European partners was the next best thing to a war; it would divert public attention from the disasters at home. Her attitude was of course inflaming British antagonism to the Community, but that did not worry her at all; it probably pleased her.

When Peter Carrington and I left Chequers, we were still at war with our leader and hostess, and the future of 'the agreement' was uncertain. Hostilities would be continued in the media. Public relations has never been my strong point, but for once I had a good idea. As we got into the car, I told Peter Carrington that I had the answer. There must be no hint of even the mildest disagreement between the Prime Minister and us. We would brief the press that the agreement was a great triumph for Mrs Thatcher: her tenacity and firmness, her insistence on getting 'my money back' and her diplomatic skills had in the end prevailed over all the machinations of those rapacious Europeans. This worked well. The poodle Thatcher press lapped it up – even by their standards Thatcher triumphs were rare delicacies. So this time, for a change, the Foreign Office 'screwed' Bernard Ingham's Downing Street propaganda machine, and the media were overwhelmingly favourable to the agreement.

By Monday the battle was virtually over. At the meeting of the cabinet that morning – one of the very few not to be held on a Thursday – Mrs Thatcher had not changed her mind, but only one cabinet minister followed her line. All the others who spoke were strongly in favour of what we had agreed, and the Prime Minister had to acquiesce. That afternoon the House of Commons was almost as easy. Peter Shore fulminated in his usual anti-European manner, but our case was so strong and the Labour record in office so weak that I nearly enjoyed myself.[23]

Probably almost all the negotiators in Brussels went further than their governments expected. But the man who had most clearly exceeded his instructions was Klaus von Dohnanyi. The German Finance Minister who had to pay for it threatened to veto the agreement, which under the German constitution he was fully entitled for a short time to do. Helmut Schmidt himself was none too pleased. Yet he saw the advantage of ending a dangerous row, and he liked and admired Dohnanyi. So he gave his consent.

We had not achieved a final settlement. That was never on offer. But we had got one which pleased virtually everybody except the Prime Minister.

The Falklands War

The Falkland Islands were a third issue on which the views and prejudices of the Prime Minister strongly conflicted with those of her Foreign Office ministers. Unlike Rhodesia and the May 30 Agreement, however, Mrs Thatcher's view on the Falklands prevailed. This resulted in the worst failure and the biggest triumph of her administration.[24]

The traditional Foreign Office view of the Falklands, caricatured by its enemies as merely wanting to get rid of the Islands as soon as possible, was based on a careful assessment of the situation. The Islands, which were dependent upon Argentina for their communications, were deteriorating economically because of Argentinian hostility and refusal to take part in collaborative measures. Argentina's claim to the 'Malvinas' was widely accepted in Latin America as legitimate. The long-standing tension between us and Argentina benefited, therefore, neither the few hundred Falkland Islanders nor the United Kingdom. And finally, with the sparse forces at our disposal, the Islands could not be defended against an Argentinian attack, which unless the Argentinians believed Britain was negotiating with good faith, was possible at any time (though some warning period was always expected). Accordingly, the Foreign Office always aimed for some arrangement with Argentina that would remove the danger of invasion.[25]

If the Foreign Office had had £3,000 million to spend on the defence of the Falklands (the sum that was spent between 1982 and 1987), its policy would no doubt have been different. It would then have said to ministers: the islands are now safe, and if you want to spend your money in that way, we have little to worry about. Yet, since before 1982 there was no money available and Britain was incapable of preventing an Argentinian invasion, the Foreign Office would have been gravely at fault had it not sought ways of preventing an invasion and war.[26]

A more plausible criticism than the Foreign Office's alleged defeatism is made in the best book on the Falklands War: 'A compromise settlement was never achieved because the British Foreign Office proved far more competent at negotiation with another government than with its own.' American diplomats, Max Hastings and Simon Jenkins continued, 'take it for granted that an essential function of their job is to lobby politicians, to sell policies that they consider desirable or essential to those who have to implement them. In Britain, the Foreign Office existed in a world of its own. Diplomats failed to mobilize any constituency of public opinion for a compromise over the Falklands ... the Foreign Office's legitimate concern to protect British interests in Latin America spurred them to keep the negotiating process in being. The flaw was that a political strategy was never evolved to complement the diplomatic one.'[27]

Yet, for better or worse, the British and American systems of government are hardly comparable. In the US, officials have to mobilize support in order to get money from Congress for their policies. The task of British civil servants is different. Their job is to give advice on policy to ministers and to carry out the policies that those ministers eventually decide upon; it is for the ministers to carry them through parliament. British civil servants are not supposed on their own initiative to lobby opposing politicians or outside interest groups, and they would get into trouble if they did. The Foreign Office can not fairly be blamed for not behaving like, say, the Pentagon in Washington.

When we came into office in 1979 we could choose for the Falklands one of four policies. We could propose to Argentina a 'sovereignty freeze', whereby she would waive her claim of sovereignty and agree to economic collaboration. We could fortify the Falklands and make them impregnable. Thirdly we could seek some accommodation with the Argentinians. Or, finally, we could do nothing and just hope for the best. In practice a sovereignty freeze was out of the question since the Argentinians, who had been becoming increasingly impatient over the 'Malvinas', would not accept it. The second policy was equally unrealistic: a government which was trying to cut public expenditure everywhere was not going suddenly to sanction a spending spree on the Falklands.[28]

The only available policies, therefore, were fecklessly to hope for the best or to seek an accommodation with the Argentinians. In view of the current Argentinian attitude the former alternative was likely to lead to eventual disaster, and Nicholas Ridley, the minister in immediate charge, quickly came to the same conclusion that the Labour government had reached in 1977: 'leaseback' was the only feasible option. Britain would cede sovereignty over the Islands to Argentina which would then lease them back to Britain for a long period – possibly ninety-nine years. In view of previous commitments, the consent of the islanders would be necessary, but after two visits Ridley thought that, while a substantial minority was opposed to leaseback and others were undecided, consent could be forthcoming; many of the islanders he had met appreciated the advantages of the stability that an agreement would bring.[29]

As on other issues, the difficulty lay in convincing the Prime Minister and government supporters. It is a commonplace that at the end of empire Britain has found it easier to settle the future of the main imperial territories – India, Malaya, large tracts of Africa – than small or relatively unimportant outposts. That was as true of the Falklands as of Gibraltar.

The Falklands aroused powerful emotions in the breasts of some. When Peter Carrington broached the subject of leaseback to Mrs Thatcher, her reaction was described as 'thermonuclear'. (Apparently she also asked her friend and great admirer Nicholas Ridley to abandon his proposals; much to his credit Ridley refused.) And when Nick Ridley made a statement in the House on 2 December 1980, the reaction of the Falklands lobby was similarly explosive. The statement was short and anodyne:

> We have no doubt about our sovereignty over the islands. The Argentines, however, continue to press their claim. The dispute is causing continuing uncertainty, emigration and economic stagnation in the islands . . . I therefore visited the islands between 22 and 29 November . . . Various possible bases for seeking a negotiated settlement were discussed. These included both a way of freezing the dispute for a period or exchanging the title of sovereignty against a long lease of the islands back to Her Majesty's Government.
>
> The essential elements of any solution would be that it should preserve British administration, law and way of life for the islanders while releasing the potential of the islands' economy and of their maritime resources, at present blighted by the dispute. It is for the islanders to advise on which, if any option should be explored in negotiations with the Argentines . . . Any eventual settlement would have to be endorsed by the islanders and by this House.

There followed the silliest half hour that I ever heard in parliament. The blimps of all parties rushed in. From the Labour front bench Peter Shore set the tone. He had been an intelligent opponent of our Rhodesian negotiations and had always been careful to avoid doing anything that might wreck them. Now he behaved very differently. Undaunted by having recently sat in a cabinet which had decided only three years before that leaseback was probably the only solution, he said that 'prospects for a leasing arrangement represent a major weakening of our long held position on sovereignty in the Falkland Islands'. Sir Bernard Braine was no better, maintaining that 'the precedent of Hong Kong is an insult to Falkland islanders'; Ridley had not mentioned either Hong Kong or a precedent. The Liberal spokesman talked about 'the shameful schemes for getting rid of these islands which have been festering in the Foreign Office for years'.[30]

Of the nineteen interventions, three – two Labour and one Conservative – were neutral or friendly; the rest were hostile. Leaseback was almost certainly the only way of avoiding a war, so those MPs and their vociferous supporters have a lot to answer for. Did they ever reflect, one wonders, that their conduct might have helped to cause the death of 255 brave British Servicemen – one for every seven inhabitants of the Falkland Islands? (Arguably the same question could be asked of the Foreign Office ministers for proposing leasehold. But we would have a more convincing answer: short of a massive expenditure programme, leaseback was the only sure way of warding off an invasion.) In any case it was a distasteful episode. Imperial pretensions are not impressive when you do not have an empire.

A fortnight later in an adjournment debate Nick Ridley went into greater detail. He pointed out that the economy of the Islands was stagnating, that their population had declined in the past year from 1800 to 1700, and that a solution of these problems required 'an overall settlement'. It was 'the dead hand of the dispute' which stood in the way of economic progress. In conclusion he implored the backbencher who had opened the debate not to 'behave as if the problem did not exist'. But that was precisely how the Falklands lobby – and the Prime Minister – did behave. For the time being at least, the Falklands lobby had killed the leaseback proposal; the strength of their reaction in parliament naturally hardened opinion among the islanders.[31]

In consequence the British government was not able to negotiate seriously with Argentina over the Falklands' future and, since it was not able to defend them adequately, its only hope of avoiding a war, sooner or later, was deterrence. Other than British resolve not to accept Argentinian annexation, the government had very little available that was likely to deter the Argentinians. We had only one ship stationed in the area, but having HMS _Endurance_ there did at least maintain some sort of naval presence. Unfortunately, at this crucial time, monetarist dogma extended its malign influence to the

South Atlantic. John Nott, Francis Pym's successor, who was making the extensive defence cuts that Francis had refused to make, decided to withdraw *Endurance*. Peter Carrington, Nick Ridley and I strongly opposed this move, but John Nott was backed by the Prime Minister, and the decision was announced on 30 June 1981.[32]

The announcement that *Endurance* would be withdrawn at the end of its 1981–82 tour of duty was a demonstration not of British resolve to defend the Falklands but of the government's belief that expenditure cuts were its highest priority. Argentina might well still have invaded even if that announcement had never been made, but it unquestionably gave the wrong signal that Britain was not really interested in the islands. The Falkland Islands Council complained that Britain appeared to be 'abandoning its defence of British interests in the South Atlantic and Antarctica' and felt that the withdrawal 'would further weaken British sovereignty in this area in the eyes not only of islanders but of the world'. The Argentinians took the same view. The British embassy in Buenos Aires reported that the theme in all the newspaper articles was that Britain was abandoning the protection of the Falkland Islands.[33]

The Prime Minister preferred verbal intransigence to concessions but had then decided to remove the one instrument that appeared to give substance to her intransigence. As her admiring biographer, Kenneth Harris, wrote: 'the financial dogmatism of the MTFS meant the sacrifice of *Endurance*'. Remarkably, at the same time, the government gave another damaging signal to Argentina. The new British Nationality Act deprived about half the Falkland Islanders of their British citizenship.[34]

'In the summer of 1981,' as Peter Carrington later wrote, 'Argentine impatience was visibly mounting, and we had a certain sense of sands running out.' Foreign Office ministers discussed the Falklands as well as other subjects on 7 September. As I was going to be sacked the following week I was, as the lawyers say, *functus officio*, but was present nevertheless. Obviously we would have to go on negotiating, but as we had nothing of substance to offer, the Argentinians would before long realize that we were wasting their time. Nick Ridley recommended a more public and active campaign to educate the islanders and British public opinion. But since that would be interpreted as the Foreign Office putting pressure on the islanders as a prelude to overriding their wishes we needed first to educate the Prime Minister and her ministerial and parliamentary colleagues, and the learning process was likely to be slow. We also discussed the possibility of making another attempt at leaseback, which provided the only chance of an agreement. But the same objections applied even more strongly. For any such attempt to be workable, Peter Carrington would have to persuade Margaret Thatcher that the concession had to be made. Otherwise he would not have got the policy through the cabinet – foreign policy was normally kept away from the cabinet, but the Prime Minister would have insisted on taking this issue to cabinet and opposing it there – and it would have fallen foul of the parliamentary party. Peter thought the chances of successful persuasion were nil. So any readoption of leaseback would have been little more than a gesture, but in retrospect I wish we had decided that the attempt should be made.[35]

Richard Luce, who succeeded Nick Ridley in the September reshuffle, negotiated ably with a very weak hand. The British strategy, as our ambassador in Buenos Aires commented, was one of general Micawberism. At the beginning of 1982 Peter Carrington tried again to get the decision to withdraw *Endurance* reversed, but once again John Nott and the Prime Minister turned him down. British policy had effectively been reduced to relying on Argentinian restraint or incompetence. Unfortunately, the Argentinian military junta had little restraint and, though it had incompetence in abundance, it chose to demonstrate this by launching a bungled war, rather than by simply failing to start one.[36]

The British government, too, has been accused of incompetence in the last few days before the invasion. Certainly, adequate intelligence was not provided, and paralysis seems to have descended on Whitehall. The government failed to send an ultimatum to the Junta, warning it that an invasion would not be allowed to succeed and that Britain would retake the Islands by force, if necessary. Such an ultimatum could have done no harm, yet even when the British Task Force was on its way to the Falklands the Argentinians were still convinced, as General Galtieri told a US State Department official, that 'the British won't fight'. Hence an ultimatum at a time when the British had only one (about to be withdrawn) ship in the area would probably not have impressed the Junta.[37]

Like many other people I was against Peter Carrington resigning, but in retrospect I am sure he was right to do so. 'The whole country,' as he wrote later, 'felt angry and humiliated . . . There were hysterical outbursts in Parliament and yells of betrayal. . . .' Although the Foreign Office as an institution was certainly not to blame, Thatcherite and class resentment welled up against it in the tabloid press – there was a particularly nasty and ignorant article in the *Daily Mail*. A sacrifice was required. Mrs Thatcher was clearly not going to go, and John Nott would not have been a sufficiently large scapegoat. So Carrington it had to be.[38]*

Mrs Thatcher's immediate decision to send a Task Force to the South Atlantic received the backing of a massive majority of the British people. Indeed the enthusiasm almost threatened to get out of hand. By 12 May 12 per cent supported an

---

* John Nott did honourably offer his resignation, but the Prime Minister refused it. Because of his earlier plans to cut it, the Navy was hostile to the Defence Secretary and regretted that his resignation had not been accepted. Hence allowance has to be made for its bias. While the Task Force was steaming south, Admiral Woodward wrote in his diary: 'None of our plans seems to hold up for more than twenty-four hours, as Mr Nott footles about, wringing his hands and worrying about his blasted career.' Woodward's outburst was probably largely due to his having been told earlier in the day by Admiral Fieldhouse, the C-in-C Fleet, that the Defence Secretary wanted to replace him with a more senior commander, because, as Fieldhouse put it, 'when – not if – it all goes sour, he wants somebody important enough to sack'.[39]

invasion of the Argentine itself, and in another poll 5 per cent favoured the use of nuclear weapons.[40] Some people thought, however, that the Task Force and the ensuing war were a disproportionate response to an essentially trivial incident. In their view the situation had not changed all that much since 1770 when Dr Johnson had decided that the Spanish invasion of the Falklands and expulsion of the small British garrison did not merit a war. 'What continuance of happiness can be expected,' Johnson asked, if a war should result from 'a contention for a few spots of earth, which, in the deserts of the ocean, had almost escaped human notice . . . ?' It is an island, he continued, 'not even the southern savages have dignified with habitation.'[41]

At the beginning of the crisis, President Reagan described the Falklands, rather similarly, as 'that little ice-cold bunch of land down there', and the attitude of many in the State Department, though not Alexander Haig, the Secretary of State, was that it was 'a Gilbert and Sullivan battle over a sheep pasture between a choleric old John Bull and a comic dictator in a gaudy uniform'. Although they were certainly not opposed to the war, many British servicemen in the South Atlantic, an eye witness has recorded, also 'perceived an underlying absurdity in a struggle so far from home for a leftover of Empire'.[42]

Yet the inhabitants of the Falklands, even if there were only 1700 of them, were British, and the invasion was an act of unprovoked aggression by a particularly unattractive military Junta. No British government could have sat back and said 'all right we got it wrong, you've won', perhaps in a futile attempt to save face referring the issue to the United Nations. The Commander of the Task Force, Admiral Sandy Woodward, surely got it right when, as he steamed towards the islands, he wrote in his diary: 'of course there's no way the Falklands are worth a war, whether we win it or not – equally there's no way you should let the Argentinians (or anybody else for that matter) get away with international robbery'. Any British government would have felt the same way about international robbery, if not about the worth of the Falklands.[43]

If before the war Margaret Thatcher got virtually everything wrong, during it she got virtually everything right. Unlike Neville Chamberlain in 1937–39, she did not even try to prevent war taking place. Yet she was like Winston Churchill during it. Even allowing for the war being a very minor one, she was a strong and inspiring war leader who made the correct decisions.

No doubt she and Britain were lucky. The brave and skilful Argentinian pilots hit a number of our ships with their bombs and would have sunk many more of them, had their engineers had the sense to alter the fuses on their bombs so that they exploded on impact. An Exocet might have hit one or both of our aircraft carriers. When the Argentinians aimed to launch a pincer attack on the Task Force by the cruiser, *Belgrano*, and the aircraft carrier, *Veintecinco de Mayo*, there was most unusually for that time of year in the South Atlantic not a breath of wind, with the result that their aircraft could not take off, and the attack had to be aborted. Had any of these matters turned out differently, unacceptable losses would probably have been inflicted on the British fleet and the repossession of the islands abandoned. The Prime Minister was also lucky in having at her disposal such magnificent sailors, soldiers and airmen. But Napoleon knew the importance of luck in war, and Mrs Thatcher, relying on the courage, fortitude and skill of the armed forces, deserved hers.[44]

No doubt, too, much of the rhetoric used by her and others to justify the war was more than a trifle overblown. The idea that liberty is indivisible and that, if aggression was allowed to succeed in this case, aggressors would be encouraged elsewhere, was far-fetched. So far from our retaliation against the Argentinian Junta deterring other aggression, Israel used it as a useful diversion of international attention to invade Lebanon; and later on Saddam Hussein was in no way discouraged from attacking Kuwait by knowledge of what had happened to Argentina.[45]

Yet war and post-war oratory tends to be florid, and what the Prime Minister said suited the temper of the time; furthermore it was certainly superior to what Admiral Woodward calls 'the lunatic nationalistic pride' of the tabloid newspapers. The important point was that her conduct of the war was almost impeccable.[46]

Mrs Thatcher has been much criticized for giving permission for the nuclear-powered submarine HMS *Conqueror* to sink the *Belgrano*, a decision allegedly made in order to make a peaceful outcome to the conflict impossible. In fact when Admiral Woodward asked for the *Belgrano* to be sunk and his request was backed by the Chief of the Defence Staff, the war cabinet had no option but to accede to it. The sinking of the *Belgrano* was not the opening of hostilities; the Argentinians had attacked the British Task Force the day before. In his account of the war Admiral Woodward makes an unanswerable case for the decision to torpedo the Argentianian cruiser. The *Belgrano* posed a genuine threat. The fact that, when permission was given, it had changed course and was heading for home (which Woodward did not know) is largely irrelevant; it might well have changed course again. The loss of life was tragic, but in consequence of the sinking the Argentinian navy never again ventured out of port. Had it not been torpedoed, the *Belgrano* and many other Argentinian ships would have tried to attack the British fleet, and the loss of life would probably have been far greater.[47]

The allegation that the *Belgrano* was sunk in order to eliminate the possibility of a peaceful solution is similarly baseless. Mrs Thatcher may well have relished the thought of war more than her colleagues, but she did not rule out negotiations. The Argentinian Junta not the British Prime Minister spurned the American attempts to mediate. Furthermore the Peruvian initiative, which the *Belgrano* sinking was alleged to have wrecked, had made little progress, was not known to the British government and was not ended by the attack. Even more conclusive, a fortnight after the *Belgrano* went to the bottom, at a time when the British military position was better than it had previously been, Mrs Thatcher accepted Sir Anthony Parsons' proposal for a compromise settlement of remarkable generosity.[48]

The Falklands War greatly enhanced British prestige – the

US navy considered the re-capture of the Falklands a military impossibility – and it transformed Mrs Thatcher's reputation, at home and abroad. She undoubtedly deserved her triumph because of the way she had conducted the war. Yet the war should never have been necessary, a view which was strongly held by many of those who won it – 'You don't mind dying for Queen and Country,' said Brigadier Julian Thompson, second-in-command of the land forces, after it was over, 'but you certainly don't want to die for politicians.'[49]

The verdict of the Franks Committee of distinguished Privy Councillors which was set up to inquire into the origins of the war was that 'we would not be justified in attaching any criticism or blame to the present government for the Argentinian Junta's decision to commit an act of unprovoked aggression in the invasion of the Falkland Islands on April 2nd 1982.' There are two explanations for that astounding conclusion. The first is the political atmosphere of the time it was written. The Franks report was published in January 1983. While the committee was deliberating, public enthusiasm for what had been achieved remained high. The committee did not want to tarnish a great victory; had the Falkland operation failed, we can be confident that it would have come to a different conclusion.[50]*

The second explanation is more particular. The verdict of

* Something of the sort happened in the United States after America's small war against Spain in 1898. The US acquired the Philippine Islands amid much controversy as to whether the American constitution applied there – that is to say whether the US constitution followed the US flag wherever it flew, or whether the Philippines were not entitled to its protection. The Supreme Court waited until after the Republican victory in the elections of 1900 before laying down, in a dubious decision, that only so much of the American constitution followed the flag as did not hamper the bearing of the white man's burden. The American humourist 'Mr Dooley' commented: 'no matter whether the constitution follows the flag or not, the Supreme Court follows the election returns'. The Franks Committee followed the flag rather than the election results. But it was not at variance with 'Mr Dooley's' observation. Like the Supreme Court it seems to have been influenced by political considerations.[51]

the Franks Committee demonstrated the well-known truth that if you ask yourself a silly question you are likely to get a very silly answer. The committee asked the question: 'Could the government have foreseen the invasion on 2 April?' To which the answer is: of course it could not know what was going to happen on 2 April, unless it had possessed unique powers of clairvoyance. The proper question to ask was: did the government through its actions and its inaction run an unnecessarily large risk of war being started? And the answer to that question, as we have seen, is undoubtedly, yes.[52]

Relations with President Reagan

United States assistance was of vital importance in the Falklands War. Without the use of the American facilities on Ascension Island the Task Force would have had no forward base, and the logistics of the enterprise would have been almost impossible. The new American air-to-air missile, Sidewinder, proved a decisive weapon in air combat, and American fuel and ammunition were provided, as well as help with satellite communications.[53]

America's early attempt to remain roughly neutral also benefited Britain. American satellite intelligence over the South Atlantic initially was virtually non-existent. But taking seriously the remarks of the US Ambassador to the UN, Mrs Kirkpatrick, Argentina believed that the United States would maintain neutrality. As a result Argentinian officials and service officers gave much intelligence information to the CIA and to the American military attachés in the Argentine capital. This was immediately passed on to London by the pro-British head of the CIA, William Casey, and by other American sources.[54]

Almost certainly the United States would in any event have been forced to side with Britain. After all it was Argentina not Britain who undeniably was guilty of unprovoked aggression, and, as Alexander Haig soon discovered, it was Argentina not Britain who blocked every attempt to negotiate a compromise solution. Furthermore, by a brilliant piece of diplomacy, Sir Anthony Parsons had within two days of the invasion persuaded the United Nations Security Council to pass Resolution 502 exactly in the form that he himself had drafted. That resolution called for Argentina's immediate withdrawal, and it gave Britain under Article 51 of the UN Charter 'the inherent right of individual and collective self-defence if armed attack occurs ... until the Security Council has taken measures necessary to maintain peace and security'. (Britain similarly gained a statement of political support and the imposition of trade sanctions by the EEC in Brussels.)[55]

While Sir Anthony Parsons was lining up the United Nations, the British ambassador in Washington, Sir Nicholas Henderson, was making similar efforts with the American government and public opinion. 'During the Falklands crisis,' a commentator wrote, 'the British Ambassador in Washington saw the National Security Adviser, went daily to Capitol Hill, lobbied the individual members of the Senate Foreign Relations Committee, and appeared on television seventy-three times. It was a masterly example of diplomatic skill.' Thus the leader of the pro-Argentinian faction in the American government, Mrs Kirkpatrick, still besotted by her earlier much-publicized distinction between totalitarian dictatorships, which were beyond the pale, and contemporary right-wing non-totalitarian ones, which she regarded as pretty benign, was heavily outgunned.[56]

Mrs Kirkpatrick accused Alexander Haig of 'having a boy's club view of gang loyalty' with London, and her admiration of the State Department was no greater than Mrs Thatcher's of the Foreign Office, though Mrs Thatcher might usefully have learned something from it. Jeane Kirkpatrick regarded the State Department as 'Brits in American clothes'; 'why not,' she asked, 'just disband the State Department and have the British Foreign Office make our policy?' Haig, who on his travels had seen the irrationality of the Argentinian Junta and knew the rights and wrongs of the issue, evidently thought that Mrs Kirkpatrick was scarcely more rational. He replied that she was 'mentally and emotionally incapable of thinking clear on this issue because of her close links with the Latins'. Like Haig, American public opinion preferred the British Foreign Office view to that of Mrs Kirkpatrick. Sixty per cent supported Britain, and 19 per cent Argentina.[57]

Yet, however strong the forces pushing the United States in the same direction, the American tilt towards Britain was certainly influenced by the close rapport between President Reagan and Mrs Thatcher. That relationship had been forged well before either of them had attained the highest office. A common ideology had brought Margaret Thatcher and Ronald Reagan together, and despite the occasional blip it proved a lasting bond. Mrs Thatcher was Reagan's first visitor in the White House, and on his last morning there he wrote her a letter of appreciation. Significantly, the first dignitary to meet his successor was Helmut Kohl.[58]

Mrs Thatcher did not consult Reagan over her decision to send the Task Force, which was understandable, even though important American interests were affected. Britain under Mrs Thatcher was America's most reliable ally, and Reagan could not afford to see her fall over the Falklands issue. On that occasion what Mrs Thatcher called the 'very, very special' relationship was of great value both to herself and to Britain. Sometimes, whatever its impact on their two countries, its chief use was personal to the two leaders.[59]

The President could rely on Mrs Thatcher's help to fight his battles, and the Prime Minister could rely on Reagan for timely electoral support. During the run up to the 1987 election Neil Kinnock paid an ill-advised visit to Washington. The President gave Kinnock an icy reception, greeting Denis Healey with the words, 'Nice to meet you, Mr Ambassador.'* The visit could hardly have been a greater contrast to Mrs Thatcher's

---

* Reagan's mistaking of Healey for the ambassador was probably not intentional. The week before, Healey later learned, the President had mistaken his Deputy National Adviser, General Colin Powell, for the janitor.

triumphant tour of the USSR. In return Mrs Thatcher refused to comment on the Iran–Contra scandal.[60]

Their close friendship did not inhibit Mrs Thatcher from giving Reagan a piece of her mind if she thought he deserved it. When Reagan announced the lifting of the grain embargo on the USSR – which had been imposed by President Carter after the invasion of Afghanistan – at a time when the American government was trying to prevent the Europeans from participating in the Siberian gas pipe-line, he was given a severe lecture which eventually led to a change of policy.[61]

As well as ideology, the President and the Prime Minister shared both a robust patriotism and a fervent nationalism. Patriotism may be taken to be a love of one's country, and nationalism a dislike of foreigners. The first is a positive emotion, while the other is primarily negative. Patriotism, in this sense, is best exemplified by Burke's maxim that 'to make us love our country, our country ought to be lovely';[62] nationalism means 'My country right or wrong'. The nationalist is all for conflict, and indeed cannot live without enemies; the patriot prefers to be left in peace to enjoy his country's advantages or repair its deficiencies. The attention of the nationalist is fixed abroad. So long as foreign lands supply him with satisfactory objects for his envy or derision, he rests content. The patriot spends more time looking inward. He knows that whatever the nation's position in the league tables of inflation or economic growth, the health and happiness of his countrymen cannot be quantified; if he finds something wanting in the mood of the nation, he is not compensated by reading about greater misery elsewhere in the world. In supporting the interests of 'Britain' the nationalist thinks he is merely cheering on an abstraction; he does not care about the parts so long as there are statistics which show that the whole is doing well. The patriot is concerned for the well-being of all his people. In this sense, at least, the patriot is the true individualist when he looks for healthy signs in society. The nationalist is little more than a purveyor of rhetoric.

Margaret Thatcher's nationalism chiefly took the form of a strong dislike of international organizations or groupings like the United Nations, the Commonwealth and the European Community. Ronald Reagan's nationalism took the form of foreign adventurism.

Reagan had not yet transformed the United States from being the largest creditor nation in the world to being the largest debtor, and America seemed all powerful. In reaction to the quietism of the Carter era, US foreign policy became ultra-active in both word and deed. Reagan's adventurism went down well with the voters, making them think their country invincible and diverting their attention from its less 'lovely' aspects. American public opinion was intensely proud that the most powerful nation in the world had managed a successful invasion of the tiny island of Grenada. There was similar exultation when the resources of the US Sixth Fleet proved capable of forcing down an unarmed Egyptian airliner. The process was circular and dangerous. The administration stirred up American public opinion, and in turn public opinion spurred on the administration to further adventures. With the USSR seemingly too powerful to take on directly, American military adventures were necessarily directed against smaller powers.[63]

In October 1983 Maurice Bishop's Marxist regime in Grenada was overthrown, and on the 19th Bishop himself was murdered, by a more extreme left-wing faction. One of Reagan's fantasies was that Grenada was going to be used by the USSR and Cuba to bring Marxist domination to the Caribbean, and the coup might anyway have caused him to order an invasion. But, four days after the murder of Bishop, 241 American servicemen were killed by a suicide bomber in Beirut. Revenge and punishment were clearly necessary. The difficulty was that nobody knew who was responsible for the Beirut massacre, and retaliation might well add to America's already serious problems in the Middle East.[64]

Retaliation against Grenada, however, would cause no such complications. The Speaker of the House of Representatives,

Tip O'Neill, thought that it was the Beirut massacre which caused the US to invade the island. Certainly America's successful capture of Grenada provided a successful distraction from the American disaster in Beirut, and enhanced Reagan's popularity. The trouble was that Grenada was a Commonwealth country, and nobody had bothered to warn the Queen or the British government that the US was about to descend on the island in force – let alone consult them.[65]

Reagan's fears of being upbraided by Mrs Thatcher and the fears of his advisers that she would make him change his mind may have been the cause of the American failure to consult her on this occasion (and on others).* Another possible reason why Britain was not warned in advance may have been that not even the US State Department was aware of the planned invasion, and therefore could not have kept the British government informed even if it had wanted to.[66]

Whatever the cause, Mrs Thatcher was naturally very angry. As was said above, she herself did not consult Reagan over sending a Task Force to the South Atlantic. But the two cases were not comparable. Mrs Thatcher was reacting to unprovoked aggression; moreover there was a long interval between the decision to dispatch the fleet and the outbreak of hostilities. Reagan was reacting to a serious incident in another part of the world; there was no compelling reason for him to do so immediately; and his invasion had begun before the British had heard about it.

Grenada was not the only occasion on which Reagan did not consult his most faithful ally, but it was the most blatant. We do not know what view Mrs Thatcher would have taken of Reagan's plans for Grenada, had she been consulted. But, as it was, she condemned the invasion; pointing out that, while

* Even the threat of a telephone call could influence him. Frank Carlucci, Caspar Weinberger's successor as Defence Secretary, once reminded Reagan during the Irangate scandal that, if he took a particular course of action, Mrs Thatcher would contact him immediately. 'Oh, I don't want that', was his petrified response.[67]

many countries would like to be free of Communism, that did not mean 'we can just walk into them and say now you are free'.[68]

That very reasonable point of view brought down on the Prime Minister's head some harsh abuse from her more extreme supporters — which probably helped to remove any remaining doubts in some minds that the stand she had taken was right. Rupert Murdoch opined that 'she's run out of puff', adding with the restraint of language that distinguishes his popular newspapers, 'she has gone out of her mind'. Paul Johnson was equally outraged that the British Prime Minister should have dared to criticize one of America's most glaring pieces of trigger-happiness. The attitude she had adopted made Mrs Thatcher (temporarily) in his eyes 'not particularly intelligent' and 'a very ordinary woman'. She has little imagination, he added, 'lacks tact and cunning and many routine political skills'.[69]

Just over two years later, at Christmas 1985, Americans were killed in two terrorist atrocities in Europe for which Colonel Gaddafi's Libya was widely believed to be responsible. (There had also been much terrorist activity in the previous two years.) The United States seemed ready to take retaliatory action — it had had plans ready since 1981 when, on mainly false information about alleged Libyan assassination squads, it had considered attacking Libya in that year — but Mrs Thatcher did not favour the idea. 'I do not believe in retaliatory strikes that are against international law', she told American correspondents; furthermore they were unlikely to do any good and might produce 'much greater chaos' than did terrorism. She added, 'I uphold international law very firmly.'[70]

Unfortunately, three months later, those admirable sentiments were forgotten or changed. When, after another terrorist outrage in Berlin, Reagan told the Prime Minister that he was going to attack Tripoli and would like permission to use British bases for the attack, she not only gave him the permission he sought, but decided that such an action was, after all, in accordance with international law and would also be effective.[71]

In view of the American help in the Falklands War, Mrs Thatcher's change of mind and her anxiety not to be 'a fairweather friend' of the United States was understandable, but still, I think, mistaken. Like Grenada, Libya was not comparable to the Falklands. In 1982 Reagan was helping his ally to do the right thing in defending itself against attack; in 1986 Mrs Thatcher helped her ally to do the wrong thing in raiding another country. The middle ages and the sixteenth century had the word for what the United States was trying to do: tyrannicide; the Americans were aiming to assassinate Colonel Gaddafi. At least thirty-two bombs were supposed to hit his compound, though only two actually did so. Two of Gaddafi's sons were wounded and his fifteen-month-old adopted daughter was killed. Gaddafi himself was unscathed. One of the chief reasons the Prime Minister gave for allowing the use of British bases was that the F111s which flew from them would be more accurate in confining the bombing to military targets than the US carrier-based aircraft. In the event the F111s hit no fewer than four foreign embassies; it is difficult to believe that the bombers from the American Sixth Fleet would have hit many more. The reason in fact why the United States wished to involve Britain was not military at all but political; the Americans did not want to be the only culprits.[72]

When a country is about to take a mistaken course of action, it is surely the duty of a good ally to try to dissuade it, not first to support it and then shower it with praise, as did Mrs Thatcher – despite the views of the cabinet.[73] If the Prime Minister felt that because of the Falklands she had to allow use of the British bases, the very least she should have done was to make clear, at the time and later, Britain's strong disapproval of such blatantly careless and foolish behaviour. No doubt President Reagan saw himself as the sheriff dealing with a cattle rustler, but at that time America was financing terrorism in Central America. It is no good being the sheriff in the Middle

East and the rustler elsewhere. In fact American hands were not even clean in the Middle East: a CIA-sponsored car bomb killed ninety-two people in Beirut in 1985. Copying terrorism is not the way to defeat it.[74]

The American action was accurately described by the Prime Minister's former foreign policy adviser, Sir Anthony Parsons, as a 'kind of vigilantism more likely to provoke than prevent terrorism'. That, after all, was much the same as Mrs Thatcher herself had thought only three months before. British complicity in the American action led to the killing of British hostages in Lebanon and to a large supply of Libyan arms and aid to the IRA. And predictably the American bombing did nothing to curb terrorism. The Libyans were evidently responsible for the destruction of the Pan Am airliner over Lockerbie.[75] Thus Mrs Thatcher's decision to collaborate with President Reagan over the Tripoli bombing, instead of trying to stop him, not only did not serve British interests; it did not serve American interests either.

The Anglo-American relationship has been an unequal one since shortly after America's entry into the last war, and the inequality has grown. Mrs Thatcher was able to influence Reagan from time to time, on occasions crucially, as on nuclear weapons after the President's meeting with Gorbachev at Reykjavik. But if as a rule she was, personally, the senior partner, Britain remained very much the junior one and generally conformed to American leadership.[76]

The Commonwealth and Europe

Margaret Thatcher's usual readiness to follow the United States was in stark contrast with her attitude to the Commonwealth and the EC. There were a number of reasons. Two of the characteristics of Thatcherism mentioned in Chapter I were its method of controversy and Mrs Thatcher's compulsion to have her own way. Both the vast disparity in power between America and Britain and the Prime Minister's affection for President Reagan muted or eliminated those Thatcherite features in her dealings with the United States. Furthermore her general superiority to the President in power of argument, commitment and knowledge did much to soften the pains of Britain being heavily subordinate to her mighty ally. Two other factors helped to reconcile her to American domination: her ideological affinity with Reagan's United States and her distaste for the Commonwealth and the European Community.

Which of those two organizations she disliked more is hard to decide. After her early outbursts at Dublin and Luxembourg, her Commonwealth rows were more spectacular than those with Europe. But the Commonwealth conferences were much less frequent than the meetings of the European heads of government, and the EC was a much more consistent obstacle to her freedom of action at home than was the intermittent opposition of the Commonwealth. In addition Britain was much the most influential and powerful member of the Commonwealth, whereas in Europe she was not even *primus inter pares*. So Europe was probably at the top of Mrs Thatcher's hierarchy of dislikes, though the Commonwealth was not far below.

The Prime Minister did not like collective decision making. The Council Chamber, for her, was not a place for intelligent discussion, for improving mutual understanding or for attempting to achieve a meeting of minds, which would inevitably require some shift of position and compromise by those taking part, including, from time to time, herself. Whether the institution was the Commonwealth, the European Community (with occasional exceptions) or her own cabinet, its function was to be dominated by her. If she was successful, then her 'victories' were trumpeted by Bernard Ingham and the obedient Conservative press. If the foreigners for some reason proved recalcitrant, then their failure to fall into line and her rigid adherence to her own views were also trumpeted as a victory for 'Maggie' – demonstrating her indomitable courage and her resolve to stand up for Britain. In all these bodies, victory or triumphant refusal to submit to the collective view was much more important to Thatcherism than the securing of agreement; British interests (which were always identified with hers) might or might not be served by this procedure, but they were anyway secondary to the need for the Prime Minister to be seen to be striving *contra mundum* for personal victory. This was conceived to be a great electoral bonus for Mrs Thatcher, though on the evidence of her usual low standing in the opinion polls the validity of that idea is questionable.

The perennial cause of rows with the Commonwealth was the treatment of South Africa and the question of sanctions. Initially I had a good deal of sympathy for Mrs Thatcher's opposition to mandatory sanctions being imposed on South Africa. I was very doubtful that they would be economically effective, feared that they would make the Afrikaaners still more intransigent, and anticipated that they would be a potent cause of increased misery to much of the black population. The evidence suggests, however, that all those fears were mistaken. Sanctions and economic pressure turned out to be strikingly effective in converting South Africa's leaders to the need for reform.

Even if, however, the anti-sanctions argument had been wholly correct, the way it was presented and the manner in which the government handled the Commonwealth would not have gained applause. An association of largely non-white countries was bound to feel strongly about apartheid, but the British Prime Minister never seemed to take proper account of their sensitivities. While there is no reason to doubt her own dislike of apartheid, she conducted her opposition to it with none of the fervour she exhibited on other issues. Indeed her enthusiasm for a multi-racial society in South Africa or elsewhere was rarely evident – it was something like the passion for truth of the great American trial lawyer, Clarence Darrow, which in H L Mencken's view was 'exactly comparable to what a man feels for an amiable maiden aunt'.

Britain had the most to lose from a loosening or severance of economic ties, but Zambia and Zimbabwe were not the only African countries to be in various ways heavily dependent on

South Africa. To have discovered from those countries what they were prepared to do, as opposed to say, about sanctions and for Britain then to make a similarly limited response should have been perfectly possible. Instead, the British government behaved as though all the right was on one side and everybody on the other side was just plain wrong, or hypocritical as well. Yet the protagonists of sanctions did not have a monopoly of self-righteousness or hypocrisy. Britain's stand was based on her economic interests (which any government would have had to take account of); at the same time, wrote Hugo Young, 'opposing Commonwealth demands was a respectable way of aligning oneself with latent racialism at home'. In addition, the British case was bolstered by ill-founded optimism about alleged improvements in South Africa and about British influence over President Botha.[77]

Since Canada and Australia favoured sanctions, Commonwealth conferences usually took the form of Mrs Thatcher against the rest. She made no more attempt to seek a consensus in the Commonwealth than she did anywhere else. As she graphically put it, 'if I were the odd man out and I were right, that would not matter, would it?' Although it was treated in much the same way as Thatcherism treated offending British institutions at home, fortunately the Commonwealth survived.

Thatcherite policy towards the European Community went through the same phases as the Thatcherite handling of the economy. In each case there was a slump at the beginning and end, and a boom in the middle.

The period of European boom, which roughly coincided with Mrs Thatcher's second term, also saw Mrs Thatcher's most creative statesmanship elsewhere. When Mr Gorbachev, at the insistence, of course, of the Foreign Office, visited Britain in December 1984, he and the Prime Minister immediately hit it off. 'I like Mr Gorbachev', she memorably said, 'we can do business together.' In view of her 'iron lady' image and the volume of anti-socialist rhetoric (much of it justified) that Mrs Thatcher had spoken over the years, that remark was a tribute not only to Mr Gorbachev's intelligence and open-mindedness and the Prime Minister's ability to spot a remarkable man, but to her willingness, on occasion, to change her mind. Dogma was abandoned to the advantage of all.[78]

The friendship between Mrs Thatcher and Mr Gorbachev was of great mutual benefit — being for Margaret Thatcher a useful counter-balance to what many thought was her too close and over-effusive bond with Ronald Reagan and the United States. But much more importantly it led to a significant improvement in East–West relations, and Mrs Thatcher soon became in Eastern Europe easily the most revered foreign leader.

'Had I said in 1979', Mrs Thatcher wrote in August 1991, ' "Elect me! In ten years the Berlin Wall will be down, the Warsaw Pact will have collapsed, you will have a friendly person in the Soviet Union, communism will be crumbling world-wide. Vote for me and Mr Reagan and all that will come about!", they would have said: "You're crazy." '

They would indeed! 'But', she added, 'it came out just that way.' And if Margaret Thatcher inordinately confused the sequence of events — the election of 'me' and Mr Reagan and the subsequent end of the cold war — with their causation, she undoubtedly deserves much credit for giving a helping hand to the basic causes of the collapse of Communism and the break-up of the Soviet Union.[79]

She was surely right, too, to curb Ronald Reagan's enthusiasm when in his 'anti-nuclear phase' and his infatuation with the Strategic Defence Initiative (or Star Wars) he turned against deterrence and proposed a ban on all nuclear missiles. On any view it was high-handed of Reagan to attempt unilaterally to revolutionize NATO's strategy overnight. Many American officials had doubts as to whether the President really knew what he was doing. In any case the Prime Minister soon straightened him out.[80]

On a much lower level of importance but on a similar level of statesmanship was the Anglo–Irish agreement of 1985. Under the Thatcher government, as under preceding governments, events in Northern Ireland continued their bloody course. A tragic prelude to the 1979 election was the assassination of Airey Neave, Mrs Thatcher's Chief of Staff and her probable Northern Ireland Secretary. The murder of Lord Mountbatten soon followed. As well as the ordinary terrorist outrages, the government had also to contend with the IRA hunger-strikers – Bobby Sands and others. I wanted to have the hunger-strikers force-fed, which always used to be the custom. Force-feeding is clearly objectionable, but less so, in my view, than people starving themselves to death. However, nobody seemed to agree with me, and I was probably wrong.

Relations between London and Dublin were nevertheless surprisingly good. In December 1980 the British and Irish governments began a series of Anglo–Irish discussions to consider their relationship 'within these islands', and almost a year later an Anglo–Irish Inter-Governmental Council was established to express in institutional form the 'unique character of the relationship between the two governments'.[81]

The relationship was a good deal less than unique during the Falklands conflict, when the Republic called upon the United Nations to take action against the British whom it branded as colonial aggressors. After that absurd and self-wounding gesture, however, the Irish government soon returned to present-day reality, and after a time good relations resumed. In the summer of 1985, Chris Patten, Under-Secretary in Northern Ireland, stated that the government of the Republic had a 'legitimate interest in Northern Ireland, and a special part to play in the politics of the minority there'.[82]

Later that year came the Anglo–Irish agreement which, according to Ian Paisley, 'rode to victory on the back of IRA terrorism'. The Unionist reaction was indeed explosive and to some extent understandable: they had not been consulted. Yet, if they had been consulted, there would not have been an agreement. Contrary to Unionist claims, the agreement did not give joint authority for Northern Ireland to the Republic. Its object was to promote 'peace and stability' in the province and to help reconcile the 'two main traditions in Ireland'.

The agreement formalized inter-state cooperation and gave, as Brendan O'Leary has written, 'formal notice that, while the Unionist guarantee remained, Unionists have no veto on policy formation with Northern Ireland'. Its results so far have been meagre, but the agreement was an important step on the route to a tolerable solution of the Ulster problem. In making it Mrs Thatcher showed herself to be brave and far-sighted.[83]

In the European Community itself Mrs Thatcher's creative period saw an extension of European political cooporation together with the solemn Declaration of Stuttgart and final victory on the British budget contribution at Fontainebleau in 1984. That victory, wrote Sir Michael Butler, our talented ambassador to the EC from 1979 to 1985, was due 'to her courage and persistence'. The achievement has turned out to be even more important than it seemed at the time. In 1992 the European Commission recommended that the British budget rebates should continue because Britain had become poorer in relation to its EC partners in the eight years since the Fontainebleau Agreement was signed.[84]

Surprisingly, however, the Prime Minister's hostility to the EC, which had been so conspicuous from 1979–81, did not subside. 'In all the innumerable meetings and discussions with her ministers and officials', wrote Sir Michael Butler who attended them, Mrs Thatcher 'showed a deep-seated prejudice against the European Community'. Notwithstanding that prejudice Mrs Thatcher agreed in 1986 to the Single European Act which gave new powers to the European parliament and abolished the right of veto of a single government, thus allowing majority voting over a large field of single-market legislation. The Single European Act was therefore a considerable infringement of the 'sovereignty' that, later, so worried Mrs Thatcher.[85]

The reasons for her relatively pro-European period of 1983–87 and for its fairly abrupt ending are a matter for her biographers. Probably her different advisers at the various times had something to do with it. More important, almost certainly, was the Conservative victory of 1987 and the growing Conservative conviction, hardening into certainty, that the Conservative party would inevitably win the next election.

That conviction, as was mentioned earlier, fed the view that the Conservative government – with a seemingly endless vista of power before it – could and should do virtually what it liked. In such an atmosphere the EC became a prime target of Mrs Thatcher's dislike of pluralism. As it could not be absolutely controlled and was a brake on Thatcherite power, it was the international equivalent of a British intermediate institution and was treated as such.

Jacques Delors was denounced as though he was the socialist successor to Ken Livingstone as leader of the Greater London Council. In her celebrated speech at Bruges on 20 September 1988, Mrs Thatcher unfolded what Michael Butler called 'perhaps the most misleading political manifesto of the decade'. The signatory of the Single European Act, only two years earlier, had suddenly discovered that, as Ghita Ionescu has written, we were 'menaced by a federalist and socialist conspiracy'. The Single European Act and the directives of the Community on competition had in fact ruled out not only the possibility of 'socialism' but also Mrs Thatcher's favourite prescription for the future: a Europe of totally independent sovereign states cooperating with each other. Once again as in 1979–80, if with limited success, the Prime Minister was fuelling anti-European prejudices in Britain. Even the British monarchy, it seemed, was threatened – a particularly improbable scare since half the states in the Community are monarchies.[86]

Margaret Thatcher was finally brought down by her European policy and by the poll tax, two issues which had one thing in common: British local government and the European Community prevented the untrammelled exercise of plebiscitary democracy. The poll tax would effectively destroy what remained of the independence of local government, and an anti-Brussels crusade would emasculate the European Community. Neither policy was popular, and both offended a large part of the Conservative party.

The EC helped to destroy Mrs Thatcher, but her legacy may in turn help to destroy the Community. Her 'anti-federalist' campaign has contributed to introducing a fatal contradiction into the Community's proposals for Economic Monetary Union and into the Maastricht Treaty. As long ago as 1977 the European Commission published a report of a study group chaired by Sir Donald MacDougall, which was based on the study of eight existing monetary unions – five federations (the United States, Canada, West Germany, Switzerland and Australia) and three unitary states (France, Italy and the United Kingdom). The MacDougall report showed that economic and monetary union required a far larger Community budget than existed then or has existed since. That is because if European governments lose the power to devalue or use monetary or fiscal policy adequately to deal with their economic difficulties, they will need considerable help from the centre to make social conditions tolerable and to engineer economic recovery. That of course is what happens in all existing federations and indeed in unitary states. New England in America and Northern Ireland in the United Kingdom are prime examples.[87]

Unfortunately anti-federalist prejudice has prevented an increase in the European budget that would be anywhere near sufficient for such a vital purpose. Similarly that prejudice has prevented the creation of a political union or a structure at the Community's centre which could deal with the problem. That, as Martin Feldstein recently wrote, 'is a formula for economic costs without any of the supposed political benefits'.[88]

The irony of the current controversy over Europe's future is that much of the Maastricht Treaty which Mrs Thatcher so ardently opposes is constructed on thoroughly Thatcherite principles. That is not surprising, since the proposals for monetary union are based on the recommendations of the Delors Committee which was inappropriately dominated by Central Bankers – the governor of the Bank of England and no less than twelve of his peers. Hence the proposals are strong on eliminating inflation and budget deficits, but weak to the point of indifference on avoiding unemployment.[89] Greater

European unity is highly desirable, but a mere 'Bankers' union' or a Bankers' Europe is not an inviting prospect. Apart from the economic and social objections, such a set-up would, because of the massive discontent it produced, lead not to the economic integration of Europe but to its break-up.

The remedy is not to leave the EC. Thatcherism 'in one country' would work no better than did 'socialism in one country'. Nor is the remedy so to dilute the Community that it is effectively disbanded. The best course could be to build the international political institutions that would enable economic union to work. The idea that MPs who favour such institutions are betraying their constituents and undermining the sovereignty of parliament is a defiance of economic and political reality. No nation today is economically sovereign. And in chapter VIII we saw how the Thatcher government (and previous administrations) treated parliament. Mrs Thatcher goes on and on about the House of Commons being the oldest parliament in the world – usually misquoting John Bright in the process* – but it is also one of the parliaments which is most under the control of the executive.

A sharing of power with Brussels and Strasbourg would in some ways mean less power to Whitehall, but except formally it would have little effect on Westminster. And just as a sharing of power in Britain with the intermediate institutions should reduce the power of the government but would probably help the individual and the governed, the same would very likely be true of greater power for Community institutions in Brussels. But that, of course, would depend on the existence of such institutions. A 'Bankers' Europe' would not have them.

Outside Europe, Mrs Thatcher had a much surer touch. She reacted with characteristic energy and decisiveness to Iraq's seizure of Kuwait. And in view of her proven aptitude for war her supporters, when the leadership struggle loomed, could argue with some plausibility that it would be wrong

---

* The House of Commons is not 'the Mother of Parliaments'. John Bright said: 'England, Mother of Parliaments.'

to change prime ministers in the middle of the struggle with Saddam Hussein. The precedents however were against them. In every major war (save one) that Britain has fought since 1688, she has changed her political leadership at least once. The exception was the American War of Independence, and that was the only war that Britain decisively lost. In any case Mrs Thatcher's successor proved a good war leader.

Mrs Thatcher's foreign policy record was therefore mixed. It contained a number of large achievements but, as in internal policy, Thatcherism looked backwards. The Anglo–American special relationship continues, but to base British foreign policy upon it is an anachronism. The disparity in power between the two countries is far too great. The Anglo–American special relationship is a grandiose term for British dependence on the United States. Britain is a European power, and its future lies with our European partners. A fragmented Europe will be in no position to compete successfully with the advancing countries of the Pacific basin and probably not even with the United States.

Mrs Thatcher undoubtedly improved Britain's stature in the world, but she had little idea how to put that enhanced standing to its best use. And because of economic failure Britain's heightened stature was not matched by increased British power.

X

Harmony or Discord?

Do not say it is time for something else! Thatcherism is not for a decade. It is for centuries!

Margaret Thatcher, October 1990[1]

You have to keep a steady nerve in politics. If you're guided by opinion polls, you're not practising leadership, you're practising followership. But, you expect your party to stay with you when the going gets rough. Some of them didn't. Some of them didn't. Absurd. We've had unpopularity in between elections before, but some of them didn't. They got scared. So be it. So be it. I wouldn't have changed. I believe you win elections, and I believe we would have won the next one . . . I'm sure that's what would have happened. But, they just ran away, they were frightened.

Margaret Thatcher, March 1991[2]

All Power, each Tyrant, every Mob
Whose head has grown too large,
Ends by destroying its own job
And works its own discharge
Rudyard Kipling: The Benefactors

IN NOVEMBER 1990 the Conservative parliamentary party performed almost the ultimate anti-Thatcherite act: it got rid of Margaret Thatcher. Whether or not that amounted to 'a defeat' for Mrs Thatcher matters little. In claiming that she was never defeated, Mrs Thatcher is right to point out that she got more votes in the leadership contest than anybody else.[3] Yet the side that is forced to leave the field is usually the one which is deemed to have been vanquished. The Conservative party's removal of its leader was only 'almost' the ultimate anti-Thatcher act, because it baulked at choosing as her successor the only avowed anti-Thatcher contender (whom I supported). It elected instead the candidate who was her chosen successor.

The field was a very good one. All three candidates would have made excellent prime ministers. In any case the party's choice of leader proved well judged. John Major quickly united the party, won the respect of international leaders and was popular at home. Having put a human face on Thatcherism and abolished the poll tax, he won the 1992 election even though the odds seemed stacked against him. Yet Thatcherism even with a human face is still Thatcherism, and John Major and the Conservative party will sooner or later have to make a choice of comparable importance to the one that was made in November 1990. But before considering that crucial choice, a look needs to be taken at where the party is now and how it got there.

The Nature of Thatcherism

Mrs Thatcher's first words in Downing Street, 'where there is discord, may we bring harmony . . .', though allegedly by St Francis of Assisi, were, as we saw, written much later. Was the sentiment she expressed as bogus as the source? Jim Prior thinks her words were 'so totally at odds with Margaret's belief in conviction politics and the need to abandon the consensus style of government' that they were 'the most awful humbug'. Certainly they were at variance, too, with most of her actions as Prime Minister. But a more likely explanation for her making this 'prayer' is that it had only recently been provided by her speech writer, Ronald Miller, and the Prime Minister had not had the time to give it much thought.[4]

There is a third explanation, however, which is more charitable than either humbug or inadvertence. Mrs Thatcher may well have had a very different idea of harmony from that normally held by Conservatives and most other people. To her, 'harmony' may have been whatever the free market happened to produce. Where others might see social conflict, poverty and misery, she saw merely the benevolent working of an invisible economic providence. If that is right and Mrs Thatcher wanted to mention Harmony and Discord, then instead of furnishing her with the false St Francis, her speech writer should have armed her with genuine Pope:

> All Nature is but Art, unknown to thee;
> All Chance, Direction, which thou canst not see;
> All Discord, Harmony, not understood;
> All partial Evil, universal good.

Pope may not have known it, but his deity was really the free market, and he well expressed Mrs Thatcher's views. Only, however, when the Prime Minister was securely in power would she have endorsed Pope's next two lines.

> And, spite of Pride, in erring Reason's spite,
> One truth is clear: Whatever is, is right[5]

At the beginning of this book one key question was left open: the nature of Thatcherism. Numerous attempts have been made elsewhere to provide an answer; one study outlines six possible approaches to the subject. Authoritative observers have emphasized the importance of 'statecraft', 'instinct' and a 'hegemonic project'. Each of those approaches obviously has substance. Like most politicians Mrs Thatcher was anxious to win elections, she had a distinctive 'style of government', and she was interested in eliminating 'socialism' and establishing hegemony. Thatcherism is many-sided.[6]

Yet its ideological content is the common thread of Thatcherism which can be traced through most of the features identified by other commentators. Margaret Thatcher identified herself so closely with her beliefs that her statecraft, her instinct and her desire for hegemony can not be separated from the ideological fervour which inspired them. It chose her friends and enemies for her, it dictated her goals, and it brought about her downfall. Mrs Thatcher was unique among British prime ministers in gaining the dubious accolade of having an 'ism', because none of her predecessors were so wedded to a set of abstract ideas.

But what is meant by calling Margaret Thatcher an ideologist? Her devotion to Manchester Liberalism is not in doubt and, as was seen above, she once said that 'we must have an ideology' to test our 'policies against', like the Labour party had.[7] Despite that ambition, many commentators deny that ideology was at the core of Thatcherism.[8] Hostile as well as friendly critics claim that Mrs Thatcher's beliefs were too inconsistent to qualify her as an ideologue. Yet ideologies do not have to be consistent. Liberals disagree about tolerating the intolerant; Marxists 'rig the dialectic' to ensure that the proletariat wins in the end; Fascists have trawled for ideas in diverse and murky waters; Mussolini even founded a Fascist faculty of political science at Perugia and then a 'School of Fascist Mysticism' at Milan, but neither of those distinguished bodies was able to make Fascist ideas coherent. Towards the end of his life the Duce himself admitted that fascism had been merely a means for him to achieve power; it was nothing more than *Mussolinismo*.[9]

In other words, if inconsistent belief-systems cannot be classed as ideologies, and if an 'ism' is prevented from being an ideology by its being adapted to serve the personal ends of its founder or leading exponent, then virtually nothing can be deemed an ideology. By the standards normally applied to the study of ideologies, Thatcherism easily qualifies. Apart from the importance of ideas, the psychological evidence points in the same direction. For example, ideologists commonly embrace their beliefs through a 'leap of faith', and there are numerous examples of the Thatcherite elect undergoing such a mysterious and holy experience.[10]

The 'New Right' is heterogeneous. Its views cover a wide area from Utopia to near-pragmatism. Outsiders think most of their ideas are mistaken, and a number might have provoked widespread violence. Not surprisingly, Mrs Thatcher baulked at some of the New Right's more cranky schemes, but that does not rule her out from being an ideologue. All governments, however dogmatic, eventually come up against political impossibilities. Even the Jacobins could not maintain the purity of their revolutionary zeal during the terror of 1792–94, and their use of price controls was tactical. Lenin's sporadic toleration of capitalism did not mean that he had become a part-time lackey of the bourgeoisie. The ideological consistency of the study can not be maintained in the council chamber or the corridors of power.[11]

The New Right may have been dismayed by what they regarded as Mrs Thatcher's backsliding, but academics and journalists are not always best placed to appreciate the problems of infusing a dogma into the spirit and laws of a nation. Margaret Thatcher was necessarily less ideologically infatuated than some of her disciples. After all, she had to maintain herself in power; otherwise the return to *laissez-faire* and the establishment of an enterprise culture would be jeopardized. Occasional compromise was unavoidable. All the same, the nature of Mrs Thatcher's beliefs and the depth of her attachment to them still mark her down as an ideologue.

The Anatomy of Dogmatism

Like all ideologies, Thatcherism is based on a simplistic view of human nature, which reflects more the qualities of the ideologist than any common attributes of mankind. The Thatcherite theory is unusually unconvincing, however, since it manages to be both too pessimistic and too optimistic. It is too pessimistic, in that it assumes that everyone is driven by selfish motives; it is too optimistic, in that it asserts that everyone pursues his selfish interests in a rational manner.

These assumptions are vital, of course, to free-market ideas.

Unfortunately, in so far as they are meaningful, they are false. 'Selfishness' (doing something for our own *exclusive* pleasure) is not the same as 'following self-interest' (doing something because we *want* to, even if it is primarily intended to benefit others). This distinction has been well known at least since the time of Hume, Bishop Butler and Adam Smith. The Thatcherite failure to appreciate the difference explains why Thatcherism was so widely suspected on welfare matters: for the well-off, supporting the welfare state is wholly compatible with self-interest but not with selfishness. This tendency to clutch at the lowest common denominator of human conduct also explains why Mrs Thatcher was not at her most persuasive when discussing 'elevated' motives – she once revealingly expressed her contempt for 'people [who] just drool and drivel that they care'.[12]

The notion of 'rational' conduct is equally flawed. Textbooks may offer their versions of rationality in the marketplace – consumers and producers can be trusted to make the right economic choice to further their own economic interests – but such work only describes rationality from one, very narrow, point of view. Other people may think that instead of maximizing profits, the only rational course is to fight famine in Africa, help to prevent global warming or sacrifice everything for the revolution.

Not content with mistaken ideas about individuals, the Thatcherites contrived to be in error about society, too. Their leader's notorious denial that there was any such thing may have been an inadvertent caricature of her views. Yet it was seized upon, because it reflected an essential element in her creed; that the individual should be treated in abstract isolation. Although they expressed much admiration for the operations of the market, Thatcherites were blind to the existence of collectives. They saw people as living in a condition reminiscent of Hobbes's state of nature, locked into a relentless competition for material resources, and growing every day more solitary, nasty, brutish and rich. For the more extreme among the priesthood, every man was an island: when the bell of unemployment tolled they paid no heed, for it generally tolled for someone else.

For the Conservative, common sense suggests that the actions of individuals should be examined for their impact upon others: both the individual and society have to be taken into account by governments. Unfortunately, in fleeing as far as possible from socialism, the Thatcherites also ended up some distance away from common sense. Much as socialists forgot the individual, the New Right were determined to forget society. 'Hell is other people' for Thatcherites, as for Jean-Paul Sartre.[13]

Mrs Thatcher was unprecedentedly successful at winning elections, but Thatcherism took little hold on the English people (and none at all on the Scots). That was partly because, as Mr Gladstone told the dons of All Souls over breakfast, 'the English people are extraordinarily difficult to work up to excitement on any question'. (They took three million unemployed in their stride, which was fortunate for the Thatcherites.) But the main reason was that they did not find Thatcherism appealing. While Mrs Thatcher was shifting national policy and the Conservative party far to the right, public opinion did not follow her. If anything, indeed, public opinion moved to the left during the Thatcher era.[14]

Apart from its failure to engage the affections of the British people, Thatcherism also managed to contravene the warnings of the country's foremost Conservative thinker. In his book *On Human Conduct*, Michael Oakeshott discussed the danger of a state compelling its citizens to join what he called an 'enterprise association'. Such an association is 'human beings joined in pursuing some common purpose, in seeking the satisfaction of some common want or in provoking some common substantive interest', and is valid only when individuals are able to contract out of it when it suits them. Under normal conditions the state should only perform a managerial function, and should not bully its citizens into conformity with its goals. In view of the hectoring nature of the Thatcherite regime, it is little wonder that Oakeshott did not consider Margaret Thatcher to be a true Conservative ruler.*

Thatcherism jarred British sensibilities not only in its style and tone, but also in its content and objective. The country probably became more selfish in the Thatcher years – it certainly believed it had done so – yet the British are not by nature just selfish individuals. They have a considerable feeling for the community and society, and while they are far too sensible not to value material prosperity – it was their preoccupation with it that persuaded Talleyrand in 1792 that the French Revolution would not spread to England – they have other values as well. To them life is more than a supermarket.[15]

Of course they could (in Oakeshott's phrase) have contracted out of the Thatcherite enterprise association. And if the voters did not like Thatcherism, why, it may fairly be asked, did they go on voting Conservative? The answer is they did so, despite their dislike of Thatcherism and despite the unpopularity of Mrs Thatcher herself. Margaret Thatcher seemed to feel that she had some profound and intimate bond with the British people. That feeling was not reciprocated. As was seen earlier, she was an unusually unpopular prime minister. In 1979 and probably in 1987 the Conservatives would almost certainly have fared better with another leader. British elections are not presidential, and the Conservatives won in 1979, 1983, 1987 (and also 1992) by default. In 1979 the Labour government was on the ropes; in 1983 and 1987 the

---

* The quotation comes from pages 98–99 of my book *Inside Right*, where there is an excellent summary of Oakeshott's argument in his *On Human Conduct*. That claim is less conceited than it sounds, since the summary was written by the great man himself. When I sent Oakeshott my chapter on him for comment, he returned it with a very nice letter and an alternative passage to the one in which I had tried to summarize *On Human Conduct*. The next day I got an equally nice letter asking me to disregard the first one, since, on reflection, he had decided it was unpardonably presumptuous to have rewritten those two pages. Naturally I disregarded his second letter.

opposition was split, and the policies put forward by Labour were so palpably unsuited to their time and country that they made the government look moderate. So the electorate (or 43 per cent of it) voted Conservative even though they were never in sympathy with Thatcherism's more ambitious objectives – as the Thatcherites themselves well recognized. In 1987 Mrs Thatcher thought that 'the reforms of the NHS were too sensitive a topic to expose to the electorate'.[16]

The Choice

The evidence is that the voters did not want Thatcherism, yet by voting for the Conservatives under Margaret Thatcher (who thought they 'voted for me'), Thatcherism is what they got. As a result, Britain is now probably the most right-wing state in Western Europe – something she has never been before. After 1688 she and the Netherlands were easily the most advanced countries politically and socially. In the era of the French Revolution she was the only country to avoid both revolution and extreme reaction. In the nineteenth century she was the most liberal major European state. If Imperial Germany introduced old-age pensions and some other social legislation while Britain still lagged behind, Britain was in every other way still ahead. Britain had super tax before either France or the United States had income tax. Between the world wars, as has been said, she introduced the most advanced social services in the world. And, after 1945, she remained in the vanguard socially, despite her poor economic record.[17]

The Conservative party having won four elections running – the last one in particularly unfavourable circumstances – may well go on winning them. There is no law of the pendulum in democratic politics. Electoral dominance by one party is much more the rule than the exception in democratic states.[18]

So the Conservatives now have to decide whether to continue in their unaccustomed role of being the most right-wing governing party in Western Europe, with an outlook more akin to the Republicans in the United States than to the Christian

Democrats in Europe, or whether to revert to their traditional much more centrist position.

In a sense it is a choice between the nineteenth and the twentieth or twenty-first centuries. Thatcherism was often described by its devotees and by its opponents as radical. We should never be goaded, Sir Karl Popper has warned, 'into taking seriously problems about words and their meanings'. Nevertheless, the rhetoric about Thatcherite 'radicalism' is seriously misleading. The so-called right-wing 'radicals' looked back to the Victorian age. While Thatcherites may have been radical, if not Jacobin, in their disregard of opposing views and institutions, Thatcherism, as Dr Ramsden has shown, was 'a conscious attempt to put the clock back'. It was neither radical nor conservative; it was reactionary.[19]

Now that the Labour party has finally, it seems, abandoned nineteenth-century socialism, it should not be too much to expect the Conservative party soon to abandon nineteenth-century liberalism. But the omens are not favourable. The government's recent abolition of the NEDC amid tribal cries of getting rid of the relics of 'corporatism' suggest that the Treasury still has not noticed what damage its policies have caused since 1979; it is still in the grip of neo-Ricardian dogma.

After Adam Smith, David Ricardo was the greatest of the political economists, but he 'had one of the most abstract minds the world has ever seen'. However suitable or unsuitable Ricardo's dogmatic *laissez-faire* ideas were for the early nineteenth-century Britain of small firms and partnerships, they have no relevance to the late twentieth-century British economy, in which some one hundred large companies produce about half of all manufacturing output and every industry is dominated by a small number of firms.[20]

In any case nineteenth-century Britain saw a prolonged retreat from *laissez-faire*. Victorian prosperity was closely linked to increasing state intervention. Nostalgic Thatcherism might see Victorian Britain as an age in which Britain stood tall among nations, and boy chimney sweeps merrily sold themselves in the dearest market. But contemporaries, such as the seventh Lord Shaftesbury, Dickens, Ruskin and Morris, saw the reality at first hand. They could not shut their eyes to the misery, squalor and cruelty of Victorian Britain, and they eloquently advocated reform. Even the Victorian hero of Thatcherism, the diligent Samuel Smiles, sounded many notes of caution which have been overlooked by his present-day admirers.

Perhaps all creeds need a mythical golden age to which their adherents long to return. But neither economically nor socially does the Victorian Age produce an acceptable model for contemporary Britain. Hence Thatcherite neo-liberalism – misleadingly called radicalism – was doomed to failure. The giddy dance of dogma has now been halted, but the Conservative party has not yet regained its balance. It still has to choose between the nineteenth and the twentieth centuries, between two-nation Thatcherism and one-nation Toryism. The record of Thatcherism – and also the Conservative tradition – should be its guide.

Britain's sudden swing to the far right under Mrs Thatcher might just have been defensible had it transformed the economy. Arguably, some social sacrifice would have been justified for the achievement of an economic miracle, though even then it would have been difficult to explain why all the sacrifices had to come from the poor. But, as this book has shown, the sacrifice imposed upon the poor produced nothing miraculous, except for the rich. Instead of experiencing an economic miracle, Britain experienced the lowest growth rate since the war. The lunge to the right caused social retreat without economic advance.

If the Conservative party continues to be Thatcherite, more or less, that will not in itself stop it winning elections. As Professor Galbraith has recently shown, 'the haves' when they are in a plurality can be just as selfish as they were when they were a small minority. They can easily be brought to ignore what is happening to the other one-third of the population – 'the have-nots'. And a continuance of Thatcherism would probably bring nothing as dreadful as the Los Angeles riots of 1965 and 1992, but it would take us ever closer to the 'Clockwork Orange' society in which the country is divided between the fortunate skilled majority (who can get work) and the unfortunate unskilled minority (who can do so only rarely). Those who are effectively excluded from the benefits of society can not be expected to remain passive indefinitely.[21]

If, instead, the Conservatives readopt one-nation Toryism, no longer will they be stuck with the once fashionable view (which was comprehensively refuted by experience in the eighties and early nineties) that markets are always right and therefore governments should not interfere. Conservatives will then take a more 'hands-on' approach to the economy, rather than the 'hands-up' attitude of Thatcherism. The state cannot desert the economic front; talk of 'rolling back its frontiers' makes better rhetoric than practical sense. Despite its Self-Denying Ordinance in the economic sphere, the Thatcherite New Model Army made frequent forays into it: for all the *laissez-faire* dogma, individual companies were often ruthlessly coerced, as was vividly demonstrated by the treatment of British Aerospace during the Westland saga; and probably many citizens (especially, of course, the unemployed) were more shamelessly bullied by the state during those heroic years of 'minimal interference' than ever before. If the state is to play an active role in society after all, its activities should at least be benevolent in intention.[22]

Nothing in logic, equity or history suggests that the state should confine itself to providing a free market. If it does so, it merely protects the rich, and leaves the poor to look after themselves — as Adam Smith pointed out, if it were not for the protection of the state, the rich could not 'sleep a single night in security'. A true Conservative state should protect everybody. Hence it has the duty to mitigate the operation of market forces. To everybody except neo-Liberals, non-market forces are every bit as legitimate and often no less 'automatic' than market ones. As most of our European partners recognize, the 'free-market' is crucially dependent upon the constructive intervention of the state. Once all this is acknowledged, the limits of government become a matter of judgement and prudence. There is no place at all for dogma.[23]

The abandonment of neo-Liberalism entails recognition that unemployment in the region of three million for the foreseeable future is not something which can be accepted with just a shrug of the shoulders or, perhaps, a murmur of regret. For Conservatives the reduction of unemployment should be as important as the conquest of inflation. The Thatcherite (and current) approach is to treat very low inflation as the overriding economic objective, if not as an end in itself. At best, however, it is a means to the end of a more prosperous and peaceful society. While a moderate level of inflation (3 or 4 per cent, say) is compatible with widespread contentment, for the jobless man 'unemployment is one hundred per cent'. For his family and friends it is unacceptably high, too. Oddly, the Thatcherites' obsession with the individual did not enable them to comprehend such an obvious point. Whether 'full employment' is practicable or not, the lowest possible unemployment should be a vital objective.

Yet, low unemployment will not be achieved with an overvalued exchange rate. Mrs Thatcher's last economic action as Prime Minister was to join the European Exchange Rate Mechanism at far too high a rate. That the rate was and is too high is proved by Britain still having a high balance of payments deficit even at the bottom of the longest recession since the 1930s. When Britain made a similar mistake in 1925, Keynes correctly pointed out that it would lead to years of deflation and unemployment. The same will happen again until the mistake is rectified.[24]

Economic dogma should be the first to go. The Conservative party must learn from the mistakes of the 1980s, not repeat them – let alone repeat those of the 1920s as well. The Thatcher era saw a grim failure of economic management. The two worst slumps and the most irresponsible boom since the war is a record no-one should be proud of. All three of those phases of economic management inflicted severe damage on the economy. And that harm will certainly not be repaired by a continued application of the nineteenth-century dogma that caused it.

The government does not necessarily have to admit error in public, but with the election safely out of the way it should at least face it in private. 'Things are what they are', wrote that good conservative, Bishop Butler, in the eighteenth century, 'and the consequences of them will be what they will be. Why then should we seek to be deceived?' At present the government is still deceiving itself and a declining number of other people. Once it discards the dogma, its self-deception will be ended.

But it was not just the economics of the Thatcher experiment that was at fault. Much social damage was also done. That, too, will take long to repair, but a start must soon be made. And the damage was not only social. As was seen earlier, Margaret Thatcher wanted, through her economic policies, to change 'the heart and the soul of the nation'.[25] She did achieve a transformation, but not, presumably, the one she intended. Britain did not change to an enterprise society. The transformation was in sensibility. British society became coarser and more selfish. Attitudes were encouraged which would even have undermined the well-being of a much more prosperous society.

Many people did well out of Thatcherism, and in consequence still support it, though their numbers, also, are in decline. Because of the coarsening of society and the bombast of Thatcherite propaganda, the beneficiaries of Thatcherite policies believe that some benign process was at work. They did not realize – and apparently still do not – that what had happened was a large redistribution of wealth from the poor to the rich.

The Thatcherite treatment of the poor was unforgivable. Once again the author of the disaster was dogma: firstly the economic dogma which conscripted a vast army of unemployed and then banned active steps to disband it by pursuing policies that would create jobs; and secondly, the social dogma which decreed that the newly unemployed would be more likely to seek work if their social-security payments were kept low.

Improving the condition of the people sounded a quaintly old-fashioned phrase in the jargon-clad and dogma-dominated politics of the 1980s. But it is the inspiration, or should be, for most public service. Above all, it should be the guiding-light for Conservatives, because it is the key to the other great object of the party that Disraeli laid down: to maintain the institutions of the country. Put at its most down-to-earth, those who wish to 'conserve' the fabric of society and avoid the shocks of violent upheavals must look to the contentment of all our fellow countrymen. The key to the survival of any social order is its ability to satisfy the aspirations of people in all walks or layers of life.

The relief of poverty and the maintenance of social well being are not optional extras or luxuries to be indulged only when times are good. The welfare state, when properly devised and administered, is not a dead-weight on the economy; it is the opposite. By providing a measure of security, it helps society to adapt to change, and it therefore promotes economic efficiency.

John Major's ambition to make the nation at ease with itself is admirable and genuinely Conservative. Yet a nation can be at ease with itself only when all its citizens feel that their government takes an interest in them and is sympathetic to their concerns. The true purpose of Conservatism is to work for harmony – the pseudo prayer of St Francis was correct. That aim can be attained, however, only by policies which are based on practical wisdom and judicious generosity, not on the cold abstractions of the dogma of discord.

So, whether or not Thatcherism continues to be preached 'the world over', it should no longer be practised at home.[26]

Notes

Preface & Acknowledgements

1 Finchley, 4 March 1991.

I Introduction: Harmony and Discord

1 cf Ridley: 'My Style of Government', pp 13, 30.
2 Wapshott & Brock: Thatcher, p 179; Watkins: A Conservative Coup, p 36.
3 cf Young: One of Us, p 510; Prior: A Balance of Power, pp 134–35.
4 cf Middlemas: Power, Competition and the State, III, p 220; K Harris: Thatcher, pp 42, 96–97; Britton: Macroeconomic Policy in Britain 1974–1987, p 23; Gilmour: Inside Right, pp 11–27; Gilmour: Britain Can Work, pp 96–101.
5 Joseph: Reversing the Trend, p 4; Halcrow: Keith Joseph, A Single Mind, pp 56, 62–66; K Harris, pp 33–37; Middlemas, III, p 24; Young, pp 105–6, 112.
6 Pym: The Politics of Consent, pp 2, 7; Foot: Another Heart and Other Pulses, pp 26–27; Prior, p 134; Wapshott & Brock, 189–90.
7 K Harris, p 133 (quotation); cf Morgan: The People's Peace, pp 4, 17; Gilmour: Inside Right, pp 33–34.
8 Gilmour: Guardian, 12 November 1984.
9 Prior, p 134; Observer, 25 February 1979; Wapshott & Brock, p 181; K Harris, pp 109, 118.

10 cf St John Stevas: *The Two Cities*, pp 18–19; Young, p 157; K Harris, pp 120–21, 138; Vincent: 'The Thatcher Government', in Hennessy & Seldon (eds): *Ruling Performance*, p 284.

11 Young, p 224; cf K Harris, pp 137–38; Gilmour: Blackpool, 14 October 1981; Patten: *The Tory Case*, p x; cf Pym, pp 177–78; Fowler: *Ministers Decide*, p 150.

12 Churchill: *Triumph and Tragedy*, p 509; Seldon: *Churchill's Indian Summer*, pp 34–35.

13 Sabine: *A History of Political Theory*, 3rd edition, p 753.

14 Oakeshott: *Rationalism in Politics*, p 48; cf Patten, p 18.

15 K Harris, pp 121, 133; cf Gilmour: *The Times*, 23 September 1981; Wapshott & Brock, pp 191–92; King: 'Margaret Thatcher', in King (ed): *The British Prime Minister*, pp 124–25.

16 cf Geoffrey Smith: *The Times*, 13 March 1981; K Harris, p 138.

17 Prior, p 132; Young, pp 218–20; *The Economist*, 20 June 1981.

18 Jennings: *Cabinet Government*, p 212; Carter: *The Office of Prime Minister*, pp 223–24; St John Stevas, pp 18–19; Churchill: *Lord Randolph Churchill*, p 337; Junor: *Listening for a Midnight Tram: Memoirs*, p 259.

19 Young, p 408; cf Ingham: *Kill the Messenger*, p 384.

20 eg Ridley; *op cit* n 1, pp 27–30, 214.

21 Gilmour: HC 17 December 1987, cols 1275–77.

22 Lawson: *Daily Telegraph*, 4 March 1991; Walker: *Staying Power*, p 186; Peter Jenkins: *Independent*, 18 July 1989.

23 cf Shepherd: *The Power Brokers*, p 202; Hennessy: *The Cabinet*, pp 94–95, 99, 103; C Johnson: *The Economy under Mrs Thatcher*, pp 251–52; Ranelagh: *Thatcher's People*, p 54.

24 Young, p 406; Chevenix Trench: *Portrait of a Patriot*, p 354; K Harris, pp 9–10.

25 HC 15 January 1988, col 572.

26 Butler and Kavenagh: *The British General Election of 1979*, pp 265, 316, 323; Gallup Political Index, Report 344, April 1989; *idem*, Report 363, November 1990; *idem*, Report 367, December 1991; Riddell: *The Thatcher Decade*, p 7; Vincent, p 281; K Harris, pp 113–17; Young, pp 241, 296, 303, 482.

27 Speech at Finchley 4 March 1991; Thatcher: *Newsweek*, April 1992.

28 Thatcher: Finchley 4 March 1991.

II Economic Policy to 1981

1 HC col 1597.

2 Seldon (ed): *Crisis '75*, p 17.

3 Churchill: *Great Contemporaries*, p 223; Morgan: *The People's Peace*, pp 6, 65–67, 93; Daalder: *Cabinet Reform in Britain in 1914–1963*, p 224.

4 Donoghue: 'The Conduct of Economic Policy' in King (ed): *The British Prime Minister*, pp 59–60, 69; Morgan, pp 7, 245 (quotation), 386–87, 389–90; Eccleshall: *Political Ideologies*, p 19; Barnett: *Inside the Treasury*, p 35; Middlemas, III, p 152.

5 Leach: *British Political Ideologies*, pp 46–48; Finlayson: *The Seventh Earl of Shaftesbury*, pp 72–86, 119–24, 176–88, 256–60, 276–301, 352–61, 545–51; Gilmour: *Britain Can Work*, pp 48–55.

6 Disraeli: *Tory Democrat* (Disraeli's Manchester and Crystal Palace speeches, 1950), pp 46–47.

7 Beer: *Modern British Politics*, p 271; Rhodes James: *Anthony Eden*, pp 328–29.

8 Perkin: *The Rise of Professional Society*, p 223; Gilmour: *BCW*, pp 70–83.

9 The phrase 'the Keynesian social democratic state' is David Heald's in *Public Expenditure*, pp 4, 257–61; it is also used by David Marquand: *The Unprincipled Society*, pp 2–3.

10 Hahn: 'On Market Economics' in Skidelsky (ed): *Thatcherism*, pp 107–12, 114, 120–21; K Smith: *The British Economic Crisis*, pp 148–53; Heseltine: *Where There's A Will*, pp 5–6, 83–84; Gilmour: *BCW*, pp 168, 217.

11 Douglas: *The Conservative Party* in Berrington (ed): Change in British Politics, pp 64–66; Ford: *Monetary Aggregates and Economic Policy*, p 1; Britton, *Macroeconomic Policy in Britain*, pp 4, 143, 149; Leach: *British Political Ideologies*, pp 8–9; Howell: *Freedom and Capital*, pp 26–27.

12 Burk & Cairncross: *Goodbye Great Britain*, pp xii–xiii; Donoghue in King (ed), pp 69–70; Gilmour: *BCW*, pp 137–38; see James Callaghan's remark on page 10; Middlemas, III, pp 139, 152, 165; Callaghan: *Time and Chance*, p 477.

13 Gilmour: *Inside Right*, p 241; cf Hirst: *After Thatcher*, pp 19–20.

14 Keynes: *The General Theory of Employment, Interest and Money*, p 383.

15 Walters: *Britain's Economic Renaissance*, pp 101, 111.

16 Gilmour: *BCW*, pp 117–18, 237–38; cf Friedman: *Capitalism and Freedom*, pp 2–3, 34–49, 92–100, 177–85, 196–202, and *passim*.

17 Britton, pp 95–98, 103–4; D Smith: *The Rise and Fall of*

Monetarism, pp 53–55, 154; Kaldor: *The Scourge of Monetarism*, p 27; cf Memorandum by the Swiss National Bank, HC 1979–80, 720, p 42, para 6.

18 eg Prior: *Sunday Times*, 5 November 1978; Prior: *A Balance of Power*, p 104; Gilmour: *IR*, pp 231–36.

19 D Smith, pp 76–81, 84; Britton, pp 98–102.

20 Keegan: *Mrs Thatcher's Economic Experiment*, pp 124–25; Bulpitt: *The Discipline of the New Democracy: Mrs Thatcher's Domestic Statecraft*, p 34; S Brittan in Keegan: *Mr Lawson's Gamble*, p 73.

21 Hahn: 'On Market Economies' in Skidelsky (ed), pp 113, 120, 123.

22 Friedman: *The Optimum Quantity of Money and Other Essays*, p V.

23 Friedman: *The Counter-Revolution in Monetary Theory*, p 24; Outhwaite, *Inflation in Tudor and Early Stuart England*, pp 49–55; Gilmour: *BCW*, pp 128–31.

24 *Observer*, 26 September 1982 in Leach, p 112.

25 Friedman: *op cit* n 23, p 67; Gilmour: *BCW*, pp 118, 154–57.

26 Letter to *The Times*, 4 March 1980; Lord Cockfield: HL 2 April 1980, col 1362; Gilmour: *BCW*, pp 137, 240.

27 Joseph: *Monetarism is Not Enough*, pp 5–6, 18–19; Kavanagh & Morris: *Consensus Politics from Attlee to Thatcher*, p 44.

28 *Observer*, 31 August 1980; letter to *The Times*, 3 March 1980.

29 Walters: *Britain's Economic Renaissance*, pp 113, 122; Congdon: *Monetarism*, p 6.

30 Bulpitt, p 32; C Johnson: *The Economy under Mrs Thatcher*, p 33; Browning: *Economic Images*, pp 208–9.

31 cf Sir Douglas Wass, the permanent secretary at the Treasury, in Young, p 146; Keegan: *Mrs Thatcher's Economic Experiment*, p 205.

32 Keegan, pp 110–17; Gilmour: *BCW*, p 138.

33 cf S Nickell in Matthews & Minford: *Mrs Thatcher's Economic Policies 1979–1987*, p 93.

34 K Harris, p 122.

35 Tebbit: *Upwardly Mobile*, p 208; Keegan, pp 119–27; Gilder: *Wealth and Poverty*, pp XIX–XX.

36 Brittan: *A Restatement of Economic Liberalism*, p 277; Prior, pp 119–20; Keegan, p 122; Britton, p 45.

37 Hicks: *What is Wrong with Monetarism?*, pp 5, 7; Kaldor: *The Economic Consequences of Mrs Thatcher*, p 48; Gilmour: *BCW*,

pp 128–29; HC 1 July 1980, cols 1396–97; Browning: *Economic Images*, pp 117, 133.

38 Walters: *Britain's Economic Renaissance*, pp 76–79. Sir Alan's defence was a little undermined by his getting the figures wrong: he thought VAT had only gone up from '10 or 12 per cent'. Professor Maynard imprudently accepted Sir Alan's figures but differed from his conclusions. Maynard: *The Economy under Mrs Thatcher*, pp 58–59.

39 Bean & Symons: *Ten Years of Mrs Thatcher*, p 37; C Johnson, pp 127–29.

40 C Johnson, p 48.

41 K Harris, pp 122–24; Prior, p 119.

42 Churchill: *The World Crisis*, pp 791–811; Hankey, *The Supreme Command*, p 625; Wolff: *In Flanders Fields*, pp 41–67.

43 Maynard, pp 43–46, 51–53.

44 K Harris, p 142; Howell: *Blind Victory*, pp 148–50; K Smith: *The British Economic Crisis*, pp 24–25.

45 Walters, pp 162–63; Britton, pp 186, 302.

46 Kaldor, *op cit* n 38, p 66; D Smith, p 94.

47 Britton, p 49; Gilder, pp XIX–XX.

48 Walker: *Staying Power*, p 161.

49 Cambridge, 7 February 1980; *Sunday Times*, 10 February 1980; *The Times*, 26 February 1980; King in King (ed), p 118; Young, pp 200–1; Wapshott & Brock, p 194.

50 cf K Harris, pp 137–38; Young, p 151; C Johnson, p 251.

51 Butler & Kavanagh: *The British General Election 1979*, p 155 (where the title is incorrect).

52 Kavanagh & Morris: *Consensus Politics*, pp 47–48; cf Howell: *op cit* n 44, p 151.

53 Financial Statement and Budget Report, March 1980.

54 Middlemas, III, pp 246, 547.

55 Lawson: *The New Conservatism*, pp 4–5.

56 Treasury Bulletin, December 1991.

57 *Private Eye, passim*.

58 Professor Willem Buiter in Walters, p 40.

59 The Government's Expenditure Plans 1979/80–1982/3, Cmnd 7439; Heald: *Public Expenditure*, pp 29–32, 44–46, 51–52; Burk & Cairncross, p 223; Bean & Symons, pp 8–10; Kaldor: *op cit* n 38, pp 39, 64–65; HC 1979–80, 720, table 6, p 116, and Kaldor's memorandum, paras 87–96.

60 HC 1979–80, 720, pp 56–57.

61 Walters, p 150.
62 Gilmour: *BCW*, p 147.
63 Thatcher: Lord Mayor's Banquet, 15 November 1982; Ridley, p 163.
64 Mill: *Essays on Some Unsettled Questions of Political Economy*, p 51.
65 Gilmour: *BCW*, pp 145–46.
66 cf Memorandum from the Austrian National Bank, HC 1979–80, 720, p 44.
67 Keynes: *The Economic Consequences of Mr Churchill*, p 19.
68 Browning: *Economic Images*, p 115; Middlemas, III, p 246.
69 Prior, pp 130–32; Wapshott & Brock, pp 196–98; Middlemas, III, p 248.
70 Junor: *Listening for a Midnight Tram: Memoirs*, p 259.
71 Cambridge, 8 March 1980.
72 Walters, pp 140–45; Riddell: *The Thatcher Decade*, p 18; Wapshott & Brock, pp 280–82; Ranelagh, pp 227–28; cf Middlemas, III, pp 234–35.
73 K Harris, pp 147–50; cf Walters, pp 86–88, 140–41; Keegan: *op cit* n 31, pp 132, 169; D Smith, p 100; Burns: 'The UK's Financial Strategy' in Eltis & Sinclair (eds): *Keynes and Economic Policy*, p 435.
74 Riddell: *op cit* n 72, p 19; C Johnson, p 45; Keegan: *Mr Lawson's Gamble*, pp 82–84; Budd: *Thatcher's Economic Performance*, p 32; Tebbit, pp 227–28; Howell: *op cit* n 44, p 150.
75 cf Walters, p 86n.
76 Alan Budd, *Independent*, 15 April 1991; Buiter & Miller: *The Macroeconomic Consequences of a Change in Regime: The UK under Mrs Thatcher*, p 3; Keegan: *op cit* n 74, p 84; Minford: 'Mrs Thatcher's Economic Reform Programme' in Skidelsky (ed), p 96; Gilmour: HC 15 March 1984, col 536; Howell: *op cit* n 44, p 151; Britton, pp 57, 301.
77 Coutts, Godley, Rowthorn & Zezza: *Britain's Economic Problems and Policies in the 1990s*, pp 16–17; Britton, p 62; Keegan: *op cit* n 31, p 214; Browning: *The Treasury*, pp 164, 355; C Johnson, pp 46–47; D Smith, pp 110–11; Gilmour: HC 17 March 1983, col 374; Young, p 341.
78 Keegan: *op cit* n 74, p 102; Minford: 'Mrs Thatcher's Reform Programme' in Skidelsky (ed), pp 97–98.
79 Middlemas, III, pp 208, 237, 542; Riddell: *The Thatcher Government*, pp 91–92; Britton, p 50.

80 Riddell: *op cit* n 79, pp 74–75; Keegan: *op cit* n 74, p 108.
81 Pratten: *Mrs Thatcher's Economic Experiment*, pp 40–41 (quotation); K Smith: *The British Economic Crisis*, pp 18, 33–34; Coutts *et al*, p 8.
82 S Brittan in Kavanagh & Seldon (eds), pp 2, 21–23; Matthews & Minford: 'Mrs Thatcher's Economic Policies', p 62, and Maynard, p 159.
83 Riddell: *op cit* n 72, p 15; Hannah: 'Mrs Thatcher, Capital-Basher?' in Kavanagh & Seldon (eds), pp 38–39; Layard & Nickell: *The Thatcher Miracle?*, pp 10–13; Kaldor: *op cit* n 38, p 78; Keegan: *op cit* n 74, pp 201–3; C Johnson, p 25.

III Why the Moderates Lost

1 Young, p 223.
2 *All Trivia*, p 62.
3 Phelps-Brown: *Egalitarianism and the Generation of Inequality*, pp 317–20; Beer: *Britain Against Itself*, p 217; HC 22 July 1981 col 132.
4 K Harris, p 141.
5 cf Riddell: *The Thatcher Government*, pp 44–45; Young, pp 204–5; K Harris, p 151.
6 Middlemas, III, pp 249–50; Browning: *The Treasury*, pp 169–70; Gilmour: Blackpool, 14 October 1981.
7 Oakeshott: *Rationalism in Politics*, p 21.
8 K Harris, p 122.
9 Aspinall: *The Cabinet Council 1783–1835*, pp 174–77; cf Professor Hahn's Memorandum to the Treasury and Civil Service Committee, HC, 1979, 72, p 81, para 1.8; and Middlemas, III, pp 234–35; cf Keegan: *Mr Lawson's Gamble*, pp 184–88; Hennessy, pp 95–96.
10 Templewood: *Nine Troubled Years*, pp 291–92, 301–18.
11 Ridley: 'My Style of Government', pp 27–31; N Malcolm in *The Spectator*, 13 July 1991; Morley: *The Life of Walpole*, p 157; Hennessy, pp 111, 122; Gilmour: *The Body Politic*, pp 205–9, 215–16, 220 (Powell).
12 Young, p 223.
13 cf Ridley, pp 30, 264; King: 'Margaret Thatcher as a Political Leader' in Skidelsky (ed), p 58; Shepherd: *The Power Brokers*, p 179; Ingham, *Kill the Messenger*, pp 172, 385.
14 cf Middlemas, III, p 252; Young, p 157.
15 Cecil: *The Life of Lord Salisbury*, III, p 202; Macmillan: *Winds of*

Change, pp 23–24; Gilmour: *The Body Politic*, p 212; according to Norman Tebbit, ministerial departmentalism had much to do with the Thatcher cabinet's acceptance of the Single European Act in 1986; Tebbit: *Unfinished Business*, p 46.

16 Prior, pp 140, 133; cf Geoffrey Smith: *The Times*, 6 June 1981; Prior, p 140; Gilmour: *The Times*, 23 September 1981.

17 Gilmour: *The Times*, 23 September 1981; Prior, pp 154–71; St John Stevas, pp 52–63; Gilmour: *BCW*, pp 170–71; Young, p 210; Pym, p 105.

18 Morgan: *The People's Peace*, pp 444–45; Montgomery Hyde: *Carson*, p 389; Hugo Young in *The Sunday Times*, 25 March 1979; P Jenkins: *Mrs Thatcher's Revolution*, p 183; Vincent in Hennessy and Seldon (eds), p 288.

19 cf Carrington: *Reflect on Things Past*, pp 275–76, 280, 308–10; and Whitelaw: *The Whitelaw Memoirs*, pp 2, 186, 329–30, 342–3; Kavanagh: *Thatcherism and British Politics*, pp 261, 282–83.

20 Hailsham: *A Sparrow's Flight*, pp 392–96.

21 Young, p 210; defence spending did rise but much less than the Labour government had planned.

22 Butler & Pinto-Duschinsky: *The British General Election of 1970*, p 156n.

23 Trevelyan: *Grey of Falloden*, pp 95–97.

24 K Harris, p 149; cf Young, pp 214–15.

25 Evans: *Good Times, Bad Times*, pp 283–89, 274.

26 cf Pym: *The Politics of Consent*, p 18.

27 Walker: *Staying Power*, p 159; Prior, p 140; *The Economist*, 13 March 1981; Geoffrey Smith, *The Times*, 13 March 1981; cf Wapshott in *The Times*, 2 June 1981; Wapshott & Brock, p 204; Pym, p 18.

28 Prior, p 140; Walker, pp 159–60.

29 Horne: *Macmillan 1894–1956*, p 2; Mackintosh: *The British Cabinet*, p 497; Gilmour, *Guardian*, 12 November 1984.

30 Young, pp 218–20; Prior, p 132; Keegan: *op cit* n 9, pp 171–72; Middlemas, III, pp 253–54.

31 Gilmour: *Observer*, 30 July 1989; cf Fowler: *Ministers Decide*, p 342; and P Jenkins: *Mrs Thatcher's Revolution*, p 184.

32 eg Junor, p 259.

33 *Guardian*, 14 September 1981.

34 *Daily Telegraph*, 13 February 1980; *Daily Mirror*, 14 February 1980; Aspinall, pp 189–90; Gilmour: *The Body Politic*, p 221.

35 Alderman & Cross: *The Tactics of Resignation*, pp 17–18, 27–28,

37, 48, 53–57; Bonham Carter: *Winston Churchill as I Knew Him*, p 361; Templewood: *Ambassador on Special Mission*, p 282; Mackintosh: *The British Cabinet*, pp 392–93.

36 Gilmour: *The Body Politic*, pp 209–12.

37 Young, pp 227–29; Middlemas, III, pp 253, 292–93; cf Norman Strauss & Geoffrey Howe in Ranelagh: *Thatcher's People*, pp 17–18.

38 See chapter II above; N Wapshott: *The Times*, 2 June 1981.

39 Longford: *Victoria RI*, p 157.

40 Quoted by Anthony King in Skidelsky (ed), p 58.

41 cf King: 'Margaret Thatcher', pp 148–49, in King (ed), and King in Skidelsky (ed), pp 58–59.

42 cf Walker: *Staying Power*, p 124; Pym, pp 105, 107; and Ridley: *op cit* n 11, p 6; Ranelagh, p 111.

43 R Johnson: *The Politics of Recession*, pp 247–48; Patten, p 175; Shepherd, p 183.

44 cf HC 1979–80, 720, pp 208–9 (James Tobin); Gilmour: *BCW*, p 137.

IV Economic Policy from 1981 to 1990

1 *Newsweek*, 15 October 1990.

2 *Church and State*, pp 51–52.

3 cf Britton, p 230.

4 Gilmour, HC 12 November 1985, col 491; Keegan: *Britain Without Oil*, passim.

5 e.g. Nigel Lawson in Eltis & Sinclair (eds): *Keynes and Economic Policy*, p xvi; HC 14 March 1989 cols 293–94; Eccleshall: 'Conservatism' in Eccleshall et al (eds): *Political Ideologies*, pp 85–86, 108.

6 Kings, I, 18: 25–28.

7 e.g. HC 17 March 1983, col 332; cf Ridley: 'My Style of Government', p 195.

8 Gilmour: Building Employers Federation, 6 March 1984; Riddell: *The Thatcher Decade*, pp 19–22; cf Britton, pp 61, 76.

9 Lawson: *The British Experiment*, Fifth Mais Lecture, HM Treasury, 18 June 1984, pp 5–6.

10 Lawson, pp 17, 2, 23–24; Lawson in Eltis & Sinclair (eds), pp xvi–xvii.

11 Rentoul: *Me and Mine*, p 87.

12 HC 15 March 1988, col 993; HC 21 March 1988, col 109; HC 14 March 1989, cols 293–94.

13 cf Keith Joseph in P Jenkins, p 98.
14 Gilmour: *BCW*, p 153.
15 Birmingham Town Hall, 19 April 1979 and Finchley 11 April 1979; HC 28 February 1980, col 1593; Gilmour, *BCW*, p 9; Young, p 140.
16 Maynard, pp 41–42; Matthews & Minford, p 62; D Smith, pp 84–85; HC 1979–80, 720, p 61.
17 Burns: 'The UK's Financial Strategy', in Eltis & Sinclair (eds): *Keynes and Economic Policy*, p 434; Keegan: *Mr Lawson's Gamble*, p 81; cf Walters: *Britain's Economic Renaissance*, pp 160–61; Walters: *Sterling in Danger*, p 90 (quotation); Browning: *The Treasury*, p 262.
18 Gilmour: Blackpool, 14 October 1981; Keegan: *Mrs Thatcher's Economic Experiment*, p 196.
19 Ridley: Oxford, 14 November 1981; *Guardian*, 15 October 1981; Walters, p 91; Gilmour: HC 9 November 1981, cols 330–31; Gilmour: *Guardian*, 19 November 1981; Gilmour: HC 28 January 1982, cols 1054–55.
20 Britton, p 73; Gilmour: London TRG, Paddington, 25 September 1984.
21 Ridley, p 195; Wynne Godley: *The Times*, 28 May 1991; Browning: *Economic Images*, pp 117–19; Britton, pp 268–69, 280, 306.
22 Schumpeter: *A History of Economic Analysis*, p 668; Allen & Hall: 'Money as a Potential Anchor for the Price Level', p 45; Kaldor: *The Economic Consequence of Mrs Thatcher*, pp 34, 42–43, 47–48; HC 1979–80, 720, pp 112–14; Richardson: *Reflections on the Conduct of Monetary Policy*, pp 8–9; Gilmour, *BCW*, pp 137–38; Dow: *A Critique of A Monetary Policy* in *Lloyd's Bank Review* October 1987, p 28; cf Hicks: *A Market Theory of Money*, p 103.
23 D Smith, pp 137–38.
24 Congdon: letter to *The Financial Times*, 19 July 1991; I have of course used the figures in the *Treasury Bulletin*.
25 Beckerman & Jenkinson: *Commodity Prices, Import Prices and the Inflation Slowdown: A Pooled Cross-country Time Series Analysis*; Gilmour: *BCW*, pp 147–48; Gilmour: HC 15 March 1984, col 537; Walters: *Britain's Economic Renaissance*, p 149; Howell: *Blind Victory*, pp 153–54; Britton, pp 64, 304; C Johnson, p 69.
26 Browning: *The Treasury*, p 240.

27 D Smith, pp 132–42; Britton, pp 137–39; Gilmour: London TRG, Paddington, 25 September 1984.

28 Keegan: *Mr Lawson's Gamble*, pp 136–38; D Jay: *Sterling*, p 250; D Smith, pp 133–42; Lawson, pp 5–6; Gilmour: London TRG, Paddington, 25 September 1984; Gilmour: Queen Mary College, 30 January 1985.

29 Burk & Cairncross: *Goodbye Great Britain*, pp 55–56; Gilmour: Queen Mary College, 30 January 1988.

30 Peter Rees: HC 24 November 1983, col 546; Barnett: *Inside the Treasury*, pp 22, 124; cf Browning: *The Treasury*, pp 232–33; Britton, pp 61, 65; Gilmour: HC 24 November 1983, cols 491–4; Gilmour: HC 12 November 1985, col 490; Gilmour: *Guardian*, 5 December 1983.

31 The phrase is Paul Hirst's in his *After Thatcher*, p 148.

32 C Johnson, pp 46–47; Keegan: *op cit* n 28, pp 177–81; D Smith, pp 110–11; Middlemas, III, p 258; Gilmour: HC 12 March 1983, col 374; Shakespeare: sonnet no 143.

33 Pollard: *The Wasting of the British Economy*, pp 39–50, 71, 75; Marquand: *The Unprincipled Society*, pp 44–50; Gilmour: *BCW*, pp 88–89.

34 Kavanagh & Morris, pp 48–49; cf Jackson: 'Economic Policy', in Marsh & Rhodes (eds): *Implementing Thatcherite Policies*, pp 16, 22.

35 Alan Budd: *Independent*, 15 April 1991; Grant: *The Political Economy of Industrial Policy*, pp 17, 24, 29, 74–77; Grant: *Government and Industry*, pp 8, 62–64; Pym, pp 184–85; Prior, p 253; Keegan: *op cit* n 28, pp 149, 207; Heseltine, pp 93–95; House of Lords Select Committee on Science and Technology: Innovation in Manufacturing Industry, HL 1990–91, 18–I, pp 5, 46; cf Middlemas, III, p 383; C Johnson, pp 186, 215 (quotation); Gilmour: *Guardian*, 5 December 1983; Gilmour: Nottingham University, 26 January 1984; Gamble: *The Free Economy and the Strong State*, pp 125–26, 195, 226.

36 Layard & Nickell, pp 3–6; Crafts: *British Economic Growth Before and After 1979*, pp 1–3, 23–24.

37 Coutts et al, pp 7–11; Sir John Harvey Jones: HL 1984–85, 238–II, p 452; Marquand, p 92; Gilmour: HC 12 November 1985, col 491.

38 HL 1985–86, 238-I, para 15; R Freeman, *The Future of UK Manufacturing*, pp 6–8; Grant: *Government and Industry*, pp 5–6; Coutts et al, p 9; Riddell: *The Thatcher Decade*, pp 81–84.

39 Gilmour: Paddington, 25 September 1984; Maynard, p 51; Keegan: *op cit* n 28, p 131.

40 HL 1984–85, 238-I, paras 96–97.

41 HL 1984–85, 238-II, pp 553–74; Lawson: HC 13 November 1985, col 590; Young, p 362; *Cambridge Bulletin*, March 1986; P Jenkins, p 257.

42 Keegan: *op cit* n 28, pp 71, 139; Ridley, p 71; Britton, p 286.

43 J Harvey Jones in Grant: *Government and Industry*, pp 5–6; HL 1984–85, 238–I, paras 72–73, 92–95; 238–II, p 474; UK National Accounts 1991, table 2.1.

44 Gilbert: *Winston S Churchill*, V, p 98; Gamble: *The Free Economy and the Strong State*, p 227; Prior, pp 122–23; Kaldor: *The Economic Consequences of Mrs Thatcher*, p 76; C Johnson, pp 132–33; Howell: *Freedom and Capital*, pp 13–14, 52 (published in 1981 but written before the election); Ridley, p 71; R W Johnson: *The Politics of Recession*, p 29 (Friedman).

45 Brian Pearce: *Guardian*, 18 March 1992.

46 HC March 1986, col 168; Keegan: *op cit* n 28, p 185; Gilmour: HC 20 March 1986, col 472.

47 Dickes: *What Remains of Thatcherism*, pp 32–33; Gilmour: HC 19 March 1986, col 498.

48 Keegan: *op cit* n 28, pp 182–86, 196; HC 12 December 1985, col 1085; P Jenkins, p 217; Britton, p 173, 240.

49 Keegan: *op cit* n 28, pp 155–57, 165, 168–71, 181; Dow: *A Critique of Monetary Policy*, p 25; cf S Brittan in Kavanagh & Seldon (eds), pp 32–3; Britton, p 76; Lawson's resignation speech: HC 31 October 1989, cols 208–9; Howe's resignation statement: HC 13 November 1990, cols 461–62; Watkins, pp 132–33, 139; Ridley, pp 27–30, 210; see introduction above.

50 cf Britton, pp 77–78; Hahn in Skidelsky (ed), pp 120–23; C Johnson, pp 103–6.

51 Young, p 503; Harris, p 257; P Jenkins, pp 280–81; D Smith, p 128.

52 Keegan: *op cit* n 28, p 213.

53 Vincent in Hennessy & Seldon (eds), p 288.

54 Dicks, pp 32–33; Middlemas, III, pp 274–75, 549; Keegan: *op cit* n 28, pp 208–9; Ridley, p 197.

55 Hicks: *A Market Theory of Money*, pp 94–96; Mill: *Principles of Political Economy*, vol II, Bk III, Ch xii, pp 53–58.

56 Keegan: *op cit* n 28, p 221; Ridley, pp 133, 200; Gilmour: HC 16 March 1988, col 1143.

57 Britton, p 81; Cripps et al, p 11; Keegan: *op cit* n 28, pp 209–10; Ridley, pp 203, 213.

58 Cripps et al, pp 11, 17; Ridley, pp 203–5.

59 Keegan: *op cit* n 28, pp 223–24; cf Ridley, pp 206–7; Gilmour: HC 7 June 1989, cols 282–83; HC 21 March 1990, col 1150.

60 Hicks: *A Market Theory of Money*, p 95; Gilmour: HC 7 June 1989, cols 282–83; HC 21 March 1990, col 1150.

61 Ridley, p 204.

62 Ridley, pp 204, 196.

63 e.g. HC 17 March 1983, col 372; Gilmour: HC 17 March 1983, col 373; HC 16 March 1988, col 1143.

64 Young, p 219; Gilmour: HC 16 March 1988, cols 1142–43.

65 C Johnson, pp 172, 301; Britton, p 79; Keegan, pp 208–10; Coutts et al, pp 16–17.

66 Coutts et al, p 17; C Johnson, p 21.

67 Ridley, pp 196, 201; Keegan, p 201; Watkins, pp 110, 123; Ranelagh, p 269.

68 Robin Leigh Pemberton: Birmingham, 18 September 1991.

69 Gilmour: HC 7 June 1989, cols 281–82.

70 cf Peter Jay: *Independent*, 23 September 1991; Lloyd's Bank Economic Bulletin September 1984 in HL 1984–85, 238–I, para 67; Gilmour: London TRG, Paddington, 25 September 1984; Gilmour: HC 16 November 1986, cols 498–99; HC 7 June 1989, cols 281–82.

71 Layard & Nickell, pp 17–19; Wells: *Guardian*, 18 December 1990.

72 Coutts et al, pp 7–8; Gilmour: *Observer*, 12 May 1985.

73 Layard & Nickell, pp 7, 19–20; Coutts et al, pp 13–16.

74 National Institute Economic Review, May 1990, p 99; Crafts, pp 22, 27–33; Coutts et al, pp 14–15; Layard & Nicholl, pp 3–6, 15; Bean & Symons, pp 3, 45–46; Riddell: *op cit* n 8, pp 40–42.

75 OECD Main Economic Indicators, Historical Edition; Coutts et al, pp 8, 14.

76 House of Lords Committee on Science and Technology: Innovation in Manufacturing Industry, HL 1990–91, 18–I, pp 5–6 (quotation), 48–49; Coutts et al, pp 12–13, 17; Shepherd, p 218.

77 Layard & Nickell, abstract pp 21–23; Bean & Symons, pp 46, 50–51; Gilmour: HC 20 March 1986, cols 469–70; see chapter VI below.

78 cf Dunn (ed): *The Economic Limits to Modern Politics*, p 38.

79 Coutts et al, p 17; Gilmour: Queen Mary College, London, 30 January 1985, and Cambridge, 9 August 1988.
80 Ian Aitken: *Guardian*, 24 October 1988.
81 Keegan: *op cit* n 28, p 174; Gilmour: HC 15 March 1984, col 536; and 20 March 1986, col 471.
82 OEDC Main Economic Indicators, Historical Edition.
83 Gilmour: *Observer*, 12 May 1985.
84 Ibid.
85 cf Layard & Nickell: *The Thatcher Miracle?*, p 2; Heath et al, *Understanding Political Change*, p 8; Hirst: *After Thatcher*, pp 115–16, 120; Watkins: *A Conservative Coup*, pp 29–30.
86 cf Nigel Lawson in Keegan: *op cit* n 28, p 140.
87 Keegan: *Britain without Oil*, p 17; Gilmour: HC 16 March 1988, cols 1143–44; Perkin, *The Rise of Professional Society*, p 220.
88 Kings I, 18: 28.

V Trade Union Reform, the Miners' Strike and Privatization

1 *The Financial Times*, 15 February 1988.
2 Hugo Young: *One of Us*, p 371.
3 Henderson: 'Britain's Decline: the Causes and Consequences', *The Economist*, 2 June 1979, reprinted in *Channels and Tunnels*, p 43; K Morgan, pp 422–23.
4 K Morgan, p 418; Skidelsky in Skidelsky (ed), pp 9–10; Marquand: *The Unprincipled Society*, pp 54–55; Prior, p 158; Gilmour: *Daily Telegraph*, 5 February & 13 March 1979.
5 Callaghan: *Time and Chance*, p 474; Barnett, pp 162–63; Hammond: *Maverick*, p 158; Morgan, pp 416–17; Gilmour: *Mr Callaghan and the 5 per cent*, Portsmouth, November 1979.
6 Callaghan: *Time and Chance*, pp 474, 514–34; *Contemporary Record*, vol I, no 3, pp 35–36; Butler & Kavanagh, pp 43–46; K Morgan, pp 418–20; Healey: *The Time of My Life*, pp 462–63, 467.
7 Philip Barrett: *Financial Times*, 15 February 1988.
8 Middlemas, III, p 167; Healey, p 467; Callaghan, pp 534–37, 540; *Contemporary Record*, p 35; Barnett: *Inside the Treasury*, pp 172–77; K Morgan, p 420; Gilmour: Amersham, 26 January 1979; Gilmour: *Daily Telegraph*, 5 February 1979; Fowler, pp 101–2; K Harris, p 102.
9 Donoghue in King (ed), pp 70–71; Barnett, pp 172–77; K Morgan, p 420; *Contemporary Record*, vol I, no 3, Autumn

1987, pp 35, 41–43; Callaghan, pp 539–40; Gilmour: Amersham, 26 January 1979; Gilmour: *Daily Telegraph*, 5 February & 13 March 1979.

10 Butler & Kavanagh, p 85; Healey, p 467; Kavanagh, pp 130–31, 162–63, 205; Young, p 129 (quotation); A Maude (ed): *The Right Approach to the Economy*, p 16 (quotation); Moran: 'The Conservative Party and the Trade Unions Since 1974', pp 48–49; Gilmour: *Daily Telegraph*, 13 March 1979.

11 cf HC 1979–80, 720, p 212 (James Tobin); Gilmour: *BCW*, p 149.

12 Middlemas, III, p 167; Butler & Kavanagh, pp 130–31; Vincent in Hennessy & Seldon, p 280; Shepherd, p 186.

13 *The Economist*, 10 January 1976; Gilmour: *Inside Right*, p 237.

14 Prior, pp 158–61; Roberts in Kavanagh & Seldon, pp 65–66; Riddell: *The Thatcher Decade*, p 47.

15 Prior, pp 157–69; Middlemas, III, pp 320–21; Shepherd, p 185.

16 Young, pp 192–97; *Sun*, 26 February 1980; Prior, pp 128–29.

17 Prior, pp 163–67; Shepherd, p 185; Young, pp 196–97; Tebbit: *Upwardly Mobile*, p 231.

18 Tebbit, pp 233–41, 252, 259, 263, 266; Fowler, p 293; Middlemas, III, pp 325–26; Kavanagh & Seldon (eds), pp 66–67.

19 Tebbit, pp 250–51, 262–66; Riddell: *op cit* n 14, pp 47–48.

20 Middlemas, III, pp 335, 347; *Employment Gazette*, May 1988, p 276; Riddell: *The Thatcher Government*, p 191; Riddell, *The Thatcher Decade*, pp 45–46; Marsh: 'Industrial Relations' in Marsh & Rhodes (eds): *Implementing Thatcherite Policies*, pp 40, 45–46; Kavanagh & Morris, p 68; Kavanagh & Seldon (eds), pp 69–70.

21 Middlemas, III, pp 336, 340; Riddell: *The Thatcher Decade*, p 57.

22 Middlemas, III, pp 347–48; Riddell: *op cit* n 21, pp 49–51; Kavanagh & Seldon (eds), p 78.

23 Dicks: 'What Remains of Thatcherism?', p 35; Britton, pp 288–90; Crafts, pp 19, 33; Layard & Nickell, pp 11–16; Bean & Symonds, pp 37–41; Minford in Skidelsky (ed), pp 98–99.

24 Roberts in Kavanagh & Seldon (eds), p 69; Crewe in *idem*, pp 247–48; Ewing in Graham & Prosser (eds), pp 151–52.

25 Prior, pp 126–27; M Holmes, p 34; Young, pp 195–97; Marsh & Rhodes (eds), pp 37–38; Tebbit: *op cit* n 17, p 224; see chapter III above.

26 Adeney & Lloyd: *The Miners' Strike*, pp 2, 19–21, 75–77, 145; Goodman: *The Miners' Strike*, pp 21–24; Prior, p 169.

27 Young: *Stanley Baldwin*, p 99 (quotation); Middlemas & Barnes: *Baldwin*, pp 387–90; Walker, p 169; Adeney & Lloyd, pp 20, 36, 49–50; Goodman, pp 13, 50.

28 Keegan: *Mr Lawson's Gamble*, p 95; Adeney & Lloyd, pp 77–79, 145–46; Goodman, pp 24–33; Young, pp 367–68 (quotation); Tebbit: *op cit* n 17, pp 302–3.

29 King (ed), pp 119–20; Adeney & Lloyd, pp 70, 72; P Walker: *Staying Power*, p 166; Goodman, p 41.

30 Ewing & Gearty: *Freedom under Thatcher*, pp 130–36; Watkins, p 113; Adeney & Lloyd, pp 25–27, 42, 59–62; Goodman, pp 39–40; Walker, pp 168–69; Gilmour: London TRG, Paddington, 25 September 1984.

31 Goodman, pp 67–74; Walker, p 172; Adeney & Lloyd, pp 86–87.

32 Jimmy Reid: Barnsley's Lenin, *The Spectator*, 13 October 1984; Young, p 367 (quotation): Lloyd & Adeney, pp 33–39; Goodman, pp 46–49.

33 Adeney & Lloyd, p 92; P Jenkins, pp 227–28; Reid: *The Spectator*, 13 October 1984.

34 Adeney & Lloyd, pp vii (quotation), 22, 41, 82; Reid: *The Spectator*, 13 October 1984; Goodman, pp 47–48; Walker, p 166.

35 Adeney & Lloyd, pp 40–44, 81–84, 87–90; Goodman, p 46.

36 Walker, pp 169–70, 178; Michael Stewart: 'The Miners' Strike' in *London Review of Books*, 6–19 September and 18–31 October 1984; Peter Paterson: 'Not a Merry Old Soul', *The Spectator*, 18 October 1986; Goodman, pp 46–48; Adeney & Lloyd, p 89.

37 Goodman, pp 25–27, 115–16, 133, 139–54; Adeney & Lloyd, pp 93, 96–99, 122–25, 196–99; Walker, p 175.

38 Adeney & Lloyd, pp 89, 128, 138–39, 144, 152; Goodman, pp 76, 105; Hammond: *Maverick*, pp 42, 46–48.

39 Adeney & Lloyd, pp 133–35, 142–44; Goodman, pp 93, 97, 109; Hammond, pp 49–53.

40 Tebbit: *op cit* n 17, p 280; Reid: *The Spectator* 13 October 1984; Goodman, p 123; Adeney & Lloyd, pp 160, 166.

41 Walker, pp 172–73; Adeney & Lloyd, p 157; Goodman, p 124.

42 Adeney & Lloyd, pp 135–36, 158; Goodman, p 123; Young, p 370.

43 Adeney & Lloyd, pp 157–58, 180–82; Goodman, pp 123–4.

44 Adeney & Lloyd, pp 155, 159–74.

45 Ewing & Gearty, p 103; Goodman, pp 79–89; Adeney & Lloyd, pp 120–28; Walker, p 170; P Jenkins, pp 233–34.

46 Adeney & Lloyd, pp 93–94, 106–7, 111–17; Goodman, pp 107–9;

P Jenkins, p 233; National Workers' Miners' Committee: *The Miners' Dispute, A Catalogue of Violence*.

47 Adeney & Lloyd, pp 128, 100.

48 Hammond, pp 44–45; Adeney & Lloyd, p 152; Goodman, p 119; Ewing & Gearty, pp 109–11.

49 John Lyons, General Secretary of the Electrical Power Engineers Association, in Adeney & Lloyd, p 152; Hammond, pp 44–45; Lloyd: *Claiming Victory* in *LRB*, 21 November 1985; Goodman, pp 198–99; Gilmour: London TRG, Paddington, 25 September 1984.

50 HL 13 November 1984; Hammond (who ascribes the phrase to von Hindenburg), p 45; A Clark, *The Donkeys*, epigraph; Goodman, pp 196–97; Christmas, p 200.

51 Adeney & Lloyd, pp 202–11; P Jenkins, p 232.

52 Young, pp 372–73; Adeney & Lloyd, 241–46, 290; Whitelaw, pp 332–33.

53 Adeney & Lloyd, pp 299–300 (Benn); Goodman, p 200 (Scargill).

54 Kelf-Cohen: *Nationalisation in Britain*, pp 15–18, 99–100, 305–6; Bullock & Shock (eds): *The Liberal Tradition*, p 255; Gilmour: *The Body Politic*, pp 51–52.

55 R Miliband, *Parliamentary Socialism*, pp 276–78; Kellner & Hitchins: *Callaghan, The Road to Number 10*, p 16; Gilmour: *The Body Politic*, pp 52, 112.

56 HC 30 January 1946, col 972.

57 Gilmour: HC 11 November 1968, cols 132–45.

58 Veljanowski: *Selling the State*, pp 64–65; Heseltine, p 64; Gilmour: *The Body Politic*, p 53.

59 Riddell: *op cit* n 21, pp 90–91; Heseltine, pp 64–65; Grimstone: 'Privatisation, the Unexpected Crusade', p 23.

60 Brittan: 'The Politics and Economics of Privatisation', p 109; Veljanowski, pp 1–6, 65–66; Ridley, p 60; Grimstone, p 23.

61 Grimstone, p 23; Veljanowski, pp 6–7; Keegan: *Mrs Thatcher's Economic Experiment*, p 173.

62 Veljanowski, p 9 (quotation).

63 Veljanowski, pp 65–66, 192, 210; Brittan: *op cit* n 60, pp 110–12; Brittan: 'A Comment on Kay and Thompson', p 35; Ridley, p 61.

64 Riddell: *op cit* n 21, p 87; Ridley, p 64; Ranelagh, p 307.

65 Brittan: 'A Comment on Kay & Thompson', p 33; Veljanowski, pp 8–9; Kay & Thompson, p 19.

66 John Moore, MP in 1986 in Graham & Prosser (eds): *Waiving the Rules*, p 74; Riddell: *op cit* n 21, p 88.

67 Kay & Thompson: *Privatisation: A Policy in Search of a Rationale*, pp 23–25; Middlemas, III, pp 359–61; Riddell: *op cit* n 21, pp 87–96; Maynard, pp 163–64; Minford in Skidelsky (ed), pp 99–100; Layard & Nickell, p 9; V Keegan: *Guardian*, 10 February 1992.

68 Kay & Thompson, pp 23–25; Brittan: *op cit* n 60, p 117; Veljanowski, p 141; Ridley, p 162.

69 Riddell: *op cit* n 21, p 98 (quotation); Veljanowski, p 18; Kay & Thompson, pp 29–30.

70 Kay & Thompson, pp 30–31; Veljanowski, pp 10–31, 32, 118–19, 147.

71 P Walker: *Staying Power*, pp 188–93; Veljanowski, pp 118–19, 140, 143.

72 NOP in *Independent on Sunday*, 6 November 1991; cf Christmas, pp 268–69; Gilmour: TRG, Cambridge, 9 November 1989.

73 Graham & Prosser (eds), pp 74, 80, 86; Gilmour, HC 18 January 1984, cols 43–45.

74 C Johnson, pp 164–65; Middlemas, III, pp 360–64.

75 Ridley, p 60; Brittan: *op cit* n 60, p 116.

76 Walker: *Staying Power*, pp 184–85 (quotation); cf Barnett: *Inside the Treasury*, pp 22, 124; Heald, p 311; Howell: *Blind Victory*, pp 72–73, 120–21.

77 Kay & Thompson, pp 27–28; C Johnson, pp 172–73; Brittan: *op cit* n 60, pp 113, 122; Brittan: *op cit* n 65, pp 35–36; Maynard, pp 74–75; Rowthorn: 'Government Spending and Taxation in the Thatcher Era', in Michie (ed), pp 266–67.

78 Grimstone, p 24 (quotation); National Audit Office: *Sale of the Water Authorities in England and Wales*, pp 6, 8; Heath et al, pp 7, 120–1; Rentoul, p 107; Riddell: *The Thatcher Era*, pp 116–22, 233; C Johnson, p 171.

79 Brittan: *op cit* n 60, pp 121–26; Veljanowski, pp 105–6.

80 Veljanowski, p 105; Graham & Prosser (eds): *Waiving the Rules*, p 74 (quotation).

81 Brittan: *op cit* n 60, pp 121–25; Brittan: *op cit* n 65, pp 36–37; Veljanowski, p 153.

82 Vickers & Yarrow: *Privatisation: An Economic Analysis*, pp 174–7; C Johnson, pp 162–63.

83 Ridley, p 59 (quotation); Kay & Thompson, pp 28–29; Veljanowski, pp 93–102, 209.

84 Sedgewick (ed): *The House of Commons 1715–54*, II, p 159.

85 Heath et al: *Understanding Political Change*, pp 122–26; Rentoul, pp 100–7.

86 Veljanowski, pp 10, 192, 210; Riddell: *op cit* n 78, p 109; Mrs Thatcher: Finchley, 4 March 1991.

VI Poverty

1 *The Sunday Times*, 3 May 1981, in Holmes: *The First Thatcher Government*, p 209.

2 'Of Commerce', *Essays*, p 266.

3 cf Popper: *Unended Quest*, p 36; Hume: *An Enquiry Concerning Human Understanding*, S3, pt II, p 193; Hume: 'Of Commerce', *Essays*, pp 271–72; Burke: *Reflections on the Revolution in France* (ed O'Brien), pp 194–95; Blake: *Disraeli*, p 482.

4 Gash: *Mr Secretary Peel*, p 622; Gash: *Sir Robert Peel*, pp 312–22; Gash in Butler (ed): *The Conservatives*, p 88; Patten, p 182.

5 Disraeli: *Sybil, or The Two Nations*, Bk I, ch v; Disraeli: *Tory Democrat*, pp 30, 46–47; Blake: *Disraeli*, p 553.

6 P Smith (ed): *Lord Salisbury on Politics*, p 49; Mackay: *Balfour*, pp 71–72, 86, 95, 112–13, 195; Southgate: *The Conservative Leadership 1832–1932*, p 202; Feiling: *Neville Chamberlain*, pp 126–48; Macleod: *Neville Chamberlain*, pp 113–16; Addison: *The Road to 1945*, p 33.

7 Bellairs: *Conservative Social and Industrial Reform*, pp 55–113; P Addison, p 14; Halcrow, pp 50–51, 55; HC 28 January 1974, col 115.

8 Robbins: *Political Economy: Past and Present*, p 109 (quotation); Runciman: *Relative Deprivation and Social Justice*, pp 68–69; Pym, pp 112–13.

9 cf C Johnson, pp 76, 79; E Halsey: 'A Sociologist's View of Thatcherism' in Skidelsky (ed) pp 182–84; Riddell, pp 174–75; Middlemas, III, p 280; Eccleshall, pp 17–18.

10 MacGregor: *Poverty, the Poll Tax and Thatcherite Welfare Policy*, p 57; Piachaud: *Revitalising Social Policy*, pp 205–6; *The Times*, 5 May 1983 (quotation) in Riddell: *The Thatcher Government*, p 1; Hirst, p 234.

11 cf Middlemas, III, p 443; Ridley, pp 79–81, 98; C Johnson, pp 258–59; Riddell: *The Thatcher Decade*, pp 129–30, 135–36; HC 27 March 1990, cols 165–66; HC 6 March 1992, cols 317–18; HC 22 June 1992, col 90.

12 Phelps-Brown: *Egalitarianism and the Generation of Inequality*, pp 126–30; Holmes: *Politics, Religion and Society in England, 1679–1742*, pp 281–308; Mathias: *The Transformation of England*, pp 171–89; cf Perkin, pp 237, 241.

13 Herbert Spencer in Perkin: *The Rise of Professional Society: England Since 1880*, pp 142–43; Dahrendorf: 'Social Values under Mrs Thatcher' in Skidelsky (ed), p 200; Minogue: 'The Emergence of the New Right' in Skidelsky (ed), pp 126, 134 (quotation); Lord Thomas of Swynnerton: 'Our Place in the World' in Riddell: *The Thatcher Government* (quotation), p 229.

14 Friedrich: *The Political Thought of Neo-Liberalism*, pp 509–12, 525.

15 Willetts, p 141; Simon: *Retrospect*, p 70.

16 Keegan: *Mr Lawson's Gamble*, p 102; see chapter IV above.

17 © 1992 by Calvin Trillin and reproduced by kind permission of the author: it originally appeared in *The Nation*: cf Phillips: *The Politics of Rich and Poor, Wealth and the American Electorate in the Reagan Aftermath, passim*.

18 Human Development Report 1990, pp 32–33, 42–44, 59; cf Bradshaw: *Child Poverty and Deprivation in the UK*; Jackson: *Economic Policy* in Marsh & Rhodes (eds), p 28.

19 HC 17 May 1988, col 801.

20 Moore: 'The End of the Line for Poverty', Speech, 11 May 1989.

21 Bosanquet: *After the New Right*, p 14; Mrs Thatcher in *Woman's Own*, 31 October 1987.

22 Moore: *op cit* n 20; A Smith: *The Wealth of Nations*, Bk V, ch 15, pt ii, art iv; Runciman: *Relative Deprivation and Social Justice*, p 266; cf EC Commission's Final Report on the Second European Poverty Programme, p 2.

23 Lynda Chalker, HC 6 November 1979, cols 167–68.

24 Barr & Coulter: 'Social Security', in Hills (ed): *The State of Welfare*, pp 303–4, 310; Bradshaw: 'Social Security' in Marsh & Rhodes (eds): *Implementing Thatcherite Policies*, pp 88–89; Perkin, pp 426–27; Christmas, p 82.

25 Sinfield: *What Unemployment Means*, p 150; Gilmour: *BCW*, p 7.

26 J Harris: *William Beveridge*, p 424; *Social Trends*, 1992, p 107; Oppenheim: *Poverty: The Facts*, p 23; cf The Low Pay Unit's price index for low-income families.

27 Atkinson: *What is Happening to the Distribution of Income in the UK?*, pp 3–4; Bradshaw, p 90.

28 Bradshaw, pp 90–91; Barr & Coulter: *op cit* n 24, p 310; Oppenheim: *Poverty*, pp 19, 23; Piachaud, p 216; Households Below Average Income, A Statistical Analysis 1979–1988–89, p 2.

29 Social Security Committee First Report 1990–91: Low-Income

Statistics: Households Below Average Income Tables 1988 HC 1991, 401, p vi; Atkinson, pp 6–7; Oppenheim, pp 20, 38; cf S Brittan in Kavanagh & Seldon (eds) p 35; Pym, p 127.

30 Perkin, pp 242–47; *Economic Trends*, January 1992, p 164; Atkinson & Micklewright: *Economic Transformation in Eastern Europe and the Distribution of Income*, Table B15; S Jenkins: *Income Inequality and Living Standards: Changes in the 1970s and 1980s*, pp 11–13, 18; Atkinson, p 22; P Townsend: *The Poor are Poorer*; Households Below Average Income, A Statistical Analysis, 1979–1988–89.

31 Report of the Archbishop of Canterbury's Commission on Urban Priority Areas 'Faith in the City', p 359; Middlemas, III, pp 308, 553; Martin: 'The Churches', in Kavanagh & Seldon (eds), p 338.

32 Young, pp 416–17; Tebbit: *Upwardly Mobile*, p 342; Bosanquet: *After the New Right*, p 102; Piachaud, pp 223–4; R Lister: *The Exclusive Society: Citizenship and the Poor*, p 68.

33 The Breadline Britain 1990's Survey, undertaken by MORI for London Weekend Television; Cohen et al: *Hardship Britain, passim*.

34 Low Income Statistics, HC 1990–1, 401, pp vii, xxvi, xlv, lxxv; Johnson & Webb: *UK Poverty Statistics: A Comparative Study*; Barr & Coulter: *op cit* n 23, pp 306–7 (quotation), 314; Bradshaw, p 97; Townsend: *Meaningful Statistics on Poverty* No2; Townsend in Becker (ed): *Windows of Opportunity*, p ix; Households Below Average Income, A Statistical Analysis 1979–1987–88, pp 1–2, 29.

35 Paul Harrison: *Inside the Inner City* (1985), p 11; Wright: *A Journey Through Ruins*, p 7; Cohen et al, *passim*.

36 Bradshaw, p 88; Oppenheim, p 19; S Brittan in Kavanagh & Seldon (eds), p 35; Riddell, p 156; Shepherd, p 189; Middlemas, III, p 262.

37 cf Alan Budd: *The Independent*, 21 March 1991: '. . . the Thatcherite policy of allowing, if not actually encouraging, a redistribution of income from the lower to the higher paid'.

38 Middlemas, III, p 438; Macgregor, pp 57–58; K Harris, p 291; Pimlott: 'The Future of the Left' in Skidelsky (ed), pp 91–92; Becker (ed), p 9; D J Smith (ed): *Understanding the Underclass*, pp 4–7, 15–20, 25, 88; Riddell, p 166.

39 EC Final Report on Second European Poverty Programme, February 1991, pp 3 (quotation), appendix I, p 12; Becker (ed), pp 55–56.

40 Dahrendorf in Skidelsky (ed), p 195; Berlin: *Two Concepts of Liberty*; Heald: *Public Expenditure*, pp 61–68; MacCallum: *Negative and Positive Preedom*, pp 312, 318–20; W Churchill: *Lord Randolph Churchill*, pp 217–18.

41 Lord Wyatt of Weeford: *The Times*, 9 April 1991.

42 D J Smith (ed), pp 36–37, 45, 90–91; *Social Trends*, 1992, pp 40–46; Bradshaw, p 85.

43 C Johnson, p 235; see chapters II and IV above.

44 *Guardian*, 6 February 1992.

45 Britton, pp 256–57; Barr & Coulter: *op cit* n 23, pp 277, 280–81, 295, 315–17; Gilmour: *BCW*, p 4; David J Smith (ed), pp 90–91.

46 Christmas: *Chopping Down the Cherry Trees*, pp 124–25; Heseltine, pp 246–47; Tebbit, p 242; Minford & Peel: *Is the Governmment's Strategy on Course?*, pp 15–17; House of Lords Select Committee on Unemployment 1982, 142, vol I, pp 130–31; David Sheppard: The 1984 Richard Dimbleby Lecture, *Listener*, 19 April 1984 (quotation); Gilmour: *BCW*, pp 4–5.

47 Hahn & Skidelsky, in Skidelsky (ed), pp 19–20, 118–19; Barr & Coulter: *op cit* n 23 , p 277; cf Perkin, p 167.

48 HL 1982, 142, p 51; 'The Health Divide' in M Whitehead: *Inequalities in Wealth*, pp 240–42.

49 HC 25 July 1988, cols 71–72; Gilmour: *BCW*, pp 6–7.

50 Berrington: *Change in British Politics*, p 4; Gordon: 'Forms of Exclusion' in Becker (ed), p 80; in 1979 just under 7 per cent of those interviewed supported the National Front or British Movement. In 1982, 14 per cent did so. If second-party preferences are included, more than 30 per cent expressed some sympathy for a party of the extreme right. Economic and Social Research Council Report on Youth in Britain.

51 Lord Scarman: *The Brixton Disorders*, Cmnd 8427; HC 14 April 1981, cols 146–48; Macgregor, p 64; Heseltine, pp 188, 244–45; Beer: *Britain Against Itself*, p 217; Young, pp 233–34, 238–39; Gilmour: Cardiff, 13 November 1985.

52 Tebbit: *Unfinished Business*, p 33 (quotation); Willetts: p 151.

53 Maynard Smith, p 13.

54 Middlemas, III, p 450; Barr & Coulter: *op. cit.* n 23, p 281; *Social Trends*, 1992 Table 5.10; cf Eccleshall et al, p 101.

55 Gilmour: Greater London TRG, 5 December 1981; Gilmour: *BCW*, p 8; Barr & Coulter: *op. cit.* n 23, pp 280–81, 295; Middlemas, III, p 255.

56 Gilmour: *BCW*, p 8.
57 Atkinson & Micklewright: *Turning the Screw: Benefits for the Unemployed 1979–1988*; CPAG: *What's Happened to Benefits?*; Bradshaw, p 87; Barr & Coulter: *op. cit.* n 23, pp 280–83, 289.
58 Mrs Thatcher: *Independent*, 5 January 1988; Local Prosperity and the North–South Divide; *Social Trends*, 1992, pp 92–3, 100; Oppenheim, p 314; Heseltine, p 168; Grant: *Government and Industry*, p 69.
59 Oppenheim, p 114; Rose: 'Divisions that Unite Britain' in Kavanagh & Seldon (eds), pp 252–54; Christmas, p 129.
60 *Poor Britain: Poverty, Inequality and Low Pay in the Nineties* (Low Pay Unit 1992); Wilkinson, pp 12–14; Bradshaw, p 86; Becker (ed), p 28.
61 C Johnson, p 246.
62 Wilkinson, pp 1–4, 34–37 and *passim*; Michie & Wilkinson: 'Inflation Policy and the Restructuring of Labour Markets' in Michie (ed), pp 211–12; Kavanagh, p 235; Ramsden, p 2; Gilmour: *London Review of Books*, 25 October 1990.
63 The Relationship between Employment and Wages, Review by Treasury Officials, January 1985.
64 Cobban, p 214.
65 Churchill: *Winston S Churchill, Young Statesman, 1901–1914*, pp 278, 298–99, 301; HC 28 April 1909, col 388; Prior, p 253; Middlemas, III, pp 324–25; Tebbit: *Upwardly Mobile*, pp 238, 243; Riddell, p 61; Wilkinson, pp 34–37.
66 Charles Evan Hughes in Finer, p 68.
67 Orwell: *England Your England*, p 175.
68 J Hughes & R Simpson: 'Social Rights of Part Time Workers in Europe' in *Poverty* (1990–91), pp 10–13.
69 Low Pay Unit Parliammentary Briefing, pp 198–99.
70 *Economic Trends*, January 1992, pp 115–26; C Johnson, pp 141–43, 292; Hills: *Changing Tax*, p 15; HC 28 January 1991, col 390.
71 Hills: *Changing Tax*, p 11.
72 *Economic Trends*, January 1992, pp 132–33.
73 HC 17 May 1988, cols 424–30; *Social Trends*, 1992, Table 5.16; Bradshaw, p 23; Riddell, pp 152–54; cf Halsey in Skidelsky (ed), p 173.
74 Esam & Oppenheim: *A Charge on the Community*, p 77; Young, p 490; Gilmour: HC 18 January 1990, col 452; Ridley, p 133.
75 Phelps-Brown, p 219; Cornford in D J Smith (ed): *Understanding the Underclass*, p 59; *The Sunday Times*, 26 November 1989.

76 Lawson: Scottish Conservative Conference, Perth 1985; Crewe: 'Values: The Crusade that Failed' in Kavanagh & Seldon (eds), p 244; Rentoul, pp 108–40.

77 Bradshaw, p 93.

77 Mrs Thatcher: Conservative Women's Conference, 25 May 1988; Eccleshall et al: *Political Ideologies*, p 109; Cooke (ed): *The Revival of Britain*, p 55; Perkin, pp 356–57; Bradshaw, pp 93–96.

78 Fowler, pp 201–3, 206–8, 216–17; Bradshaw, pp 86–87; Kavanagh, pp 212–16.

79 P Jenkins, pp 263–64; Christmas, pp 173–74; *The Observer*, 10 April 1988.

80 Gilmour: CPAG, Blackpool, 8 October 1985; Barr & Coulter: *op cit* n23, p 296.

81 Barr & Coulter: *op cit* n 23, pp 284–93; *Social Trends*, 1992, Table 1.5, pp 27, 117; Bradshaw, pp 87–89; Becker (ed), p 31.

82 cf Nicholas Timmins: *Independent*, 6 April 1988.

83 Fowler, p 223; Barr & Coulter: *op cit* n 23, p 282; Becker (ed), p 31; Esam & Oppenheim, p 49.

84 cf Riddell, p 157; Gilmour: Blackpool, 8 October 1985.

85 Ehrman: *The Younger Pitt, II*, pp 473–74; Phelps-Brown, p 162 (quotation); Woodward: *The Age of Reform*, p 15 (quotations); Hinde: *Castlereagh*, p 236 (quotation); Blake: *The Conservative Party from Peel to Thatcher*, p 50; Grigg: *Lloyd George, The People's Champion*, p 177n; Harris: *William Beveridge*, pp 412–14, 448–50; Barr & Coulter: *op cit* n 23, p 280; Gilmour: Blackpool, 8 October 1985.

86 *Social Trends*, 1989; HC 24 May 1989, col 705; Public Expenditure White Paper (Social Security), February 1991, table 30.

87 Letter to National Council for One Parent Families, February 1978 in HC 24 April 1989, col 913; George Thomas Society Lecture, 17 January 1990; Parker & Sutherland: *Child Tax Allowances?*; *Social Trends*, 1992, p 95; C Johnson, p 122.

88 Ridley, p 101.

89 Barr & Coulter: *op cit* n 23, pp 300–1; Gilmour: Oxford TRG, 20 October 1987.

90 Gilmour, ibid.

91 Tebbit: *Upwardly Mobile*, pp 95, 278; Ridley, p 101.

92 Gilmour: CPAG, York, 5 November 1988.

93 Gilmour: Child Poverty Action Group AGM, York, 5 November 1988.

94 Ridley, p 101.

95 Willetts: 'The Family', in Kavanagh & Selden (eds), p 271 (quotation); Gilmour, HC 17 December 1987, col 1276.

96 *Evening Standard*, 24 July 1991.

97 Cornford in D J Smith (ed), pp 60–61 (quotation); Fowler: HC 17 June 1985, col 159; & 1991; Gilmour: Oxford TRG, 20 October 1987.

98 John Kay, IFS 1984; HC 14 March 1984, col 479; Fourteenth Report of the Treasury and Civil Service Committee on the 1984 Budget: Minutes of Evidence, p 48; Gilmour: Blackpool, 8 October 1985.

99 Hermione Parker: 'The Great Jobs Robbery', *The Times*, 25 July 1987; Piachaud, pp 220–21; Rentoul, pp 110–20; Becker (ed), pp 42, 52.

100 Ridley, p 99 (quotation); Barr & Coulter: *op cit* n 23, pp 315–17, 328–31, 332.

101 National Audit Office: *The Social Fund*, pp 1, 19; G Craig:'The Social Fund', *Poverty*, winter 90/91.

102 National Audit Office: *The Social Fund*, pp 2, 20; Bradshaw, p 87; cf Sir David Steel in *The Sunday Times*, 9 June 1985.

103 National Audit Office: *The Social Fund*, pp 1, 5, 15.

104 Ibid, pp 1–3, 10–11, 15–16, 27; Fowler, pp 223–24; *Guardian*, 15 February 1991.

105 Speech by John Moore, 23 April 1988; DHSS Impact of the Reformed Structure of Income Related Benefits', October 1987; Bradshaw, pp 88–89, 94; Becker (ed), p 57; The Social Security Consortium: *From Cradle to Grave?*, pp 3, 9.

106 Ibid, p 8; Barnardo's report on 1988 benefit reforms, *Poverty*, spring 1991, p 5.

106 Johnson & Stark: *Taxation and Social Security 1979–1989; the Impact on Household Incomes*; Poverty in Official Statistics: Two Reports; Riddell, pp 154–56.

107 Gilmour: HC 16 March 1988, col 1141.

108 Fowler: *Ministers Decide*, pp 209, 224; Gilmour: CPAG, Blackpool, 8 October 1985.

109 Parker: *Instead of the Dole*; Parker & Sutherland: *Child Tax Allowances?*; and Parker (ed): *Basic Income and the Labour Market*.

110 Anthony Barber: HC 5 November 1973, cols 634–38; The Right Approach (Conservative Party document, 1976); Patrick Jenkin: Brighton, 7 October 1976; Lords Select Committee on Unemployment, 1982, 142 vol I, p 131; Young, pp 522–23.

111 Britton, p 256; Heath: 'The Attitudes of the Underclass', in D J Smith (ed), pp 35–37; Cornford in *idem*, pp 59–61.
112 See chapter IV above.
113 Galbraith: *The Culture of Contentment*, pp 13–15, 97, 102.
114 Hume: 'Of Commerce', *Essays*, p 266.

VII Housing, Health and Education

1 *The Times*, 9 February 1984 in Rentoul: *Me and Mine*, p 6.
2 *Egalitarianism and the Generation of Inequality*, p 527.
3 *Social Trends*, 1992, pp 145–49; Hills & Mullings: 'Housing' in Hills (ed): *The State of Welfare*, pp 173–83, 202.
4 Tebbit: *Upwardly Mobile*, pp 124–25; Stewart & Stoker (eds): *The Future of Local Government*, p 78.
5 Walker: *The Ascent of Britain*, pp 30–33, 163–76; Walker: *Staying Power*, pp 140–41.
6 Heseltine: *Where There's a Will*, pp 78–81; Ridley, pp 87–89; Riddell: pp 114–15; Graham & Prosser (eds), pp 117–18; *Social Trends*, 1992, pp 145, 147; Kemp: 'Housing', in Marsh & Rhodes (eds): *Implementing Thatcherite Policies*, p 71; Rentoul: *Me and Mine*, pp 61–68.
7 Gyford: *The Politics of Local Socialism*, p 11; Major C R Attlee: 'Local Government and the Socialist Plan', in Addison et al: *Problems of a Socialist Government*, p 196.
8 Hills & Mullings, pp 136–38, 146, 149; A Murie in Kemp, pp 66 (quotation), 67–72; Heseltine, pp 153–54.
9 Murie: 'Housing and the Environment', in Kavanagh & Seldon (eds), pp 215–17; Hills & Mullings, pp 141–49 (quotation), 161, 191–94, 201; Riddell, p 147; *Social Trends*, 1992, pp 155–56.
10 Hills (ed), pp 2, 26; Titmuss: *Essays on 'The Welfare State'*, pp 44–46, 50.
11 Kemp, pp 72, 78; Hills & Mullings, pp 154–59.
12 Ridley, pp 87–89; Kemp, pp 67–75, 79; Christmas, pp 67–69.
13 *Independent*, 7 May 1991.
14 Kemp, p 78; Oldman: *Who Says There's No Housing Problem?*, pp 10, 29; J Greve with E Currie: *Homelessness in Britain*; Heseltine, p 199; Hills & Mullings, p 169.
15 Ridley, p 90.
16 Official figures quoted in Oldman: *Who Says There's No Housing Problem?*, p 3.
17 Salvation Army Report on Homelessness in London (Summer 1989); Hills & Mullings, p 168; *Social Trends*, 1992, pp 150–51;

Becker (ed), pp 33, 36.

18 Hills & Mullings, pp 168–69; Kemp, p 77; Simon Randall in 'Housing London's Homeless' Report; cf J Hulls (ed), p 332.

19 'Prescription for Poor Health', 1988 in Oldman: *Temporary Accommodation, The Permanent Story*, pp 8, 13.

20 HC 23 February 1989, col 741; Shelter: *Homelessness*, report 1989, p 2.

21 *Sunday Telegraph*, 10 February 1991; Gilmour: *BCW*, pp 3–4.

22 Kemp, p 78; Hills & Mullings, p 173; Riddell, p 158; Randall: *Homeless and Hungry – A Sign of the Times* (quotation); cf Dahrendorf in Skidelsky (ed), p 200.

23 Randall: *Homeless and Hungry*.

24 Oldman, p 13; Greve with Currie, p 9.

25 *Social Trends*, 1992, p 154; Riddell: *The Thatcher Legacy*, p 224.

26 Piachaud, p 220; Greve with Currie, p 9; Smith (ed), p 93; *Financial Times*, 17 February 1989.

27 Kemp, p 75; Oldman, p 14.

28 *Unfinished Business*, p 97; Ridley, p 91; cf Sir Alfred Sherman in Wright: *A Journey Through Ruins*, pp 6–7.

29 Heseltine, pp 156, 195–97; Heath et al, p 130; Smith (ed), p 94; Hills & Mullings, pp 170–71; Kemp, p 76; Macgregor, p 63.

30 C Johnson, p 149; Heseltine, pp 209–11; Muellbauer: *The Great British Housing Disaster*, pp 23–25; Ridley, pp 178–79; Murie in Kavanagh & Seldon (eds), pp 217, 225.

31 Murie in Kavanagh & Seldon (eds), pp 224–5.

32 HC, 3 series CCXXII, col 100 in McDowell: *British Conservatism 1832–1914*, p 148.

33 Webster: 'The Health Service', in Kavanagh & Seldon (eds), pp 167, 180; Riddell: *The Thatcher Era*, p 239.

34 Butler & Kavanagh: *The British General Election of 1979*, pp 300–1.

35 *Economist*, 18 September 1982; K Harris, pp 200–1; Young, pp 299–301; Fowler, pp 61–62, 181–87; Prior, p 152.

36 Rousseau: *Le Contrat Social*, ch vii (quotation); cf Fowler, p 190; Webster, pp 167, 182; cf Tebbit: *op cit* n 26, pp 109–17.

37 Hahn in Skidelski (ed), pp 119–20; S Goodwin: 'Poverty and the Health Debate', *Poverty*, winter 1988–89.

38 Gilmour: *Inside Right*, pp 183–84.

39 J Le Grand, J Winter & F Worthy: 'The NHS: Safe in Whose Hands?', in Hills (ed): *The State of Welfare*, p 93; *Daily Telegraph*,

8 January 1986.

40 *Social Trends*, 1992, pp 140, 143; Rowthorn: 'Government Spending and Taxation in the Thatcher Era', in Michie (ed): *The Economic Legacy 1979–92*, pp 267–76; C Johnson, pp 94–5; Wistow: 'The National Health Service' in Marsh & Rhodes (eds), pp 102, 111–12; Le Grand et al, pp 94–97, 100–1, 126–27; Webster, pp 169–71; Fowler, p 166; Ridley, pp 83–84; Social Services Committee, Sixth Report 1987–88, HC 1687.

41 *Observer*, 29 March 1987.

42 Ibid.

43 Crewe in Skidelsky (ed), p 43; Kavanagh & Morris, pp 86–87; Webster, p 171; Kavanagh, p 217; *Guardian*, 15 January 1988; *Social Trends*, 1992, pp 122–23.

44 G Davey Smith, M Bentley & J Black: 'The Black Report on Socioeconomic Inequalities in Health Ten Years On', *BMJ* no 6748, 18 November 1990; Le Grand et al, pp 89, 92; *Social Trends*, 1992, pp 121–23; Riddell, p 158; cf Phelps Brown, p 234.

45 Inequalities in Health: The Black Report (1980) and The Health Divide (1987), p 12.

46 The Under-Secretary for Health, Ray Whitney, MP, in P Townsend, N Davidson and M Whitchurch: *Introduction to Inequalities in Health*, 1988, pp 10, 12; *Evening Chronicle*, 10 October 1986.

47 Le Grand et al, p 93; Wistow, pp 106–8, 114–15; Webster, pp 179–80; Piachaud, p 20; Christmas, p 224.

48 Webster, p 176.

49 Ridley, pp 86, 95–96.

50 Munsche: *Gentlemen and Poachers*, pp 76, 93; cf Fowler, pp 187, 190, 205, 210; Kavanagh & Seldon (eds), p 104.

51 Watkins, p 44.

52 Fowler, pp 187, 205 (quotation), 210.

53 Le Grand et al, pp 93–94.

54 Webster, pp 180–81; Michael Prowse: *Financial Times*, 22 March 1989.

55 Harriet Harman, MP: *Observer*, 8 May 1988.

56 *Independent*, 25 March 1991.

57 Department of Health: *NHS Directly Employed Non-Medical Manpower*, 31 December 1990; *Financial Times*, 8 June 1991.

58 *The NHS Reforms and You*, DHS 1991; *Observer*, 13 May 1991; *Independent*, 13 May 1991.

59 *Independent*, 3 May 1991.

60 Social Services Committee 1988–89 Eighth Report, HC 214–111,

paras 7.23–7.25; *Independent*, 23 March 1989.

61 Eighth Report, para 7.25; Titmuss: *Essays on 'The Welfare State'*, pp 29, 33; cf Hahn in Skidelsky, pp 120–21.

62 Wright, p 219.

63 L Bilmes & J Shaw in *Financial Times*, 8 June 1991; Morgan: *The People's Peace*, p 38.

64 cf Wistow, pp 109–11, 115–16; Webster, pp 181–82.

65 *BMJ*, September 1991 in James Le Fanu: 'The Doctors' Dilemma', *The Spectator*, 12 October 1991.

66 Scott: 'Higher Education', in Kavanagh & Seldon (eds), pp 199–202, 205–10; Glennerster & Low: 'Education', in Hills (ed), *The State of Welfare*, p 41–44; Morgan: *The People's Peace*, pp 480–81; Ranelagh, pp 59–60; Young, pp 401–3 (quotation); P Jenkins, pp 271–72.

67 Luttwak in *London Review of Books*, 12 September 1991; Perkin, p 487.

68 *New York Times*, 22 November 1988; *Higher Education into the 1990s*, Cmnd 9524; Young, p 414; Scott, p 205; Kavanagh, p 291 (Powell); Wilkie: 'The Thatcher Effect in Science', in Kavanagh & Seldon, pp 325–26; Mrs Thatcher: Newcastle-on-Tyne, 23 March 1985, in Kavanagh, p 292, and in Perkin, pp 486–87.

69 Bradbury in *Cuts*, pp 40–41.

70 Mary Warnock: *Observer*, 5 November 1989; P Johnson, *The Spectator*, 7 September 1991; Gilmour: HC 24 March 1988, cols 605–6.

71 Perkin, pp 394–98; West: *Education and the State*, p 88 (quotation); Wilkie, p 319; Conrad Russell, *Independent*, 4 November 1989; for the Thatcherite view of universities and the market, see Tebbit: *Unfinished Business*, pp 106–9.

72 Lord Porter of Luddenham: *Independent*, 24 May 1991; Wilkie, p 316 (quotation), pp 322–29; 'Science Watch', *Independent*, 13 March 1991; Heseltine, p 234.

73 Scott, p 205; Christmas, p 234.

74 Sir Claus Moser: Speech to Science 90, Swansea, August 1990, p 33; P Jenkins, p 272; I Crawford, Information Officer of the LSE, in *Good Housekeeping*, March 1991.

75 Alan Howarth, MP, Minister for Higher Education: *Independent*, 2 March 1991.

76 Macgregor, p 59; PAC, *Observer*, 24 February 1991; *Independent*, 11 May 1991.

77 Scott, pp 203–10 (quotation); Perkin, p 452; Dahrendorff in Skidelsky, p 188; *Independent*, 11 April and 11 May 1991.

78 Mackay: *Balfour*, p 86; cf P Jenkins, p 267.

79 Tebbit: *Unfinished Business*, p 99.

80 *Education: A Framework for Expansion*, 1972, Cmmd. 5174; Glennerster & Low: *Education* in Hills (ed) pp 34, 53–55; Wapshott & Brock, pp 94–102.

81 Riddell, p 142; Kaldor: *Economic Consequences*, p 86.

82 Glennerster & Low, pp 34–35.

83 Tomlinson: 'The Schools', in Kavanagh & Seldon (eds) p 183; Patten, pp 88, 97; Ridley, pp 92–94 (quotation); Young, p 514.

84 Ridley, pp 92–93.

85 Miliband: *Markets, Politics and Education*, pp 15–16 (quotation); 'Opting for What?', *The Times* leading article, 28 May 1992.

86 Ridley: '*My Style of Government*', p 93.

87 Wright: *A Journey through Ruins*, p 29.

88 Robbins: *Political Economy, Past and Present*, pp 8, 120–21, 128; A Smith: *The Wealth of Nations*, bk v, ch I pt III, Art II; West: *Education and the State*, pp 8, 112, 116–17; Phelps-Brown, p 152.

89 Lord Radcliffe: the Georgian Group, July 20 1954; Bogdanor: 'The Constitution', in Kavanagh & Seldon (eds) pp 140–41; Burke: *Speech to the Electors of Bristol*, 3 November 1774; Hills (ed) pp 28–29.

90 Gilmour; HC 17 December 1987, col 1276; Piachaud, p 210; Miliband, p 11.

91 Titmuss, p 187; Riddell, pp 144–45.

92 Tomlinson, pp 193–95.

93 Piachaud: pp 212–15; Views of Conservative councillors: *Observer* schools report, 23 June 1991.

94 Wallas: *Human Nature in Politics*, p 13.

95 Riddell, pp 146–47.

96 Letter to *Observer*, 3 March 1991.

97 Glennerster & Low: *op cit* n 66, pp 60–65, 76; The Prince of Wales Shakespeare's Birthday Lecture, 22 April 1991; Sir Claus Moser: Speech to Science 90, Swansea, August 1990; Brittan, pp 258–59; P Jenkins, p 267.

98 Glennerster & Low: *op cit* n 66, pp 54–65; P Jenkins, p 270; *Independent*, 13 May 1991.

99 Rowthorn in Michie (ed), pp 267–76; C Johnson, pp 94–95; Glennerster & Low: *op cit* n 66, pp 37–39, 46, 79–82; Tomlinson, pp 190–91; Ridley, p 84; Riddell, p 142.

100 Glennerster & Low: *op cit* n 66, Hills (ed), pp 80–81; Rowthorn, pp 210–11; *Independent*, 13 May 1991.

101 Sir Claus Moser: *op cit* n 97; Glennerster & Low: *op cit* n 66, pp 37–39.

102 Rowthorn in Michie (ed), p 273–74; Heseltine, p 222.

103 Sir Claus Moser: *op cit* n 97, p 32; Rowthorn in Michie (ed), pp 272–73.

104 Gallup poll in *The Sunday Times*, 2 July 1989.

105 Crewe in Kavanagh & Seldon, pp 239–47; Crewe in Skidelsky (ed), pp 33–43.

106 Crewe & Searing: *Ideological Change in the British Conservative Party*, pp 376–78; Heath et al, pp 175–76; Le Grand: 'The State of Welfare', in Hills (ed), pp 355–56; Ridley, pp 92–94; Hirst, p 25.

107 Le Grand in Hills (ed), p 339–40, 361.

VIII Means and Ends

1 *Newsweek*, April 1992.

2 In Whitefield: *Machiavelli*, p 138.

3 *Newsweek*, 15 October 1990.

4 Mrs Thatcher: *Newsweek*, April 1992.

5 Scruton: *The Meaning of Conservatism*, pp 53–58; Patten, p 70.

6 Hailsham: *The Dilemma of Democracy*, pp 9, 126–30 and *passim*; Hailsham: *A Sparrow's Flight*, pp 391–96; Gilmour: 'Review of the Dilemma of Democracy', in *Books and Bookmen*, June 1978.

7 Southgate in Butler (ed): *The Conservatives*, pp 142–43 (quotation); Gilmour, *BCW*, pp 196–97; for the contrary view, see Norton: *The Constitution in Flux*.

8 Disraeli: *Tory Democract*, p 41.

9 R W Johnson's phrase in *The Politics of Recession*, p 237; Middlemas, III, p 571; Speech on the Frame-Work Bill, 27 February 1812; Moore (ed): *Byron's Works*, vol vi, p 320; Stewart & Stoker (eds): *The Future of Local Government*, p 2; Riddell, p 177.

10 Gilmour: *Guardian*, 16 February 1989.

11 Ramsden: *Thatcher and Conservative History*, p 3; Gilmour: *Guardian*, 16 February 1989; Mount: *The Constitution Now*, pp 162–64; Gamble: *The Free Economy and the Strong State*, p 205.

12 Mrs Thatcher: 'What's Wrong with Politics?', CPC lecture, 10 October 1968, in Wapshott & Brock, p 271; Gilmour: *Inside Right*, pp 206–7; Gilmour: *The Body Politic*, p 147.

13 Browning: *The Lost Leader*.

14 Michael Latham: *Economist*, 3 August 1991.

15 Mrs Thatcher to Bruce Gyngell, the Chairman of TV-AM, in all London papers 18 October 1991; Churchill, 26 October 1930 in Gilbert: *Winston S Churchill*, vol v, p 1021; Gilmour: *Guardian*, 12 November 1984.

16 Gilbert, vol v, p 1004; HC 14 April 1986, cols 584–702.

17 See chapter I above; Riddell in Kavanagh & Seldon (eds), pp 103–5; Young, pp 475–77; Mount: *The British Constitution Now*, pp 122–23; HC 15 April 1986, cols 729–31.

18 Young, p 439; Walker, pp 202–3.

19 e.g. Peter Jenkins: *Independent*, 21 June 1989 (quotation); Gilmour: *The Observer*, 30 July 1989; *Independent*, 31 July 1988; Carlyle: *The French Revolution*, Bk vii, ch 1.

20 Gilmour: 'The False Doctrine of Thatchocracy', *Observer*, 30 July 1989; Mount, p 139; cf Young pp 229–31.

21 Halcrow: *Keith Joseph*, pp 135–37; King (ed), p 126; Prior, p 136; Hennessy in Kavanagh & Seldon (eds), pp 120–23; Young, pp 161–62.

22 Vansittart: *The Mist Procession*, p 313; Gilmour: *The Body Politic*, p 198.

23 cf Roy Jenkins: *Mr Balfour's Poodle*, p viii.

24 Mount, pp 32, 162–63, 188; Gilmour, HC 18 March 1991, cols 52–55.

25 Ridley, p 33 (quotation); Margaret Thatcher: letter to Charter 88, 26 May 1989 in Keane: *The Media and Democracy*, p 112.

26 Keeton: *The Passing of Parliament*; Hollis: *Can Parliament Survive?*; Carter: *The Office of Prime Minister*, pp 112–13 (quotation); *Economist*, 3 August 1991.

27 R Harris: *Good and Faithful Servant*, pp 5, 83, 99, 122–23, 126.

28 R Harris, pp 89–91, 114, 134 (quotation), 174–75.

29 e.g. *Economist*, 20 June 1981; Cockerell, p 266; R Harris, p 122.

30 R Harris, pp 89–91, 144–50, 174–75; for Bernard Ingham's explanation and defence see Ingham: *Kill the Messenger*, pp 319–333.

31 R Harris, pp 152–55; cf Ingham, pp 196–206.

32 R Harris, pp 175, 192; HC 31 October 1989, col 175; HC 2 February 1989, col 488; Hetherington: 'The Mass Media', in Kavanagh & Seldon, pp 294–95.

33 R Harris, pp 11, 99, 114–16; cf Ingham, pp 187–89.

34 Young, pp 454–57; Linklater & Leigh: *Not with Honour*, pp 172–73; R Harris, p 136; Ingham, p 337.

35 Linklater & Leigh, pp 127–28; Ingham, pp 334–35; R Harris, p 130; Young, p 440.

36 Linklater & Leigh, pp 128–30, 133–35; R Harris, p 130.

37 Linklater & Leigh, pp 135–40; R Harris, pp 131–33.

38 Harris, pp 134–36; Linklater & Leigh, pp 139, 142, 154–55, 164; Young, pp 441–42.

39 Ingham, pp 335–36; Young, pp 450–51; Linklater & Leigh, p 164; Harris, pp 133–34.

40 Harris, pp 135, 140–41; Linklater & Leigh, pp 158, 164.

41 Linklater & Leigh, pp 136–37; Harris, pp 131–32; Ingham, p 337.

42 *The Thatcher Factor*, Channel 4, 6 April 1989 (Brittan); A Howard: *Independent*, 8 April 1989; R Harris: *The Sunday Times*, 9 April 1989; R Harris: *Good and Faithful Servant*, pp 132–41 (Brittan); Linklater & Leigh, pp 152–54, 165; Ingham, pp 335–37.

43 cf Linklater & Leigh, pp 216–17.

44 Orwell: *England Your England*, p 34; Orwell: *Shooting an Elephant*, p 122; I have been unable to trace the 'crooks and charlatans' reference; Booth: *British Hustings 1924–1950*, p 254 (quotation).

46 Evans: *Good Times, Bad Times*, pp 165–66.

47 Hammond: *Maverick*, pp 73–90; Hetherington: 'The Mass Media', in Kavanagh & Seldon (eds), p 292.

48 Hetherington, pp 292–93.

49 Liebling: *The Press*, p 8; Snoddy, pp 124–28, 192–93; Evans, p 217; Worsthorne: *Sunday Telegraph*, 30 April 1989; cf R Knight Bruce: 'The Royal Confidants', *Spectator*, 13 July 1991; H Porter: 'Exposing the Rat Pack,' *Spectator*, 6 June 1992.

50 Snoddy, pp 128–29 (quotation); Mr Black repeated his views in the *Guardian*, 22 June 1992.

51 *Financial Times*, 1986 in Edward Whitley: 'A Very Private Person', *Spectator*, 26 October 1991.

52 Interview with Derek Malcolm, *Guardian*, 11 July 1991.

53 Johnson: 'Gall of the Tabloids', *Spectator*, 3 August 1991.

54 Johnson, ibid; Jenkins: *Independent*, 25 January 1989; Snoddy, p 109 (quotation).

55 cf Hetherington in Kavanagh & Seldon (eds) pp 20–91; Jack O'Sullivan & Steve Connor: *Independent*, 29 June 1992.

56 Dryden: *Absalom and Achitophel*, ll 539–40.

57 Hugo Young: 'Rupert Murdoch and *The Sunday Times*: A Lamp Goes Out', *Political Quarterly*, vol 55, no 4, (1984), p 384.

58 Snoddy, pp 159–60; 194–95.

59 Auberon Waugh: *Spectator*, 2 September 1989; Snoddy, pp 100, 160–61.

60 J Morgan (ed): *The Backbench Diaries of Richard Crossman*, pp 628–33 (which contain an admission but far from the whole truth); Adamson: *The Old Fox*; Bernard Levin: *The Times*, 10 March 1981; Carter Ruck: *Memoirs of a Libel Lawyer*, pp 107–15; but cf Foot: *Aneurin Bevan 1945–1960*, pp 546–47.

61 Butler, in Skidelsky (ed), p71; Lewis: *International Herald Tribune*, 3 April 1992.

62 Sir David Nicholson: *Guardian* 23 December 1991; Leach, p 22; Templewood: *Ambassador on Special Mission*, p 55.

63 cf Middlemas, III, pp 415–19, 431.

64 Burke: *Reflections*; Burke: *Letter to M Dupont, 1789*.

65 Burke: *Reflections*; Gilmour: *Inside Right*, p 64.

66 Peregrine Worsthorne: 'The New Right v The Queen', *Sunday Telegraph*, 30 April 1989; Mount, p 95 (quotation).

67 Enthronement sermon, *The Times*, 26 March 1980; Gilmour: *Independent*, 5 November 1986; See chapter VI above.

68 Cockerell: *Live from Number 10*, p 277 (quotation); Young, p 282; cf Ingham, pp 311–12.

69 Mrs Thatcher: Church of Scotland, 21 May 1988; Rentoul, pp 143–44 (quotation).

70 Mrs Thatcher: *Sunday Telegraph*, 28 June 1987, in Young, p 420; Wesley: *Letters*, pp 138–39; Vulliamy: *John Wesley*, p 270; Pollock: *John Wesley*, p 231; Hempson: *Methodism and Politics in British Society 1750–1850*, pp 232–33; Gilmour: *Riot, Risings and Revolution*, p 92; Wearmouth: *Methodism and the Working-Class Movement of England 1800–1850*, pp 160 (quotation), 162–63.

71 cf Tebbit, p 341.

72 See chapter VI above; Ortega y Gasset: *The Revolt of the Masses*.

73 Ewing & Gearty: *Freedom under Thatcher*, pp 2, 58, 156–69; Graham & Prosser, pp 192–93.

74 Peter Wright: *Spycatcher, passim*; Ewing & Gearty, pp 152–53; Young, p 461; Ingham, p 319; Gilmour: HC 15 July 1988, cols 593–96.

75 Ewing & Gearty, pp 154–60; Graham & Prosser, pp 192–93.

76 Weekly Law Reports, 28 August 1987, p 1286; Ewing & Gearty, pp 158–60.

77 Lord Scarman: 'Wright: How the Law Lords got it Wrong', *The Times*, 19 August 1987.

78 G Lewis: *Lord Atkin*, p 137.

79 The House of Lords judgment, 13 October 1988, Lord Griffiths at p 19.

80 Lord Beloff & Michael Beloff: 'Reforms that threaten Executive Control over Judges and Lawyers', *Independent*, 16 March 1989.

81 Hailsham: 'How to Ruin The Professions', *Spectator*, 26 March 1988; Middlemas, III, pp 415–19; Holmes: *Augustan England, Professions, State and Society 1680–1730*, pp3–18, and *passim*.

82 Robert Alexander: 'True Cost of the Law Reforms', *Independent*, 18 April 1989; Zellick: 'The Law', in Kavanagh & Seldon (eds), pp 286–88.

83 Hailsham, *Spectator*, 26 March 1988; Gamble, pp 165, 215; Piachaud, p 289.

84 J M Thompson (ed): *French Revolution Documents 1789–94*, p 11.

85 Steve Milligan: *What Shall We Do About the BBC?*, p 3 (quotation).

86 Whitelaw, pp 345–50.

87 Cockerell, pp 152, 155; Cooke (ed): *The Vintage Mencken*, p 70.

88 Cockerell, p 134; R Harris, p 122; Hetherington in Kavanagh & Seldon (eds), pp 297–99; Milne, pp 163–66, 218 (quotation), 217–35.

89 Cockerell, pp 297, 310; Milne: *The Memoirs of a British Broadcaster*, pp 109, 163–72.

90 Letter from Norman Tebbit to the BBC, 30 October 1986; The BBC's response to Norman Tebbit, 5 November 1986; Tebbit, pp 324–25; Ingham pp 351–55; Milne, pp 218, 252–56.

91 Cockerell, p 285; see the epigraph of this chapter.

92 Tebbit, p 326; Milne, pp 255–56; Cockerell, p 257.

93 Milne, pp 103–4, 109, 116–25, 186–99, 247; Linklater & Leigh: *Not With Honour*, p 67 (quotation); Hetherington, pp 295, 301; Cockerell, pp 295–98.

94 Ewing & Gearty, pp 147–51; Graham & Prosser (eds), p 192; Cockerell, p 315.

95 Ewing & Gearty, p 151; Milne, pp 266–68; Cockerell, pp 315, 268–69.
96 Milne, p 202.
97 Ewing & Gearty, pp 237–38; Cockerell, p 335–36.
98 Ewing & Gearty, pp 238–41; Hetherington, p 296.
99 Hetherington, pp 299–301; Cockerell, pp 332–34; Andrew Stephens: *Observer*.
100 Hetherington, pp 299–301.
101 Simon Jenkins: Revenge: 'Yet Another Killing Hits TV', *The Sunday Times*, 13 November 1988; Peter Jenkins: *Independent*, 9 November 1988; G Walden: *Sunday Telegraph*, 3 December 1989.
102 Hetherington, p 301.
103 Michael Grade: *Guardian*, 17 October 1991; Mrs Thatcher to Bruce Gyngell in the newspapers of 18 October 1991.
104 Hetherington, pp 291 (quotation), 297, 299; Margaret Thatcher: *Newsweek*, April 1992 (quotation).
105 Swift: *On Poetry: A Rhapsody*, ll 185–90.
106 de Tocqueville: *Democracy in America*, p 586; Kennedy: *Salisbury 1830–1903*, p 178; Young: 'Local Government', in Kavanagh & Seldon (eds), p 124; Gyford: *The Politics of Local Socialism*, p 70.
107 King: 'The New Right, the New Left and Local Government', in Stewart & Stoker (eds): *The Future of Local Government*, pp 188–89; Hayek: *The Constitution of Liberty*, pp 263–64.
108 Gyford, p 114.
109 *Putting Britain First: A National Policy from the Conservatives*, 1974; Young, p 82.
110 Halcrow, pp 75–76 (quotation); Young, p 83.
111 Jackson: *Local Authority Budgets and Economic Stability*, pp 2–7, 41–43; Jones: *Local Government and The Social Market*, pp 14–15; Jones & Stewart: *The Case for Local Government*, p 11; Howell, *Blind Victory*, pp 185–86; Gilmour, *BCW*, pp 73–74.
112 Gifford, pp 25–27; Kavanagh, p 170; Rhodes: 'Local Government Finance', in Marsh & Rhodes (eds) p 52; Goldsmith & Newton: 'Central-Local Government Relations', in Berrington (ed), pp 226–27.
113 Robson: *Local Government in Crisis*; Gilmour: *The Body Politic*, p 331 (quotation); Mount, p 251; Ridley: *The Local Right*, pp 18–22; Gyford, pp 33, 43, 102–3; Walsh: 'Competition and Service in Local Government', in Stewart and Stoker

(eds), pp 31–34, 51–52; Stewart: 'Changing Organisation of Local Authorities', in *idem*, pp 172, 177.

114 Jones & Stewart: *The Case for Local Government*, pp 12, 53–55; Jackson, pp 10, 18–19, 32–34, 41–43; Rhodes: 'Local Government Finance', in Marsh & Rhodes (eds), pp 53–54.

115 Jones & Stewart, p 33: Rhodes in Marsh & Rhodes, pp 54–55, 61; Howell, p 86; Goldsmith & Newton: *op cit* n 112, pp 220–21.

116 Jones & Stewart, pp 3, 37; Enoch Powell: *Sunday Express*, 11 October 1981 in Rhodes, p 61; Letter from Roger Parker-Jervis, chairman of Bucks County Council; *The Times*, 19 January 1983.

117 Goldsmith & Newton: *op cit* n 112, p 217; Gilmour: *Guardian*, 2 April 1984.

118 Prior, pp 150–51; Rhodes, p 55.

119 Ramsden: *Thatcher and Conservative History*, p 3; Marsh, pp 54–55; Gilmour: *Guardian*, 2 April 1984.

120 Rhodes, p 56; Gilmour: HC 11 April 1984, col 451; HC 10 May 1984, col 1007.

121 Gyford, p 19.

122 Rhodes, p 56 (quotation); Goldsmith & Newton: *op cit* n 112, p 229; Gilmour: Annual conference of the Chartered Institute of Public Finance and Accountancy, Brighton, 5 June 1984; Gamble, pp 132–33.

123 Gilmour: HC 20 July 1986, cols 70–73.

124 Macgregor: *Poverty, the Poll Tax and Thatcherite Welfare Policy*, p 447; Gibson: 'Why Block Grant Failed', in Ranson et al (eds): *Between Centre and Locality*, p 58; Jones & Stewart, pp 63–71; Rhodes, p 61.

125 Ridley, pp 122–23; Gibson, p 63; Rhodes, pp 50–51, 58–59, 62–63; cf Barnett: *Inside the Treasury*, pp 75–76.

126 Gilmour: *Guardian*, 2 April 1984; Jones & Stewart, pp 156–57.

127 Jones & Stewart, pp 57–58, 98.

128 Watkins, pp 56–67; Shepherd, pp 189–90; Mount, p 139; see chapters I and VI above.

129 HC 20 January 1986, col 73.

130 Travers: 'Community Charge and Other Financial Changes', in Stewart & Stoker, pp 14–29; Macgregor, p 445; Rhodes, p 60.

131 Jones: *Local Government and the Social Market*, p 9; Gilmour: HC 17 December 1987, col 1276.

132 Jones, pp 5–6; Jackson, pp 7–8; Hirst, pp 202–3; Stewart & Stoker, pp 164–65, 237–40.

133 Mount, pp 204, 243, 251–2.

134 Conservative Research Department: Campaign Guide 1977, pp 518–20.

135 Ibid, p 520; Gilmour: *The Body Politic*, pp 335–36; *Inside Right*, pp 219–21.

136 B Crick: 'On Scottish Nationalism', *Government and Opposition*, summer 1992, pp 386–88; Bogdanor: 'The Constitution', in Kavanagh & Seldon (eds), pp 137–38.

137 Ferdinand Mount makes this case well and at length in *The British Constitution Now*, pp 198–202; I argued it briefly and much less well in *Inside Right*, pp 219–20.

138 Gilmour: *Inside Right*, p 220.

139 Tebbit: *Unfinished Business*, p 61; cf Young in Kavanagh & Seldon (eds), p 132; Jones: *Local Government and the Social Market*, pp 10–11.

140 Gamble: *The Free Economy and the Strong State*, pp 31–37, 203–6, 231–33; Marquand: *The Unprincipled Society*, pp 82–83; Halsey: 'A Sociologist's View of Thatcherism', in Skidelsky (ed), pp 182–83; Barry: 'The Continuing Relevance of Socialism', in *idem* (ed), p 146; R Johnson: *The Politics of Recession*, pp 239, 248.

141 Hayek: *The Road to Serfdom, passim*; Gilmour: *London Review of Books*, 25 October 1990; Finer: *The Road to Reaction*, pp 9, 22, 29–30, 50, 70, 74–75, 90–91, 116–19 and *passim*; cf Middlemas, III, pp 463–67; Bogdanor: *op cit* n 136, p 158; Rousseau: *Le Contrat Social*, Bk I, ch 6.

142 Oakeshott: *Rationalism in Politics*, p 48; Pulzer: *Do We Need a Constitution?* LRB, 5 December 1991; Dobrée (ed); *The Letters of George III*, p 128; Burke: *Speech on Conciliation with America* in Maccunn, pp 267–68; Mathiot: *The British Political System*, p 333.

143 Burke: *Letter to M Dupont, 1789*; Gilmour: *Inside Right*, pp 64–65; Bogdanor: *op cit* n 136, pp 137–38, 141–42; Gamble, pp 234–35, Hirst; pp 49–50, 63–64; Pymm, p 97.

IX Foreign Policy

1 Interview with Barbara Walters, ABC, 8 March 1991.

2 Giscard d'Estaing: *Le Pouvoir et La Vie*, vol II.

3 Henderson: *Channels and Tunnels*, p 143.

4 Jenkins: *European Diary 1977–1981*, pp 440–41.

5 Ridley, p 162.

6 Carrington: *Reflect on Things Past*, pp 285, 371; Ridley,

pp 41–44; R Johnson: *The Politics of Recession*, p 248; Dickie: *Inside the Foreign Office*, pp 267–68; and see section on the Falklands War below.

7 HC 25 July 1979, col 732.
8 Carrington, pp 271–73, 287–91; Cosgrave: *Carrington*, p 142; Young, p 176.
9 HC 25 July 1979, cols 623–24.
10 Young, p178; HC 25 July 1979, cols. 620–30.
11 HC 25 July 1979, col 733.
12 Carrington, pp 296–97.
13 Jenkins: *A Life at the Centre*, p 492.
14 Ibid.
15 Young, p 184; Jenkins: *European Diary*, p 511; Jenkins: *Life at the Centre*, p 493.
16 For Giscard, see epigraph above; for Schmidt, see Young, p 187.
17 Jenkins: *Life at the Centre*, p 495.
18 Tugendhat: *Making Sense of Europe*, p 121; Young, pp 186–87; Jenkins: *European Diary*, pp 529–30.
19 cf Nicholas Comfort: *Daily Telegraph*, 28 February 1980.
19a R Jenkins: *European Diary 1977–1981*, p 557.
20 Jenkins: *European Diary*, pp 592–93; Young, pp 188–89.
21 Jenkins: *European Diary*, p 604.
22 R Harris: *Good and Faithful Servant*, pp 88, 102 (quotations); Prior, p 145; Young, p 189.
23 Young, pp 189–90; HC 2 June 1980, cols 1143–57.
24 cf Hastings & Jenkins: *The Battle for the Falklands*, pp 336–37; Young, p 258.
25 Carrington, pp 348–52.
26 Little: 'Anglo-Argentine Relations', in Byrd (ed), pp 153–54.
27 Hastings & Jenkins, pp 325–26.
28 Carrington, pp 348–54.
29 Hastings & Jenkins, pp 38–39; Carrington, pp 354–55; *Franks Report*, paras 71–72, 81.
30 HC 2 April 1980, cols 128–34; *Franks Report*, para 61.
31 HC 18 December 1980, cols 650–52.
32 Carrington, pp 359–60; Hastings & Jenkins, pp 42–43, 53; Young, pp 260–62, 265; *Franks Report*, paras 114–18.
33 *Franks Report*, paras 115–16; Carrington, pp 359–60.
34 Hastings & Jenkins, pp 42–44, 326; K Harris, pp 175–76; Little in Byrd (ed), p 137; Carrington, pp 359–60.
35 *Franks Report*, paras 90, 96, 98–99; Carrington, pp 357–58.
36 *Franks Report*, paras 104, 117–18.

37 Haig: *Caveat*, p 280 (quotation); Henderson: *Channels and Tunnels*, p 91; Hastings & Jenkins, pp 322, 336.

38 Carrington, pp 370–71.

39 Woodward, p 94.

40 Friedman: *Britain and the Falklands War*, p 98.

41 Johnson: 'Thoughts on the Late Transactions respecting Falkland's Islands', in *The Works of Samuel Johnson*, vol 8, pp 86, 107; Boswell: *Life of Johnson*, pp 449–50; P Jenkins, p 162.

42 Henderson, p 85 (quotation); Haig, p 266 (quotation); Hastings & Jenkins, p 315 (quotation).

43 S Woodward: *The Hundred Days*, p 81; Hastings & Jenkins, p 339.

44 S Woodward, p xviii; Hastings & Jenkins, p 323.

45 P Jenkins, p 161; Young, p 273; Fisk: *Pity the Nations*, pp 193–242; Pym, pp 29–30.

46 S Woodward, p 165.

47 S Woodward, pp 149–62; Henderson, pp 93–97.

48 Henderson, pp 90–91, 97–99, 198; Hastings & Jenkins, pp 172–73; Prior, pp 148–49; K Harris, pp 189–90.

49 Young, pp 282–83 (quotation); Hastings & Jenkins, pp 336–37.

50 *Frank Report*, para 229; S Jenkins: 'A Very British Foul-Up', *The Times*, 2 April 1992; Young, pp283–85; Hastings & Jenkins, p 347.

51 F P Dunne: 'Mr Dooley's Opinions', in Brogan: *The American Political System*, p29.

52 *Franks Report*, para 260.

53 S Woodward, pp xviii, 126; Henderson, p 108.

54 B Woodward: *Veil, the Second War of the CIA 1981–1988*, p 212; G Smith: *Reagan and Thatcher*, p 84; Hastings & Jenkins, p 58.

55 Hastings & Jenkins, pp 98–102; Dickie, pp 194–95; Ionescu, p 200; K Harris, pp 180–81.

56 Z Steiner: 'Decision Making in American and British Foreign Policy', in *An open and shut case*, p 15 in M Smith; 'Britain and the United States: Beyond the Special Relationship?', in Byrd (ed) p22; Hastings & Jenkins, pp112–13.

57 Hastings & Jenkins, pp 113, 258 (quotation); Henderson, pp 86, 92–93, 107; Smith in Byrd (ed), p 22.

58 G Smith, pp 252, 254; Young, pp 249–51.

59 M Smith, in Byrd (ed), p 9.

60 Healey: *The Time of My Life*, p 534.

61 Henderson, p 78; G Smith, pp 212–13.

62 Burke: *Reflections*, p 172.

63   B Woodward, pp 299–300; Andrew & Ian Gilmour: 'Terrorism', *London Review of Books*, 23 October 1986.

64   B Woodward, pp 285–92.

65   Young, pp 345–46; Ionescu, p 246.

66   M Smith, in Byrd (ed), p 23.

67   G Smith, p 245.

68   Young, pp 347–48 (quotation).

69   Murdoch quoted by Terence Lancaster in *Daily Mirror*, 24 November 1985; Paul Johnson: 'Margaret Thatcher the Lost Leader', *Observer*, 20 November 1983; for other extracts from Murdoch and Johnson, see Young, pp 349–55.

70   B Woodward, pp 184–87; Young, pp 474–75; Parsons in Byrd (ed), pp 91–92.

71   Young, pp 474–76; B Woodward, pp 445–46.

72   Young, pp 475–76; Hitchens: *Blood, Class and Nostalgia*, pp 350–51; Gilmour: HC 16 April 1986, col 918.

73   See chapter VIII above.

74   J Adams: *The Financing of Terror*, pp 20–23, 31–34; Gilmour: HC 16 April 1986, cols 918–19; Gilmour: 'Terrorism', *London Review of Books*, 23 October 1986.

75   M Smith: 'Britain and the United States', in Byrd (ed) pp 21–22; HC 15 April 1986, col 730 (Parsons); Gilmour: HC 17 April 1986, cols 917–19.

76   Friedman: 'Thatcherism and Defence', in Kavanagh & Seldon (eds) p 149; M Smith, in Boyd (ed), pp 24–32.

77   Young, pp 484–85.

78   P Jenkins, pp 288–89; Young, pp 392–93.

79   Friedman: *op cit* n 76, p 145; Margaret Thatcher: *Evening Standard*, 28 August 1991, reprinted from *Newsweek*.

80   Friedman, pp 148–49; Young, pp 479–81.

81   Boyce: 'The Irish Connection', in Kavanagh & Seldon, p 228.

82   Ibid, pp 228–33.

83   Brendon O'Leary: 'The Anglo-Irish Agreement, Folly or Statecraft?', pp 5–32, *West European Politics*, vol 10, No 1, January 1987; Boyce: *op cit* n 81, pp 232–37; Bulpitt: 'Rational Politicians and Conservative Statecraft', in Byrd (ed), p 198.

84   Michael Butler: 'Simply Wrong about Europe', *The Times*, 26 November 1991; *Independent*, 23 July 1992; Thomas: *Ever Closer Union*, p 8; Allen: 'British Foreign Policy and West European Cooperation', in Byrd (ed), pp 36–43, 46–48.

85   Butler, ibid; Ionescu, pp 200–1; Thomas: *Ever Closer Union*, pp 8, 26–27; Vincent in Hennessy & Seldon, pp 287–93.

86 Ionescu, p 203; Butler, ibid.

87 *The MacDougall Report 1977*: Sir Donald MacDougall: 'Economic and Monetary Union on the European Commission Budget', *National Institute Economic Review*, May 1992.

88 *Economist*, 13 June 1992.

89 G Smith: *Full Employment in the 1990s*, p 63; MacDougall: *op cit* n 88.

X Harmony or Discord?

1 *Newsweek*, 15 October 1990.

2 Interview with Barbara Walters, ABC, 8 March 1991.

3 Ibid.

4 Prior, p 113.

5 Pope: *An Essay on Man*, Epistle I, ll 289–94.

6 Jessop et al: *Thatcherism: A Tale of Two Nations*, pp 6–9; Bulpitt: *The Discipline of the New Democracy: Mrs Thatcher's Domestic Statecraft*, pp 19–39; Riddell: *The Thatcher Era*, pp 2–3; Gamble: *The Free Economy and the Strong State*, esp. pp 174–207; Ridley: '*My Style of Government*'; pp 23–53.

7 See Chapter I above; Young p 406.

8 Ionescu: *Leadership in an Interdependent World*, pp 153–55; Minogue & Biddis (eds): *Thatcherism: Personality and Politics*, pp 38–54; and n 6 above.

9 Sandell (ed): *Liberalism and Its Critics*, introduction; A J P Taylor, *Introduction to K A Marx and F Engels: The Communist Manifesto*, p 10; Mack Smith: *Italy*, p 412; Mack Smith: *Mussolini*, pp 103, 302.

10 Cormack (ed): *Right Turn*, *passim*; Graham Turner: *Sunday Telegraph*, 28 June 1992.

11 Schama: *Citizens*, pp 805–15; Soboul: *The Parisian Sans-Culottes and the French Revolution 1793–94*. pp 52–54; Carr: *The Bolshevik Revolution 1917–1923*, II, pp 276–79; Ulam: *Lenin and the Bolsheviks*, pp 622–25, 683–86.

12 T B Macaulay: 'Review of Mill's Essay on Government' in *Complete Works*, vol VII, pp 365–76; eve of poll interview with David Dimbleby in 1987 in Cockerell, pp 330–31.

13 Jean-Paul Sartre: *Huis Clos*, scene 5.

14 C R L F: *Mr Gladstone at Oxford, 1890*, p 96; Crewe & Searing: *Ideological Change in the Conservative Party*, pp 375–78; Butler and Kavanagh: *The British General Election of 1987*, p 6; Crewe: 'Has the Electorate become Thatcherite?', in Skidelsky

(ed), pp 33–43; Heath et al: *Understanding Political Change*, pp 171–82.

15 Crewe: 'Value: The Crusade that Failed', in Kavanagh & Seldon (eds) pp 239–50; Christie: *Stress and Stability in Later Eighteenth-Century Britain*, p 93.

16 See nn 14 and 15 and chapter I above; Young, p 545; Ridley, p 86 (quotation).

17 Mrs Thatcher, *Newsweek*, April 1992 (quotation).

18 Bogdanor: 'The 1992 General Election and the British Party System', p 299; Crewe in Skidelsky (ed), p 30.

19 Popper: *The Unending Quest*, p 19; Ramsden: *Thatcher and Conservative History*, p 3; Perkins, p 501; but cf M Garnett: *In Defence of Reactionaries*, pp 14–16.

20 Maccunn: *The Political Philosophy of Edmund Burke*, p 9 (quotation); Gilmour: *BCW*, pp 12–13, 18; Perkin, pp 12, 501, 504.

21 Galbraith: *The Culture of Contentment*, *passim*; Gilmour: Cambridge, 8 March 1980; see chapter II above.

22 See chapters VI and IX above; Linklater & Leigh: *Not with Honour*, pp 145–48, 160–62, 187; Wilson: *A Very British Miracle*, pp 161–65.

23 Perkin, pp 13, 499–501; Hirschman: *Exit, Loyalty, Voice*, p 18 and *passim*.

24 Keynes: *The Economic Consequences of Mr Churchill*; Gilbert: *Winston Churchill*, V, pp 92–100; Gilmour: *BCW*, pp74–75.

25 Epigraph of chapter VI, and also chapter VII.

26 Mrs Thatcher: Finchley, 4 March 1991; and see preface above.

Bibliography of Works Cited

Place of publication London unless otherwise stated.

Adams, James: *The Financing of Terrorism* (1986)

Adamson, Iain: *The Old Fox: A Life of Gilbert Beyfus* (1963)

Addison, Christopher et al: *Problems of a Socialist Government* (1933)

Addison, Paul: *The Road to 1945* (1975)

Adeney, Martin & Lloyd, John: *The Miners' Strike 1984–5* (1986)

Alderman, A K & Cross, J A: *The Tactics of Resignation* (1967)

Allen & Hall: Money as a Potential Anchor for the Price Level (*LBS Economic Outlook*, February 1991)

Aspinall, A: *The Cabinet Council 1783–1835* (1952)

Atkinson, A B: What is Happening to the Distribution of Income in the UK? (Keynes Lecture at the British Academy, 1991)

Atkinson, A B & Micklewright, J: *Economic Transformation in Eastern Europe and the Distribution of Income* (Cambridge, 1992)

Atkinson, A B & Micklewright, J: *Turning the Screw: Benefits for the Unemployed 1979–1988* (1988)

Barnett, Joel: *Inside the Treasury* (1982)

Bean, Charles & Symons, James: *Ten Years of Mrs Thatcher* (Centre for Economic Policy Research, 1989)

Becker, Saul (ed): *Windows of Opportunity* (1991)

Beckerman, Wilfrid & Jenkinson: *Commodity Prices, Import Prices and the Inflation Slowdown* (1983)

Beer, Samuel H: *Britain Against Itself* (1982)

Beer, Samuel H: *Modern British Politics* (1965)

Bellairs, Charles E: *Conservative Social and Industrial Reform* (1977)

Berlin, Isaiah: *Two Concepts of Liberty* (Oxford, 1958)

Berrington, Hugh (ed): *Change in British Politics* (1984)

Blake, Robert: *The Conservative Party from Peel to Thatcher* (1985)

Blake, Robert: *Disraeli* (1966)

Bogdanor, Vernon: 'The 1992 General Election and the British Party System' (*Government and Opposition*, summer 1992)

Bonham Carter, Violet: *Winston Churchill as I Knew Him* (1965)

Booth, A H: *British Hustings 1924–1950* (1956)

Bosanquet, Nick: *After the New Right* (1983)

Boswell, James: *Life of Johnson* (Oxford, 1952)

Bradbury, Malcolm: *Cuts* (1987)

Bradshaw, Jonathan: *Child Poverty and Deprivation in the UK* (1990)

Brittan, Samuel: A Comment on Kay and Thompson (*Economic Journal*, March 1986)

Brittan, Samuel: The Politics and Economics of Privatisation (*Political Quarterly*, 1955)

Brittan, Samuel: *A Restatement of Economic Liberalism* (1988)

Brittan, Samuel: *The Role and Limits of Government* (1983)

Britton, A J G: *Macroeconomic Policy in Britain 1974–1987* (Cambridge, 1991)

Brogan, D W: *The American Political System* (1943)

Browning, Peter: *Economic Images* (1983)

Browning, Peter: *The Treasury and Economic Policy 1964–1985* (1986)

Budd, Alan: Thatcher's Economic Performance (*Contemporary Record*, vol 2, no 2, summer 1988)

Buiter, William H & Miller, Marcus H: *The Macroeconomic Consequences of a Change in Regime: Britain under Mrs Thatcher* (1983)

Bullock, Alan & Shock, Maurice (eds): *The Liberal Tradition* (1956)

Bulpitt, Jim: The Discipline of the New Democracy, Mrs Thatcher's Domestic Statecraft (*Political Studies*, XXXIV, 1986)

Burk, Kathleen & Cairncross, Alec: *Goodbye Great Britain* (1992)

Burke, Edmund: *Reflections on the Revolution in France* (C C O'Brien ed, Harmondsworth, 1986)

Butler, David & Pinto-Duschinsky, Richard: *The British General Election of 1970* (1971)

Butler, David & Kavanagh, Dennis: *The British General Election of 1974* (1975)

Butler, David & Kavanagh, Dennis: *The British General Election of 1979* (1980)

Butler, David & Kavanagh, Dennis: *The British General Election of 1987* (1988)

Butler, Lord (ed): *The Conservatives* (1977)

Byrd, Peter (ed): *British Foreign Policy under Thatcher* (Deddington, Oxford, 1988)

Callaghan, James: *Time and Chance* (1987)

Carlyle, Thomas: *The French Revolution* (1837)

Carr, E H: *The Bolshevik Revolution 1917–1923*, vol 2 (1952)

Carrington, Lord: *Reflect on Things Past* (1988)

Carter, Byron E: *The Office of Prime Minister* (1956)

Carter-Ruck, Peter: *Memoirs of a Libel Lawyer* (1990)

Cecil, Lady Gwendoline: *The Life of Lord Salisbury*, 4 vols (1921–32)

Chevenix Trench, Charles: *Portrait of a Patriot* (1962)

Christie, Ian R: *Stress and Stability in Late Eighteenth Century Britain* (Oxford, 1984)

Christmas, Linda: *Chopping Down the Cherry Trees* (1991)

Churchill, Randolph S: *Winston S Churchill, Young Statesman 1901–1914* (1967)

Churchill, Winston S: *Great Contemporaries* (1942)

Churchill, Winston S: *Lord Randolph Churchill* (1907)

Churchill, Winston S: *Triumph and Tragedy* (1954)

Churchill, Winston S: *The World Crisis 1911–1918* (abridged and revised edition, 1960)

Clark, Alan: *The Donkeys* (1961)

Cobban, Alfred: *Edmund Burke and the Revolt Against the Eighteenth Century* (1929)

Cockerell, Michael: *Live from Number 10* (1988)

Cohen, Ruth et al: *Hardship Britain: Being Poor in the 1990s* (1992)

Coleridge, Samuel Taylor: *On the Constitution of the Church and State* (J Barrett ed, 1972)

Congdon, Tim: *Monetarism, An Essay in Definition* (1978)

Congdon, Tim: *Monetarism Lost, and Why it must be Regained* (1989)

Cooke, Alistair (ed): *Mencken: The Vintage* (New York, 1955)

Cooke, C (ed): *The Revival of Britain: Speeches on Home and European Affairs 1975–88* (1989)

Cormack, Patrick (ed): *Right Turn* (1978)

Cosgrave, Patrick: *Carrington* (1985)

Coutts, Ken, Godley, Wynne, Rowthorn, Bob Zezza, Gennarro: *Britain's Economic Problems and Policies in the 1990s* (1990)

Crafts, Nick: *British Economic Growth Before and After 1979* (Centre for Economic Policy Research, March 1988)

Crewe, Ivor & Searing, Donald: Ideological Change in the British Conservative Party (*American Political Science Review*, vol 82, no 2, June 1988)

Daalder, Hans: *Cabinet Reform in Britain 1914–1963* (Stanford, 1964)

Dickie, John: *Inside the Foreign Office* (1992)

Dicks, Geoffrey: What Remains of Thatcherism? (*LBS Economic Outlook*, Oxford, July 1991)

Disraeli, Benjamin: *Sybil, or The Two Nations* (1845)
Disraeli, Benjamin: *Tory Democrat, Disraeli's Manchester and Crystal Palace Speeches* (1950)
Dobrée, Bonamy (ed): *The Letters of George III* (1935)
Dow, Christopher: *A Critique of Monetary Policy* (Lloyds Bank Review, October 1987)
Dunn, John (ed): *The Economic Limits to Modern Politics* (Cambridge, 1990)

Eccleshall, Robert et al: *Political Ideologies, An Introduction* (1984)
Education: A Framework for Expansion (Command 5174, 1972)
Ehrman, John: *The Younger Pitt*, vol II (1983)
Eltis, Walter & Sinclair, Peter (eds): *Keynes and Economic Policy, the Relevance of the General Theory after Fifty Years* (1988)
Esam & Oppenheim, C: *A Charge on the Community* (1989)
Evans, Harold: *Good Times, Bad Times* (1985)
Ewing, K J & Gearty, C A: *Freedom under Thatcher* (Oxford, 1990)

CRLF: *Mr Gladstone at Oxford*, 1890 (1908)
Feiling, Keith: *The Life of Neville Chamberlain* (1946)
Fforde, Matthew: *Conservatism and Collectivism 1886–1914* (Edinburgh, 1990)
Finer, Herman: *Road to Reaction* (1946)
Finlayson, Geoffrey B A M: *The Seventh Earl of Shaftesbury* (1981)
Fisk, Robert: *Pity the Nation* (Oxford, 1991)
Foot, Michael: *Aneurin Bevan 1945–1960* (1975)
Foot, Michael: *Another Heart and other Pulses* (1984)
Ford, J L: *Monetary Aggregates and Economic Policy* (Birmingham, 1982)
Fowler, Norman: *Ministers Decide* (1991)
Franks Report: Falkland Islands Review (Command 8787, 1983)
Freedman, Lawrence: *Britain and the Falklands War* (Oxford, 1988)
Freeman, Richard: *The Future of UK Manufacturing* (1990)
Friedman, Milton: *Capitalism and Freedom* (Chicago, 1962)
Friedman, Milton: *The Counter-Revolution in Monetary Theory* (1970)
Friedman, Milton: *The Optimum Quantity of Money and Other Essays* (1967)
Friedrich, Carl J: The Political Thought of Neo-Liberalism (*American Political Science Review*, 49, 1955)

Galbraith, John Kenneth: *The Culture of Contentment* (1992)
Gamble, Andrew: *The Free Economy and the Strong State* (1988)

Garnett, Mark: In Defence of Reactionaries (*Salisbury Review*, December 1991)

Gash, Norman: *Mr Secretary Peel* (1961)

Gash, Norman: *Sir Robert Peel* (1972)

Gilbert, Martin: *Winston S Churchill*, vol V, 1922–1939 (1976)

Gilder, George: *Wealth & Poverty* (1982)

Gilmour, Ian: *The Body Politic* (1969)

Gilmour, Ian: *Britain Can Work* (1983)

Gilmour, Ian: *Inside Right* (1977)

Gilmour, Ian: *Riot, Risings and Revolution* (1992)

Goodman, Geoffrey: *The Miners' Strike* (1985)

Graham, Cosmo & Prosser, Tony: *Waiving the Rules* (Milton Keynes, 1988)

Grant, Wyn: *Government and Industry* (Aldershot, 1981)

Grant, Wyn: *The Political Economy of Industrial Policy* (1982)

Gray, John: *Liberalisms* (1989)

Greve, J with Currie, E: *Homelessness In Britain* (1990)

Grigg, John: *Lloyd George, The People's Champion 1902–1911* (1978)

Grimstone, Gerry: Privatisation, the Unexpected Crusade (*Contemporary Record*, vol I, no 1, spring 1987)

Gyford, John: *The Politics of Local Socialism* (1985)

Haig, Alexander: *Caveat* (1984)

Hailsham, Lord: *The Dilemma of Democracy* (1975)

Hailsham. Lord: *A Sparrow's Flight, Memoirs* (1990)

Halcrow, Morrison: *Keith Joseph, A Single Mind* (1989)

Hamilton, Malcolm B: The Elements of the Concept of Ideology (*Political Studies*, XXXV, 1987)

Hammond, Eric: *Maverick* (1992)

Hankey, Lord: *The Supreme Command*, 2 vols (1961)

Harris, José: *William Beveridge* (Oxford, 1977)

Harris, Kenneth: *Thatcher* (1989)

Harris, Robert: *Good and Faithful Servant* (1990)

Harrison, Paul: *Inside the Inner City* (1985)

Hastings, Max & Jenkins, Simon: *The Battle for the Falklands* (1983)

Hayek, F A: *The Constitution of Liberty* (1960)

Hayek, F A: *The Road to Serfdom* (1944)

Heald, David: *Public Expenditure* (Oxford, 1983)

Healey, Denis: *The Time of My Life* (1989)

Heath, Anthony et al: *Understanding Political Change* (Oxford, 1991)

Hempton, David: *Methodism and Politics in British Society 1750–1850* (1987)

Henderson, Nicholas: *Channels and Tunnels* (1987)

Hennessy, Peter: *Cabinet* (Oxford, 1986)

Hennessy, Peter & Seldon, Anthony (eds): *Ruling Performance* (Oxford, 1987)

Hershman, Albert O: *Exit, Voice and Loyalty* (Cambridge, Mass, 1970)

Heseltine, Michael: *Where There's a Will* (1990)

Hicks, John: *A Market Theory of Money* (Oxford, 1989)

Hicks, John: *What is Wrong with Monetarism?* (Lloyds Bank Review, October 1975)

Higher Education into the 1990s (Command 9525)

Hills, John: *Changing Tax* (1988)

Hills, John (ed): *The State of Welfare* (Oxford, 1990)

Hinde, Wendy: *Castlereagh* (1981)

Hirst, Paul: *After Thatcher* (1989)

Hitchens, Christopher: *Blood, Class and Nostalgia* (1990)

Hollis, Christopher: *Can Parliament Survive?* (1949)

Holmes, Geoffrey: *Augustan England, Professions, State and Society 1680–1730* (1982)

Holmes, Geoffrey: *Politics, Religion and Society in England, 1679–1742* (1986)

Holmes, Martin: *The First Thatcher Government 1979–1983* (1985)

House of Commons Social Security Committee, First Report 1990–1, Low Income Statistics

House of Commons Social Services Committee, Sixth Report 1987–8 (HC 1687)

House of Commons Social Services Committee, Eighth Report 1988–9 (HC 214–111)

House of Lords Select Committee on Science & Technology: Innovation in Manufacturing Industry (HL 18–1, 1990–1)

House of Lords Select Committee on Overseas Trade (HL 238–1–3, 1984–5)

Households Below Average Income, A Statistical Analysis 1979–88-9 (CSO, 1992)

Households Below Average Income, Tables 1988 (HC 401, 1990–1)

Howell, David: *Blind Victory* (1986)

Howell, David: *Freedom and Capital* (Oxford, 1981)

Hume, David: *Essays, Moral Political and Literary, 1741–2* (Oxford, 1975)

Hume, David: *An Inquiry Concerning Human Understanding* (posthumous edition, 1777)

Hyde, Montgomery: *Carson* (1953)

Ingham, Bernard: *Kill the Messenger* (1991)

Ionescu, Ghita: *Leadership in an Interdependent World* (1991)

Jackson, P M: *Local Government Budgets and Economic Stability* (Leicester, 1991)

Jay, Douglas: *Sterling: Its Use and Misuse* (1985)

Jenkins, Peter: *Mrs Thatcher's Revolution* (1987)

Jenkins, Roy: *European Diary 1977–1981* (1989)

Jenkins, Roy: *A Life at the Centre* (1991)

Jenkins, Roy: *Mr Balfour's Poodle* (1954)

Jenkins, S: 'Income, Inequality and Living Standards: Changes in the 1970s and 1980s' (*Fiscal Studies*, vol 12, no 1, February 1990–91)

Jennings, Ivor: *Cabinet Government* (third edition, Cambridge, 1959)

Jessop, B et al: *Thatcherism: A Tale of Two Nations* (1988)

Johnson, Christopher: *The Economy Under Mrs Thatcher 1979–1990* (Harmondsworth, 1991)

Johnson, P & Stark, J: *Taxation and Social Security 1979–1989: the Impact on Household Incomes* (1989)

Johnson, Paul & Webb, Steven: *UK Poverty Statistics: A Comparative Study* (1991)

Johnson, R W: *The Politics of Recession* (1985)

Jones, George & Stewart, John: *The Case for Local Government* (1983)

Jones, G W: *Local Government and the Social Market* (1991)

Joseph, Keith & Sumption, Jonathan: *Equality* (1979)

Joseph, Keith: *Monetarism is not Enough* (nd)

Joseph, Keith: *Reversing the Trend* (1975)

Junor, John: *Listening for a Midnight Tram: Memoirs* (1990)

Kaldor, Nicholas: *The Scourge of Monetarism* (Oxford, 1982)

Kaldor, Lord: *The Economic Consequences of Mrs Thatcher* (1983)

Kavanagh, Dennis & Morris, Peter: *Consensus Politics from Attlee to Thatcher* (Oxford, 1989)

Kavanagh, Dennis & Seldon, Anthony (eds): *The Thatcher Effect* (Oxford, 1989)

Kavanagh, Dennis: *Thatcherism and British Politics, The End of Consensus?* (Oxford, 1990)

Kay, J A & Thompson, D J: Privatisation, A Policy in Search of a Rationale (*Economic Journal*, 96, March 1986)

Keane, J: *The Media and Democracy* (Cambridge, 1991)

Keegan, William: *Britain Without Oil* (Harmondsworth, 1985)

Keegan, William: *Mr Lawson's Gamble* (1989)

Keegan, William: *Mrs Thatcher's Economic Experiment* (1984)

Keeton, G W: *The Passing of Parliament* (1952)

Kelf-Cohen, R: *Nationalisation in Britain* (second edition, 1961)

Kellner, Peter & Hitchens, Christopher: *Callaghan: The Road to Number 10* (1976)

Keynes, J M: *The Economic Consequences of Mr Churchill* (1925)

Keynes, J M: *The General Theory of Employment, Interest and Money* (1936)
King, Anthony (ed): *The British Prime Minister* (second edition, 1985)

Lawson, Nigel: *The New Conservatism* (1980)
Layard, R & Nickell, S: *The Thatcher Miracle?* (Centre for Economic Policy Research, April 1989)
Leach, Robert: *British Political Ideologies* (1991)
Lewis, Geoffrey: *Lord Atkin* (1983)
Liebling, A: *The Press* (New York, 1961)
Linklater, Magnus & Leigh, David: *Not with Honour* (1986)
Lister, Ruth: *The Exclusive Society: Citizenship and the Poor* (1990)
Longford, Elizabeth: *Victoria RI* (1964)
Low Pay Unit: *Poor Britain: Poverty, Inequality and Low Pay in the Nineties* (1992)

MacCallum, Gerald C, Jr: Negative and Positive Freedom (*Philosophical Review*, vol LXXV, 1967)
Maccunn, John: *The Political Philosophy of Burke* (1913)
McDowell, R B: *British Conservatism 1832–1914* (1959)
Macgregor, Susan: Poverty, The Poll Tax and Thatcherite Welfare Policy (*Political Quarterly*, Part I: vol 62, no 4, 1991; Part II: vol 63, no 1, 1992)
Mackay, Ruddock F: *Balfour, Intellectual Statesman* (Oxford, 1985)
Mack Smith, Denis: *Mussolini* (1981)
Mack Smith, Denis: *Italy, A Modern History* (Michigan, 1959)
Mackintosh, John: *The British Cabinet* (1962)
Macleod, Iain: *Neville Chamberlain* (1961)
Macmillan, Harold: *Winds of Change 1914–39* (1966)
Malcolm, Noel: *Sense on Sovereignty* (1991)
Marquand, David: *The Unprincipled Society* (1988)
Marsh, David & Rhodes, R A W (eds): *Implementing Thatcherite Policies* (Buckingham, 1992)
Marx, K A & Engels, F: *The Communist Manifesto* (ed intro A J P Taylor) (1960)
Mathias, Peter: *The Transformation of England* (1979)
Mathiot, André: *The British Political System* (1958)
Matthews, Kent & Minford, Patrick: Mrs Thatcher's Economic Policies (*Economic Policy*, 5 October 1987)
Maude, Angus (ed): *The Right Approach to the Economy* (1977)
Maynard, Geoffrey: *The Economy under Mrs Thatcher* (Oxford, 1988)
Michie, Jonathan (ed): *The Economic Legacy 1979–92* (1992)

Middlemas, Keith: *Power, Competition and the State*, vol 3 (1991)

Middlemas, Keith & Barnes, John: *Baldwin* (1969)

Miliband, David: *Markets, Politics and Education* (1991)

Miliband, Ralph: *Parliamentary Socialism* (1961)

Mill, John Stuart: *Essays on Some Unsettled Questions of Political Economy* (third edition, 1877)

Mill, John Stuart: *Principles of Political Economy*, 2 vols (1848)

Milligan, Steven: *What Shall We Do About the BBC?* (1990)

Milne, Alasdair: *DG: Memoirs of a British Broadcaster* (1988)

Minogue, Kenneth & Biddis, M (eds): *Personality and Politics* (1987)

Moore, Thomas (ed): *The Works of Lord Byron*, 17 vols (1847)

Moran, Michael: The Conservative Party and the Trade Unions Since 1974 (*Political Studies*, XXVII)

Morgan, Janet (ed): *The Backbench Diaries of Richard Crossman* (1981)

Morgan, Kenneth: *The People's Peace* (Oxford, 1990)

Morley, John: *The Life of Walpole* (1889)

Mount, Ferdinand: *The British Constitution Now* (1992)

Muellbauer, John: *The Great British Housing Disaster and Economic Policy* (1990)

Munshe, Peter: *Gentlemen and Poachers* (Cambridge, 1981)

National Audit Office: *Sale of the Water Authorities in England & Wales* (HMSO, 1992)

National Audit Office: *The Social Fund* (HMSO, 1992)

Norton, Philip: *The Constitution in Flux* (1982)

Oakeshott, Michael: *On Human Conduct* (Oxford, 1975)

Oakeshott, Michael: *Rationalism in Politics and Other Essays* (1962)

Oldman, J: *Temporary Accommodation, The Permanent Story* (1989)

Oldman, J: *Who Says there's no Housing Problem?* (1990)

O'Leary, Brendan: The Anglo–Irish Agreement: Folly or Statecraft? (*West European Politics*, vol 10, January 1987)

Oppenheim, Carey: *Poverty, the Facts* (1990)

Orwell, George: *England Your England* (1941)

Orwell, George: *Shooting an Elephant* (1950)

Outhwaite, R B: *Inflation in Early and Tudor England* (second edition, 1982)

Parker, H (ed): *Basic Income and the Labour Market* (1991)

Parker, H: *Instead of the Dole* (1989)

Parker, H & Sutherland, H: *Child Tax Allowances?* (1991)

Patten, Chris: *The Tory Case* (1983)

Perkin, Harold: *The Rise of Professional Society* (1989)

Phelps-Brown, Henry: *Egalitarianism and the Generation of Inequality* (Oxford, 1988)

Phillips, Kevin: *The Politics of Rich and Poor, Wealth and the American Electorate in the Reagan Aftermath* (New York, 1990)

Piachaud, David: Revitalising Social Policy (*Political Quarterly*, vol 1, 1992)

Pollard, Sidney: *The Wasting of the British Economy* (1982)

Pollock, John: *John Wesley 1703–91* (1989)

Popper, Karl: *Unended Quest* (1976)

Pratten, Clifford: *Mrs Thatcher's Economic Experiment* (Lloyds Bank Review, January 1982)

Prior, Jim: *A Balance of Power* (1986)

Pym, Francis: *The Politics of Consent* (1984)

Ramsden, John: Thatcher and Conservative History (*Contemporary Record*, April 1991)

Randall, G: *Homeless and Hungry – A Sign of the Times* (1989)

Ranelagh, John: *Thatcher's People* (1991)

Ransom, S et al (eds): *Between Centre and Locality* (1985)

Rentoul, John: *Me and Mine* (1989)

Rhodes James, Robert: *Anthony Eden* (1986)

Richardson, Gordon: *Reflections on the Conduct of Monetary Policy* (1978)

Riddell, Peter: *The Thatcher Decade* (Oxford, 1989)

Riddell, Peter: *The Thatcher Era and its Legacy* (Oxford, 1991)

Riddell, Peter: *The Thatcher Government* (Oxford, 1985)

Ridley, Nicholas: *The Local Right, Enabling not Providing* (1988)

Ridley, Nicholas: '*My Style of Government*' (1991)

Robbins, Lord: *Political Economy, Past and Present* (1976)

Robson, William A: *Local Government in Crisis* (1966)

Rousseau, Jean-Jacques: *Le Contrat Social* (1762)

Runciman, W G: *Relative Deprivation and Social Justice* (1966)

Sabine, G: *A History of Political Theory* (third edition, 1951)

St John Stevas, Norman: *The Two Cities* (1984)

Sandell, M (ed): *Liberalism and its Critics* (New York, 1984)

Scarman, Lord: *The Brixton Disorders, 1981* (Command 8247)

Schama, Simon: *Citizens* (1989)

Schumpeter, Joseph: *A History of Economic Analysis* (1956)

Scruton, Roger: *The Meaning of Conservatism* (1980)

Sedgwick, Romney (ed): *The House of Commons 1715–54*, 2 vols (1978)

Seldon, Anthony: *Churchill's Indian Summer* (1981)

Seldon, Arthur (ed): *Crisis '75 . . . ?* (1975)

Shepherd, Robert: *The Power Brokers* (1991)
Sheppard, David: *The 1984 Richard Dimbleby Lecture* (1984)
Simon, Viscount: *Retrospect* (1952)
Sinfield, Adrian: *What Unemployment Means* (1981)
Skidelsky, Robert (ed): *Thatcherism* (1989)
Smith, Adam: *The Wealth of Nations* (1776)
Smith, D J (ed): *Understanding the Underclass* (1992)
Smith, David: *The Rise and Fall of Monetarism* (1987)
Smith, G Davey et al: The Black Report on Socio-economic Inequality in Health Ten Years On (*British Medical Journal*, no 6748, 18 November 1991)
Smith, Geoffrey: *Reagan and Thatcher* (1990)
Smith, H Maynard: *Henry VIII and the Reformation* (1948)
Smith, John Grieve: *Full Employment in the 1990s* (1992)
Smith, Keith: *The British Economic Crisis* (1984)
Smith, Logan Pearsall: *All Trivia* (1929)
Smith, Paul (ed): *Lord Salisbury on Politics* (1972)
Snoddy, Raymond: *The Good, the Bad and the Unacceptable* (1992)
Soboul, Albert: *The Parisian Sans-Culottes and the French Revolution 1793–94* (Oxford, 1964)
Southgate, Donald (ed): *The Conservative Leadership 1832–1932* (1974)
Stewart, John & Stoker, Gerry (eds): *The Future of Local Government* (1989)

Tebbit, Norman: *Unfinished Business* (1991)
Tebbit, Norman: *Upwardly Mobile* (1989)
Templewood, Lord: *Ambassador on Special Mission* (1946)
Templewood, Lord: *Nine Troubled Years* (1954)
Thatcher, Margaret: *What's Wrong with Politics?* (1968)
Thomas, Hugh: *Ever Closer Union* (1991)
Thompson, J M (ed): *French Revolution Documents 1789–94* (Oxford, 1933)
Titmuss, Richard: *Essays on 'The Welfare State'* (1958)
Townsend, Peter: *Meaningful Statistics on Poverty 1991* (1991)
Townsend, Peter: *The Poor are Poorer: A Statistical Report on Change in the Living Standards of Rich and Poor in the UK 1979–89* (University of Bristol, 1991)
Trevelyan, G M: *Grey of Falloden* (1940)
Tugendhat, Christopher: *Making Sense of Europe* (1986)

Ulam, Adam B: *Lenin and the Bolsheviks* (1969)

Vansittart, Lord: *The Mist Procession* (1958)

Veljanowski, Cento: *Selling the State* (1987)

Vickers, J & Yarrow, G K: *Privatisation: The Economic Analysis* (1989)

Vulliamy, C E: *John Wesley* (1954)

Walker, Peter: *The Ascent of Britain* (1977)

Walker, Peter: *Staying Power* (1991)

Wallas, Graham: *Human Nature in Politics* (fourth edition, 1948)

Walters, Alan: *Britain's Economic Renaissance* (New York & Oxford, 1986)

Walters, Alan: *Sterling in Danger* (1990)

Wapshott, Nicholas & Brock, George: *Thatcher* (1983)

Watkins, Alan: *A Conservative Coup* (1991)

Wearmouth, Robert: *Methodism and the Working Class Movement in England 1800–50* (1937)

Wesley, John: *Selected Letters* (F Gill ed, 1956)

West, E G: *Education and the State* (1965)

Whitehead, M: *Inequalities in Wealth* (1988)

Whitelaw, William: *The Whitelaw Memoirs* (1989)

Whitfield, J H: *Machiavelli* (Oxford, 1947)

Wilkinson, Frank: *Why Britain Needs a Minimum Wage* (1991)

Willetts, David: *Modern Conservatism* (1992)

Wilson, Edgar: *A Very British Miracle, The Failure of Thatcherism* (1992)

Wolff, Leon: *In Flanders Fields* (1959)

Woodward, Admiral Sandy: *One Hundred Days* (1992)

Woodward, Bob: *Veil, The Secret Wars of the CIA 1981–1987* (1987)

Woodward, Llewellyn: *The Age of Reform 1815–1870* (second edition, Oxford, 1962)

Wright, Patrick: *A Journey Through Ruins* (1991)

Young, G M: *Stanley Baldwin* (1952)

Young, Hugo: *One of Us* (1989)

Young, Hugo: Rupert Murdoch and the Sunday Times: A Lamp Goes Out (*Political Quarterly*, vol 55, no 4, 1984)

Index